Paul and His Legacy

Paul and His Legacy

Collected Essays

William O. Walker, Jr.

POLEBRIDGE PRESS
Salem, Oregon

Dedication

This collection of essays is lovingly dedicated to my three children: Scott, Mary, and Neal; and my four grandchildren: Liz, Mike, Maggie, and Hannah.

Copyright © 2015 by William O. Walker, Jr.
All rights reserved. Printed in the United States of America. No part of this book may be used or reproduced in any manner whatsoever without written permission except in the case of brief quotations embodied in critical articles and reviews. For information address Polebridge Press, Willamette University, 900 State Street, Salem, OR 97301.

Cover and interior design by Robaire Ream

Library of Congress Control Number: 2014949082

Contents

Preface vii

Abbreviations xi

Part One: Studies in Galatians

    Chapter 1: Why Paul Went to Jerusalem: The
Interpretation of Galatians 2:1–5 3

    Chapter 2: Translation and Interpretation of
Ἐὰν Μή in Galatians 2:16 13

    Chapter 3: Does the "We" in Galatians 2:15–17
Include Paul's Opponents? 21

    Chapter 4: Galatians 2:8 and the Question of
Paul's Apostleship 29

    Chapter 5: Galatians 2:7b–8 as a Non-Pauline
Interpolation 37

    Chapter 6: "There Is Not Male and Female":
A Pauline Addition in Galatians 3:28 65

Part Two: Studies in the Corinthian Correspondence
and Romans

    Chapter 7: 2 Corinthians 6:14–7:1 and the
Chiastic Structure of 6:11–13; 7:2–3 91

    Chapter 8: 1 Corinthians 15:29–34 as a
Non-Pauline Interpolation 95

    Chapter 9: 2 Corinthians 3:7–18 as a
Non-Pauline Interpolation 123

    Chapter 10: Apollos and Timothy as the
Unnamed "Brothers" in 2 Corinthians 8:18–24 . . . 151

    Chapter 11: Romans 8:29–30 as a Non-Pauline
Interpolation 181

Part Three: The Book of Acts and the Letters of Paul

    Chapter 12: The Timothy-Titus Problem
Reconsidered 203

Chapter 13: Acts and the Pauline Corpus Reconsidered 213

Chapter 14: Acts and the Pauline Corpus Revisited: Peter's Speech at the Jerusalem Conference 237

Chapter 15: The Story of Peter and Cornelius as a Corrective to Galatians 2:11–14 249

Chapter 16: The Portrayal of Aquila and Priscilla in Acts: The Question of Sources 265

Addendum: The "Theology of Woman's Place" and the "Paulinist" Tradition 287

Bibliography 301

Index of Modern Authors 315

Preface

All of the essays in this volume except two were published—one in a *Festschrift* and the others in various scholarly journals—between 1981 and 2013. Except for minor editing to bring them into conformity with the Polebridge Press format and style, the correction of some typographical errors, and the re-wording of a very few sentences in the interest of greater clarity, these articles appear in the present volume exactly as they were originally published. Both of the essays that have not previously been published—"'There Is Not Male and Female': A Pauline Addition in Galatians 3:28" and "The Story of Peter and Cornelius as a Corrective to Galatians 2:11–14"—were completed in 2014.

Working through materials that I wrote during a span of more than three decades has been an interesting and, in some respects, a humbling experience. On the one hand, I still find myself in basic agreement with most of what I wrote during the earlier years of my career. On the other hand, it is now clear to me that I could have expressed myself more clearly and cogently at some points, and, in some respects, my thinking has evolved over the years. For example, in some of my earlier work, I simply assumed that Gal 2:7b–8 was written by Paul; later, I became convinced that this was a non-Pauline interpolation. Similarly, I simply assumed at one time, along with most other contemporary New Testament scholars, that the Book of Acts was written in the first century and that its author was not familiar with any of the Pauline letters; now, I am persuaded that Acts was written in the second century—perhaps as late as the middle of the second century—and that its author did know and, indeed, use a collection of the Pauline letters. A more abrupt shift in my thinking has related to Paul's attitude toward women. Until quite recently, I thought that his radical egalitarianism simply rested upon a foundation already laid by Jesus and within the pre-Pauline church. I am now persuaded, however, that the evidence regarding Jesus and the pre-Pauline church is scanty and, at best, questionable and that Paul may well have been the first to articulate the radical egalitarianism expressed in Gal 3:28: "There is neither Jew nor Greek, there is neither slave nor free, *there is not male and female*, for you are all one in Christ Jesus."

It has been particularly my interest in the question of interpolations in the Pauline letters that has informed much of my work over the past forty years. Most of this work was incorporated into my book, *Interpolations in the Pauline Letters*, which was published by Sheffield Academic Press in 2001, but the present volume includes chapters arguing that four additional passages are, in fact, later non-Pauline interpolations.

I am grateful to Larry Alexander, publisher of Polebridge Press, for accepting my proposal to publish this collection of essays on Paul and his legacy, and no words of mine can adequately express my appreciation to the team of Cassandra Farrin, Char Matejovsky, and Robaire Ream for the skillful and highly professional way in which they have moved my materials through the process of publication. It is to them that I attribute much of the quality of this volume; whatever problems there are, however, should be laid at my door.

My thanks to the following journals and publishers for permission to include previously-published materials in this volume:

- *The Catholic Biblical Quarterly*: "Why Paul Went to Jerusalem: The Interpretation of Galatians 2:1–5"; "Galatians 2:7b–8 as a Non-Pauline Interpolation"; "First Corinthians 15:29–34 as a Non-Pauline Interpolation"; and "Apollos and Timothy as the Unnamed 'Brothers' in 2 Corinthians 8:18–24."
- *Journal of Biblical Literature*: "Translation and Interpretation of Ἐὰν Μή in Galatians 2:16"; and "Galatians 2:8 and the Question of Paul's Apostleship."
- *New Testament Studies* (Cambridge University Press): "Does the 'We' in Galatians 2:15–17 Include Paul's Opponents?"; "Second Corinthians 6:14–7:1 and the Chiastic Structure of 6:11–13; 7:2–3"; and "The Portrayal of Aquila and Priscilla in Acts: The Question of Sources."

- *Journal for the Study of Paul and His Letters* (Sage Publications): "Second Corinthians 3:7–18 as a Non-Pauline Interpolation"; and "Romans 8:29–30 as a Non-Pauline Interpolation."
- *Journal for the Study of the New Testament* (Sage Publications): "Acts and the Pauline Corpus Reconsidered."
- *The Expository Times* (Sage Publications): "The Timothy-Titus Problem Reconsidered."
- *Trinity University Studies in Religion* (Trinity University Department of Religion): "The 'Theology of Woman's Place' and the 'Paulinist' Tradition."
- Mercer University Press: "Acts and the Pauline Corpus Revisited: Peter's Speech at the Jerusalem Conference."

Abbreviations

1–2 Clem.	1–2 Clement
1–2 Cor	1–2 Corinthians
1–2 Pet	1–2 Peter
1–2 Thess	1–2 Thessalonians
1–2 Tim	1–2 Timothy
A	Codex Alexandrinus
AB	Anchor Bible
ABD	*Anchor Bible Dictionary*. Edited by D. N. Freedman. 6 vols. New York, 1992
B	Codex Vaticanus
BADG	Bauer, W., W. F. Arndt, F. W. Gingrich, and F. W. Danker. *Greek-English Lexicon of the New Testament and Other Early Christian Literature.* 2nd ed. Chicago, 1979.
BDAG	Bauer, W., F. W. Danker, W. F. Arndt, and F.W. Gingrich. *Greek-English Lexicon of the New Testament and Other Early Christian Literature*. 3rd ed. Chicago, 1999
BDF	Blass, F., A. Debrunner, and R. W. Funk. *A Greek Grammar of the New Testament and Other Early Christian Literature.* Chicago, 1961
BEvT	Beiträge zur evangelischen Theologie
Bib	*Biblica*
BJRL	*Bulletin of the John Rylands Library of Manchester*
BNTC	Black's New Testament Commentaries
BRev	*Bible Review*
BTB	*Biblical Theology Bulletin*
C	Codex Ephraemi
CBQ	*The Catholic Biblical Quarterly*
Col	Colossians
D	Codex Claromontanus
Did.	*Didache*

DPL	*Dictionary of Paul and His Letters.* Edited by G. F. Hawthorne and R. P. Martin; Downers Grove, 1993
EKKNT	Evangelisch-katholischer Kommentar zum Neuen Testament
Eph	Ephesians
ExpT	*The Expository Times*
F	Codex Augiensis
FBBS	Facet Books, Biblical Series
FRLANT	Forschungen zur Religion und Literatur des Alten und Neuen Testaments
G	Codex Boernerianus
Gal	Galatians
Gen	Genesis
Gos. Phil.	*Gospel of Philip*
Haer.	Irenaeus, *Adversus haereses*
Heb	Hebrews
Hist. eccl.	Eusebius, *Historia ecclesiastica*
HNT	Handbuch zum Neuen Testament
HNTC	Harper's New Testament Commentaries
Hom. 1 Cor.	John Chrysostom, *Homiliae in epistulam i ad Corinthios*
Hos	Hosea
HR	*History of Religions*
HTKNT	Herders theologischer Kommentar zum Neuen Testament
HTR	*Harvard Theological Review*
IBC	Interpretation: A Bible Commentary for Teaching and Preaching
ICC	International Critical Commentary
IDB	*The Interpreter's Dictionary of the Bible.* Edited by G. A. Buttrick. 4 vols. Nashville, 1962
Ign. *Eph.*	Ignatius, *To the Ephesians*
Ign. *Rom.*	Ignatius, *To the Romans*
Ign. *Trall.*	Ignatius, *To the Trallians*
Int	*Interpretation*
Isa	Isaiah
JAAR	*Journal of the American Academy of Religion*

JAOS	*Journal of the American Oriental Society*
Jas	James
JBL	*Journal of Biblical Literature*
JSNT	*Journal for the Study of the New Testament*
JSNTSup	Journal for the Study of the New Testament: Supplement Series
JSPL	*Journal for the Study of Paul and His Letters*
JTS	*Journal of Theological Studies*
KEK	Kritisch-exegetischer Kommentar über das Neue Testament (Meyer-Kommentar)
K	Codex Mosquensis
LSJ	Liddell, H. G., R. Scott, H. S. Jones, *A Greek-English Lexicon*. 9th ed. with revised supplement. Oxford, 1996
LXX	Septuagint
Marc.	Tertullian, *Adversus Marcionem*
Mart. Pol.	Ignatius, *Martyrdom of Polycarp*
Matt	Matthew
MeyerK	See KEK
MNTC	Moffatt New Testament Commentary
Neot	*Neotestamentica*
NIB	*The New Interpreter's Bible*
NICNT	New International Commentary on the New Testament
NIDB	*New International Dictionary of the Bible*. Edited by J. D. Douglas and M. C. Tenney. Grand Rapids, 1987
NIGTC	New International Greek Testament Commentary
NovT	*Novum Testamentum*
NT	New Testament
NTL	New Testament Library
NTS	*New Testament Studies*
Onom.	Pollux, *Onomasticon*
Pan.	Epiphanius, *Panarion (Adversus haereses)*
Phaen.	*Phaenomena*
Phil	Philippians
Phlm	Philemon
Praescr.	Tertullian, *De praescriptione haereticorum*

Ps(s)	Psalm(s)
Res.	Tertullian, *De resurrection carnis*
Rev	Revelation
Rom	Romans
SBLDS	Society of Biblical Literature Dissertation Series
SBLMS	Society of Biblical Literature Monograph Series
SBT	Studies in Biblical Theology
SNTSMS	Society for New Testament Studies Monograph Series
SP	Sacra Pagina
TCGNT	Metzger, Bruce M. *A Textual Commentary on the Greek New Testament.* London/New York, 1971.
TDNT	*Theological Dictionary of the New Testament.* Edited by G. Kittel and G. Friedrich. Translated G. W. Bromiley. 10 vols. Grand Rapids, 1964–76
ThT	*Theologisch Tijdschrift*
Tit	Titus
TLZ	*Theologische Literaturzeitung*
TRu	*Theologische Rundschau*
TS	*Theological Studies*
TUGAL	Texte und Untersuchungen zur Geschichte der altchristlichen Literatur
UNT	Untersuchungen zum Neuen Testament
VF	*Verkündigung und Forschung*
WMANT	Wissenschaftliche Monographien zum Alten und Neuen Testament
WUNT	Wissenschaftliche Untersuchungen zum Neuen Testament
ZKG	*Zeitschrift für Kirchengeschichte*
ZNW	*Zeitschrift für die neutestamentliche Wissenschaft und die Kunde der älteren Kirche*
ZTK	*Zeitschrift für Theologie und Kirche*

Part One

Studies in Galatians

Chapter 1

Why Paul Went to Jerusalem
The Interpretation of Galatians 2:1–5

The interpretation of Gal 2:1–5 (and indeed of vv. 1–10 as a whole)[1] involves a number of important and perplexing exegetical, historical, and theological problems. Among these is the question of the syntactical relations among the various sections of vv. 1–5: (a) the account of Paul's Jerusalem trip in vv. 1–2; (b) the mention of circumcision in relation to Titus in v. 3; and (c) the reference to the "false brothers" in vv. 4–5. Particularly problematic is the fact that vv. 4–5 (usually translated as "but[2] because of the false brothers secretly brought in . . .") constitute an elaborate prepositional phrase that appears, at least initially, to have no syntactical relation to what precedes or follows. Thus, most commentators treat the verses as some type of anacoluthon, ellipsis, or parenthesis.[3]

"Why Paul Went to Jerusalem: The Interpretation of Galatians 2:1–5." *CBQ* 54,3 (July 1992) 503–10. Copyright © 1992 Catholic Biblical Association of America. Reprinted with permission.

1. Ramsay, among others, maintains that "though one may thrust in a period here or there, it is really one sentence that runs through verses 1–10" (*Historical Commentary*, 289).

2. I shall suggest below that the more appropriate translation of *de* in this case is "and"; see BAGD, 171: "Most common translations: *but*, when a contrast is clearly implied; *and*, when a simple connective is desired, without contrast."

3. A notable exception is O'Neill (*Recovery of Paul's Letter*, 32–33), who regards the *de* of v. 4 as a later addition to the text and translates vv. 3–4 as follows: "for not even my companion who was a Greek was compelled to be circumcised on account of the false intruding brothers who came in to spy out the freedom we have in Christ Jesus. . . ." For a thorough discussion of the issues, see Burton, *Critical and Exegetical Commentary*, 77–86. Burton (pp. 79–82) mentions three possible types of construction for the prepositional phrase: (1) "those which make it limit some following word"; (2) "those which make [it] limit what precedes, introducing an epexegetic addition to the preceding statement"; and (3) "those which make [it] limit something supplied from the preceding." His own conclusion is that a form of the third type "alone brings this portion of

Hans Dieter Betz, for example, regards vv. 4–5 as "a grammatical anacoluthon" and interprets the verses as a "digression" from the primary discussion in vv. 1–3: "After Paul had reported the outcome of the confrontation in 2:3, the digression in 2:4–5 returns to that confrontation and gives a more detailed account of it." Linking vv. 4–5 logically to the immediately preceding v. 3,[4] Betz apparently assumes that the activity of the "false brothers" occurred in Jerusalem at the time of Paul's visit and was directly related to the question of the circumcision of Titus. Thus, he proposes to translate vv. 4–5 as follows: "Now this happened because of the false brothers secretly brought in . . ."[5]

Bernard Orchard, on the other hand, argues that vv. 3–5 represent an "ellipsis" or parenthesis within vv. 1–10 and that vv. 4–5 comprise a secondary parenthesis within vv. 3–5. According to Orchard, Paul interrupts his account of the trip to Jerusalem (vv. 1–2, 6–10) to point out that the issue of Titus' circumcision was not even raised in Jerusalem, as would have been expected had the leaders there been in disagreement with Paul's version of the law-free gospel (v. 3). This parenthetical statement is then further interrupted by the elliptical "But because of the false brothers . . ." of vv. 4–5, which Orchard proposes to complete with some such words as "the liberty of the Gentiles is now in danger" or "this question has now arisen."[6] Orchard's argument is, for the most

---

the paragraph into line with the apostle's general argument by which he aims to show his entire independence, even of the other apostles" (pp. 81–82); thus, Burton suggests (p. 77) the following translation: "And not even Titus . . . was compelled to be circumcised, and (what shows more fully the significance of the fact) it was urged because of the false brethren."

4. In principle, the particle *de* could "throw the reference" either forward (beginning a new sentence, which, for some reason, Paul never completes) or backward (introducing a subordinate clause that is somehow related to what immediately precedes); most scholars opt for the latter.

5. Betz, *Galatians: A Commentary*, 89–92.

6. Orchard, "Note on the Meaning of Galatians ii.3–5"; "New Solution," esp. pp. 165–67; "Ellipsis between Galatians 2,3 and 2,4," with reaction by Blommerde, "Is there an Ellipsis?," and reply by Orchard, "Once Again the Ellipsis"; idem., "Ellipsis and Parenthesis," 249–58. Note that Bruce (*Epistle of Paul to the Galatians*, 116) prefers to fill in the ellipsis with "the question of circumcising Gentile converts was first raised."

part, accepted by F. F. Bruce, who suggests the following reconstruction of the course of events:

> When Paul and Barnabas visited Jerusalem on the occasion referred to in v 1, nothing was said about requiring Gentile converts to be circumcised, although Titus was with them and would have constituted a test case had any one been minded to raise the question. The question was not raised until later, when certain 'false brethren' infiltrated the church of Antioch, the headquarters of Gentile Christianity, and tried to insist on circumcision. Paul and his colleagues made no concession to those men—whatever rumours to the contrary may have been spread abroad—for a concession on this issue would have jeopardized the integrity of the gospel. And the position which Paul and his colleagues took then is the position which Paul takes now towards the crisis in the churches of Galatia.[7]

Thus, Orchard and Bruce locate the activity of the "false brothers" not in Jerusalem at the time of Paul's visit but later in Antioch or perhaps Galatia.

Contrary to Betz, Orchard, Bruce, and most other commentators, I now propose to revive a quite different interpretation of Gal 2:1–5.[8] I believe that the two prepositional phrases, *de kata apokalypsin* (v. 2) and *dia de tous pareisaktous pseudadelphous* . . . (v. 4), are syntactically parallel, that both are linked to the verb, *anebēn* (v. 2), and that, together, they indicate the twofold reason for Paul's trip to Jerusalem (note that both are introduced by *de*). Thus, in vv. 2–5, Paul asserts that he "went up in accordance with a revelation . . . *and* because of the false brothers" and comments briefly and almost parenthetically regarding each aspect of the reason after mentioning it.[9] The trip was undertaken in obedience

---

7. Bruce, *Epistle of Paul to the Galatians*, 116–17.
8. Burton notes (*Epistle of Paul to the Galatians*, 80) that the interpretation now to be proposed was "advocated by some of the older modern expositors," citing Sieffert, *Der Brief an die Galater*.
9. Note that Paul continues the parenthetical style in vv. 6–10: "what they were makes no difference to me; God shows no partiality" (v. 6b); and "for he who worked through Peter for the mission to the circumcised worked through me also for the Gentiles" (v. 8).

to a revelation that Paul should go and lay his gospel before the leaders in Jerusalem, apparently with the hope of obtaining their stamp of approval (v. 2). That he was successful in this regard is indicated by the fact that "even Titus, who was with me, was not compelled to be circumcised, though he was a Greek" (v. 3; cf. "those . . . who were of repute added nothing to me" in v. 6).[10] The historical occasion for the revelation, however, and thus in a very real sense also a part of Paul's reason for going to Jerusalem, was the prior activity (in Antioch?)[11] of the "false brothers" who had objected to his version of the gospel (v. 4). Regarding these false brothers, Paul insists that "we did not yield submission [to them] even for a moment" (v. 5).[12]

Thus understood, the meaning of Gal 2:1–5 can be set forth in "sense lines" as follows:

> Then after fourteen years I went up again to Jerusalem with Barnabas, taking Titus along with me,
>
> And I went up by revelation and laid before them—but privately before those who were of repute—the gospel that I preach among the Gentiles, lest somehow I should be

---

10. The introduction of the reference to Titus (v. 3) with the conjunction *alla* ("but") might appear to disrupt the preceding reference to Paul's Jerusalem trip and thus to relate v. 3 to what follows in v. 4. I believe, however, that the disruption points only to the last part of v. 2 ("lest somehow I should be running or had run in vain"), not to vv. 2–3 as a whole. Paul had apparently entertained at least the hypothetical fear that he might have been "running in vain" in his proclamation to the Gentles, but his apprehension was set at ease by the fact that Titus was not compelled to be circumcised.

11. Acts 15:1–2 appears to indicate Antioch (14:26–28); Gal 1:21–24, however, might suggest the broader regions of Syria and Cilicia.

12. There is a very real sense in which v. 3 and v. 5 are parallel: the former is a parenthetical statement illustrating the success of Paul's trip to Jerusalem; the latter, in similar parenthetic fashion, emphasizes Paul's refusal to yield to the "false brothers." This parallelism is in no way destroyed by the fact that v. 3 refers to what happened in Jerusalem, while v. 5 points to what had happened earlier, probably in Antioch. As to why Paul mentions first what happened later (vv. 1–3) and only later what had occurred earlier (vv. 4–5), see below.

running or had run in vain (but even Titus, who was with me, was not compelled to be circumcised, though he was a Greek);

and [it is also true that I went up] because of the false brothers secretly brought in, who slipped in to spy out our freedom that we have in Christ Jesus in order that they might enslave us (to whom we did not yield submission even for a moment) in order that the truth of the gospel might be preserved for you.

The advantages of such an interpretation of Gal 2:1–5 are obvious: it eliminates the need to regard vv. 4–5 as an anacoluthon, ellipsis, or parenthesis by providing a clear syntactical link with the immediately preceding material (vv. 1–3). It also makes possible a clear and consistent chronological reconstruction of the course of events narrated in vv. 1–5: (a) the activity of the "false brothers"; (b) Paul's refusal to submit to them; (c) the revelation that he should go to Jerusalem; and (d) the actual trip and its results. Finally, this interpretation of Gal 2:1–5 is consistent with the account in Acts 15:1–3, which cites the activity of Judaizers from Judea and the resulting controversy (in Antioch) as the occasion for Paul's trip to Jerusalem.[13] In this regard, I am by no means suggesting that the exegesis of Galatians (or any of Paul's letters) should be controlled or even guided by the narrative in Acts. Nevertheless, all other things being equal, an interpretation of Galatians that is in harmony with Acts would appear, *prima facie*, to be preferable to one that conflicts.[14]

---

13. There is some question, of course, about whether Gal 2:1–10 and Acts 15:1–29 refer to the same occurrence; I am following what Bruce (*Epistle of Paul to the Galatians*, 108) refers to as "the majority view" in assuming that they do.

14. The question of the historical reliability of Acts is, of course, a difficult one; see, e.g., Haenchen, "Book of Acts as Source Material"; idem., *Acts of the Apostles*, 98–103; and, for a somewhat different perspective, Hengel, *Acts and the History of Earliest Christianity*. If, as some scholars still hold, Acts is based upon relatively reliable narrative sources, the interpretation of Galatians that is in harmony with Acts would certainly be

There are, however, at least three possible problems with the interpretation of Gal 2:1–5 here being proposed. The first is that Acts 15:1–3 makes no reference to divine revelation as the reason for Paul's trip to Jerusalem. This is particularly surprising in light of the fact that Acts elsewhere associates revelation with Paul's travel plans.[15] It has often been suggested, however, that the author of Acts has at times taken features of the same Jerusalem visit and divided them between two different alleged visits. John Knox, for example, argues that the two visits reported in Acts 15:1–9 and 18:22 correspond to the one visit of Gal 2:1–10 and that the two reported in Acts 11:27–30 and 21:15 correspond to the one anticipated in 1 Cor 16:3–4 and Rom 15:25–32.[16] Kirsopp Lake and others, on the other hand, have assumed that both Acts 11:27–30 and 15:1–29 deal with the visit reported in Gal 2:1–10.[17] Moreover, Ernst Haenchen has suggested that Acts 11:27–30 was artificially constructed by the author of Acts on the basis of two originally unrelated traditions: (1) Agabus' prediction of a great famine; and (2) Barnabas' and Paul's relief mission from Antioch to Jerusalem.[18] In my judgment, however, an at least equally likely possibility is that the author constructed Acts 11:27–30 on the basis of three originally unrelated traditions: (1) Agabus' prediction of a famine (revelation); (2) Paul's and Barnabas' trip to Jerusalem in response to a divine revelation (Gal 2:1–2); and (3) Paul's carrying of a gift of money to the Christians in Jerusalem (1 Cor 16:3–4; Rom 15:25–32). If my suggestion is correct, it then becomes clear why Acts 15:1–3 makes no reference to revelation as the reason for

---

preferable. This might also be true, however, if, as Morton Scott Enslin suggests (*Reapproaching Paul,* 26–27), "the letters of Paul . . . appear to have been the principal source used by Luke in reconstructing the activities of the man who brought to reality the Gentile mission"; in this case, what we would have at many points in Acts is an early interpretation of materials in the Pauline letters. See also Chapter 13 in this volume, "Acts and the Pauline Corpus Reconsidered."

15. Acts 11:27–30; 13:1–4; 16:9–10; 23:11.
16. Knox, *Chapters in a Life of Paul,* 43–52.
17. Lake, "Note XVI. The Apostolic Council of Jerusalem," 199–204.
18. Haenchen, *Acts of the Apostles,* 378–79.

Paul's trip to Jerusalem: the author of Acts has already used the tradition of divine revelation as the reason for a trip to Jerusalem in the account of the alleged earlier trip reported in Acts 11:27–30.

A second possible problem with my interpretation of Gal 2:1–5 is the order in which the revelation and the false brothers are mentioned in the narrative. If the activity of the "false brothers" was the *occasion* for the revelation, why does Paul mention the revelation first and refer to the false brothers only in the midst of his account of the events in Jerusalem? Does this not suggest, as many have argued, that the activity of the false brothers occurred only after Paul's arrival in (or perhaps even after his departure from) Jerusalem and thus had nothing to do with his reasons for going? The answer, I believe, lies in Paul's rhetorical strategy in the first sections of Galatians. From the very beginning of the letter, Paul insists that his gospel came directly from God, not from humans.[19] As a part of his argument, he explicitly notes his limited contact with the apostles in Jerusalem. Following his call, he "did not confer with flesh and blood nor go up to Jerusalem to those who were apostles before [him]," but rather "went away into Arabia and returned again to Damascus" (1:16–17). When, after three years, he did go to Jerusalem (apparently for the first time!), he remained with Cephas for fifteen days but "saw none of the other apostles except James the Lord's brother" (1:18–19). The importance of this limited contact with the Jerusalem apostles is emphasized by the affirmation in 1:20, "In what I am writing to you, before God, I do not lie!"[20] Thus, it is not at all surprising that when Paul refers to this second visit to Jerusalem, he goes to great pains to insist, at the very beginning of the account, that he went *only* because of a divine revelation (2:2). Once this is made clear and something is said about the purpose and outcome of the visit, he can reflect

---

19. See, e.g., "an apostle—not from humans or through a human but through Jesus Christ and God the Father" (1:1); and "the gospel that was preached by me is not a human gospel, for neither did I receive it from a human nor was I taught it, but it came through a revelation of Jesus Christ" (1:11).

20. For similar affirmations, see 1 Thess 2:5; 2 Cor 1:23; 11:31.

back on the historical context of the revelation, which, as the occasion of the revelation, was also, in effect, a part of the reason for his trip to Jerusalem.[21]

A third possible problem with this interpretation of Gal 2:1–5 was pointed out a number of years ago by Burton. Burton acknowledged that the proposed interpretation "yield[s] a not unreasonable sense, and avoid[s] many of the difficulties encountered by the other constructions"; nevertheless, he dismissed it as "scarcely call[ing] for discussion" because "it is hardly conceivable that the reader would be expected to supply mentally a word left so far behind."[22] The word "left so far behind," of course, is the *anebēn* (or possibly the *anethemēn*)[23] of v. 2. This appears to be a rather serious problem, at least initially. I believe, however, that it can be resolved along essentially the same lines as was the previous one. As was suggested above, Paul's rhetorical strategy early in Galatians is to insist that his gospel originated not with humans but with God. Central to this strategy is the emphasis upon his limited contact with the church's Jerusalem leadership. The central issue at hand, then, is Paul's visits to Jerusalem. Thus,

---

21. Perhaps an imperfect analogy might be seen in 1 Cor 1:14–16, where Paul first asserts what is most important to him at the moment—"I am thankful that I baptized none of you except Crispus and Gaius, lest any one should say that you were baptized in my name"—and then in effect says, almost as an afterthought, "Well, the truth is in fact a bit more complicated than this." This analogy fails, however, in the sense that Paul does not here pursue the second point further, as is the case in Gal 2:4–5.

22. Burton, *Critical and Exegetical Commentary*, 80–81.

23. In his expanded paraphrase of Gal 2:1–10, Ramsay (*St. Paul the Traveller*, 55–56) suggests that the prepositional phrase of vv. 4–5 is to be linked not with *anebēn* but rather with *anethemēn*: "Now *I may explain that* I went up on account of a revelation *(which shows how completely my action was directly guided by the Divine will, and how independent it was of any orders or instructions from the Apostles)*. And I communicated to them with a view to consultation the gospel which I continue preaching among the Gentiles. . . . Further, the occasion *of my consulting the leading Apostles* was because of certain insinuating false brethren . . ." It is possible, of course, that the prepositional phrase is dependent upon both *anebēn* and *anethemēn*.

in chap. 2, Paul first notes the simple fact (and timing) of the second visit (v. 1); immediately thereafter comes his insistence that the visit was undertaken only in response to divine revelation (v. 2a); then follow the purpose and something of the outcome of the visit (vv. 2b–3). Only after making it clear both that the visit was ordained by God and that it was successful does Paul apparently feel comfortable disclosing that human activity (that of the "false brothers") played any part, even indirectly, in his decision to go to Jerusalem. Thus, in vv. 4–5, he describes briefly the occasion for the revelation and therefore also for the trip: the activity of the "false brothers" and his refusal to yield to them.[24] Having thus completed his explanation of his reason for going to Jerusalem, Paul then (vv. 6–10) returns to the point first raised in v. 3, that is, the outcome of the meeting.

A final point is of interest but cannot here be explored in any detail: Paul's understanding of "revelation" and the relation between divine revelation and the events of human activity and experience. Paul speaks of his own call in terms of God's "revelation" of Christ (Gal 1:12; cf. 1:16), and he also speaks of ongoing "revelation" in the life of the Christian (1 Cor 14:6, 26, 30; 2

---

24. Paul could, of course, have repeated the verb *anebēn* at the beginning of v. 4. I can only speculate why he did not. He had already used the verb twice (vv. 1 and 2), and he may simply have thought it unnecessary or even stylistically displeasing to use it yet a third time within the same sentence. If my reading of Gal 2:1–5 is correct, one might also wonder why *anebēn* was not added to the text by one or more later scribes in an attempt to make the passage more easily understandable. Again, I can only speculate. Scribes may have regarded repetition of the verb as unnecessary or undesirable for the same reasons as did Paul. On the other hand, they may (as has been the case with most modern interpreters) not have understood that *anebēn* was related to the second prepositional phrase. This latter alternative is perhaps strengthened by the fact that the textual tradition reflects various attempts to clarify the beginning of v. 5 (Marcion, for example, omitted *oude*, and the original text of D omitted *hois oude*). The fact that later scribes (and modern interpreters) failed to understand Paul's meaning is no compelling argument, however, against any particular interpretation of Paul's meaning.

Cor 12:1, 7).[25] Except in the passage under consideration, the specific *content* of a revelation is never indicated (e.g., that someone should take a trip to a specified place), although 1 Cor 14:6, 26, 30, where "revelation" is closely associated with "spiritual gifts," rather clearly imply that there *is* such content. Surely it is not unreasonable to assume, however, that Paul saw divine revelation as situational, that is, as related to specific occasions, events, problems, questions, and the like, in much the same way as Paul's own letters were addressed to the specific contemporary needs of his congregations. Thus, in Paul's mind, his own controversy with the "false brothers" in Antioch and a divine revelation instructing him to confer with the apostles in Jerusalem might well have been linked as two aspects of his reason for going to Jerusalem; indeed, the revelation would likely have been viewed as God's response to the situation.[26]

---

25. In addition, Paul speaks of the "revelation" of certain divine attributes or activities, such as righteousness (Rom 1:17), righteous judgment (Rom 2:5), wrath (Rom 1:18), and wisdom (1 Cor 2:10), as well as of various aspects of eschatological "revelation" (Rom 8:18, 19; 1 Cor 1:7; 3:13). Finally, he speaks once of the "revelation" of faith (Gal 3:23).

26. This is not necessarily to suggest that Paul viewed the situation *per se* as a revelation from God or that he "saw" the revelation *in* the situation; rather, in Paul's mind, the situation would likely have prompted the revelation in the sense that the revelation was God's response to the situation.

Chapter 2

Translation and Interpretation of Ἐὰν Μή in Galatians 2:16

Without question, Paul's letter to the Galatians has played a major role in the history of Christian thought. Indeed, Donald G. Miller once claimed—no doubt with some degree of hyperbole—that "perhaps no writing of equal length has influenced the world so mightily."[1] Along the same lines but in more restrained tones, John Knox observed that Galatians "is one of the most significant of early Christian documents, not only because of the light it throws upon Paul and the primitive churches, but also because of the influence it has exerted in subsequent history."[2]

Within the letter, it is generally agreed that one particular verse—2:16—is of crucial importance. Carolyn Osiek, for example, declares that this verse "states in one sentence the core of Paul's conviction about the salvation brought by Christ vis-à-vis salvation as promised by the Law," and Thomas C. Geer, Jr., asserts that "Galatians 2:16 is generally regarded to be the theological center of Paul's letter to the Galatians."[3]

If this is true, then the accurate translation and correct interpretation of the verse are clearly matters of the utmost concern. As Geer points out, however, both the translation and the interpretation of Gal 2:16 are fraught with difficulties. At issue are such questions as: (1) the meaning of δικαιοῦν, ἔργα νόμου, and πίστις (Ἰησοῦ) Χριστοῦ; (2) the translation of ἐὰν μή; and (3) the relation of vv. 15–16 to the preceding verses in the chapter.[4] Obviously, different answers to these difficult questions will

---

"Translation and Interpretation of Ἐὰν Μή." *JBL* 116,3 (Fall 1997) 515–20. Copyright © 1997 Society of Biblical Literature. Reprinted with permission.

1. Miller, *Live As Free Men*, 11.
2. Knox, "Galatians, Letter to the," 338.
3. Osiek, *Galatians*, 26; Geer, "Galatians 2:16," 1.
4. Geer, "Galatians 2:16," 1.

lead to quite diverse understandings of the meaning of the verse. For example, as Geer notes, "the recent discussion between James D. G. Dunn and Heikki Räisänen about Paul's relationship to his former religious life has focused primarily on Galatians 2:16." Dunn believes that the verse demonstrates Paul's basic continuity with Judaism, while Räisänen views it as indicating the apostle's essential break with Judaism.[5]

To be sure, the debate between Dunn and Räisänen involves all of the questions mentioned above; moreover, the questions are themselves interrelated to such an extent that a definitive answer to one would be impossible without attention also to the others. Nevertheless, it is clear that the question of the correct translation of ἐὰν μή lies at the heart of the debate between Dunn and Räisänen and, in fact, is central to an understanding of the verse as a whole. Thus, I shall focus on the question of the translation of ἐὰν μή and how this might affect the translation and interpretation of the verse as a whole.

The usual translation of the Greek phrase ἐὰν μή is "if not," "unless," or "except."[6] In Gal 2:16, however, it is almost always translated as "but only" or simply "but."[7] The rationale for this was articulated many years ago by Ernest de Witt Burton:

> ἐὰν μή is properly exceptive . . . , but it may introduce an exception to the preceding statement taken as a whole or to the principal part of it—in this case to οὐ δικαιοῦται ἄνθρωπος ἐξ ἔργων νόμου or to οὐ δικαιοῦται ἄνθρωπος alone. The latter alternative is clearly to be chosen here, since the former would yield the thought that a man [*sic*] can be justified by works of law if this be accompanied by faith, a thought never expressed by the apostle and wholly at variance with his doctrine as unambiguously expressed in several pas-

---

5. Geer, "Galatians 2:16"; see Dunn, "New Perspective on Paul," esp. 103–18; and Räisänen, "Galatians 2.16 and Paul's Break with Judaism."
6. BAGD (211) gives only "if not" and "unless" as meanings.
7. See, e.g., BDF §376: "Ἐὰν μή is seldom used for 'but, save' (Att. likewise) and always without verb." Cited as examples are Gal 2:16 and Mark 4:22. In the latter case, I regard "except" as the preferable translation; the former, of course, is the verse under present consideration.

sages. . . . But since the word "except" in English is always understood to introduce an exception to the whole of what precedes, it is necessary to resort to the paraphrastic translation "but only."[8]

Apparently following this rationale, the NRSV, for example, reads: "a person is justified not by works of the law *but* through faith in Jesus Christ"; and F. F. Bruce has: "it is not by legal works that any human being is justified *but only* by faith in Jesus Christ."[9] Räisänen accepts this translation of ἐὰν μή and maintains that "justification by works of the law . . . is denied throughout verse 16, as it is in the rest of the letter."[10] Dunn, on the other hand, argues that ἐὰν μή in Gal 2:16 should be translated in its usual sense of "except" or "unless."[11] Thus, in his view, Paul appears to be saying that justification is impossible on the basis of the law *unless* faith in Christ is also present.[12]

It is my own judgment that Dunn is technically correct as regards the *translation* of ἐὰν μή in Gal 2:16: it carries its usual meaning of "except" or "unless." It is also my judgment, however, that Burton is correct as regards the *reference of the exception* introduced by ἐὰν μή: the exception refers only to the words "a person is not justified," not to "a person is not justified by works of law." Paul is *not* saying that "a person is not justified by works of law except through faith in Jesus Christ";[13] rather, he *is* saying (in this part of the verse) that "a person is not justified except through faith in Jesus Christ."

Is it possible, however, to explain the syntax of Gal 2:16 in such a way as to make this clear? I believe it is. I suggest that in Gal 2:16

---

8. Burton, *Critical and Exegetical Commentary*, 121.
9. Bruce, *Epistle of Paul to the Galatians*, 136.
10. Räisänen, "Galatians 2.16 and Paul's Break with Judaism," 547.
11. Dunn, "New Perspective on Paul," 112.
12. This is, to be sure, an oversimplification of Dunn's view.
13. It is not my purpose in this study to enter the debate regarding the correct translation of πίστις (Ἰησοῦ) Χριστοῦ (i.e., whether the genitive is a subjective or an objective genitive); thus, I follow the more generally accepted view and translate the phrase as "faith in (Jesus) Christ."

we have an example of an "ellipsis"[14] within a parenthesis, and that the verse makes perfectly good sense if the omitted words are added and the parenthesis is so indicated. Thus, I would render Gal 2:16 as follows (with the added words in brackets):[15]

> Knowing that a person is not justified by works of law ([a person is not justified] except through faith in Jesus Christ), we also have come to faith in Christ Jesus in order that we might be justified by faith in Christ and not by works of law, because by works of law no one is justified.

In short, I suggest (1) that "a person is not justified" is intended to serve *double duty* by introducing *both* "by works of law" (i.e., "a person is not justified by works of law") *and* "except through faith in Jesus Christ" (i.e., "a person is not justified except through faith in Jesus Christ") and (2) that "a person is not justified except through faith in Jesus Christ" is intended as a parenthetical aside, included to clarify and amplify the statement, "a person is not justified by works of law."

To support this interpretation, I offer the following brief observations:

1. It is clear that what I am calling "parenthetical asides," or simply "parentheses,"[16] are by no means rare in the letters of

---

14. According to BDF §§479–80, "Ellipsis (brachylogy) in the broad sense applies to any idea which is not fully expressed grammatically and leaves it to the hearer or reader to supply the omission because it is self-evident." "Ellipsis in the strict sense," however, refers to "a case in which a term neither is present nor can be supplied from some related term."

15. As already indicated, I do not here propose to deal with the meaning of δικαιοῦν, the meaning of ἔργα νόμου, or the correct translation of πίστις (Ἰησοῦ) Χριστοῦ.

16. BDF §458 defines "parenthesis" as "a grammatically independent thought thrown into the midst of the sentence," suggesting (§465) that it "usually originates in a need which suddenly crops up to enlarge upon a concept or thought where it appears in the sentence" or that "it may be due to the difficulty of adapting an afterthought which suddenly comes to mind to the structure of the sentence as it was begun."

Paul.[17] Indeed, in the Galatian letter itself, the RSV has parentheses at 1:20; 2:2, 6, 8 (the last three in the same chapter as 2:16!), and the NRSV includes all of these except 1:20; in addition, T. Baarda, for example, has found parentheses at 1:12[18] and 5:11b.[19] Thus, there is no a priori reason for denying the presence of a parenthesis also at Gal 2:16.

2. It is also clear that there are numerous examples of ellipsis in Paul's letters.[20] Within the Galatian letter, I argued some years ago for the presence of ellipsis in Gal 2:1–5 (just a few verses prior to 2:16).[21] Similarly, a few verses later, in Gal 3:5, it is likely that "he who supplies the Spirit . . ." is intended to be repeated (in slightly different form) before "by works of law or by hearing with faith."[22] Recently, J. Lambrecht has argued convincingly for the presence of an ellipsis in Gal 5:11b.[23] Thus, as in the case of parenthesis, there is no a priori reason for denying the presence of ellipsis at Gal 2:16.

3. More specifically, quite apart from my proposed translation of the verse, it is clear that an ellipsis already occurs in Gal

---

17. BDF §465 suggests possible parentheses at Rom 1:13; 2:15–16; 3:5; 2 Cor 11:21; 6:2, 13; 10:10.

18. Baarda, "Openbaring-Traditie en Didachè," esp. 157–59.

19. Baarda, "Ti eti diōkomai in Gal. 5:11"; but for a rebuttal, see Lambrecht, "Is Gal 5:11b a Parenthesis?"

20. See, e.g., BDF §481: "Ellipses dependent on individual style and choice go much farther, especially in letters, where the writer can count on the knowledge which the recipient shares with himself and where he imitates ordinary speech. In the latter there is likewise an abundance of elliptical expressions, both conventional and those more dependent on individual preference." Here, it may be relevant to note that Paul's letter to the Galatians was apparently *dictated* (see Gal 6:11), that is, delivered orally. In Paul's letters, BDF §§479–83 finds ellipsis (of various types) at Rom 4:9; 5:3, 11, 18; 8:23; 9:6, 10; 11:18; 13:7; 14:21; 1 Cor 1:31; 3:2; 4:6; 10:24, 31; 14:19, 34; 2 Cor 1:24; 3:5; 5:13; 8:15, 19; 9:6, 7; 10:9; Gal 2:9; 3:5, 19; 5:13; Phil 3:13:4:17.

21. Walker, "Why Paul Went to Jerusalem" (chapter 1 in this volume).

22. See, e.g., BDF §479.

23. Lambrecht, "Is Gal 5:11b a Parenthesis?"

2:16. Strictly speaking, as the introduction to the protasis of an implied conditional statement, ἐὰν μή should be followed by a verb. Because it is not, it represents an elliptical construction "with the verb of the protasis omitted."[24] Both the implied verb and its subject, however, are almost certainly to be inferred from the δικαιοῦται ἄνθρωπος earlier in the verse.[25] Thus, the completed protasis would read ἐὰν μὴ δικαιῶται (subjunctive mood following ἐάν) ἄνθρωπος διὰ πίστεως Ἰησοῦ Χριστοῦ ("unless a person is justified through faith in Jesus Christ").[26]

---

24. LSJ, 481 (VII.3). This is by no means rare, either in classical Greek or in the NT. See, e.g., Smyth, *Greek Grammar*, 530–31; Goodwin, *Greek Grammar*, 300; and BDF §376.

25. This means, of course, that, as I propose to translate the verse, the verb δικαιοῦται actually serves *triple* (not just double) duty: it introduces both "by works of law" and "except through faith in Jesus Christ," and (in the subjunctive mood following ἐάν) it is the verb to be inferred after ἐὰν μή.

26. Gal 2:16 is in some respects similar to Gal 1:19, where the verb of the protasis is also missing and must be supplied from the verb εἶδον earlier in the sentence (here, it might be said that εἶδον does *double duty*, with both ἕτερον τῶν ἀποστόλων and Ἰάκωβον τὸν ἀδελφὸν τοῦ κυρίου serving as its direct objects). Cf. also Gal 1:7, where, however, the verb appears both in the protasis and earlier in the sentence. In neither 1:19 nor 1:7 is it entirely clear what the implied *apodosis* might be. Except for the absence of ἄν in the apodosis, 1:19 might be regarded as a contrary-to-fact condition: "If I had not seen James the brother of the Lord, I would not have seen another of the apostles [besides Cephas]." In the case of 1:7, Burton suggests that εἰ μή introduces not a protasis but rather an "exception" and translates the verse, "which is not another except in the sense that . . ." (*Critical and Exegetical Commentary*, 23). Here again, however, except for the absence of ἄν and the *present* tense of the verbs, the verse might be regarded as a contrary-to-fact condition: "If there were not some troubling you and wishing to pervert the gospel of Christ, [there] would not be another [gospel]." For the possibility that both 1:19 and 1:7 might in fact *be* contrary-to-fact conditions, see, e.g., Lambrecht ("Is Gal 5:11b a Parenthesis?," 238–39) on Gal 5:11b: "The protasis (εἰ . . . κηρύσσω) is grammatically speaking a so-called 'realis', a simple condition, but one expects here an irrealis, a condition contrary to fact: 'if I were still preaching circumcision'. There can be no doubt, since his becoming a Christian Paul does no longer preach circumcision. Notwithstanding the simple condition of this protasis Paul refers to an irreal hypothesis, a condition contrary to fact." See also, e.g.,

4. Logically, of course, a protasis implies an apodosis. In different ways, both Dunn and Burton suggest that the apodosis of the conditional statement in Gal 2:16 is stated at the beginning of the verse. For Dunn, it is οὐ δικαιοῦται ἄνθρωπος ἐξ ἔργων νόμου; for Burton, only οὐ δικαιοῦται ἄνθρωπος. Both in classical Greek and in the New Testament, however, it is not uncommon for the apodosis of a conditional statement to be omitted, particularly if it can easily be inferred from the context.[27] Thus, it is by no means clear, on a priori grounds, that the apodosis is in fact stated in Gal 2:16. If not, is it possible to reconstruct an implied apodosis? I submit that it is. As already noted, the verb of the protasis in Gal 2:16 is omitted and must be inferred from the verb earlier in the sentence (δικαιοῦται). It is a general rule of Greek syntax, however, that "the verb of the protasis is usually omitted when the apodosis has the same verb."[28] This suggests that the most likely verb for the apodosis in Gal 2:16 would be the appropriate form of the verb in the protasis (δικαιῶται). In the context, it suggests further that the most likely subject of this verb would be the same as the subject of the verb in the protasis (ἄνθρωπος). Thus, the most likely apodosis would be simply οὐ δικαιοῦται ἄνθρωπος. The complete conditional statement, then, would read, οὐ δικαιοῦται ἄνθρωπος ἐὰν μὴ δικαιῶται ἄνθρωπος διὰ πίστεως Ἰησοῦ Χριστοῦ ("A person is not justified unless he/she is justified through faith in Jesus Christ").[29]

Burton, *Critical and Exegetical Commentary*, 286: "The conditional clause εἰ . . . κηρύσσω, though having the form of a simple present supposition, evidently expresses an unfulfilled condition."

27. See, e.g., Smyth, *Greek Grammar*, 532; Burton, *Syntax*, 110; and Dana and Mantey, *Manual Grammar*, 291.

28. Smyth, *Greek Grammar*, 530.

29. Despite what has just been said about omission of the apodosis in conditional statements, it could be argued that the apodosis in Gal 2:16 is *not* actually omitted; it has already been stated earlier in the verse and is simply not repeated. This, however, leaves unanswered the question of whether the apodosis consists of οὐ δικαιοῦται ἄνθρωπος ἐξ ἔργων νόμου or simply οὐ δικαιοῦται ἄνθρωπος. This must be resolved on other grounds.

5. Not only is my proposed interpretation of Gal 2:16 plausible in terms of Greek syntax and Pauline style; it also provides a clear and consistent picture of Paul's views regarding the basis for justification (i.e., justification is based not on works of law but rather on faith in Christ). Although this latter point might be regarded as "begging the question" or some form of "circular argumentation," nevertheless, in my judgment, it should not be ignored.[30]

6. Finally—and this may be as much a conclusion to be drawn from my interpretation as it is an argument for it—the structure of Gal 2:16 can be seen as forming a chiasm if my reading of the verse is correct:

  A — a person is not justified by works of law
   B — ([a person is not justified] except through faith in Jesus Christ)
    C — we also have come to faith in Christ Jesus
   B¹ — in order that we might be justified by faith in Christ
  A¹ — and not by works of law because by works of law no one is justified

---

30. Indeed, it is essentially the argument used by Burton to support his view that ἐὰν μή in Gal 2:16 introduces an exception only to "the principal part" of the preceding statement, not to the statement "taken as a whole" (*Critical and Exegetical Commentary*, 121).

Chapter 3

Does the "We" in Galatians 2:15–17 Include Paul's Opponents?

Introduction

Generally speaking, J. Louis Martyn is rather dubious regarding recent attempts to interpret Paul's Galatian letter in terms of ancient rhetorical canons.[1] He does, however, express considerable interest in the rhetorical strategies employed in Galatians. Of particular concern in the present study is Martyn's understanding of Paul's rhetorical use of "we" (ἡμεῖς) in Gal 2:15–17.

Because it immediately follows Paul's reported rebuke of Cephas in v. 14b, Gal 2:15–17 appears, at least initially, to be simply a continuation of what Paul said. If so, the "we" in vv. 15–17 may well refer solely to Paul and Cephas. According to Martyn, however, it is clear by the end of chapter 2 that Paul is addressing a larger audience than just Cephas.[2] This suggests that vv. 15–17 are not a continuation of Paul's statement to Cephas.[3] Nevertheless, it is still possible that the "we" of these verses refers specifically to Paul and Cephas—representing simply Paul's acknowledgement or reminder to his Galatian readers that he and Cephas share both a common Jewish heritage (v. 15) and a common Christian faith (vv. 16–17).

It is also possible, however, that the "we" is more inclusive. Thus, it might also include Barnabas and "the other Jews" mentioned in v. 13. More broadly, it might refer to all Jews who, like

---

"Does the 'We' in Gal 2.15–17 Include Paul's Opponents?" *NTS* 49,4 (Oct 2003) 560–65. Copyright © 2003 Cambridge University Press. Reprinted with permission.

1. Martyn, *Galatians: A New Translation*, 20–23. For attempts at such an interpretation, see, e.g., Betz, *Galatians: A Commentary*; Longenecker, *Galatians*; and Witherington, *Grace in Galatia*.

2. Martyn, *Galatians: A New Translation*, 229.

3. Note that both the RSV and the NRSV end Paul's statement to Cephas with v. 14 and, indeed, the latter ends the paragraph at this point.

Cephas and Paul, have become Christians.[4] Martyn asserts, however, that vv. 15–21 are in fact "a speech" addressed to Paul's opponents in Galatia and that the "we" of vv. 15–17 is specifically intended to include these opponents.[5] Indeed, he sees the entire phrase, ἡμεῖς φύσει Ἰουδαῖοι καὶ οὐκ ἐξ ἐθνῶν ἁμαρτωλοί, as "a rhetorical convention, the *captatio benevolentiae*, in which the speaker captures his audience by means of a friendly reference to something he shares with them"—in this case, a common Jewish heritage.[6] Thus, presumably, Paul hopes to establish a common bond with his opponents in the hope of winning them over to his own position.

The purpose of the present study is to argue that Martyn's interpretation of the "we" in Gal 2:15–17 is incorrect—that it does not, in fact, include Paul's opponents. The argument will be based upon five considerations: (1) Paul's use of the first person plural elsewhere in Galatians; (2) the significance of the first two words in Gal 2:15; (3) the possibility that Paul's opponents in Galatia were not Christians; (4) Paul's use of the third person when referring to his opponents elsewhere in Galatians; and (5) the tenor of Paul's actual statements regarding his opponents.

Paul's Use of the First Person Plural Elsewhere in Galatians

Elsewhere in Galatians, Paul employs the first person plural[7] in three different ways: (1) in a clearly *inclusive* sense, referring simply to all Christians, whether Jewish or Gentile;[8] (2) in an *implicitly inclusive* sense, referring specifically to Jewish Christians but

---

4. E.g., Matera, *Galatians*, 92; and Betz, *Galatians: A Commentary*, 115.

5. Martyn, *Galatians: A New Translation*, 230, 248. Martyn (pp. 117–26) prefers the more neutral label "teachers" rather than "opponents," though he acknowledges (p. 117) that Paul views them as opponents.

6. Martyn, *Galatians: A New Translation*, 246. For a similar interpretation, see, e.g., Das, "Another Look at ἐὰν μή," 536–39.

7. Included under "first person plural" are both the first person plural of the personal pronoun ("we" or "us") and the first person plural form of verbs.

8. Gal 1:3, 4; 4:26, 31; 5:1, 5, 25; 6:14, 18.

with language immediately following that draws Paul's Gentile readers in Galatia into the picture;[9] and (3) in a clearly *exclusive* sense, referring to Paul himself (and one or more of his associates?) in such a way as to distinguish him (them?) from certain other people.[10] Clearly, the first and second usages are not applicable to Gal 2:15–17, because the phrase "Jews by birth and not Gentile sinners" (φύσει Ἰουδαῖοι καὶ οὐκ ἐξ ἐθνῶν ἁμαρτωλοί) makes it clear that the "we" of these verses refers to Jews but not to Gentiles. The third usage, which I have termed the "exclusionary" usage, may, however, provide something of a precedent for the "we" of 2:15–17.[11]

The exclusionary use of the first person plural suggests a dichotomy between the "we" and a "they." Moreover, it implies some degree of tension or even conflict between the two. Finally, in each of the three passages employing this usage, the "they" apparently refers to Paul's fellow Jews; and, in at least two of the three, it refers to fellow Jewish Christians. Thus, the first person plural in Gal 1:8–9 distinguishes Paul (and his associates?) from his opponents in Galatia, who almost certainly are Jews but who may or may not be Jewish Christians.[12] In Gal 2:4–5, it distinguishes Paul (and one or more associates?) from the "false brothers" (ψευδάδελφοι), who almost certainly are Jewish Christians[13] and whom Paul clearly regards as opponents. In Gal 2:9–10, the first person plural distinguishes Paul and Barnabas from James, Cephas, and John, who, of course, are Jewish Christians. In this passage, although no actual controversy is indicated, there is a clear differentiation

---

9. Gal 3:13–14, 23–25; 4:3–6. Specific reference to Jewish Christians is indicated by mention of the Law, but see "the Gentiles" in 3:14, "you" in 3:26, and "you" in 4:6–7.

10. Gal 1:8–9; 2:4–5; 2:9–10.

11. Note that all three of the passages employing the third usage occur prior to 2:15–17.

12. Most scholars assume that they are Jewish Christians, but Nanos has recently argued rather convincingly that they were non-Christian Jews (*The Irony of Galatians*).

13. The label ψευδάδελφοι suggests that they are—or at least claim to be—Christians (cf. 2 Cor 11:26), and the nature of their dispute with Paul probably indicates that they are Jewish Christians.

between Paul's mission and that of the Jerusalem apostles and at least the intimation of some degree of tension.

If the "we" of Gal 2:15–17 is interpreted in light of these passages—that is to say in the "exclusionary" sense, then it must be seen as suggesting a dichotomy between Paul (and any others included in the "we") and an implied "they." The dichotomy cannot be simply between Jews and Gentiles, however, as might be implied by the opening phrase of v. 15 (ἡμεῖς φύσει Ἰουδαῖοι καὶ οὐκ ἐξ ἐθνῶν ἁμαρτωλοί), because Paul immediately makes it clear (v. 16) that the "we" refers not to *all* Jews but only to Jews who "know that a person is not justified by works of law" and "have trusted in Christ Jesus." This suggests that the "they" would be people, almost certainly Jews, who do not know this and/or have not trusted in Christ—most likely, Paul's opponents in Galatia. Thus, the "we" in Gal 2:15–17 by no means includes Paul's opponents; rather, it suggests a sharp dichotomy between Paul and them.

The Significance of the First Two Words in Gal 2:15

The very presence and the placement of the first two words of Gal 2:15—ἡμεῖς φύσει—suggest that both are singled out for special emphasis. In the first place, each could have been omitted without significantly altering the denotative meaning of vv. 15–16. If these two verses form a single sentence, as appears likely,[14] then the ἡμεῖς of 16b could have served as the subject of the entire sentence, thus making the ἡμεῖς of 15 unnecessary. Similarly, if Paul's intention was simply to distinguish between Jews and Gentiles, there would have been no need for φύσει; it would simply have been understood. In the second place, the positioning of ἡμεῖς at the very beginning of the sentence and that of φύσει before rather than after Ἰουδαῖοι indicate that both words are in some way being emphasized.

---

14. See, e.g., Bruce, *Epistle of Paul to the Galatians*, 137.

The emphasis on ἡμεῖς suggests a dichotomy between the "we" and an implied "they."[15] The meaning could be either (a) "*we* are Jews but they are not" or (b) "they are Jews but so are *we*." Because the implied "they" would almost certainly be Paul's opponents and because these opponents were almost certainly Jews (whether Christian or not), it is my own judgment that the latter meaning is the correct one: Paul tacitly acknowledges the Jewish credentials of his opponents but, at the same time, asserts that his own Jewish credentials (and those of Peter and possibly others) are in no way inferior.[16] Thus, the "we" distinguishes Paul (and anyone else included in the "we") from the opponents even as it acknowledges their common Jewish heritage.

The emphasis on φύσει could mean either (a) "we are Jews *by birth* but they are not" or (b) "they are Jews by birth, but so are *we*." As regards the former alternative, Mark D. Nanos suggests that the Paul's opponents[17] may very well, in fact, have been proselytes[18]—a suggestion that I regard as worthy of serious consideration. If this is correct, then the emphasis on φύσει becomes quite striking: "We (unlike the opponents) are Jews by birth, not by conversion; thus, our Jewish credentials are even stronger than theirs." Even if this is not the case, however, the wording strongly reinforces the claim that Paul's Jewish credentials are in no way inferior to those of his opponents: "We (like our opponents) are in every sense *real Jews*."

In short, it appears that the "we" of Gal 2:15 is comparative ("we like they") and that the "by birth" is either comparative or contrastive (either "we like they" or "we unlike they"). In both cases, the other member of either the comparison or the contrast is most likely Paul's opponents in Galatia. In short, it is difficult

---

15. To be sure, the dichotomy could be between the "we" and a "you," but this would suggest that the distinction is between Paul (and others) and his Galatian readers, which appears most unlikely.
16. Cf. 2 Cor 11:22, where the situation faced by Paul is remarkably similar to that in Galatians; cf. also Phil 3:4b–5.
17. Nanos prefers the term "influencers."
18. Nanos, *The Irony of Galatians*, 6, 14–15, 239–42, and especially 277–81.

to see how these opponents could be included in the "we" of vv. 15–17.

Paul's Opponents in Galatia as Non-Christians

Nanos has recently mounted a strong argument that, contrary to the assumption of most scholars, Paul's opponents in Galatia were not Jewish Christians—indeed, that they were not Christians at all; rather, they were "members of the larger Jewish communities of Galatia entrusted with the responsibility of conducting Gentiles wishing more than guest status within the communities through the ritual process of proselyte conversion by which this is accomplished."[19] In my judgment, Nanos may very well be correct at this point. If so, then the "we" of Gal 2:15–17 cannot include Paul's opponents, for Paul declares (v. 16) that "*we* have trusted in Christ Jesus."

Paul's Use of the Third Person with Reference to His Opponents

As already noted, nowhere else in Galatians does Paul include his opponents when employing the first person plural. Moreover, he never speaks *to* these opponents in the second person. Consistently, when he has his opponents in mind, he speaks *about* them, using the third person.[20] I see no reason to view Gal 2:15–17 as an exception. Thus, it is my judgment that the "we" of these verses excludes rather than includes Paul's opponents.

The Tenor of Paul's Statements regarding His Opponents

A final consideration in the argument against inclusion of Paul's opponents in the "we" of Gal 2:15–17 is the absolutely scathing tenor of what Paul actually says about these opponents. They are "confusing" (ταράσσειν) the Galatian Christians (1:7; 5:10), "bewitching" (βασκάνειν) them (3:1), and "prevent[ing] them from

---

19. Nanos, *The Irony of Galatians* (quotation p. 6).
20. Gal 1:7, 9; 2:4–5, 12; 3:1; 4:17; 5:7, 10, 12; 6:12–13.

obeying the truth" (5:7); further, their motives in so doing are dishonorable (4:17; 6:12–13). Apparently, in Paul's view, these opponents have no redeeming features at all. Indeed, he wishes that they would castrate themselves (5:12), warns that they will face judgment (5:10), and, in fact, pronounces a curse upon them (1:9). With the possible exception of 2:15–17, this is absolutely consistent in the Galatian letter. Thus, I see no reason to suppose that, in this one passage, Paul would, "in a friendly manner,"[21] include these opponents in his invocation of a shared confessional statement—even as a rhetorical device.

Conclusion

By way of summary:

1. An examination of Paul's use of the first person plural elsewhere in Galatians suggests that the "we" of Gal 2:15–17 is employed in an exclusionary rather than an inclusionary sense—i.e., to express a sharp dichotomy between the "we" and an implied "they"; it suggests, further, that Paul's opponents in Galatia are the "they."
2. The presence and placement of the first two words in 2:15—ἡμεῖς and φύσει—suggest the same thing.
3. It may be that Paul's opponents in Galatia were not Christians at all, in which case they could not be included in the "we" of 2:15–17.
4. Elsewhere in Galatians, Paul consistently employs the *third* person, not the first, when he has his opponents in mind.
5. The scathing tenor of Paul's comments regarding his opponents makes it highly unlikely that he would include them in the "we" of 2:15–17.

In light of these considerations, it is my own judgment that the "we" (ἡμεῖς) of Gal 2:15–17 refers in the first instance to Paul and Cephas, with possibly a secondary reference to Barnabas and

---

21. Martyn, *Galatians: A New Translation*, 248.

"the other Jews" in the Galatian churches. It does not, however, include Paul's opponents. In these verses, Paul is in no way suggesting that he and his opponents are in agreement—regarding anything; quite to the contrary! Rather, his use of the "we" is intended to associate Cephas with himself—despite Cephas' temporary lapse (Gal 2:11–14)—precisely in the struggle against the opponents.

In 2:1–10, Paul has claimed the support of the "pillar" apostles (James, Cephas, and John) for his mission to the Gentiles. Now, in 2:15–17, he claims the support of Cephas in his struggle against his opponents in Galatia. As in 2:1–10, to be sure, Paul makes these claims with a certain degree of ambivalence. In 2:6–9, he refers rather snidely to the "reputation" of James, Cephas, and John as "pillars" but insists that this made no difference to him (or to God). By the same token, in 2:11–14, he sharply rebukes Cephas for his "hypocrisy." Nevertheless, in 2:7–9, he insists that James, Cephas, and John approved his mission to the Gentiles. Similarly, in his use of "we" in 2:15–17, he claims Cephas' support in his struggle against the opponents. In short, he places himself and Cephas (and possibly Barnabas and "the other Jews") on one side of the conflict and the opponents on the other. His "we" is by no means intended to include the latter but rather precisely to separate them from both himself and Cephas.

Chapter 4

Galatians 2:8 and the Question of Paul's Apostleship

It has often been noted that Gal 2:8 (ὁ ἐνεργήσας Πέτρῳ εἰς ἀποστολὴν τῆς περιτομῆς ἐνήργησεν καὶ ἐμοὶ εἰς τὰ ἔθνην) refers to Peter's missionary activity as an "apostleship' or "apostolate" (ἀποστολή) but does not explicitly apply the same label to that of Paul.[1] The omission is indeed surprising, given Paul's vehement insistence upon his own apostolic status earlier in the Galatian letter (1:1)[2] and his references elsewhere to his mission as an "apostleship" (ἀποστολή, Rom 1:5; 1 Cor 9:2). Thus, many scholars have assumed that the wording of the latter part of the verse (ἐνήγησεν καὶ ἐμοὶ εἰς τὰ ἔθνη) is to be seen as an ellipsis — "an abbreviated form of speech which would be understood by Paul's readers to explicitly attribute apostleship to Paul as well as Peter."[3] Ernest De Witt Burton, for example, asserts that "εἰς τὰ ἔθνη is manifestly a condensed expression equivalent to εἰς ἀποστολὴν τῶν ἐθνῶν, or the like, used for brevity's sake or through negligence."[4]

"Galatians 2:8 and the Question of Paul's Apostleship." *JBL* 123,2 (Summer 2004) 323–27. Copyright © 2004 Society of Biblical Literature. Reprinted with permission.

1. E.g., Betz, *Galatians: A Commentary*, 98: "Most surprisingly, the statement does not contain the parallel notion of Paul's 'apostolate of the Gentiles' (ἡ ἀποστολὴ τῶν ἐθνῶν)."

2. Gal 1:1; see also Gal 1:17; 1 Thess 2:6; 1 Cor 1:1; 4:9; 9:1–2, 5; 15:9; 2 Cor 1:1; 11:5; 12:11–12; Rom 1:1; 11:13.

3. McLean, "Galatians 2.7–9 and the Recognition of Paul's Apostolic Status," 68–70 (quotation p. 70). Schlier (*Der Brief an die Galater*, 78 n. 2) and Mussner (*Der Galaterbrief*, 116 n. 91) see this as an example of a construction known as *comparatio compendiaria*; on this, see, e.g., Schwyzer, *Griechische Grammatik*, vol. 2, 99 n. 1; and BDF §479, 483.

4. Burton, *Critical and Exegetical Commentary*, 94.

To support this latter interpretation of Gal 2:8, the ellipsis in the verse immediately preceding (v. 7) is sometimes cited as a parallel. Thus, for example, Frank J. Matera insists:

> The omission of "apostleship" here [in v. 8] does not mean that Paul has an inferior position *vis à vis* Peter. Rather, there is a balance in the use of ellipsis in this and the preceding verse: Paul entrusted with *the gospel to the uncircumcised*, Peter *to the circumcised*; Peter entrusted with *apostleship to the circumcised*, Paul *to the uncircumcised*.[5]

Similarly, Richard B. Hays maintains that "the non-repetition of 'apostleship' in v. 8 is no more significant than the non-repetition of 'gospel' in v. 7."[6]

A close reading of vv. 7 and 8, however, discloses that there is no real parallel so far as the syntax of the two verses is concerned. The relevant portion of v. 7 (πεπίστευμαι τὸ εὐαγγέλιον τῆς ἀκροβυστίας καθὼς Πέτρος τῆς περιτομῆς) is carefully crafted in such a way as to leave no doubt regarding either the meaning of the statement or, indeed, the actual wording to be supplied. The parallel genitives (τῆς ἀκροβυστίας and τῆς περιτομῆς) make it clear that the words to be supplied (following Πέτρος) are πεπίστευται τὸ εὐαγγέλιον (parallel to πεπίστευμαι τὸ εὐαγγέλιον in the earlier part of the clause). Insertion of the missing words in no way disturbs the syntax of the sentence, and no further alteration is required. The resulting sense of the entire clause is then obvious: πεπίστευμαι τὸ εὐαγγέλιον τῆς ἀκροβυρτίας καθὼς Πέτρος πεπίστευται τὸ εὐαγγέλιον τῆς περιτομῆς.

Such, however, is not the case with v. 8. In the first part of the verse (ὁ γὰρ ἐνεργήσας Πέτρῳ εἰς ἀποστολὴν τῆς περιτομῆς), it is clear that ἀποστολήν (accusative case) is the object of the preposition εἰς and that τῆς περιτομῆς (genitive case) is related

---

5. Matera, *Galatians*, 77.
6. Hays, "Letter to the Galatians," 226.

to ἀποστολήν in some kind of descriptive way (e.g., "apostleship of the circumcision," "apostleship to the circumcision," "apostleship for the circumcision"). Thus, a literal translation of these words reads, "For the one who worked in Peter for an apostleship of the circumcision . . ." The second part of the verse (ἐνήργησεν καὶ ἐμοὶ εἰς τὰ ἔθνη), however, not only omits ἀποστολήν but also has the preposition εἰς followed immediately by τὰ ἔθνη. Because τὰ ἔθνη is in the accusative case, it (not an implied ἀποστολήν) would appear to be the object of the preposition εἰς, which, of course, is regularly followed by the accusative case. Thus, there is no syntactical parallelism between τῆς περιτομῆς (genitive case) and τὰ ἔθνη (accusative case) in v. 8, as there is between τῆς ἀκροβυστίας and τῆς περιτομῆς (both in the genitive case) in v. 7. Indeed, rendering ἐνήργυσεν καὶ ἐμοὶ εἰς τὰ ἔθνη as "he worked also in me for an apostleship of the Gentiles" would require not only supplying the word ἀποστολή but also changing the accusative τὰ ἔθνη to the genitive τῶν ἐθνῶν. In short, although it is clear that τὸ εὐαγγέλιον is to be repeated in v. 7, it is by no means self-evident that ἀποστολήν is similarly to be repeated in v. 8. The latter part of v. 8 may indeed be an ellipsis, but, if so, neither the meaning nor the wording to be supplied is obvious. A literal translation reads simply, "he worked also in me for the Gentiles;"[7] anything beyond this is pure speculation.

The verse immediately following Gal 2:8 also contains an ellipsis (ἵνα ἡμεῖς εἰς τὰ ἔθνη αὐτοὶ δὲ εἰς τὴν περιτομήν); thus, one might argue that the presence of ellipses in both v. 7 and v. 9 strengthens the case for such an ellipsis also in v. 8. The claim that v. 8 is syntactically parallel to v. 9, however, is even less convincing than that involving v. 7. As in the case of v. 7, the phrasing in v. 9 makes clear both the meaning of the statement and, perhaps to a somewhat lesser extent, the wording to be supplied. A verb must

---

7. Thus, Betz, for example, says: "The difference is that only Peter's mission is called 'apostolate' (ἀποστολή) while Paul's mission is not given a specific name" (*Galatians: A Commentary*, 98).

be understood in both members of the clause—presumably the same verb.⁸ The sense of the entire clause then becomes clear: ἵνα ἡμεῖς ἔλθωμεν (or perhaps εὐαγγελισώμεθα) εἰς τὰ ἔθνη αὐτοὶ δὲ ἔλθωσιν (or perhaps εὐαγγελίσωνται) εἰς τὴν περιτομήν. Again, as in v. 7, no alteration has been required except insertion (twice) of the missing word. As has already been noted, however, such is not the case if v. 8 is to be seen as an ellipsis affirming Paul's apostolic status; there, both the insertion of a word and a change in case are required. In short, neither v. 7 nor v. 9 provides an apt parallel for the alleged ellipsis in v. 8.

There are, in fact, a number of other ellipses in Paul's letter to the Galatians, and in every case, so far as I can ascertain, it is necessary only to supply the missing word or words to make clear the meaning of the statement; no other alteration is needed. Thus, for example, Gal 1:12 reads, οὐδὲ γὰρ ἐγὼ παρὰ ἀνθρώπου παρέλαβον αὐτὸ οὔτε ἐδιδάχθην, ἀλλὰ δι' ἀποκαλύψεως Ἰησοῦ Χριστοῦ. Here, as Burton notes, "a verb such as is suggested by παρέλαβον and ἐδιδάχθην is of necessity to be supplied in thought with δι' ἀποκαλύψεως,"⁹ but no further alteration is required. Similarly, Gal 2:10—immediately following the ellipsis already noted in v. 9—reads, μόνον τῶν πτωχῶν ἵνα μνημονεύομεν, ὃ καὶ ἐσπούδασα αὐτὸ τοῦτο ποιῆσαι. Here, Burton notes that "ἐθέλησαν or some similar verb might be supplied,"¹⁰ but, once again, no further alteration is required. Further, Gal 3:5 reads, ὁ οὖν ἐπιχορηγῶν ὑμῖν τὸ πνεῦμα καὶ ἐνεργῶν δυνάμεις ἐν ὑμῖν, ἐξ ἔργων νόμου ἢ ἐξ ἀκοῆς πίστεως; here, a verb such as is suggested by the participles ἐπιχορηγῶν and ἐνεργῶν is to be supplied in the second clause of the sentence, but no further alteration is needed. Other examples include Gal 2:4, where a verb is needed before διὰ δὲ παρεισάκτους

---

8. See, e.g., Burton, *Critical and Exegetical Commentary*, 96: "A verb such as ἔλθωμεν or εὐαγγελισώμεθα is to be supplied in the first part, and a corresponding predicate for αὐτοί in the second part."

9. Burton, *Critical and Exegetical Commentary*, 41.

10. Burton, *Critical and Exegetical Commentary*, 99.

Chapter 4 ※ *Gal 2:8 & the Question of Paul's Apostleship* 33

ψευδαδέλφους; Gal 3:19, where a verb is needed in the question, τί οὖν ὁ νόμος; Gal 4:12, where a form of the verb γίνεσθαι is implied before κἀγὼ ὡς ὑμεῖς; Gal 4:23, where the verb γεγέννηται is to be repeated in the second clause of the sentence; and Gal 5:13, where a verb is needed in the clause, μόνον μὴ τὴν ἐλευθερίαν εἰς ἀφορμὴν τῇ σαρκί. In none of these examples, however, is any further alteration of the sentence required. Thus, at least in his Galatian letter, Paul appears to be consistent in his construction of ellipses: in order to make the meaning clear, one need only supply the missing word or words.[11] As has been noted, however, such is not the case if Gal 2:8 is to be read as an ellipsis asserting (or implying) Paul's apostleship. This would require both the insertion of a word (ἀποστολήν) after the preposition εἰς and changing the accusative τὰ ἔθνη to the genitive τῶν ἐθνῶν.

If the author of Gal 2:8 had in fact wished to make it clear that Paul's missionary activity, like that of Peter, was an "apostleship" (ἀποστολή), the verse could easily have been worded in such a way as to accomplish this. Given Paul's insistence elsewhere upon his own apostolic status, one might expect that the relevant clause would simply spell this out, fully and explicitly: ἐνήργησεν καὶ ἐμοὶ εἰς ἀποστολὴν τῶν ἐθνῶν. If, however, for stylistic or other reasons, an ellipsis were preferred, it could have read, ἐνήργησεν καὶ ἐμοὶ τῶν ἐθνῶν (genitive rather than accusative case, with the words εἰς ἀποστολήν to be understood between ἐμοί and τῶν ἐθνῶν); in such case, Gal 2:8 would have been syntactically parallel to v. 7. In either case, the meaning would have been clear, and Paul's "apostleship," like that of Peter, would have been specified—more explicitly in the former instance, but nonetheless unambiguously in the latter. Neither of these alternatives was followed, however.

Thus, as the wording stands, only two possible conclusions appear warranted. The first is that the composition here is simply

---

11. A rather cursory examination of ellipses in the other Pauline letters suggests the same conclusion; see, e.g., Rom 5:3, 11, 18; 8:23; 9:6, 10; 12:1; 13:11; 14:21; 2 Cor 1:24; 3:5; 5:13; 8:19; 9:6; 10:16; Phil 1:28; 3:13.

incredibly sloppy[12]—that, although the intended sense is indeed εἰς ἀποστολὴν τῶν ἐθνῶν, the last two words have been drawn into the accusative case because they come immediately after εἰς, which regularly takes the accusative for its object. This, of course, is conceivable. One must then ask, however, why it is that τῆς περιτομῆς is not similarly drawn into the accusative case (τὴν περιτομήν) following the implied verb πεπίστευται in v. 7.

The other possibility is that, for whatever reason, Gal 2:8 (like the Book of Acts)[13] intentionally refrains from claiming apostolic status for Paul. Thus, some commentators believe that Paul deliberately omitted the second ἀποστολή—perhaps because he was echoing or even quoting the wording of an agreement between himself and the Jerusalem leaders "in which the term 'apostleship' was deliberately withheld from the description of Paul's missionary work."[14] In short, because Paul's primary goal in Gal 2:1-10 is simply to claim apostolic support for his Gentile mission, he "could have thought it wiser to cite [the earlier agreement] without comment, since all that he meant and claimed by 'apostleship' had been agreed to in effect, whether or not the title itself had been used."[15]

My own judgment, however, is that, for reasons already noted, Paul would have been highly unlikely to characterize Peter's missionary activity as an "apostleship" (ἀποστολή) without applying the same label to his own—even if this did reflect the language of an agreement between himself and the Jerusalem "pillars."

---

12. See the phrase "through negligence" in the above quotation from Burton.

13. Except in Acts 14:4, 14, where both Barnabas and Paul are called "apostles" (ἀπόστολοι).

14. Dunn, *Commentary on the Epistle to the Galatians*, 107. See, e.g., Dinkler, "Der Brief an die Galater," 182–183; Dinkler, "Die Petrus-Rom-Frage," 197–98; Klein, "Galater 2,6–9," 282–83; and Schlier, *Der Brief an die Galater*, 12th ed., 77 n. 2. Cf. also, e.g., Lüdemann (*Paul, Apostle to the Gentiles*, 64–80) who argues that Gal 2:7–8 reflects the wording of an agreement reached at Paul's first visit to Jerusalem (prior to the "Jerusalem Conference").

15. Dunn, *Commentary on the Epistle to the Galatians*, 107.

Furthermore, it is by no means clear that Paul would have regarded himself as bound by the specific wording of such an agreement—particularly when writing to the Christians in Galatia, which is rather far removed from Jerusalem.

This, of course, opens up the possibility that Paul may not himself have included 2:8 in his letter to the Galatians. Thus, more than seventy years ago, Ernst Barnikol argued that the verse should be viewed as part of a later, non-Pauline interpolation.[16] My own judgment is that Barnikol is correct, but this is the subject of another study.[17] For the moment, suffice it to note that Gal 2:8 does not attribute apostolic status to Paul, as it explicitly does to Peter, and, in a letter attributed to Paul, this must be seen as quite surprising.

---

16. Barnikol, "Non-Pauline Origin." According to Barnikol, the interpolation consists of v. 7b (beginning with τῆς ἀκροβυστίας) and v. 8.

17. See Walker, "Galatians 2:7b–8 as a Non-Pauline Interpolation" (chapter 5 in this volume).

Chapter 5

Galatians 2:7b–8 as a Non-Pauline Interpolation

Galatians 2:7b–8[1] confronts the interpreter with the following difficult problems: (a) the name Πέτρος, which appears nowhere else in the Pauline letters; (b) a peculiar syntactical construction with the verb ἐνεργεῖν, which is without parallel in the Pauline corpus and, indeed, in the entire New Testament; (c) a distinction between two "gospels," which appears to reflect neither Pauline language nor Pauline thought; (d) a parallelism between Peter and Paul as the two great missionaries of the Christian movement, not to be found elsewhere in Paul's writings and appearing to reflect a later stage of Christian thought; (e) a treatment of "apostleship" that fails to attribute this status to Paul; and (f) the strained connection between vv. 7b–8 and their immediate context. Indeed, these problems are sufficiently numerous and serious to call into question Pauline authorship of the material. Thus, two competing hypothesis have been proposed to account for its presence in Galatians: "the protocol hypothesis" and "the interpolation hypothesis."

In this study, I shall: (a) discuss the history, main features, and possible weaknesses of the two hypotheses; (b) describe the problems of Gal 2:7b–8, indicating my own judgment that they argue not only for non-Pauline origin of the material but also for the interpolation hypothesis as the more plausible explanation for its presence in Galatians; and (c) consider, in an "Addendum," the

---

"Galatians 2:7b–8 as a Non-Pauline Interpolation." *CBQ* 65,4 (Oct 2003) 568–87. Copyright © 2003 Catholic Biblical Association of America. Reprinted with permission.

1. Although I shall deal specifically with the last six words of v. 7 and all of v. 8, some of the discussion will necessarily involve the preceding two words in v. 7: τὸ εὐαγγέλιον.

absence of early attestation of Gal 2:7b–8. Overall, the purpose of the study is to argue that Gal 2:7b–8 is a later, non-Pauline interpolation.

The Protocol Hypothesis

Something akin to the protocol hypothesis was first proposed by Oscar Cullmann. Noting that the Greek name Πέτρος appears in Paul's letters only at Gal 2:7b–8, he suggested that Paul uses Πέτρος here because he is citing "an official document, in the Greek translation of which the form *Petros* was used."[2] As developed more fully, particularly by Erich Dinkler,[3] the protocol hypothesis argues that Paul is here citing, directly or indirectly, some official or quasi-official record or "protocol" of the division of labor worked out between himself and the "pillar" apostles when they met in Jerusalem (Gal 2:1–10; cf. also Acts 15:1–35). This hypothesis now enjoys rather widespread support, either as proposed by Dinkler,[4] in somewhat modified form,[5] or with significant alteration.[6]

Dinkler reconstructs the relevant portion of the protocol as follows: εἶδον οἱ στῦλοι ὅτι Παῦλος πιστεύει[7] τὸ εὐαγγέλιον τῆς ἀκροβυστίας καθὼς Πέτρος τῆς περιτομῆς. ὁ γὰρ ἐνεργήσας Πέτρῳ εἰς ἀποστολὴν περιτομῆς ἐνήργησεν καὶ Παύλῳ εἰς τὰ ἔθνη. Dinkler believes that Paul cited the protocol in order to claim the stamp of apostolic authority for his own missionary activities. Thus, he used the protocol's actual wording rather than

---

2. Cullmann, *Peter: Disciple · Apostle · Martyr*, 20; see also his "Πέτρος, Κηφᾶς," esp. 100 n. 6.
3. Dinkler, "Brief an die Galater," esp. 182–83; idem., "Die Petrus-Rom-Frage," esp. 197–98. Dinkler includes all except the first two words of v. 7 in the protocol.
4. E.g., Klein, "Galater 2,6–9," esp. 282–84; and Schlier, *Der Brief an die Galater*, 12th ed, 77 n. 2.
5. E.g., Betz, *Galatians: A Commentary*, 97; and Bruce, *Epistle of Paul to the Galatians*, 121.
6. E.g., Munck, *Paul and the Salvation of Mankind*, 62 n. 2; Georgi, *Remembering the Poor*, 31–33, see also 168 n. 10; and Lüdemann, *Paul, Apostle to the Gentiles*, 64–80.
7. It is unclear why Dinkler has πιστεύει rather than πεπίστευται.

paraphrasing it to fit his own vocabulary and style.[8] Indeed, Paul may have included wording and even ideas with which he was less than comfortable, precisely in order to claim such authority.

Before asking whether the protocol hypothesis accounts for the problems of Gal 2:7–8 at least as adequately as does its rival, it is appropriate to ask whether it is inherently plausible simply *qua* hypothesis. My own judgment is that it is not.

In the first place, as Richard B. Hays notes, "Paul gives no indication that he is quoting the text of a formal agreement."[9] This, of course, is an argument from silence, and Paul apparently does sometimes cite previously formulated materials without stating that he is doing so. Such citations, however, are limited to confessional formulations (e.g., Rom 1:3–4; Phil 2:6–11) or "slogans" (e.g., 1 Cor 6:12, 13; 7:1; 8:1, 4, 8; 10:23); they do not include formal agreements between himself and others. Moreover, if Paul's purpose in citing the protocol is to claim its support for his own mission, as Dinkler maintains, one would expect him to indicate as much for the benefit of his readers. That he does not do so appears to argue against the protocol hypothesis.

In the second place, there is no evidence that such a protocol ever existed. It is not mentioned in Galatians, elsewhere in the Pauline corpus, or in Acts. Indeed, Acts is silent regarding any division of labor between Paul and the Jerusalem leaders and, in fact, identifies *Peter* as the pioneer missionary to the Gentiles (Acts 10:1–11:18; cf. 15:7).[10] Further, I am unaware of any reference to such a protocol elsewhere in early Christian literature. Thus, the very notion of a protocol remains speculative, with little to recommend it except that it allegedly resolves the problems of Gal 2:7–8. If, however, a resolution of these problems that is at least as satisfactory can be found without appealing to a hypothetical document, then, all other things being equal, Ockham's Razor would appear to favor this alternate solution.

---

8. Dinkler, "Brief an die Galater," 183.
9. Hays, "Letter to the Galatians," esp. 226.
10. Of course, the division of responsibility might have occurred later.

In the third place, the protocol hypothesis assumes that the alleged document was composed in both Aramaic and Greek or, more likely, was formulated in Aramaic and then translated into Greek, and that Paul cites the Greek version because he is addressing a Greek-speaking audience.[11] Thus, Dinkler attempts to show from the Syriac Peshitta that Gal 2:7–8 betrays "Semitic" linguistic features, asserting, for example, that "in the Syriac the parallelism between verses 7 and 8 is complete."[12] Such "Semitic" features, however, might well reflect the work of the translator (from Greek to Syriac) rather than an original Aramaic version. Moreover, as Hans Dieter Betz notes, "there is no evidence . . . for an Aramaic version of the document."[13] Finally, Gunter Klein, who accepts the protocol hypothesis, confesses that the assumption of a Greek copy of the protocol is a "complication of the hypothesis,"[14] and Dinkler acknowledges that "apparently no bilingual protocols or protocol-like documents of antiquity are known in the Greek-Roman area." Thus, the idea of either a bilingual protocol or its translation from Aramaic into Greek is highly suspect.

In the fourth place, the protocol hypothesis assumes that the Greek version of the document would use the Greek Πέτρος rather than the Aramaic Κηφᾶς. This, however, is questionable. Indeed, Paul himself, writing in Greek and for Greek-speaking audiences, consistently uses Κηφᾶς, not Πέτρος, elsewhere in his letters.[15]

The strengths of the protocol hypothesis are that it recognizes the problems of Gal 2:7–8, offers a possible solution for some of them, and, indeed, acknowledges the difficulty of attributing the passage to Paul. Nevertheless, this hypothesis creates at least as many problems as it solves. Thus, I accept Hays's conclusion that,

---

11. The protocol might, of course, have been composed only in Greek, even in Jerusalem, if it was intended for circulation in the Greek-speaking world.
12. Dinkler, "Nachtrag" to "Der Brief an die Galater" in *Signum Crucis*, 281–82.
13. Betz, *Galatians: A Commentary*, 97 n. 385.
14. Klein, "Galater 2,6–9," 283; Dinkler, "Nachtrag," 281.
15. See, e.g., Barnikol, "Non-Pauline Origin," esp. 289–90.

"despite the ingenuity" of the proposal, it must be judged "finally unpersuasive."[16] This opens the door for another solution—the interpolation hypothesis—that does not depend on a hypothetical and otherwise problematic document, and to which I now turn.

The Interpolation Hypothesis

Clearly less popular then its rival,[17] the interpolation hypothesis maintains that Gal 2:7b–8[18] is a later, non-Pauline insertion. Thus, Paul is responsible for neither its wording nor its inclusion in Galatians. A brief history of this hypothesis is instructive.

In 1887, the Dutch scholar W. C. van Manen maintained that Gal 2:7b–8 (beginning with καθὼς Πέτρος τῆς περιτομῆς) was one of numerous "Catholic" (i.e., anti-Marcionite) additions to Galatians.[19] Some years later, P.-L. Couchoud also attributed the material to a "Catholic" editor, but, at about the same time, Henri Delafosse ascribed vv. 6–8 to a "Marcionite" redactor. Then, in 1931, Ernst Barnikol argued that Gal 2:7b–8 (beginning with τῆς ἀκροβυστίας) was an anti-Marcionite insertion, dating from the late second century. Finally, without reference to Barnikol, David Werner suggested that Gal 2:3–8, as a whole, was an interpolation. Thus, at least five scholars have argued that Gal 2:7b–8 is (part of) a later, non-Pauline, addition to Galatians.[20]

---

16. Hays, "Letter to the Galatians," 226. See also, e.g., Haenchen, *The Acts of the Apostles*, 466–67; idem., "Petrus-Probleme" esp. 192–93.

17. Bruce (*Epistle of Paul to the Galatians*, 121) refers to it as one of the "more radical" solutions.

18. Beginning with either τῆς ἀκροβυστίας or καθὼς Πέτρος in v. 7b and including all of v. 8. My own judgment is that the interpolation begins with τῆς ἀκροβυστίας.

19. Van Manen, "Marcions Brief," esp. 530, 513–14; Couchoud, "La première édition de Saint Paul," esp. 258; Delafosse, *Les écrits de Saint Paul*, 189–90; Barnikol, "Non-Pauline Origin"; Werner, "Galatians ii.3–8: As an Interpolation," 380.

20. See also, e.g., Schenke, "Das Weiterwirken des Paulus," esp. 517; and Schenke and Fischer, *Einleitung in die Schriften des Neuen Testaments*, 79–80. O'Neill (*Recovery of Paul's Letter*), regards only καθὼς Πέτρος τῆς περιτομῆς (v. 7b) and Πέτρῳ (v. 8) as "originally glosses to the text" (37). This, however, does remove the name Πέτρος from the material in question.

Although the views of van Manen, Couchoud, Delafosse, and Werner received little attention, Barnikol's proposal immediately provoked negative responses from such leading scholars as Hans Lieztmann, and Johannes Behm, and, more recently, from others including Heinrich Schlier, Erich Dinkler, and Günter Klein.[21] Particularly in the English-speaking world, however, commentators have tended either to summarize briefly and immediately dismiss Barnikol's view and move on to other matters[22] or to ignore it altogether.[23] To my knowledge, no one has subjected his proposal to detailed scrutiny, attempted to answer the rather cursory arguments advanced against it, or, indeed, asked whether there might be additional reasons for viewing Gal 2:7b–8 as an interpolation.

According to Barnikol, the interpolation (Gal 2:7b–8) consists of the following words: τῆς ἀκροβυστίας καθὼς Πέτρος τῆς περιτομῆς. ὁ γὰρ ἐνεργήσας Πέτρῳ εἰς ἀποστολὴν τῆς περιτομῆς ἐνήργησεν καὶ ἐμοὶ εἰς τὰ ἔθνη. With the removal of these words, the original Pauline text of Gal 2:6–9 reads as follows:

ἀπὸ τῶν δοκούντων εἶναι τι, —
ὁποῖοί ποτε ἦσαν οὐδέν μοι διαφέρει ·
πρόσωπον ὁ Θεὸς ἀνθρώπου οὐ λαμβάνει —
ἐμοὶ γὰρ οἱ δοκοῦντες οὐδὲν προσανέθεντο,
   ἀλλὰ τοὐναντίον
ἰδόντες ὅτι πεπίστευμαι τὸ εὐαγγέλιον
καὶ γνόντες τὴν χάριν τὴν δοθεῖσάν με,
Ἰάκωβος καὶ κηφᾶς καὶ Ἰωάννης,
οἱ δοκοῦντες στῦλοι εἶναι,
δεξιὰς ἔδωκεν ἐμοὶ καὶ Βαρναβᾷ κοινωνίας,

---

21. Lietzmann, *An die Galater*, 13; and "Notizen," esp. 93; Behm, Review of Barnikol, *Der nichtpaulinische Ursprung*, esp. 29; Schlier, *Der Brief an die Galater*, 12th ed., 77 n. 2; Dinkler, "Der Brief an die Galater," 182–83. Cf. also his "Die Petrus-Rom-Frage," 198; Klein, "Galater 2,6–9," 282–84.

22. E.g., Betz, *Galatians: A Commentary*, 96; and Bruce, *Epistle to the Galatians*, 121.

23. E.g., Matera, *Galatians*, 76–77; Dunn, *Commentary on the Epistle to the Galatians*, 105–6; and Martyn, *Galatians: A New Translation*, 200–202, 211–12.

ἵνα ἡμεῖς εἰς τὰ ἔθνη,
αὐτοὶ δὲ εἰς τὴν περιτομήν.[24]

According to Barnikol, viewing Gal 2:7b–8 as a later insertion not only accounts for its problems but also sheds significant light upon certain aspects of early Christian history.[25]

Before asking whether the interpolation hypothesis accounts for the problems of Gal 2:7b–8 at least as adequately as does its rival, it is important to ask whether possible objections to the interpolation hypothesis, simply *qua* hypothesis, are as weighty as those raised against the protocol hypothesis.

Two such objections might be raised. The first questions the likelihood of any interpolations in Paul's letters. I have addressed this issue elsewhere, arguing that the widespread presence of interpolations in other ancient literature, what we know or can surmise regarding the literary history of the letters, and the abundant evidence of actual textual alterations in the manuscript tradition "lead almost inescapably to the conclusion, simply on *a priori* grounds, that the Pauline letters, as we now have them, are likely to contain non-Pauline interpolations."[26] Further, it is now widely agreed that there are in fact *some* interpolations in Paul's writings.[27] Thus, there appears to be little basis for objection to the interpolation hypothesis simply as a matter of principle.

The second objection would require that any interpolation hypothesis be supported by direct text-critical evidence; that is, the suspected interpolation must either be missing from one or more

---

24. Barnikol, "Non-Pauline Origin," 293. Barnikol suggests that the original text may also have included the words εἰς τὰ ἔθνη following τὸ εὐαγγέλιον in v. 7a. The insertion, then, would have been placed between τὸ εὐαγγέλιον (v. 7a) and εἰς τὰ ἔθνη (now at the end of v. 8).

25. Barnikol, "Non-Pauline Origin," 286.

26. Walker, *Interpolations*, 26–43, here 43.

27. E.g., Strecker, *History of New Testament Literature*, 40. On 1 Cor 14:34–35, see, e.g., Fee, *First Epistle to the Corinthians*, 699–708; and Murphy-O'Connor, "Interpolations in 1 Corinthians," 90–92. On Rom 16:25–27, see, e.g., Fitzmyer, *Romans*, 753–55. See Walker, *Interpolations*, 17–20, for a listing of many proposed interpolations in the Pauline letters.

of the early witnesses or appear at different locations in these witnesses.[28] As Georg Strecker has noted, such is clearly not the case with Gal 2:7b–8.[29] I have addressed this objection elsewhere, arguing (a) "that the absence of direct text-critical evidence for interpolation must be seen as precisely what it is: the *absence* of evidence, which, in the face of otherwise compelling evidence for interpolation, should not be allowed to decide the issue"; (b) "that the Pauline letters would have been most susceptible to textual alteration, including interpolation, precisely during the period prior to the date of the oldest surviving manuscript"; and (c) that there are "plausible answers to the question of why no manuscripts not containing presumed interpolations have survived."[30] Thus, the absence of text-critical evidence for interpolation means simply that the proposed interpolation was a part of the text by the latter part of the second century. Thus, I regard this second objection to the interpolation hypothesis as by no means conclusive.

In short, it is almost certain that the Pauline letters include interpolations, and direct text-critical evidence is not essential to the identification of such interpolations. Thus, it is my judgment that, so far as Gal 2:7b–8 is concerned, the interpolation hypothesis is considerably less problematic, simply *qua* hypothesis, than is its rival. The relevant question, therefore, now becomes whether the interpolation hypothesis accounts for the problems of Gal 2:7b–8 more adequately than does the protocol hypothesis.

Problems of Gal 2:7b–8

As noted, problems posed by Gal 2:7b–8 include the name Πέτρος, a peculiar syntactical construction with ἐνεργεῖν, the distinction

---

28. E.g., Wisse, "Textual Limits to Redactional Theory," esp. 177–78; Ellis, "Silenced Wives of Corinth," esp. 220; idem, "Traditions in 1 Corinthians," esp. 488 and 498 n. 58; see also, e.g., Gamble, "Redaction of the Pauline Letters," esp. 418; Aland and Aland, *Text of the New Testament*, 295.

29. Strecker, "Das Evangelium Jesu Christi," esp. 527.

30. Walker, *Interpolations*, 55–56. The entire chapter (pp. 44–56) is devoted to a discussion of the absence of direct text-critical evidence for interpolation.

between two "gospels," the parallelism between Peter and Paul, the treatment of "apostleship," and the relation of the material to its context. Here, I shall describe these problems, indicating my own judgment that they point not only to a non-Pauline origin for Gal 2:7b–8 but also to the interpolation hypothesis as the more plausible explanation for its presence in Galatians—in short, that Gal 2:7b–8 was neither composed by Paul nor included by him in his Galatian letter.

The Name Πέτρος

According to Ernst Barnikol, "The starting point [for explaining the difficulties of Gal 2:7b–8] is the unsolved textual problem of the ten Κηφᾶς-Πέτρος passages in Paul."[31] In this regard, six interrelated phenomena are to be noted. First, the name Πέτρος, which appears twice in Gal 2:7b–8,[32] is, according to the best manuscript evidence,[33] not found elsewhere in the Pauline corpus.[34] Second, the name Κηφᾶς occurs four times in 1 Corinthians (1 Cor 1:12; 3:22; 9:5; 15:5)[35] and, according to the best manuscript evidence,[36] four times also in Galatians (Gal 1:18; 2:9, 11, 14)—a total of eight times in the Pauline corpus.

The third phenomenon is that, although Κηφᾶς is clearly the preferred reading at Gal 1:18; 2:9, 11, 14, a few witnesses read

---

31. Barnikol, "Non-Pauline Origin," 286. Unfortunately, the English translation of Barnikol's essay consistently misspells Κηφᾶς as Κεφᾶς (in the German original, Barnikol correctly has Κηφᾶς, though he sometimes transliterates into German as "Kephas"). In this study, I shall change Κεφᾶς to Κηφᾶς when quoting the English translation.

32. The manuscript evidence appears to be unanimous (note, however, that K omits καθὼς Πέτρος τῆς περιτομῆς [v. 7b] and that ὁ γὰρ ἐνεργήσας Πέτρῳ εἰς ἀποστολὴν τῆς περιτομῆς εἰς ἀποστολὴν τῆς περιτομῆς [v. 8] is missing from the original of Codex Sinaiticus as well as from F, G, and 1241).

33. For details, see n. 37 below.

34. It does, of course, appear frequently in the Gospels and Acts (also at 1 Pet 1:1 and 2 Pet 1:1).

35. The manuscript evidence appears to be unanimous.

36. For details, see n. 37 below.

Πέτρος in each case.³⁷ Almost certainly, these variants reflect the influence of Gal 2:7b–8, where Πέτρος is unanimously attested. For whatever reason, some scribes were apparently troubled by the references to Κηφᾶς in Galatians.³⁸ Apparently, too, these scribes regarded Κηφᾶς and Πέτρος as the same person but preferred the latter name.

The fourth phenomenon is actually the absence of a phenomenon. Just as some scribes changed Κηφᾶς to Πέτρος at Gal 1:18; 2:9, 11, 14, apparently for the sake of uniformity, one might have expected the reverse change in some manuscripts of Gal 2:7b–8 (i.e., Πέτρος to Κηφᾶς) — again for the sake of uniformity. After all, Κηφᾶς is the more common name in Galatians and Πέτρος is otherwise absent from the Pauline corpus. Nevertheless, Πέτρος is never changed to Κηφᾶς in the textual tradition of Gal 2:7b–8. Again, this suggests that the scribes, assuming Κηφᾶς and Πέτρος to be the same person, were, for whatever reason, more comfortable with the latter name.

The fifth phenomenon is that, although the manuscript evidence in Gal 2:9 strongly attests the listing of the "pillars" (στῦλοι) in the order Ἰάκωβος, Κηφᾶς, Ἰωάννης, some witnesses that change Κηφᾶς to Πέτρος at this point also revise the order of the listing to Πέτρος, Ἰάκωβος, Ἰωάννης — that is, they give first place to Πέτρος, not Ἰάκωβος, thereby suggesting that Πέτρος, not Ἰάκωβος, is the most important of the three. An exception here is P⁴⁶, which reads Πέτρος but maintains the order Ἰάκωβος, Πέτρος, Ἰωάννης. Thus, it appears that the original listing was Ἰάκωβος, Κηφᾶς, Ἰωάννης, that at least one (early) manuscript (P⁴⁶) changed κηφᾶς to Πέτρος³⁹ but maintained the same se-

---

37. For details, see, e.g., Elliott, "Κηφᾶς," esp. 248. Note that P⁴⁶ (generally dated ca. 200 CE) reads Πέτρος in Gal 2:9 but not in 1:18; 2:11, 14 (P⁴⁶ only came to the attention of scholars in the 1930s and thus was apparently not known by Barnikol when he published his 1931 essay).

38. Similar changes were not made in 1 Cor 1:12; 3:22; 9:5; 15:5, the only other appearances of Κηφᾶς in the Pauline corpus.

39. Only at Gal 2:9; not at 1:18; 2:11, 14.

quence, and that other (later) manuscripts (e.g., D, F, and G)[40] both changed Κηφᾶς to Πέτρος[41] and moved Πέτρος to first place in the list. This suggests that some scribes were troubled both by the reference to Κηφᾶς rather than Πέτρος and by the implication that Κηφᾶς/Πέτρος was less important than Ἰάκωβος.[42]

The sixth and final phenomenon is that the references to Πέτρος in Gal 2:7b–8 are immediately followed by a reference to Κηφᾶς (v. 9),[43] but the relation between the two is by no means clear. Both the Greek Πέτρος and the Aramaic כיפא (transliterated in Greek as Κηφᾶς) mean "rock"; thus, most interpreters have viewed the former as simply the Greek translation of the latter and have assumed Πέτρος and Κηφᾶς to be the same person.[44] Gal 2:7–9 does not intimate, however, that this is the case, and, as Kirsopp Lake observed, "To call the same man by two names in the same sentence is, to say the least, a curious device."[45] Indeed, in the absence of any evidence to the contrary, the passage appears to suggest that Κηφᾶς and Πέτρος are two different people—Κηφᾶς one of the "pillars" of the Jerusalem church and Πέτρος the leading missionary to the Jews.

In short, the name Πέτρος in Gal 2:7b–8 poses at least seven questions:

1. Are Πέτρος and Κηφᾶς the same person?
2. If not, who is Πέτρος?
3. If so, how should one explain both names in the same context (Gal 2:7b–9) with no intimation of their identity?

---

40. D is generally dated to the sixth century; F and G to the ninth century.

41. Not only at Gal 2:9 but also at 1:18; 2:11, 14.

42. Acts 15 (esp. vv. 13–21) suggests that *James* (not Peter) was the leader of the Jerusalem church; see also Acts 12:17; 21:18; Gal 2:12.

43. Regarding textual variants, see n. 37 above.

44. Apart from its eight occurrences in 1 Corinthians and Galatians, Κηφᾶς appears in the NT only in John 1:42, where he is clearly identified as Πέτρος.

45. Lake, "Simon, Cephas, Peter," esp. 96.

4. If so, why is this person called Πέτρος only at Gal 2:7b–8 and Κηφᾶς elsewhere in the Pauline corpus (including in Galatians)?
5. Why did some scribes change Κηφᾶς to Πέτρος in Gal 1:18; 2:9, 11, 14?
6. Why was the opposite change—that is, Πέτρος to Κηφᾶς—never made in Gal 2:7b–8?
7. Why did some scribes change the order Ἰάκωβος, Κηφᾶς, Ἰωάννης to Πέτρος, Ἰάκωβος, Ἰωάννης in Gal 2:9?

Various answers have been proposed. Since antiquity, some interpreters have maintained that Πέτρος and Κηφᾶς are two different people.[46] Most scholars, however, have assumed that Κηφᾶς and Πέτρος are the same person. Thus, Kirsopp Lake once suggested that Paul may simply have used the two names indiscriminately.[47] Alternatively, J. K. Elliott proposed that Paul may "refer to the apostle as Peter when he approves of his work and as Kephas when he disapproves."[48] Attempting to resolve the matter on text-critical grounds, Adalbert Merx and Karl Holl argued that an original Κηφᾶς in Gal 2:7b–8 was changed to Πέτρος when the latter became the more widely-accepted appellation.[49] Along different lines, Paul Gaechtner proposed that Πέτρος was "the

---

46. E.g., Lake, "Simon, Cephas, Peter," 95–97; Goguel, *La foi à la resurrection*, 272–75; Riddle, "Cephas-Peter Problem"; and Henze, "Cephas seu Kephas non est Simon Petrus!" For early Christian attestation of this view, see, e.g., Cullmann, *Peter: Disciple · Apostle · Martyr*, 20 n. 7.

47. Lake, *Earlier Epistles of St. Paul*, 116; see also, e.g., Zahn, *Der Brief des Paulus*, 70 n. 84. Bruce (*Epistle of Paul to the Galatians*, 120) agrees that this may indeed be the case.

48. Elliott, "Κηφᾶς," 248–50, here 250.

49. Merx, *Die vier kanonischen Evangelien*, 161–63; and Holl, *Gesammelte Aufsätze*, vol. 2: *Der Osten*, 45 n. 3. Schlier (*Der Brief an die Galater*, 77 n. 2), however, notes the unlikelihood that a "'Hellenistic' redaction of the text" (i.e., one in which Κηφᾶς was changed to Πέτρος) would have gained acceptance in Gal 2:7b–8 but nowhere else in Galatians; Dinkler agrees ("Der Brief an die Galater," 182); see also, e.g., Schulze-Kadelbach, "Die Stellung des Petrus," esp. 1.

personal name" and Κηφᾶς "the official name" for the same person,⁵⁰ and Peter Stuhlmacher suggested that Πέτρος was the title (not personal name) borne by Cephas "in his capacity as God's apostolic mandatory (only!) for the world of Israel."

In my judgment, such proposed solutions are pure speculation, with little evidence to support them. I regard it as more likely that Paul consistently wrote Κηφᾶς and that the references to Πέτρος in Gal 2:7b–8 derive from another source. If Paul were so abruptly to introduce the name Πέτρος—in a context where he has already referred to Κηφᾶς (Gal 1:18) and is to do so three more times (Gal 2:9, 11, 14) including once in the very next verse—would he not think it important either to indicate that Πέτρος and Κηφᾶς are the same person or, alternatively, to provide some identification of Πέτρος, whom he never mentions elsewhere, either in this letter or in his other extant writings? Clearly, one cannot simply assume that Paul's Galatian readers would make the connection or, alternatively, that they would know the identity of Πέτρος. Thus, it is my judgment that Paul is not responsible for the wording of Gal 2:7b–8—at least with regard to the name Πέτρος. Either he is citing some earlier source (the protocol hypothesis) or someone other than Paul added the material in question (the interpolation hypothesis).

On the face of it, the protocol hypothesis might appear to provide a plausible explanation of the Πέτρος/Κηφᾶς data, maintaining, as it does, that, despite his usual preference for Κηφᾶς, Paul here refers to Πέτρος because this is the name used in the Greek version of the protocol. In my judgment, however, the interpolation hypothesis provides a more satisfactory explanation of these data. Even if Paul did not compose Gal 2:7b–8 and is simply quoting from a source, surely he would, for the sake of his readers, either indicate that Πέτρος and Κηφᾶς are the same person or, if not, somehow identify Πέτρος! Thus, I think it probable that Gal 2:7b–8—or at least the name Πέτρος—was added by someone

---

50. Gaechter, *Petrus und seine Zeit*, 385. Stuhlmacher, *Das Paulinische Evangelium*, 94–95, here 94 (my translation).

other than Paul, at a time when it was generally understood that Πέτρος and Κηφᾶς were the same person, when Πέτρος had become the more widely-accepted name, and when it was deemed important to emphasize the importance of Peter along with that of Paul—that is to say, after the lifetime of Paul.

Once the name Πέτρος appeared in the text (i.e., Gal 2:7b–8), some scribes changed Κηφᾶς to Πέτρος elsewhere in the Galatian letter, again to create a uniformity of names and to emphasize the importance of Peter. Similarly, some scribes changed the listing of the "pillars" (2:9), again to emphasize the importance of Peter. Such alterations would, of course, make no sense if 2:7b–8 were not a part of the text, because Πέτρος does not appear elsewhere in the Pauline corpus. The opposite change would not be made in Gal 2:7b–8 (i.e., Πέτρος to Κηφᾶς) because, although it would create uniformity regarding the names, it would blunt the force of the attempt to emphasize the status of Peter as Paul's equal in the missionary work of the church.

In short, it is my judgment that the name Πέτρος argues not only against Pauline authorship of Gal 2:7b–8 but also against Paul's inclusion of these verses in his Galatian letter. Indeed, I believe Barnikol to be correct in his view that "everything is clear" regarding Πέτρος/Κηφᾶς if Gal 2:7b–8 is viewed as an interpolation:

> [Paul] wrote only Κηφᾶς not Πέτρος! The later inserted passage with the double but otherwise isolated Πέτρος leads to the mishmash of the textual attestations of all other passages, i.e., original passages in Galatians, but not in 1 Corinthians, and because of its secondary origin, remained itself unanimously attested, a sign of its non-Pauline origin.[51]

Peculiar Construction with Ἐνεργεῖν

The verb ἐνεργεῖν occurs twice in Gal 2:8. Ulrich Wilckens maintains that ἐνεργεῖν and its derivatives (ἐνέργεια, ἐνέργημα,

---

51. Barnikol, "Non-Pauline Origin," 290.

and ἐνεργής) represent characteristically Pauline vocabulary.⁵²
As Barnikol observes, however, the peculiar construction with
ἐνεργεῖν in v. 8 is without parallel in the Pauline corpus and, indeed, in the entire New Testament. Elsewhere, ἐνεργεῖν appears
either absolutely⁵³ or followed by ἐν and the dative case.⁵⁴ In Gal
2:8, however, the verb appears twice, in each case followed by the
dative without the preposition. Thus, Barnikol concludes: "This
evidence could not be any clearer: Paul writes ἐνεργεῖν ἐν ἐμοί;
he never wrote ἐνεργεῖν ἐμοί."⁵⁵ To say that Paul *never* wrote
ἐνεργεῖν ἐμοί may go too far, but this peculiar construction does
argue against Pauline authorship of Gal 2:8.

Paul might, of course, simply have taken the construction
from a source (the protocol) without alteration. Thus, this phenomenon is compatible with either the protocol or the interpolation hypotheses. My own judgment, however, is that it argues
slightly in favor of the latter. Paul never elsewhere uses ἐνεργεῖν
followed by the dative without the preposition; thus, he might
have been uncomfortable with the construction and therefore altered it to match his own usage. It appears less likely, however,
that an interpolator would be sensitive to the rather subtle difference in style; thus, the interpolator's usage might differ from that
of Paul. In short, all other things being equal, I regard the peculiar
construction with ἐνεργεῖν in Gal 2:8 as providing some support
for the interpolation as opposed to the protocol hypothesis.

Distinction between Two "Gospels"

Reflecting neither language nor thought that is typically Pauline
is the distinction in Gal 2:7b between two apparently equally-

---

52. Wilckens, "Der Ursprung der Überlieferung," 72 n. 41.

53. In the undisputed Pauline letters: Gal 5:6; 1 Cor 12:11; Phil 2:13; in the disputed letters: Eph 1:11; 2 Thess 2:7; elsewhere in the NT: Jas 5:16.

54. In the undisputed Pauline letters: Gal 3:5; Rom 7:5; 1 Cor 12:6; 2 Cor 1:6; 4:12; Phil 2:13; 1 Thess 2:13; in the disputed letters: Eph 1:20; 2:2; 3:20; Col 1:29; elsewhere in the NT: Matt 14:2; Mark 6:14 (*note*: the last two are parallel accounts).

55. Barnikol, "Non-Pauline Origin," 290. See also, e.g., Lüdemann, *Paul, Apostle to the Gentiles*, 68.

valid "gospels"—τὸ εὐαγγέλιον τῆς ἀκροβυστίας and [τὸ εὐαγγέλιον] τῆς περιτομῆς.[56] To be sure, εὐαγγέλιον and τὸ εὐαγγέλιον appear frequently in the Pauline letters, but, except at Gal 2:7b, always either absolutely[57] or qualified in terms of source and/or content[58] or of bearer[59]—never in terms of intended recipients.[60] Thus, the phrasing appears to be un-Pauline.

Wilckens argues that τὸ εὐαγγέλιον τῆς ἀκροβυστίας and [τὸ εὐαγγέλιον] τῆς περιτομῆς are Pauline in origin, on the grounds that the antithesis between "uncircumcision"/"uncircumcised" and "circumcision"/"circumcised" occurs elsewhere in the Pauline corpus[61] and, indeed, "only in the Pauline writings and in those writings influenced by Paul."[62] This is true, but the distinction between two apparently equally-valid "gospels" appears to contradict Paul's vehement insistence in Gal 1:6–9 that there is only *one* true "gospel." Paul does, of course, speak in v. 6 of "another gospel" (ἕτερον εὐαγγέλιον; cf. also εὐαγγέλιον ἕτερον in 2 Cor 11:4), but he immediately adds (v. 7) that this "other gospel"

---

56. E.g., Barnikol, "Non-Pauline Origin," 290–91; Dinkler, "Nachtrag," 282; Klein, "Nachtrag," 118 n. 3; and Betz, *Galatians: A Commentary*, 96.

57. Rom 1:16; 10:16; 11:28; 1 Cor 4:15; 9:14 *bis*, 18 *bis*, 23; 15:1; 2 Cor 8:18; 11:4; Gal 1:6, 11; 2:2, 5, 14; Phil 1:5, 7, 12, 16, 27; 2:22; 4:3, 15; 1 Thess 2:4; Phlm 13.

58. The gospel "of God" (Rom 1:1; 15:16; 2 Cor 11:7; 1 Thess 2:2, 8;), "of his son" (Rom 1:9), "of Christ" (Rom 15:19; 1 Cor 9:12; 2 Cor 2:12; 9:13; 10:14; Gal 1:7; Phil 1:27; 1 Thess 3:2), or "of the glory of Christ" (2 Cor 4:4).

59. "My gospel" (Rom 2:16; 16:25), or "our gospel" (2 Cor 4:3; 1 Thess 1:5).

60. Burton (*Critical and Exegetical Commentary*, 92–93) says that "the genitives τῆς ἀκροβυστίας and τῆς περιτομῆς cannot be more accurately described than as genitives of connection, being practically equivalent to τοῖς ἐν ἀκροβυστίᾳ (in uncircumcision) and τοῖς περιτετμημένοις." More specifically (p. 93), he speaks of the genitives as "denoting to whom the message is to be presented."

61. Gal 5:6; 6:15; Rom 2:25–29; 3:30; 4:9–12; 1 Cor 7:18–19; Eph 2:11; Col 3:11.

62. Wilckens, "Der Ursprung der Überlieferung," 72 n. 41. For the argument that the antithesis originates not with Paul but rather in pre-Pauline baptismal traditions, see Lüdemann, *Paul, Apostle to the Gentiles*, 66–68.

is not really another gospel but rather a *perversion* of the gospel of Christ. There can be only *one* true gospel—certainly not two as in Gal 2:7b! In light of this, it would be quite astonishing for Paul (indeed, in the same letter!) to differentiate so explicitly between a "gospel of the uncircumcision" and "[a gospel] of the circumcision."[63] It is my judgment, therefore, that Paul did not write these words.

For the same reasons, I find it virtually impossible to believe that Paul would accept such a distinction, even in a document composed by someone else. I conclude, therefore, that Paul neither wrote Gal 2:7b nor, having taken it from an earlier source (the protocol), included it in his Galatian letter. In short, the distinction between two apparently equally valid gospels strongly supports the interpolation hypothesis as opposed to the protocol hypothesis.

Parallelism between Peter and Paul

Gal 2:7b–8 portrays Peter and Paul as the two great Christian missionaries—Peter to "the circumcision" (ἡ περιτομή) and Paul to "the uncircumcision" (ἡ ἀκροβυστία) or "the Gentiles" (τὰ ἔθνη). There is nothing in the phrases ἡ περιτομή and ἡ ἀκροβυστία *per se* that would argue against Pauline authorship of Gal 2:7b–8, for Paul refers rather frequently to "circumcision" and "uncircumcision,"[64] often in the same context,[65] and in some cases the terms clearly are metonyms for Jews and Gentiles.[66]

Did Paul, however, see his own mission as directed either exclusively or primarily toward the Gentiles? Ernst Barnikol

---

63. Tertullian (*Praescr.* 23), however, maintains that the distinction refers to a "distribution of their spheres of work" and not "a division of the gospel." Nevertheless, for Paul to have used such wording in his letter to the Galatians must be regarded as strange.

64. Περιτομή: Gal 2:9, 12; 5:6, 11; 6:15; 1 Cor 7:19; Rom 2:25, 26, 27, 28, 29; 3:1, 30; 4:9, 10, 11, 12; 15:8; Phil 3:3, 5. Ἀκροβυστία: Gal 5:6; 6:15; 1 Cor 7:18, 19; Rom 2:25, 26, 27; 3:30; 4:9, 10, 11, 12.

65. Gal 5:6; 6:15; 1 Cor 7:19; Rom 2:25, 26, 27; 3:30; 4:9, 10, 11, 12.

66. Περιτομή as metonym for Jews: Gal 2:9, Rom 3:1 (?), 30; 4:9; 15:8 (?); Phil 3:3 (?); ἀκροβυστία as metonym for Gentiles: Rom 2:26; 3:30; 4:9.

maintains that "the popular image of Paul as the apostle to the Gentiles" only arose in the second century,[67] but this is far from certain. Although Paul at least once suggests that he also works among Jews (1 Cor 19:19–23, esp. v. 20),[68] he rather frequently specifies that his mission field is among Gentiles.[69] Thus, Barnikol appears to be at least partially in error regarding Paul's understanding of his own mission.

What, however, about Peter? Apart from Gal 2:7b–8, there is no indication that Paul regards Peter as missionary *par excellence* to the Jews. Indeed, as noted, Paul never elsewhere even refers to Πέτρος. He does, of course, speak of Κηφᾶς on several occasions (Gal 1:18; 2:9, 11, 14; 1 Cor 1:12; 3:22; 9:5; 15:5), but never specifically as envoy to the Jews. In short, while Paul likely viewed himself primarily as missionary to Gentiles, there is no evidence elsewhere in the letters that he would have characterized Peter as missionary to Jews. To be sure, this is an argument from silence, but if Paul did in fact write Gal 2:7b–8, one might expect to find elsewhere in the Pauline writings some confirmation of the picture presented there. Thus, I regard the evidence at this point as weighing against Pauline authorship of Gal 2:7b–8 and probably against Pauline inclusion of the passage as well.

Even more important is the question of whether Paul viewed himself and Peter as "the two great figures high above all other Christian missionaries of the early period," as Gal 2:7b–8 suggests. Ernst Barnikol thinks not; indeed, in his view, "the historical Paul would never have dared to place himself next to Cephas, neither in Jerusalem, nor in Antioch, not even in Corinth."[70] In this

---

67. Barnikol, "Non-Pauline Origin," 294.
68. Note that Acts consistently portrays Paul as going first to the Jews and turning to the Gentiles only because of his rejection by the Jews (e.g., Acts 13:45–49; 18:5–6; 25:25–28).
69. E.g., Gal 1:16; Rom 1:5, 13; 11:13; 15:16, 18. Observing that Rom 15:16 reflects the same idea as Gal 2:8 "almost word for word" (i.e., εἰς τὰ ἔθνη). Barnikol ("Non-Pauline Origin," 294) suggests that it too is most likely a non-Pauline interpolation that "presumably arose at the same time" as Gal 2:7b–8.
70. Barnikol, "Non-Pauline Origin," 285–86, 291–92, here 285–86 and 286 n. 5.

regard, it is noteworthy that Paul sometimes appears to subordinate himself to the Jerusalem "pillars." Even earlier in Galatians (2:1–2), he reports that he went to Jerusalem and submitted his gospel to "those who were of repute" (τοῖς δοκοῦσιν) *lest somehow I should be running or had run in vain* (μή πως εἰς κενὸν τρέχω ἢ ἔδραμον)." Further, in 1 Cor 15:9, Paul refers to himself as "the least of the apostles (ὁ ἐλάχιστος τῶν ἀποστόλων), unfit to be called an apostle."

As regards Peter, it has been noted that Paul never elsewhere even uses the name Πέτρος. Moreover, his references to Κηφᾶς provide little evidence to support the portrayal of Peter in Gal 2:7b–8. Paul gives Cephas an important role in the Christian movement both by identifying him as the first to see the risen Christ (1 Cor 15:5) and as one of the Jerusalem "pillars" (Gal 2:9) and by reporting that during his visit to Jerusalem he saw only Cephas and James (Gal 1:18–19).[71] Nevertheless, there is no indication that he assigns Cephas a unique role of leadership. Indeed, his listing of the Jerusalem "pillars" in the order James/Cephas/John suggests otherwise.

Of relevance, too, is the view, recently revived by Michael Goulder, that, far from being "the two great and *united* chief apostles," "working alongside *and* with one another,"[72] Peter and Paul were in fact leaders of two *competing* missions that "were agreed about the supreme significance of Jesus, but . . . disagreed about almost everything else."[73] To the extent that Goulder is correct, it would be difficult to regard Paul either as the author of Gal 2:7b–8 or as the one who included it in the Galatian letter.

Barnikol believes that the solitary elevation of Peter and Paul to the status of Christian missionaries *par excellence* originated only in "the proclamation of the early Catholic Church in the

---

71. 1 Cor 9:5 speaks of "the other apostles and the brothers of the Lord and Cephas," perhaps suggesting a particularly important position for Cephas.
72. Barnikol, "Non-Pauline Origin," 286.
73. Goulder, *St. Paul versus St. Peter*, ix–x.

second century."[74] Indeed, in his view, Gal 2:7b–8 reflects "a reaction against the one-sided Pauline proclamation of Marcion," the intent of which was to stress, *pace* the Marcionites, that Paul was not the only true apostle.[75] In my judgment, there is much to be said for Barnikol's view. In any case, it is difficult to locate within their own lifetime this elevation of Peter and Paul to such positions of preeminence.

In short, I find it highly unlikely that Paul would claim, or accept the claim, that the worldwide mission field had been divided between him and Peter, as Gal 2:7b–8 indicates. Thus, I seriously doubt that Paul either composed these verses or included them in his Galatian letter.

Treatment of "Apostleship"

Doubly problematic is the treatment of "apostleship" (ἀποστολή) in Gal 2:8.[76] In the first place, the phrase ἀποστολὴ τῆς περιτομῆς is without parallel in the Pauline corpus and, indeed, in the entire New Testament. The word ἀποστολή appears elsewhere in the New Testament only three times (twice in the Pauline corpus), where, in each case, it is used either absolutely (Rom 1:5; Acts 1:25) or with the possessive pronoun "my" (1 Cor 9:2: μου τῆς ἀποστολῆς)—never with a genitive indicating those on behalf of whom the apostleship is exercised as at Gal 2:8.[77] Thus, I doubt that Paul coined the phrase ἀποστολὴ τῆς περιτομῆς, although he may have taken it from an earlier source (the protocol). Thus, the phrase itself is consistent with either the protocol or the interpolation hypothesis.

---

74. See, e.g., *1 Clement* 5, where Peter and Paul are cited as "the greatest and most righteous pillars" (οἱ μέγιστοι καὶ δικαιότατοι στύλοι [sic]); see also Ign. *Rom.* 4.3, where Peter and Paul are juxtaposed as "apostles." It is worthy of note that both *1 Clement* and Ignatius list Peter first.

75. Barnikol, "Non-Pauline Origin," 285–86, 298. Except in 14:4, 14, Acts never refers to Paul as an "apostle."

76. On ἀπόστολος, see, e.g., Betz, *Galatians: A Commentary*, 74–75.

77. Cf., however, Rom 11:13, where Paul refers to himself as "apostle of [or "to"] Gentiles" (ἐθνῶν ἀπόστολος).

In the second place, given Paul's insistence upon his own apostolic status earlier in Galatians (Gal 1:1)[78] and his references elsewhere to his mission as an "apostleship" (ἀπόστολος, 1 Cor 9:2; Rom 1:5), it is striking that, although v. 8a explicitly refers to *Peter's* "apostleship," the parallel wording in 8b fails to specify apostolic status for *Paul*.[79] Ἐνήργησεν καὶ ἐμοὶ εἰς τὰ ἔθνη has often been viewed as simply an ellipsis for ἐνήργησεν καὶ ἐμοὶ εἰς ἀποστολὴν τῶν ἐθνῶν that strongly implies Paul's own apostolic status.[80] Indeed, the ellipsis in v. 7 (πεπίστευμαι τὸ εὐαγγέλιον τῆς ἀκροβυστίας καθὼς Πέτρος τῆς περτομῆς) is sometimes cited as a parallel,[81] and reference might also be made to that in v. 9 (ἵνα ἡμεῖς εἰς τὰ ἔθνη αὐτοὶ δὲ εἰς τὴν περιτομήν). These, however, are not true parallels to v. 8, because in neither instance would insertion of the missing word(s) disturb the syntax of the sentence or require further alteration. In v. 8, however, insertion of the missing word (presumably ἀποστολήν following εἰς) would require changing τὰ ἔθνη (accusative case) to τῶν ἐθνῶν (genitive case). A writer could easily have indicated apostolic status for Paul without actually repeating ἀποστολήν simply by writing ἐνήργησεν καὶ ἐμοὶ τῶν ἐθνῶν, with the words εἰς ἀποστολήν to be supplied by the reader.[82] Even this, however, would be surprising coming from Paul. The principal point of the first two chapters of Galatians is to emphasize *Paul's* (not Peter's) status as an apostle—an apostle called and commissioned by none other than God but also recognized as such by the "pillars" in Jerusalem. Surely, in such a context, Paul would not speak explicitly of Peter's apostleship without mentioning his own! Moreover, I find it most unlikely that he would incorporate such material into his letter from another source (the protocol).

---

78. See also Gal 1:17; 1 Thess 2:6; 1 Cor 1:1; 4:9; 9:1–2, 5; 15:9; 2 Cor 1:1; 11:5; 12:11–12; Rom 1:1; 11:13.
79. E.g., Betz, *Galatians: A Commentary*, 98.
80. E.g., Burton, *Critical and Exegetical Commentary*, 94.
81. E.g., Matera, *Galatians*, 77.
82. Cf. καθὼς Πέτρος τῆς περιτομῆς in v. 7b.

If, however, Gal 2:7b–8 is a later, anti-Marcionite interpolation, as Barnikol argues, it would then be precisely *Peter's* (not Paul's) apostleship that was at issue, and the wording of v. 8 would not be surprising. To have "Paul" himself attest Peter's apostolic status would negate the views of Marcion, who regarded Paul as the only true apostle. Moreover, how better to emphasize *Peter's* apostleship than by explicitly mentioning it and, at the same time, omitting any reference to that of Paul? Indeed, it may be that the interpolator—like the author of Acts—deliberately withheld the status of apostleship from Paul.[83]

Problematic for any interpretation of Gal 2:7b–8 is the fact that the contrast in v. 7b is between τῆς ἀκροβυστίας and τῆς περιτομῆς but that in v. 8 is between τῆς περιτομῆς and τὰ ἔθνη.[84] Although "the uncircumcision" and "the Gentiles" are essentially synonymous in meaning, one might expect a writer—and perhaps especially an interpolator—to repeat in v. 8 the same pair that is found in v. 7b, even if in reverse order. The proposed interpolation, however, includes not only v. 8 but also v. 7b with its contrasting of τῆς ἀκροβυστίας and τῆς περιτομῆς. Thus, the issue is not whether the interpolator was attempting to make the interpolation "fit" with what Paul had written; rather, it is simply a matter of internal consistency within the interpolation itself. Moreover, the interpolator may have formulated the latter part of the interpolation (v. 8) in light of Paul's own pairing in v. 9: τὰ ἔθνη and τὴν περιτομήν. As already noted, however, the lack of parallelism between v. 7b and v. 8 is problematic however one explains the origin of this material.

In short, it is my judgment that the treatment of apostleship in Gal 2:8 argues strongly not only against Pauline authorship but

---

83. Only in Acts 14:4, 14 is Paul (along with Barnabas) referred to as an "apostle"; elsewhere, the title is reserved for the leaders of the church in Jerusalem. On the possibility that Acts is an anti-Marcionite document, see, e.g., Knox, *Marcion and the New Testament*, e.g., 139; and now Tyson, *Marcion and Luke-Acts*.

84. Actually, as already noted, the contrast is not exact: τῆς περιτομῆς is in the genitive case, while τὰ ἔθνη is in the accusative case (following the preposition εἰς).

also against Pauline inclusion of Gal 2:7b–8 in his letter—in short, against the protocol hypothesis and in support of the interpolation hypothesis.

Galatians 2:7b–8 and Its Immediate Context

The relation of Gal 2:7b–8 to its immediate context (Gal 2:6–10) is problematic. The point of vv. 6–10 is that the "pillars" in Jerusalem agreed to a division of labor whereby Paul (and Barnabas) would carry the gospel to the Gentiles and they to the Jews.[85] Verses 7b–8 add nothing substantive to this point, and their removal would in no way affect it. The last six words of v. 7 simply draw a distinction between Paul's "gospel of the uncircumcision" and Peter's "of the circumcision"—a distinction which, as already noted, is highly problematic. As regards v. 8, Hans Dieter Betz refers to it as a "parenthetical statement" and notes that it "is very strange indeed."[86] It is in no way dependent upon what precedes or follows and, except for the conjunction γάρ, could easily stand alone as an independent statement. Moreover, the verse breaks what would otherwise be a smooth logical and syntactical transition from v. 7 to v. 9, Various scholars have noted that the deletion of v. 8 would highlight the striking parallelism between two participial clauses, ἰδόντες ὅτι πεπίστευμαι τὸ εὐαγγέλιον (v. 7) and γνόντες τὴν χάριν τὴν δοθεῖσάν μοι (v. 9), which appear to be virtually synonymous in meaning[87] Indeed, with the removal of both v. 7b and v. 8,[88] vv. 7a and 9 would read smoothly as follows: ἀλλὰ τοὐναντίον ἰδόντες ὅτι πεπίστευμαι τὸ εὐαγγέλιον καὶ γνόντες τὴν χάριν τὴν δοθεῖσάν μοι, Ἰάκωβος καὶ Κηφᾶς καὶ Ἰωάννης, οἱ δοκοῦντες στῦλοι εἶναι, δεξιὰς ἔδωκαν ἐμοὶ καὶ Βαρναβᾷ κοινωνίας, ἵνα ἡμεῖς εἰς τὰ ἔθνη, αὐτοὶ δὲ εἰς τὴν

---

85. As noted, this in itself problematic.
86. Betz, *Galatians: A Commentary*, 97. On the "parenthetical" nature of the verse, see, e.g., Burton, *Critical and Exegetical Commentary*, 93.
87. E.g., Dinkler, "Der Brief an die Galater," 183.
88. V. 7b (τῆς ἀκροβυστίας καθὼς Πέτρος τῆς περιτομῆς) is included as part of the interpolation because, as noted, both the name Πέτρος and the distinction between two "gospels" appear to be non-Pauline.

περιτομήν. In short, as Dinkler notes, one can eliminate the material in question "without causing a break in the characteristic style of the sentence."[89]

In addition, the division of labor portrayed in vv. 7b–8 differs from that in v. 9. In 7b–8, it is *Paul alone* and *Peter alone* who are the focus of attention; in v. 9, however, *both Paul and Barnabas* are to go to the Gentiles, and *James, Cephas, and John* to the circumcision. It is unlikely, in my judgment, that Paul would write or include in his letter two such different portrayals of the division of labor.

In short, the seeming awkwardness of the "fit" between Gal 2:7b–8 and its immediate context suggests that this material was composed by someone other than Paul and somewhat arbitrarily inserted at its present location. Although it is possible that Paul himself might incorporate such material into his own letter without "smoothing out" the stylistic tensions, I regard it as highly unlikely that he would include material that substantively contradicted his own portrayal of the matter at hand. Thus, I see the relation of Gal 2:7b–8 to its immediate context as arguing in favor of the interpolation hypothesis as opposed to the protocol hypothesis.

Conclusion regarding Problems of Gal 2:7b–8

Six problems have been noted in Gal 2:7b–8. Particularly serious are the references to Πέτρος, the distinction between two apparently equally-valid "gospels," the parallelism between Peter and Paul as the two great missionaries of the Christian movement, and the treatment of "apostleship." Surely, the presence of such problems in a short passage of only twenty words, in a letter otherwise regarded as Pauline, requires some explanation. In my judgment, it is highly unlikely that Paul himself composed this material; moreover, I find it exceedingly difficult to believe that he would include it, regardless of its origin, in his letter to the Galatians.

In short, I am persuaded that the interpolation hypothesis more adequately accounts for the problems of Gal 2:7b–8 than

---

89. Dinkler, "Der Brief an die Galater," 183.

does the protocol hypothesis. In addition, I have already indicated that I believe the interpolation hypothesis, simply *qua* hypothesis, to be inherently less problematic than the protocol hypothesis. I conclude, therefore, that Gal 2:7b–8 is a later non-Pauline addition to the Paul's Galatian letter.

Addendum

Ernest Barnikol points out that the earliest extant citation of or allusion to Gal 2:7b–8 appears in Irenaeus, late in the second century, in a passage that is clearly anti-Marcionite in tenor (*Haer.* 3.13.1).[90] Noting further that Marcion's version of Galatians apparently did not include 2:7b–8, Barnikol then asserts that the verses are never cited or even alluded to by Tertullian (early third century).[91] He finds this particularly significant, for the parallelism between Peter and Paul drawn in Gal 2:7b–8 would have been most useful to Tertullian in his attacks against Marcion. This can only mean, according to Barnikol, that Tertullian did not know the verses in question, even though he was familiar with the immediately following verse (Gal 2:9).[92] Thus, the interpolation, which likely originated in the West before the end of the second century, was not yet a part of "the African Bible" known by Tertullian early in the third century.[93]

Barnikol's claim that Tertullian never cites or even alludes to Gal 2:7b–8 was immediately challenged, however, by Hans Lietzmann, who asserted that Tertullian alludes to Gal 2:8 in his *De praescriptione haereticorum* 23.[94] Responding to Rudolf Bultmann's objection that Tertullian's reference is to v. 9, not v. 8,[95] Lietzmann insisted that, although the passage in question reports the con-

---

90. See Barnikol, "Non-Pauline Origin," 295–99.
91. Barnikol, "Non-Pauline Origin," 295–96.
92. Gal 2:9 is cited or alluded to at least four times in Tertullian: *Marc.* 1.20.2; 4.2.5; 5.3.6; *Praescr.* 23.9.
93. Barnikol, "Non-Pauline Origin," 295–99.
94. Lietzmann, *An die Galater*, 13; see also, e.g., Schlier, *Der Brief an die Galater*, 77 n. 2; see also, e.g., Behm, Review of Barnikol, *Der nichtpaulinische Ursprung*, 29.
95. Bultmann, Review of Barnikol, *Der nichtpaulinische Ursprung*, 555.

tent of v. 9, it also reflects knowledge of v. 8.[96] Thus, according to Lietzmann, Tertullian did in fact know Gal 2:8.

Lietzmann appears to be correct at this point. Although Tertullian's strong opposition to Marcion's insistence upon the sole apostleship of Paul might lead one to expect both more and more explicit allusions to or even citations of Gal 2:7b–8, it must be acknowledged that Tertullian apparently knew Gal 2:7b–8. It must also be noted, however, that Tertullian's writings are later in date than are those of Irenaeus. Thus, Barnikol's basic point remains: the presence of Gal 2:7b–8 in Galatians cannot be attested until near the end of the second century—in the writings of Irenaeus.

Clearly, however, Galatians as a whole was known earlier, for both Tertullian (e.g., *Marc.* 4.3) and Epiphanius (*Pan.* 42.9.4; 42.11.10) indicate that it was included (by name) in Marcion's canon. To be sure, James Moffatt speaks of "the inferiority of [the letter's] early attestation, as compared, *e.g.*, with that of I Cor. or of Rom.,"[97] but "probable reminiscences of the language of Galatians" have been found in 1 *Clement*, *Barnabas*, Polycarp's *Letter to the Philippians*, and Justin Martyr.[98] Thus, the letter was known well before the latter part of the second century. Moreover, there may even be an illusion to Gal 2:9 (the verse immediately following the suspected interpolation) in 1 *Clem.* 5.2.[99]

In any case, although the letter as a whole was known earlier, no attestation of Gal 2:7b–8 has been found prior to Irenaeus. This,

---

96. Lietzmann, "Notizen," 93. Compare Tertullian's *Petrus in circumcisionem, Paulus in nationes* with Πέτρῳ εἰς ἀποστολὴν τῆς περιτομῆς . . . καὶ ἐμοὶ εἰς τὰ ἔθνη in Gal 2:8 (note the mention only of Peter and Paul, the sequence of the names, and what Lietzmann terms "*die singularische Ausdruckweise*").

97. Moffatt, *Introduction*, 107.

98. Burton, *Critical and Exegetical Commentary*, lxviii–lxix; see also, e.g., Moffatt, *Introduction*, 107.

99. Note οἱ μέγιστοι καὶ δικαιότατοι στύλοι [*sic*]. The reference to στύλοι could hark back to Gal 2:9 and/or to Rev 3:12 (elsewhere in the NT, στύλος appears only at 1 Tim 3:15; Rev 10:1). In favor of the former is the fact that 1 *Clement* speaks immediately thereafter not of James/Cephas/John and Paul/Barnabas as in Gal 2:9 but rather only of Peter and Paul (Cephas?) as in 2:7b–8.

of course, does not confirm the interpolation hypothesis, but, in conjunction with other more positive types of evidence, it does constitute an argument from silence.

Chapter 6

"There Is Not Male and Female"
A Pauline Addition in Galatians 3:28

Galatians 3:27–28, with its reference to baptism "into Christ," is widely regarded—correctly in my judgment—as reflecting a pre-Pauline baptismal formula.[1] The verses read as follows:

ὅσοι γὰρ εἰς Χριστὸν ἐβαπτίσθητε Χριστὸν ἐνεδύσασθε. οὐκ ἔνι Ἰουδαῖος οὐδὲ Ἕλλην, οὐκ ἔνι δοῦλος οὐδὲ ἐλεύθερος, οὐκ ἔνι ἄρσεν καὶ θῆλυ, πάντες γὰρ ὑμεῖς εἷς ἐστε ἐν Χριστῷ Ἰησοῦ.

For as many of you as were baptized into Christ have put on Christ. There is not Jew or Greek, there is not slave or free, there is not male and female, for you are all one in Christ Jesus.

It has often been noted that the third pair in Gal 3:28—ἄρσην and θῆλυς ("male" and "female")—is missing in two other passages that appear to reflect the same or a similar baptismal formula: 1 Cor 12:13 and Col 3:11.[2] The former passage reads, καὶ γὰρ ἐνὶ πνεύματι ἡμεῖς πάντες εἰς ἓν σῶμα ἐβαπτίσθημεν, εἴτε

---

1. See, most recently, de Boer, *Galatians: A Commentary*, 242–47 (for arguments supporting this view, see 245–46); cf. also, e.g., Schlier, *Der Brief an die Galater*, 172–76; Lohse, *Colossians and Philemon*, 143; Bouttier, "Complexio Oppositorum"; Betz, *Galatians: A Commentary*, 181–85; Schrage, *Der erste Brief an die Korinther*, vol. 3, 207–8; and Martyn, *Galatians: A New Translation*, 378–83. For opposing views, see, e.g., Dautsenberg, "Da Ist Nicht Männlich und Weiblich," 183; and Martin, "The Covenant of Circumcision."

2. The same or a similar baptismal formula is likely also reflected in Eph 4:4–6, which, however, makes no mention of specific categories of people. It is possible, moreover, that Rom 3:9; 10:12; 1 Cor 1:22, 24; 7:18–22; 10:32; and Eph 6:8 also reflect the same or a similar baptismal formula (for bibliography, see Hansen, "'All of you are one,'" 1 n. 3). None of these passages includes "male" and "female." Thus, there may be as many as ten places in the NT that reflect the baptismal formula but fail to include "male" and "female."

Ἰουδαῖοι εἴτε Ἕλληνες εἴτε δοῦλοι εἴτε ἐλεύθεροι, καὶ πάντες ἓν πνεῦμα ἐποτίσθημεν ("For all of us were also baptized by one spirit into one body, whether Jews or Greeks, whether slaves or free, and all of us drank one spirit") with no mention of ἄρσενες or θήλειαι. Similarly, the latter passage reads, ὅπου οὐκ ἔνι Ἕλλην καὶ Ἰουδαῖος, περιτομὴ καὶ ἀκροβυστία, Βάρβαρος, Σκύθης, δοῦλος, ἐλεύθερος, ἀλλὰ [τὰ] πάντα ἐν πᾶσιν Χριστός (". . . where there is not Greek and Jew, circumcision and uncircumcision, barbarian, Scythian, slave, free, but Christ [is] all in all"), with no reference to ἄρσην or θῆλυς ("male" or "female").[3]

Less frequently noted is the possibility—I would say probability—that the same or a similar baptismal formula, without any mention of ἄρσην and θῆλυς, is also alluded to in 1 Cor 7:17–24. Here, Paul introduces the principle, ἑκάστῳ ὡς ἐμέρισεν ὁ κύριος, ἕκαστον ὡς κέκληκεν ὁ Θεός, οὕτως περιπατείτω ("let each one lead the life which the Lord has assigned to him and in which God called him"; v. 17), and then applies the principle to "circumcision" (περιτομή) and "uncircumcision" (ἀκροβυστία)—i.e., Jew and Greek—and to "slave" (δοῦλος) and "free" (ἐλεύθερος) but not to "male" (ἄρσην) and "female" (θῆλυς). To be sure, vv. 17–24 are included in a chapter that deals generally with questions regarding sex, marriage, and divorce—i.e., relations between men and women. More specifically, the verses immediately follow a section dealing with divorce (vv. 10–16) and immediately precede

---

3. 1 Cor 12:13 refers explicitly to baptism "into one body," while there is no mention of baptism in Col 3:11; nevertheless the imagery in the latter passage of "putting off the old nature" and "putting on the new nature" (vv. 9–10: ἀπεκδυσάμενοι τὸν παλαιὸν ἄνθρωπον . . . καὶ ἐνδυσάμενοι τὸν νέον) suggests a baptismal context, and the words οὐκ ἔνι are reminiscent of Gal. 3:28. Note that a number of "Western" witnesses (e.g., D*, F, G, 629, and old Latin texts), probably under the influence of Gal 3:28, include ἄρσεν καὶ θῆλυ before Ἕλλην καὶ Ἰουδαῖος in Col 3:11. On the relation among Gal 3:27–28; 1 Cor 12:13; and Col 3:11, see, e.g., Moule, *Worship in the New Testament*, 52; Bruce, *Epistle to the Galatians*, 186–87; Beasley-Murray, *Baptism in the New Testament*, 148–49; Scroggs, "Paul and the Eschatological Woman," 291–92; Martyn, *Galatians: A New Translation*, 375–80; Dunn, *Baptism in the Holy Spirit*, 109–13, 117–20, 127–31; and Hansen, "'All of you are one'."

a section setting forth reasons for not marrying (vv. 25–38). For this reason, one might assume that ἄρσην and θῆλυς were in the back of Paul's mind as he composed the material.[4] If vv. 17–24 stood alone, however, as they easily might,[5] one would be unlikely to see in them any connection to issues regarding gender.

Thus, there are at least two and probably three passages in the New Testament that apparently cite or allude to the baptismal formula cited in Gal 3:26–28 or to a similar formula without including the third pair in Gal 3:28: ἄρσην and θῆλυς.[6] It is widely assumed, however, that the original baptismal formula included all three pairs—Ἰουδαῖος/Ἕλλην, δοῦλος/ἐλεύθερος, and ἄρσην/θῆλυς—and that Paul, for some reason, simply chose to omit the third pair in 1 Cor 12:13 (and, I would add, in 1 Cor 7:17–24), as did the pseudonymous author of Colossians in Col 3:11. Questioning this assumption, Hans Dieter Betz, among others, argues that οὐκ ἔνι ἄρσεν καὶ θῆλυς in Gal 3:28 "appears to be a secondary addition to an earlier version" of the baptismal

---

4. The influence of Gal 3:28 would most likely play a role in this assumption. Indeed, Bartchy, in his discussion of 1 Cor 7:17–24 (*Mallon chrēsai*, 162–65), suggests that Jew/Gentile and slave/free relations were regularly linked in Paul's mind with male/female relations, but he cites only Gal 3:28 as evidence for this linkage. As will be noted later, it is entirely possible that it was precisely Paul's allusion to the baptismal formula in the midst of his discussion of relations between men and women in 1 Cor 7:17–24 that initially suggested to him the idea, articulated (later?) in his letter to the Galatians, of adding οὐκ ἔνι ἄρσεν καὶ θῆλυ to the formula.

5. Collins (*First Corinthians*, 274) refers to the verses as a "rhetorical digression." Fitzmyer (*First Corinthians: A New Translation*, 306) notes that "some commentators consider these verses (17–24) to be a digression because the topics treated in vv. 1–16 and 25–40 are not mentioned." Fitzmyer himself maintains, however, that "these verses . . . present a theological reflection that is fundamental to the rest, and it is best to recognize them as formulating a principle on which the other more specific topics are based." My own guess is that the verses may originally have been composed for some other context and later included in 1 Corinthians 7 because they *indirectly* provided illustrations for Paul's advice regarding marriage and divorce.

6. See n. 2 for the possibility that there may be as many as ten such passages.

formula.⁷ Betz also maintains, however, that the clause is a *pre-Pauline* addition to the formula.⁸

The purpose of the present study is (a) to argue, in agreement with Betz, that οὐκ ἔνι ἄρσεν καὶ θῆλυ is, indeed, *a secondary addition* to the pre-Pauline baptismal formula cited in Gal 3:27-28 but (b) also to argue that it was not added to the formula *qua* baptismal formula but rather only when the formula was cited as *part of a theological argument* and (c) to argue, *pace* Betz, that it most likely was *Paul* who made the addition. I shall also suggest plausible reasons why, even though Paul added ἄρσην and θῆλυς in Gal 3:28, he might *not* have included them in 1 Cor 12:13 and in 1 Cor 7:17-24.⁹

A Secondary Addition to the Baptismal Formula

Betz's argument that οὐκ ἔνι ἄρσεν καὶ θῆλυ is a secondary addition to the pre-Pauline baptismal formula cited in Gal 3:27-28 is based explicitly on the fact that the wording of the clause differs in two significant respects from that of the first and second clauses in v. 28: (1) ἄρσεν/θῆλυ are connected by καί while Ἰουδαῖος/ Ἕλλην and δοῦλος/ἐλεύθερος are connected by οὐδέ, and (2) Ἰουδαῖος, Ἕλλην, δοῦλος, and ἐλεύθερος are all masculine while

---

7. Betz, *Galatians: A Commentary*, 181-82.
8. Betz, *Galatians: A Commentary*, 195.
9. If 1 Corinthians was written *later* than Galatians, it would mean that Paul included ἄρσην and θῆλυς in the *earlier* letter but then, apparently deliberately, omitted them in the *later* letter. If 1 Corinthians was written *before* Galatians, however, it may well be the case that Paul's radically egalitarian views regarding women were a comparatively late development in his thought. It is beyond the scope of this study to enter into the vexed question of the relative dating of 1 Corinthians and Galatians, but Schnelle (*Apostle Paul*, 269-77) has recently made a strong case for dating Galatians *after* 1 Corinthians, and his position has now been cautiously accepted by Boring (*Introduction to the New Testament*, 276-79). Schnelle bases his argument on (a) close contacts between Galatians and Romans in both content and structure and (b) references to the "collection" in 1 Cor 16:1 and Gal 2:10.

ἄρσεν and θῆλυ are both neuter.[10] Typically, and in my judgment correctly, these differences are explained by assuming that οὐκ ἄρσεν καὶ θῆλυ reflects the wording, ἄρσεν καὶ θῆλυ ἐποίησεν αὐτούς, of Gen 1:27[11] — the idea being that, in baptism, the division of the first human into "male and female" has now been overcome.[12] If this assumption is correct, however, there is yet a third respect in which the wording of οὐκ ἔνι ἄρσεν καὶ θῆλυ differs from that of the preceding two clauses in v. 28: Ἰουδαῖος, Ἕλλην, δοῦλος, and ἐλεύθερος are all in the *nominative* case, but ἄρσεν and θῆλυ are in the *accusative* case as in Gen 1:27. In short, the distinctive wording of οὐκ ἔνι ἄρσεν καὶ θῆλυ — a different conjunction connecting them, different gender, and different case — suggests that the clause is a secondary addition to the baptismal formula cited in Gal 3:27–28.

Betz also calls attention to the fact, already noted, that the two other New Testament passages that appear to reflect the same or a similar baptismal formula — 1 Cor 12:13 and Col 3:11 (and I would add 1 Cor 7:17–24) — do *not* include ἄρσην and θῆλυς.[13] Although it involves an argument from silence, the omission of ἄρσην and θῆλυς in these passages provides additional evidence that οὐκ ἔνι ἄρσεν καὶ θῆλυ is a secondary addition in Gal 3:28: it indicates that *two* different authors, composing *three* different passages, either (a) were familiar with a version of the formula that did not include ἄρσην and θῆλυς or (b) chose, each independently of the other, to omit the clause containing these words when citing the formula. As between the two alternatives, I regard the former as inherently more likely.

---

10. Betz, *Galatians: A Commentary*, 181–82.
11. Cf. Gen 5:2; Matt 19:4; Mark 10:6.
12. E.g., Stendahl, *The Bible and the Role of Women*, 32; Bruce, *Epistle to the Galatians*, 189; Martyn, *Galatians: A New Translation*, 376–77.
13. Betz, *Galatians: A Commentary*, 182, 195. See n. 2 for the possibility that there may be as many as ten passages in the NT that reflect the same or a similar baptismal formula but without including "male" and "female."

Betz also notes that οὐκ ἔνι ἄρσεν καὶ θῆλυ does not appear to be relevant for Paul's argument in Gal 3:28, suggesting that Paul included it only because it was already a part of the baptismal formula.[14] It is important to note, however, that ἄρσην and θῆλυς actually *would* be relevant for the authors' arguments in both 1 Cor 12:13 and Col 3:11, where they do *not* appear. In 1 Cor 12:13, the plurals of ἄρσην and θῆλυς (ἄρσενες and θήλειαι), would be equally as appropriate as Ἰουδαῖοι/Ἕλληνες and δοῦλοι/ ἐλεύθεροι and would, in fact, strengthen Paul's argument by including a third element of diversity in the "body," which is the point of the passage. Similarly, the addition of ἄρσην and θῆλυς in Col 3:11 would add yet another dimension to unity in Christ, which is the point of the verse. This suggests that, if the pair had been included in the baptismal formula with which these two authors were familiar, they almost certainly would have included it.

As will be noted later, various possible reasons have been suggested as to why, despite the fact that it would have been relevant for his argument and, indeed, would even have strengthened it, Paul did not include ἄρσην and θῆλυς in 1 Cor 12:13. My own judgment, however, is that if ἄρσην and θῆλυς had in fact been a part of the baptismal formula, Paul's explicit reference to "baptism" (ἐβαπτίσθημεν) would almost certainly have required that he include the entire formula and not just its first two clauses.

In any case, I see no reason why the author of Colossians would have omitted ἄρσην and θῆλυς if they had been present in the baptismal formula. Initially, one might suppose that their omission stemmed from the "patriarchal" attitude of the author that is exhibited in the *Haustafel* of Col 3:18–4:1. This supposition is ruled out, however, by the fact that Col 3:11 *does* include δοῦλος and ἐλεύθερος. If the author had removed ἄρσην and θῆλυς to promote the "patriarchal" attitude set forth in the *Haustafel*, this same author would almost certainly have also removed δοῦλος and ἐλεύθερος for the same reason. This strongly suggests that

---

14. Betz (*Galatians: A Commentary*, 182, 195). He also notes that the same is true of the second clause, οὐκ ἔνι δοῦλος οὐδὲ ἐλεύθερος.

the author of Colossians knew a baptismal formula that included Ἰουδαῖος, Ἕλλην, δοῦλος, and ἐλεύθερος but not ἄρσην and θῆλυς.

The situation regarding 1 Cor 7:17–24 is somewhat more complicated. I have suggested that these verses also allude to the same or a similar baptismal formula as that cited in Gal 3:27–28 but without including ἄρσην and θῆλυς. To be sure, one might assume (a) that it was precisely the inclusion of ἄρσην and θῆλυς in the formula that prompted Paul's allusion to it in a chapter dealing with sex, marriage, and divorce—i.e., with relations between men and women, and (b) that he omitted ἄρσην and θῆλυς because the issue at hand was not "male" as opposed to "female" but rather marriage as opposed to non-marriage and/or because the question was that of changing from one status (marriage or non-marriage) to the other (changing from slave to free or *vice versa* would have been a possibility, but changing from male to female or *vice versa* would not). Nevertheless, the omission of any explicit reference to ἄρσην and θῆλυς—*in a passage dealing specifically with relations between men and women*—must be noted because it may well be another indication that Paul was familiar with a baptismal formula that did not include the pair.[15]

In light of the overall weight of the evidence, it is my conclusion that οὐκ ἔνι ἄρσεν καὶ θῆλυ simply does not "fit" alongside οὐκ ἔνι Ἰουδαῖος οὐδὲ Ἕλλην and οὐκ ἔνι δοῦλος οὐδὲ ἐλεύθερος as part of the pre-Pauline baptismal formula cited by Paul in Gal 3:27–28 and that the formula at one time existed without the clause. Betz is correct: the clause *is* a secondary addition to the formula. This conclusion, however, leads to two questions: (1) At what point was οὐκ ἔνι ἄρσεν καὶ θῆλυ added to the baptismal formula? (2) Was it a *pre-Pauline* or a *Pauline* addition?

---

15. As will be noted later, it is possible that it was precisely Paul's allusion to the baptismal formula in the midst of his discussion of relations between men and women in 1 Cor 7:17–24 that initially suggested to him the idea, articulated (later?) in his letter to the Galatians, of adding οὐκ ἔνι ἄρσεν καὶ θῆλυ to the formula.

A Theological, Not a Liturgical Addition

Although Betz sees the distinctive wording of οὐκ ἔνι ἄρσεν καὶ θῆλυ as evidence only that the clause is a secondary addition to the baptismal formula cited in Gal 3:27–28, my own judgment is that this wording also constitutes rather strong evidence that the clause was not added to the formula *qua* baptismal formula but rather only when the formula was cited as part of a theological argument. In *the liturgical language of a baptismal formula*, one would expect, simply on *a priori* grounds, that the wording of the various clauses would be parallel. Note, for example, the exact double parallelism in 1 Cor 6:11b, which also apparently refers to baptism: ἀλλὰ ἀπελούσασθε, ἀλλὰ ἡγιάσθητε, ἀλλὰ ἐδικαιώθητε ἐν τῷ ὀνόματι τοῦ κυρίου Ἰησοῦ Χριστοῦ καὶ ἐν τῷ πνεύματι τοῦ Θεοῦ ἡμῶν.[16] Thus, even if one of the clauses was a secondary addition to the formula, one would expect its wording and structure to be parallel with that of the other clauses. In the case of Gal 3:28, this means that one would expect the third clause to read οὐκ ἔνι ἄρσην οὐδὲ θῆλυς (ἄρσην and θῆλυς in the *nominative* rather than the accusative case and οὐδέ rather than καί) or perhaps even οὐκ ἔνι ἀνὴρ οὐδὲ γύνη (both ἀνήρ and γύνη being *personal* rather than neuter). Alternatively, if οὐκ ἔνι ἄρσεν καὶ θῆλυ (based on Gen 1:27) was a secondary addition to the baptismal formula *qua* baptismal formula, one would expect the first two clauses to have been changed to read οὐκ ἔνι Ἰουδαῖος καὶ Ἕλλην, οὐκ ἔνι δοῦλος καὶ ἐλεύθερος in order to maintain a symmetry among the three clauses. One would certainly *not*, however, expect οὐκ ἔνι ἄρσεν καὶ θῆλυ in the baptismal formula *qua* baptismal formula!

---

16. Indeed, if the aorist tenses are changed to present tenses, the words might well be *exactly* what was said in a baptismal liturgy. For similar parallelism in a confessional formula, see, e.g., 1 Tim 3:16: ὃς ἐφανερώθη ἐν σαρκί, ἐδικαιώθη ἐν πνεύματι, ὤφθη ἀγγέλοις, ἐκηρύχθη ἐν ἔθνεσιν, ἐπιστεύθη ἐν κόσμῳ, ἀνελήμφθη ἐν δόξῃ.

When the baptismal formula is utilized as *part of a theological argument,* however, as it is in Gal 3:27–28, such rhetorical/liturgical conformity becomes much less important than the link to Gen 1:27. Indeed, if the *theological* point being made is "that the division of the first humans into 'male and female' articulated in Gen 1.27 ha[s] been overcome in the church, the new creation,"[17] it is absolutely *necessary* to preserve the exact wording of Gen 1:27; otherwise, the point will almost certainly be missed. Apparently with this in mind, Krister Stendahl even hints that an original οὐκ ἔνι ἄρσεν οὐδὲ θῆλυ might have been *changed* to οὐκ ἔνι ἄρσεν καὶ θῆλυ precisely in order to make this point.[18] If such a change was made to the formula *qua* baptismal formula, however, it appears likely that the οὐδέ would also have been changed to καί in the other two clauses in order to preserve the symmetry appropriate to a baptismal formula. In my own judgment, therefore, it is more likely that the entire clause, οὐκ ἔνι ἄρσεν καὶ θῆλυ, was simply *added* to a formula that already contained οὐκ ἔνι Ἰουδαῖος οὐδὲ Ἕλλην and οὐκ ἔνι δοῦλος οὐδὲ ἐλεύθερος and that, because the baptismal formula was now being cited not for liturgical purposes but rather as part of a theological argument, there would have been no need to change the οὐδέ to καί in the first two clauses. In any case, the distinctive wording, οὐκ ἔνι ἄρσεν καὶ θῆλυ, makes sense only in the context of *a theological statement*, not in that of *a baptismal liturgy*.

Thus, in my judgment, the triple lack of parallelism in wording between the third and the first two clauses of Gal 3:28 and the absence of ἄρσην and θῆλυς in 1 Cor 12:13, Col 3:11, and 1 Cor 7:17–24 constitute strong evidence not only that οὐκ ἔνι ἄρσεν καὶ θῆλυ represents a secondary addition to the pre-Pauline baptismal formula but also that it was added only when the formula was cited as part of a theological argument. The remaining question, then, is whether it was a *pre-Pauline* or a *Pauline* addition.

---

17. Stendahl, *The Bible and the Role of Women*, 1–2.
18. Stendahl, *The Bible and the Role of Women*, 32.

A Pauline, Not a Pre-Pauline Addition

As has already been noted, Gal 3:28 is the *only* passage in the New Testament that includes ἄρσην and θῆλυς when citing the baptismal formula; three other passages—1 Cor 12:13; Col 3:12; and 1 Cor 7:17–28—apparently cite or allude to the same or a similar baptismal formula without including the pair.[19] The simplest explanation for this is (a) that the formula at one time did not include ἄρσην and θῆλυς, (b) that they were added to the formula not *qua* baptismal formula but rather in order to use the formula as part of a theological argument, and (c) that that it was Paul who added them to the formula. Thus, invoking the principle of Ockham's Razor, I suggest that the burden of proof lies with any claim that οὐκ ἔνι ἄρσεν καὶ θῆλυ is a *pre-Pauline* addition.

The only evidence cited by Betz to support his claim that the clause is pre-Pauline is his observation that it "is not actually used in Paul's argument" in Galatians. He concludes from this that Paul included the clause simply because it was already a part of the baptismal formula.[20] This conclusion, however, does not necessarily follow from the observation. Rather, I propose the following scenario, which I regard as more plausible than the one suggested by Betz: (a) Paul cited the baptismal formula in Gal 3:27–28 because its first clause was directly relevant for—and indeed provided strong support for—his argument that, in baptism, all ethnic distinctions are overcome and circumcision therefore becomes irrelevant; (b) because it was a *baptismal formula*, perhaps one with which the Galatians were already familiar, he thought it necessary to cite the *entire* formula, lest it not be recognized as a baptismal formula and therefore carry less weight as a basis for his argument; (c) thus, he included the second clause of the formula, even though it would appear not to be directly relevant for his argu-

---

19. See n. 2 for the possibility that there may be as many as ten such passages.

20. Betz, *Galatians: A Commentary*, 182, 195. He also notes that the same is true of the second clause, οὐκ ἔνι δοῦλος οὐδὲ ἐλεύθερος.

ment; (d) inclusion of this second clause, however, broadened the scope of Paul's argument by adding socio-economic status to ethnicity as a human distinction that is overcome in baptism; (e) this, in turn "opened the door" for further expansion of the formula; and so (f) Paul added ἄρσην and θῆλυς to the formula in order to emphasize his own conviction that, in baptism, *all* human distinctions—not only those of ethnicity and socio-economic status, but also those of gender—are overcome. Indeed, he laid the groundwork for such expansion of the formula with the "all" in v. 26: πάντες γὰρ υἱοὶ Θεοῦ ἐστε διὰ τῆς πίστεως ἐν Χριστῷ Ἰησοῦ.

It is at least possible that a clue as to *why* Paul added "male" and "female" to a baptismal formula that already included "Jew"/"Greek" and "slave"/"free" can be found in 1 Cor 7:17–24. Chapter 7 as a whole deals with matters pertaining to sex, marriage, and divorce—i.e., relations between men and women. Paul's overriding concern is to prevent πορνεία ("immorality"), and he sees two alternatives to πορνεία. One is celibacy, for which he expresses a clear preference, and the other is marriage. Despite his preference for celibacy, however, he both calls for the preservation of marriages whenever possible—even marriages between believers and unbelievers (vv. 10–16)—and stresses the importance of sexual relations between husbands and wives (vv. 2–5). In the final analysis, then, his overall counsel is that people should remain in the state in which they were "called," whether married or unmarried (vv. 17a, 24). Indeed, he speaks of this as his "rule in all the churches" (οὕτως ἐν ταῖς ἐκκλησίαις πάσαις διατάσσομαι). This suggests that Paul views celibacy and marriage as equally appropriate states for members of the Christian community. Indeed, he speaks in v. 7 of both celibacy and marriage as a "gift from God" (χάρισμα ἐκ Θεοῦ).

It may well have been this idea that both celibacy and marriage are "gifts" from God—in other words, that those who are celibate and those who are married have equal standing in the eyes of God—that prompted Paul's allusion in 1 Cor 7:17–24 to the baptismal formula, which spoke of equality between "circumcision" and "uncircumcision" (i.e., "Jew" and "Gentile") and between "slave" and free." The baptismal formula declared that, in baptism, two of the most basic human dichotomies—ethnicity ("Jew" and "Greek") and socio-economic status ("slave" and "free")—are erased. Jews and non-Jews, slaves and free people, all have equal standing in the eyes of God. Paul appealed to this formula, in the midst of a discussion of relations between men and women, to support the somewhat different notion that celibacy and marriage are equally valid options for members of the Christian community. Such use of the formula, however, would quite naturally suggest the appropriateness of adding to it a third dichotomy—one having to do with men and women. "Celibate" and "married" (the topics immediately at hand) would not be truly parallel to "Jew"/"Greek" and "slave"/"free," but "male" and "female" would. Thus, prompted by his discussion of relations between men and women in 1 Corinthians 7 and remembering his appeal to the baptismal formula in the context of that discussion, Paul quite naturally might, in the course of his argument, have added "male" and "female" to the baptismal formula.

The addition of "male" and "female" to the formula, however, introduced a human dichotomy that was even more basic than those of ethnicity ("Jew"/"Greek") and socio-economic status ("slave"/"free"). This was a dichotomy reaching all the way back to the Creation. Thus, in order to emphasize the radical import of adding "male" and "female" to the baptismal formula, Paul would have used the exact wording in Gen 1:27— ἄρσεν καὶ θῆλυ—even though this wording is not parallel with Ἰουδαῖος οὐδὲ Ἕλλην and δοῦλος οὐδὲ ἐλεύθερος. What Paul likely had in mind—and wished his readers to recall—was the wording of Gen 1:27 in its entirety: καὶ ἐποίησεν ὁ Θεὸς τὸν ἄνθρωπον, κατ' εἰκόνα Θεοῦ ἐποίησεν αὐτόν, ἄρσεν καὶ θῆλυ ἐποίησεν αὐτούς. Particularly when read in conjunction with Gen 2:18–25, which narrates the creation of Eve from Adam's rib,[21] this verse appears to suggest a

---

21. Both Paul and his contemporaries would almost certainly have read Genesis 1 and 2 as a *single* account of the creation (as have many people even into the twenty-first century).

distinction between τὸν ἄνθρωπον/αὐτόν, on the one hand, and ἄρσεν καὶ θῆλυ/αὐτούς, on the other hand—in other words, that God originally created one single being, ὁ ἄνθρωπος, and subsequently divided this single being into ἄρσην and θῆλυς.[22] Thus, by adding οὐκ ἔνι καὶ θῆλυ to the baptismal formula in Gal 3:28, with its use of this "creation" language, Paul indicated that, in baptism, that is, in the "new creation," the distinction between male and female—like that between Jew and Greek and between slave and free—is overcome and the original unity of ὁ ἄνθρωπος is restored. That Paul had the new creation in mind as he composed the letter to the Galatians and that he associated it with the elimination of distinctions among various classes of humans is indicated quite clearly in Gal 6:15, near the very end of the letter, which reads, οὔτε γὰρ περιτομή τί ἐστιν οὔτε ἀκροβυστία ἀλλὰ καινὴ κτίσις ("for neither is circumcision anything or uncircumcision, but a new creation"). It is noteworthy that a majority of the early manuscripts have ἐν γὰρ Χριστῷ Ἰησοῦ at the beginning of 6:15, and this phrase ties the verse quite closely to the πάντες γὰρ ὑμεῖς εἷς ἐστε ἐν Χριστῷ Ἰησοῦ of 3:28.[23] Indeed, 6:15 could almost be seen as an abbreviated paraphrase of the baptismal formula cited in 3:27–28.[24]

In support of the scenario I have just proposed, I offer the following considerations:

1. There is little, if any, clear evidence that the pre-Pauline church, or any segment of it, was, in fact, as radically egalitarian as οὐκ ἔνι ἄρσεν καὶ θῆλυ would suggest.

---

22. This has often been suggested; see, e.g., Meeks, "Image of the Androgyne." For a similar idea in Gnostic Christianity, see, e.g., *Gos. Phil.* 76, 86.

23. Of the early manuscripts, only P[46] (ca. 200 CE) and B (fourth century) omit ἐν γὰρ Χριστῷ Ἰησοῦ at the beginning of 6:15. The NRSV omits it in the text but includes a footnote that reads, "Other ancient authorities add *in Christ Jesus*." Metzger (*Textual Commentary*, 2nd ed., 530) says, "The shorter reading has limited but adequate support."

24. Cf. also Gal 5:6: ἐν γὰρ Χριστῷ Ἰησοῦ οὔτε περιτομή τι ἰσχύει οὔτε ἀκροβυστία ἀλλὰ πίστις δι' ἀγάπης ἐνεργουμένη.

2. Quite apart from Gal 3:28, there are clear indications in the Pauline letters that Paul himself was—or at least became—radically egalitarian in his attitude toward the status and role of women.
3. As has already been suggested, there is some evidence that Paul may have known a version of the baptismal formula that did not include ἄρσην and θῆλυς.
4. As has already been noted, the distinctive wording οὐκ ἔνι ἄρσεν καὶ θῆλυ is appropriate and even necessary for Paul's *theological argument* in Galatians but would not be appropriate in *a baptismal formula*, whether as an original part of the formula or as a secondary addition.

The third and fourth considerations have already been addressed, but it is necessary to provide some explication of the first and second.

The Pre-Pauline Church as Egalitarian?

Some scholars have argued that οὐκ ἔνι ἄρσεν καὶ θῆλυ reflects the attitude both of the historical Jesus and of the pre-Pauline church, or at least of some segments of the pre-Pauline church,[25] and thus would already have been a part of the pre-Pauline baptismal formula cited in Gal 3:27–28. My own judgment, however, is that the evidence regarding both Jesus and the pre-Pauline church is limited, ambiguous at best and, in any case, unreliable so far as actual history is concerned.

All of the Gospels were written after Paul's lifetime, and each has its own theological, apologetic, and/or "political" agendas. Thus, even many feminist scholars, who might be expected to be open to a picture of Jesus as radically egalitarian, are quite cautious in their assessment of the evidence. As Mary Rose D'Angelo puts it:

---

25. See, e.g., Schüssler Fiorenza, *In Memory of Her*, 105–59 on the Jesus movement and 160–204 on the early Christian missionary movement. Others have argued similarly.

Chapter 6 ❧ *A Pauline Addition in Gal 3:28* 79

The Jesus of the gospels acts in and speaks to and for communities of the late first and early second centuries. Sayings of Jesus have been revised to suit their needs, and questions or objections that are put to him often articulate the issues the communities understand themselves to be facing. The other figures in the gospels, both the unnamed antagonists and recipients of miracles and the named disciples who figure in individual stories, tend to represent positions within or related to the evangelists' communities. Titles and practices, like disputes, may reflect the practices and decisions of the early Christian churches.[26]

Thus, D'Angelo concludes that the portrayals of women and of issues relating to gender in the Gospels of Mark and John—and the same can be said of Matthew and Luke-Acts—"give the lie to simplistic claims that Jesus was a campaigner against the gender prescriptions of his time."[27]

It is equally difficult to reconstruct attitudes regarding women in the pre-Pauline church. The only canonical narrative of the times, the Book of Acts, was written a generation or more after the events it purports to describe (probably in the early-to-mid-second century),[28] and its theological, apologetic, and "political" agendas are becoming increasingly evident.[29] It is clear from Paul's incidental references that certain women played a prominent role in the life and leadership of the church of Paul's time, but, as Margaret Y. MacDonald observes:

---

26. D'Angelo, "Reconstructing 'Real' Women from Gospel Literature," 106.

27. D'Angelo, "(Re)presentations of Women in the Gospels: John and Mark," 145; cf. D'Angelo, "(Re)presentations of Women in the Gospels of Matthew and Luke-Acts." They also rule out, in her judgment, the view that Jesus selected twelve male disciples in order to create an all-male ministry.

28. Pervo (*Dating Acts*) dates Acts ca. 125–130 CE. My own judgment is that it may have been written as late as the middle of the second century.

29. E.g., Tyson (*Marcion and Luke-Acts*) suggests that Acts was motivated in part by the need to provide the church with material that would serve in its fight against Marcionite Christianity in the second century.

Comparative studies have illustrated . . . that the appearance of women in leadership roles should not be seen as unique in ancient society. Rather, early Christian women acted in ways that were in keeping with the leadership of women in other communities in the Roman imperial world.[30]

In short, we have *very* little reliable information regarding the pre-Pauline church—certainly not enough to warrant characterizing it, or any segment of it, as radically egalitarian with regard to the status and role of women. It *may* have been, but we cannot with any confidence say that it *was*!

Evidence of Paul's Radical Egalitarianism

Until rather recently, Paul was typically seen not as a radical egalitarian but rather as a vigorous defender of the patriarchal system that characterized first-century society in general. This view was based, however, on four quite dubious foundations: (1) certain passages in the pseudo-Pauline writings,[31] (2) two passages in 1 Corinthians that, in my judgment, most likely are later non-Pauline interpolations,[32] (3) what is now widely regarded as a misreading of 1 Corinthians 7, and (4) a disregard for or, in some cases, a misreading of certain of Paul's more-or-less incidental references to particular women with whom he was associated in the

---

30. MacDonald, "Reading Real Women," 218.
31. Col 3:18; Eph 5:22–33; 1 Tim 2:9–15; Titus 2:4–5.
32. 1 Cor 11:3–16; 14:34–35. The latter passage is now rather widely regarded as an interpolation, see, e.g., Fee, *First Epistle to the Corinthians*, 699–705; and Payne, *Man and Woman, One in Christ*, 225–67. On the former passage, which is still widely regarded as authentically Pauline, see, e.g., Hawkins, *Recovery of the Historical Paul*, 187–88; Walker, "1 Corinthians 11:2–16 and Paul's Views regarding Women"; Cope, "1 Cor 11:2–16: One Step Further"; Trompf, "On Attitudes toward Women"; Munro, *Authority in Paul and Peter*, 69–75; Munro, "Women, Text, and Canon," 26–28; Walker, "Vocabulary of 1 Corinthians 11.3–16"; Walker, *Interpolations*, 91–126; Mount, "1 Corinthians 11:3–16: Spirit Possession and Authority"; Dewey et al., *Authentic Letters of Paul*, 110–11; and Milinovich, *Beyond What Is Written*, 144–52.

work of the churches. Apart from the pseudo-Pauline writings, the two likely interpolations in 1 Corinthians, and the misreading of 1 Corinthians 7, there is simply no evidence that Paul supported the patriarchal system. Indeed, a more accurate reading of 1 Corinthians 7 and the incidental references to particular women indicates the exact opposite.[33] These latter two points, therefore, call for brief elaboration.

Paul's discussion of sex, marriage, and divorce in 1 Corinthians 7 was, in the past, typically seen as reflecting a negative attitude toward women, but this interpretation is now widely disavowed. There is now widespread agreement that v. 1b—καλὸν ἀνθρώπῳ γυναικὸς μὴ ἅπτεσθαι ("It is well for a person not to touch a woman")[34]—is a quotation of what certain people in Corinth are saying, that Paul himself does not agree with the statement, and, indeed, that he quotes it in order to argue against it in the following verses.[35] Moreover, a careful reading of the chapter as a whole reveals: (a) Paul's insistence that husbands and wives have precisely the same rights and responsibilities within the marriage relation—i.e., that the marriage relation is one of complete mutuality and equality;[36] and (b) perhaps most significantly, his encouragement for those women and men who so desire to remain unmarried[37]—not because marriage and sexuality are in any way sinful but rather because of the nearness of the end and for the sake of their "undivided devotion to the Lord."[38] This latter point was truly revolutionary, for it represented a radical break with the most basic of all patriarchal institutions: the patriarchal family. Thus, a careful reading of 1 Corinthians 7 indicates not a negative

---

33. For discussion, see Walker, "Paul on the Status and Role of Women."

34. So far as I am aware, commentators have not attempted an explanation of why ἄντρωπος ("person") is used rather than ἀνήρ ("man").

35. For arguments supporting this view, see, e.g., Thiselton, *First Epistle to the Corinthians*, 498–501. I note that the NRSV places the statement in quotation marks.

36. 1 Cor 7:2–4, 10–16.

37. 1 Cor 7:8.

38. 1 Cor 7:29–35.

attitude toward women but rather a radical egalitarianism on the part of Paul.

Also to be noted are Paul's more-or-less incidental references to certain particular women. These include (a) references to women as his "fellow workers" or as "workers in the Lord" who have "worked hard" or "labored side by side" with him in various of the churches[39]—references that employ the same terminology that Paul applies to male associates who were clearly regarded as leaders in the churches;[40] (b) his praise for a wife and husband, Prisca and Aquila, as "his fellow workers in Christ Jesus, who risked their necks" for him and in whose home a community of Christians meets for worship;[41] (c) his identification of a certain Phoebe both as a "deacon" or "minister" (διάκονος),[42] a title that he elsewhere applies generally to leaders in the church,[43] and as προστάτις,[44] which likely indicates a position of leadership and/or authority; and (d) most striking of all, his reference to his "fellow prisoners" Andronicus (a man) and Junia (a woman!) not only as "apostles" but as "prominent among the apostles" (ἐπίσημοι ἐν τοῖς ἀποστόλοις).[45] All of these references, in my judgment, are expressions of Paul's radical egalitarianism with regard to the status and role of women.

In light of such evidence, I conclude that, quite apart from Gal 3:28, there is ample reason to characterize Paul's attitude toward the status and role of women as radically egalitarian. This, coupled with the lack of evidence for such egalitarianism in the pre-Pauline church, makes it likely, simply on *a priori* grounds, that

---

39. Phil 4:2–3; Rom 16:3, 6, 12.
40. 1 Thess 3:2; 1 Cor 3:9; 2 Cor 8:23; Phil 2:25; Phlm 1, 24; Rom 16:9–21.
41. 1 Cor 16:19; Rom 16:3–5. Aquila is named first in 1 Cor 16:19 and Prisca in first in Rom 16:3; this suggests that Paul regarded them as equals in the life and work of the church.
42. Rom 16:1. Διάκονος is often mistranslated as "deaconess."
43. Phil 1:1; with reference to himself: 1 Cor 3:5; 2 Cor 3:6; 6:4; 11:23.
44. Rom 16:2.
45. Rom 16:7. For a convincing argument in favor of the feminine "Junia" rather than the masculine "Junias," see Epp, *Junia*.

it was Paul who added οὐκ ἔνι ἄρσεν καὶ θῆλυ to the baptismal formula cited in Gal 3:27–28.

Preliminary Conclusion

In my judgment, the cumulative weight of the evidence points to the conclusion (a) that οὐκ ἔνι ἄρσεν καὶ θῆλυ is *a secondary addition* to the baptismal formula cited by Paul in Gal 3:27–28, (b) that it was added only when the formula was incorporated into *a theological argument* and (c) that it most likely was *Paul* who made the addition. The remaining question, then, is why Paul did not also include ἄρσην and θῆλυς in the other two passages—1 Cor 7:17–24 and 1 Cor 12:13—in which he apparently alluded to the same or a similar baptismal formula.

Absence of ἄρσην and θῆλυς in 1 Cor 7:17–24 and 1 Cor 12:13

As Joseph A. Fitzmyer observes, "speculation runs wild when commentators try to determine why [Paul] omits the third [pair], 'male or [sic] female,' [in 1 Cor 12:13]."[46] At least five possible reasons come to mind, none of which can be definitively ruled out, and these would apply also to 1 Cor 7:17–24:

1. The clause οὐκ ἔνι ἄρσεν καὶ θῆλυ in Gal 3:28 reflects the outlook of "a liberating pre-Pauline movement," and Paul's own views are more accurately represented in 1 Cor 7:17–24 and 1 Cor 12:13.[47] If Galatians was written *prior to* 1 Corinthians, this may suggest that, between the time of Galatians and that of 1 Corinthians, Paul revised his views on male/female relations in the church or at least developed some reservations regarding the egalitarianism expressed in Galatians and, for this reason, omitted ἄρσην and θῆλυς in 1 Cor 7:17–24 and 1 Cor 12:13.[48] This

---

46. Fitzmyer, *First Corinthians: A New Translation*, 478.
47. MacDonald, *There Is No Male and Female*, 4–5.
48. I regard it as likely, however, that Galatians was written *after* 1 Corinthians (see n. 9 above).

possibility would appear to be ruled out, however, by what Paul says regarding three particular women in Romans, which is certainly *one* of the last, if not *the* last, of his extant letters. Here, as has already been noted, he refers to Phoebe as a "deacon" or "minister" (διάκονος) and "leader" (προστάτις) in the church (16:1–2), speaks warmly of his "fellow workers in Christ Jesus," Prisca and Aquila, in whose house a church meets for worship (16:3–4), and says that Junia, along with Andronicus (presumably her husband), are "prominent (ἐπίσημοι) among the apostles" (16:7).[49] Of particular interest is the fact that he names Prisca *first*, before her husband Aquila, unlike in 1 Corinthians, which clearly was written earlier than Romans, where it is Aquila who is named first (1 Cor 16:19). These references suggest that, if anything, Paul's views became *more* rather than less egalitarian as time passed.

2. The Galatian churches were familiar with a form of the baptismal formula that included ἄρσην and θῆλυς, the church in Corinth knew a formula that omitted them, and Paul, in each case, simply used the form with which his readers were familiar. There is, however, no evidence for this possibility.

3. Paul omitted ἄρσην and θῆλυς in 1 Cor 7:17–24 and 1 Cor 12:13 to avoid calling attention again to a major issue apparently dividing the Corinthian church—the nature of human sexuality—that he had already addressed earlier in the letter.[50] A rather strong case has been made for this possibility.[51] It must be noted, however, that this applies only to 1 Cor 12:13, because 1 Cor 7:17–24 is all about human sexuality.

---

49. To be sure, all of these references are in chap. 16, which some scholars regard as part of an originally separate letter (perhaps to Ephesus) that was subsequently appended to Romans, in which case it may well have been written earlier than chaps. 1–15. The majority opinion, however, now appears to reject this view; see, e.g., Myers, "Romans," 818–19; Moo, "Romans," 844.b.

50. 1 Cor 5:1–8; 6:13b–20; cf. 11:3–16, which, however, may be a non-Pauline interpolation (see n. 32).

51. See, e.g., Hays, *First Corinthians*, 214; and Collins, *First Corinthians*, 463.

4. 1 Corinthians was written *earlier* than Galatians, at a time when Paul's own thinking had not yet arrived at the radically egalitarian view reflected in Gal 3:28. The dating of Galatians has long been a matter of scholarly debate, with proposed dates ranging from as early as 49 CE, which would make it one of the earliest, or possibly the earliest, of Paul's extant letters, to as late as 58 CE, which would make it one of the latest. As has already been noted, it is my own judgment that a strong argument has been made for dating Galatians *later* than 1 Corinthians,[52] and this provides a reasonable explanation of the presence of ἄρσην and θῆλυς in Gal 3:28 and their absence in 1 Cor 7:17–24 and 12:13.[53]

5. The baptismal formula with which Paul was familiar did not, in fact, include ἄρσην and θῆλυς, but he added them in Gal 3:28 to make a particular theological point. The bulk of the present study has been an attempt to demonstrate that this—along with option four above—is most likely the case. In short, it is my judgment (a) that 1 Corinthians was likely written *earlier* than Galatians, (b) that 1 Corinthians 7:17–24 and 12:13 do not include "male" and "female" because they were not included in the baptismal formula with which Paul was familiar and he had not yet developed the radically egalitarian attitude expressed in Gal 3:28, (c) that it may well have been his allusion to the baptismal formula in 1 Cor 7:17–24 that suggested the appropriateness of adding "male" and "female" to the formula, and finally (d) that he added οὐκ ἔνι ἄρσεν καὶ θῆλυ—based on Gen 1:27—to the formula in Gal 3:28 to express his mature conviction that, in baptism, *all* distinctions—ethnic, socio-economic, and gender-related—were overcome.

With regard to 1 Cor 7:17–24, there is yet another reason why Paul might have omitted ἀνήρ and θῆλυς. In this passage, he is using "circumcision"/"uncircumcision" and "slave"/"free" to

---

52. See n. 9.

53. The matter is complicated, of course, if any of the "partition" theories regarding 1 Corinthians are accurate. This might mean that part of 1 Corinthians was written before Galatians and part of it after.

illustrate his preference that the married should remain married if possible and the unmarried remain unmarried. A move from uncircumcision to circumcision and even *vice versa* would have been possible; similarly, a move from slavery to freedom and *vice versa* would have been possible. Changing one's status from male to female or *vice versa*, however, would not have been possible. Thus, the third pair in Gal 3:28—ἄρσην and θῆλυς—would simply not have been relevant in 1 Cor 7:17–24. This might account for the omission of the pair. If, however, Galatians was written *later* than 1 Corinthians, as I think was likely the case, then the following scenario becomes plausible:

a. Paul was familiar with a baptismal formula that included "Jew"/"Greek" and "slave"/"free" but not "male"/"female."
b. Although his concern in 1 Corinthians 7 was with sex, marriage, and divorce (i.e., relations between men and women), not ethnicity or socio-economic status, he invoked this formula to support his principle: "Let each of you remain in the condition in which you were called."
c. His invocation of the formula to support his views regarding sex, marriage, and divorce suggested that the formula might also have something to say directly regarding relations between women and men.
d. This led him eventually to add "male and female" to the baptismal formula.
e. His discussion of sex, marriage, and divorce in 1 Corinthians 7 might easily have led him to word the third pair "married or unmarried," but "male or female" would more closely parallel the deep-seated socio-economic implications of "Jew or Greek" and "slave or free."
f. The phrase "male or female," however, would almost inevitably bring to mind Gen 1:27 (καὶ ἐποίησεν ὁ Θεὸς τὸν ἄνθρωπον, κατ' εἰκόνα Θεοῦ ἐποίησεν αὐτόν, ἄρσεν καὶ θῆλυ ἐποίησεν αὐτούς).
g. Thus, in order to emphasize that *all* of the most basic human distinctions—not only ethnicity and socio-economic

status but also gender (not marital status)—have been overcome in the new creation, Paul added "male and female" (not "celibacy and marriage") to the baptismal formula that already included "Jew or Greek" and "slave or free," using the exact wording of Gen 1:27 (i.e., ἄρσεν καὶ θῆλυ rather than ἄρσην οὐδὲ θῆλυς).

Conclusion

In light of the foregoing considerations, it is my judgment (a) that οὐκ ἔνι ἄρσεν καὶ θῆλυ is, as Betz argues, a secondary addition to the pre-Pauline baptismal formula cited in Gal 3:27–28, (b) that the clause was not added to the baptismal formula *qua* baptismal formula but only when the formula was incorporated into a theological argument, (c) that, *pace* Betz, it most likely was Paul himself who added the clause to the baptismal formula, and (d) that there are plausible reasons why Paul might have not have included ἄρσην and θῆλυς in 1 Cor 7:17–24 and 12:13.

"So What?"

I have argued that οὐκ ἔνι ἄρσεν καὶ θῆλυ is a secondary addition to the baptismal formula cited in Gal 3:26–28 and that it most likely was Paul who added the clause. In the process, I have also argued that the absence of the ἄρσην/θῆλυς pair in 1 Cor 7:17–24 and 1 Cor 12:13 can be accounted for without in any way weakening my primary arguments, suggesting along the way that Galatians was likely written *later* than 1 Corinthians. If I am correct, then it would appear that Paul's views regarding the status and role of women became, in fact, increasingly egalitarian as time passed but that it was only in Galatians that he articulated this egalitarianism in an unmistakably clear and forceful manner.[54]

---

54. But see also the references in Romans 16 to Phoebe (vv. 1–2), Prisca (vv. 3–4), Mary (v. 6), Junia (v. 7), Tryphsena and Tryphosa (v. 12), Persis (12), the mother of Rufus (v. 13), Julia (v. 15), and the sister of Nereus (v. 15).

Part Two

Studies in the Corinthian
Correspondence and Romans

Chapter 7

2 Corinthians 6:14–7:1 and the Chiastic Structure of 6:11–13; 7:2–3

New Testament scholars have long debated whether 2 Cor 6:14–7:1 originally stood at its present location in 2 Corinthians and, indeed, whether the passage should even be attributed to Paul. The verses have variously been viewed as (a) composed by Paul specifically for inclusion at their present location, (b) composed by Paul for some other occasion[1] but subsequently included at their present location either by Paul or by someone else, (c) composed by someone other than Paul but included at their present location by Paul, or (d) both composed by someone other than Paul and included at their present location by someone other than Paul (not necessarily the same person).[2] It is not my intention in this brief study to address the question of authorship; rather, I propose simply to look at one aspect of the question as to whether this passage originally stood at its present location in 2 Corinthians—that is, at the relation between 2 Cor 6:14–7:1 and its immediate context (6:11–13 and 7:2–3).

The relation of 2 Cor 6:14–7:1 to its immediate context has long been regarded as problematic. It is possible, of course, that the verses represent simply a "dictation pause, a sudden digression (unrelated to context), or an *ad hoc* response to lingering problems

---

"2 Cor 6.14–7.1 and the Chiastic Structure of 6.11–13; 7.2–3." *NTS* 48,1 (Jan 2002) 142–44. Copyright © 2002 Cambridge University Press. Reprinted with permission. Some of the material appeared earlier in Walker, *Interpolations*, 202, and was included in the *NTS* article with permission from Sheffield Academic Press.

1. Perhaps as part of the earlier letter mentioned in 1 Cor 5:9–11.
2. For a good summary of scholarship since the Reformation, see Webb, *Returning Home*, 16–30; see also, e.g., Furnish, *II Corinthians*, 375–83.

at Corinth (due to external factors)"[3] and thus are to be seen as original to the text at this point,[4] but the arguments for viewing them as a secondary insertion are impressive. The passage appears to interrupt what would otherwise be a syntactically smooth and logically clear transition from the immediately preceding verses (6:11–13) to those that immediately follow (7:2–3) and could easily stand alone as a self-contained independent unit.

This has long been recognized, of course, by New Testament scholars. What has not previously been noted, however, at least to my knowledge, is that the removal of 6:14–7:1 leaves a perfect chiasmus in the now (re-)unified material immediately preceding and immediately following (6:11–13; 7:2–3):[5]

> **A¹** *Assurance of affection* (6:11): "Our mouth has opened to you, Corinthians, our heart has been widened" (τὸ στόμα ἡμῶν ἀνέῳγεν πρὸς ὑμᾶς, Κορίνθοι, ἡ καρδία ἡμῶν πεπλάτυνται).
>> **B¹** *Disclaimer of responsibility for alienation* (6:12): "You are not restricted by us, but you are restricted by your affections" (οὐ στενοχωρεῖσθε ἐν ἡμῖν, στενοχωρεῖσθε δὲ ἐν τοῖς σπλάγχνοις ὑμῶν).[6]
>>> **C¹** *Appeal for affection* (6:13): "And in return—I speak as to children—be also yourselves widened" (τὴν δὲ αὐτὴν ἀντιμισθίαν, ὡς τέκνοις λέγω, πλατύνθητε καὶ ὑμεῖς).

---

3. Webb, *Returning Home*, 163.

4. For a significant attempt to show that 6:14–7:1 is closely related to its immediate context, see Webb, *Returning Home*; see also, e.g., Thrall, "The Problem of II Cor. VI.14–VII.1"; and Murphy-O'Connor, "Relating 2 Corinthians 6.14–7.1 to Its Context."

5. This is noted in my *Interpolations in the Pauline Letters* (202), but without any real argumentation.

6. Ἐν τοῖς σπλάγχνοις ὑμῶν is generally translated "in your affections." The clear parallelism between this phrase and ἐν ἡμῶν, however, suggests the same translation of ἐν in both cases. What is left unstated is the object of the Corinthians' "affections." Presumably, it was affection for something other than Paul (and his companions?) and other than what Paul would have approved.

C² *Appeal for affection* (7:2a): "Make room for us" (χωρήσατε ἡμᾶς).

B² *Disclaimer of responsibility for alienation* (7:2b): "We wronged no one, we corrupted no one, we took advantage of no one" (οὐδένα ἠδικήσαμεν, οὐδένα ἐφθείραμεν, οὐδένα ἐπλεονεκτήσαμεν).

A² *Assurance of affection* (7:3): "I do not say this to condemn you, for I have said before that you are in our hearts, to die together and to live together" (πρὸς κατάκρισιν οὐ λέγω,⁷ προείρηκα γὰρ ὅτι ἐν ταῖς καρδίαις ἡμῶν ἐστε εἰς τὸ συναποθανεῖν καὶ συζῆν).

It might be possible to argue that 6:11–13; 7:2–3 represents not an example of chiasmus but simply a repetition of ideas and even terminology. For example, v. 12a ("You are not restricted by us"), which is the first part of what I have labeled *disclaimer of responsibility for alienation*, might be viewed not as the beginning of a new point but simply a restatement and elaboration of v. 11 (*assurance of affection*). Verse 12a is immediately followed, however, by 12b ("but you are restricted by your affections"), and the pointed contrast between ἐν ἡμῖν ("by us") and ἐν τοῖς σπλάγχνοις ὑμῶν ("by your affections") makes it clear that 12a and 12b belong together as a single unit. Thus, a new point is in fact being made in v. 12: it is the Corinthians themselves who are responsible for the alienation, not Paul (and his companions?).⁸ Clearly, this is a different point than that made in v. 11.

---

7. See, e.g., Bultmann, *Second Letter to the Corinthians*, 178: "The πρὸς κατάκρισιν οὐ λέγω in verse 3—'I do not say this in order to condemn you'—does not intend to remove a misunderstanding. It is only an (superfluous) expression of Paul's love, his suing for trust. That this is the motive is stated in the words which follow—προείρηκα γὰρ ὅτι ἐν ταῖς καρδίαις ἡμῶν ἐστε εἰς τὸ συναποθανεῖν καὶ συζῆν. The meaning is, 'Indeed I have just told you . . .' that is, in 6.12 or in 6.11f."

8. It is unclear whether the "we" here and elsewhere is an "editorial we," referring only to Paul, or whether it includes one or more of his companions or co-workers.

One might also argue that 7:2b represents not a disclaimer of responsibility for the alienation but simply a claim of innocence that provides the grounds for the appeal in 7:2a—in short, that v. 7 as a whole makes a single point: "Make room for us [because] we wronged no one . . ." In response, however, it should be noted that the same might be said regarding 6:12–13 (or, indeed, regarding all of 6:11–13): i.e., that the Corinthians should "be widened" because of Paul's (and his companions'?) affection for them and because he has not "restricted them." In this case, the chiasmus would remain but with different elements:

A^1 *Basis for appeal for affection* (6:11–12)
  B^1 *Appeal for affection* (6:13)
  B^2 *Appeal for affection* (7:2a)
A^2 *Basis for appeal for affection* (7:2b–3)

It appears much more likely, however, that 7:2b, which might be paraphrased as "We have done nothing wrong," is intended to parallel 6:12a, which could be rephrased as "We are not restricting you." Thus, 7:2b points to 6:12a, which, as already noted, is closely linked to 6:12b. Therefore, 7:2b parallels 6:12 in its entirety and, like the latter, can appropriately be labelled a *disclaimer of responsibility for alienation*.

In short, 2 Cor 7:2–3 represents not only a repetition of the points made in 6:11–13 but also a repetition in reverse sequence (*ABC* in 6:11–3 and *CBA* in 7:2–3), and it is precisely such a repetition of points in reverse sequence, of course, that constitutes a "chiasmus."

The appearance of this chiasmus when 2 Cor 6:14–7:1 is removed would appear to strengthen significantly the case for viewing these verses as a later insertion into the text of Paul's letter to the Corinthians! In and of itself, however, this phenomenon says nothing at all regarding the authorship of the passage.

Chapter 8

1 Corinthians 15:29–34 as a Non-Pauline Interpolation

In a clear understatement, Raymond F. Collins observes that the interpretation of 1 Cor 15:29–34 is "difficult." More bluntly, Hans Conzelmann characterizes the verses as "one of the most hotly disputed passages in the epistle."[1] Particularly troublesome are the references to baptism on behalf of the dead (v. 29) and fighting with beasts in Ephesus (v. 32a), but there are other problems as well.

The purpose of this study is to argue that 1 Cor 15:29–34 is an interpolation, neither composed by Paul nor included by him in his Corinthian letter. The argument is based upon considerations of (a) context, (b) vocabulary, and (c) content, with attention as well to (d) the self-contained unity of the verses when removed from their present context, (e) the essential irrelevance of the absence of text-critical evidence for interpolation, (f) the inevitably cumulative nature of any argument for interpolation, and (g) the possible origin of the interpolation.

Context

The topic of 1 Corinthians 15 as a whole is resurrection from the dead. This is also the topic of vv. 29–32 and, albeit less directly, arguably that of vv. 33–34 as well.[2] Thus, vv. 29–34 would appear to "fit" in chap. 15 insofar as subject matter is concerned. An examination of the logic of the chapter, however, suggests that this may not be the case.

"1 Corinthians 15:29–34 as a Non-Pauline Interpolation." *CBQ* 69,1 (Jan 2007) 84–103. Copyright © 2007 Catholic Biblical Association of America. Reprinted with permission.

    1. Collins, *First Corinthians*, 556; Conzelmann, *1 Corinthians: A Commentary*, 275.

    2. On vv. 33–34, see below.

Verses 1–28 proclaim the fact of Christ's resurrection "as the common ground of all Christian preaching and faith"[3] (vv. 1–11), insist that a denial of resurrection negates Christ's resurrection and thus invalidates Christian faith itself (vv. 12–19), and assert that Christ's resurrection guarantees the future resurrection of believers and the final destruction of death (vv. 20–28). Verses 35–58 address a possible objection regarding the nature of the resurrection body (vv. 35–53), concluding with a ringing affirmation of victory and an exhortation to faithful endurance (vv. 54–58). The flow of the argument in vv. 1–28, 35–58 is logical, clear, and complete.

This flow is abruptly interrupted, however, by vv. 29–34, which contain "very little in the way of theology," are "pure[ly] *ad hominem*" and indeed "*ad hoc*" in nature,[4] and, at best, represent "something of an interlude, a brief respite from dense and involved argumentation."[5] Paul Ellingworth and Howard Hatton suggest, therefore, that "Paul is digressing [in v. 29] from the main subject of the resurrection of Christ and of the believers,"[6] and Conzelmann asserts that "the new argument [introduced at v. 29] has nothing to do with the one advanced so far." Even Gordon D. Fee, while maintaining that the "rhetoric" of vv. 29–34 "follows naturally . . . from the preceding argument," acknowledges that it does "not necessarily [follow] logically."[7] The removal of vv. 29–34 would in no way alter or weaken the force of Paul's overall argument in chap. 15; indeed, the logic of the argument would be considerably clearer without these verses.

If vv. 29–34 logically "belong" in chap. 15 at all, it would appear to be after v. 19, not after v. 28. In vv. 12–19, Paul discusses certain *theological* and *soteriological* implications of denying the resurrection, and this might appropriately be followed by refer-

---

3. Fee, *First Epistle to the Corinthians*, 737.
4. Fee, *First Epistle to the Corinthians*, 761, 762.
5. Wright, *Resurrection of the Son of God*, 338.
6. Ellingworth and Hatton, *Translator's Handbook*, 308; Conzelmann, *1 Corinthians: A Commentary*, 277.
7. Fee, *First Epistle to the Corinthians*, 763.

ence to some *practical* and *ethical* implications of such denial (vv. 29–34). Indeed, the reference to "those who have died in Christ" (vv. 18–19) might lead logically to the question regarding "those who are baptized on behalf of the dead" (v. 29). Verses 29–34 do not appear after v. 19, however. They come after the "majestic contemplation of God's ordered eschatological, sovereign purposes"[8] in vv. 20–28, and the logical connection between this triumphant scenario and baptism on behalf of the dead is by no means clear. Thus, in their present location, vv. 29–34 are, at best, a digression on the part of Paul.

It is possible, of course, that such a digression would not pose a problem. Collins suggests that "to a large extent [1 Corinthians] as a whole is constructed according to a pattern of chiastic parallelism" whereby "Paul offers some general considerations (A), then a digression that supports his argument (B), and finally a further reflection that specifies the general reflection and responds to the particular issue at hand (A^1)." Collins suggests, further, that "Paul's use of digression [in 1 Corinthians] in support of his argument is consistent with the ancient rhetoricians' understanding of digression."[9] As examples of such a chiastic pattern involving digression, however, Collins cites 1 Cor 1:10–3:23; 5–7; 8–10; and 12–14, *but not 15:29–34*.[10] Furthermore, it is not at all clear that these verses, even as a digression, would logically support Paul's argument in vv. 1–28. Thus, I regard 1 Cor 15:29–34 not as a digression but rather as an interruption.

This does not prove, of course, that the verses are non-Pauline, but it surely raises the possibility. The possibility is strengthened, moreover, by attention to the conjunctions at the beginning of vv. 29 (ἐπεί) and 34 (ἀλλά).

---

8. Thiselton, *First Epistle to the Corinthians*, 1240.
9. Collins, *First Corinthians*, 14. According to Collins, Quintillian states that digression can be "used to amplify an argument's principal point, to abridge an argument, to make an emotional appeal, or to introduce such topics as would add charm and elegance to the composition."
10. Collins, *First Corinthians*, 14–16.

Elsewhere in Paul's letters, ἐπεί ("because," "since," or "for") appears nine times.[11] In every case it serves as a direct causal link between the immediately preceding clause or sentence and what is to follow—sometimes, indeed, as an ellipsis, meaning "for if it were different" or "otherwise."[12] Only at 1 Cor 15:29 do the RSV and the NRSV place their translation of ἐπεί at the beginning of a new paragraph. Elsewhere, it always appears either within a sentence[13] or at the beginning of a sentence within a paragraph.[14] In either case, the connection between that which precedes and that which follows is logical and clear. In 1 Cor 15:29, however, the logical connection with what precedes is anything but clear. Nothing has previously been said about baptism on behalf of the dead, and the last explicit reference to resurrection was six verses earlier, in v. 23. If ἐπεί here does provide a link with what precedes, it would have to be with the entire line of argumentation in vv. 20–28 (or perhaps even vv. 1–28). This, however, would be contrary to Paul's consistent use of ἐπεί elsewhere in the letters, where, as noted, it serves as a direct causal link between the immediately preceding clause or sentence and what is to follow. Thus, if Paul was the author of vv. 29–34, these verses most likely appeared originally either in some other letter or elsewhere in 1 Corinthians, where the immediately preceding material was more closely related to the question of baptism on behalf of the dead, or at least explicitly to that of baptism.

It is also significant that the verse immediately following 1 Cor 15:29–34 begins with the adversative conjunction ἀλλά ("but"), which normally indicates a strong contrast between that which precedes and that which follows.[15] Such a contrast makes little sense following v. 34, however, which is simply an admonition to

---

11. Rom 3:6; 11:6, 22; 1 Cor 5:10; 7:14; 14:12, 16; 2 Cor 11:18; 13:3.
12. Rom 11:6, 22; 1 Cor 7:14; 14:16.
13. Rom 11:6, 22; 1 Cor 5:10; 14:12; 2 Cor 11:18; 13:3.
14. Rom 3:6; 1 Cor 7:14; 14:16.
15. See, e.g., BDF 231–32: "A distinction is to be observed between general contrast (δέ) and that which is directly contrary (ἀλλά), which is roughly comparable to German *aber* and *sondern*."

right thinking and sinless living, or even following vv. 29–34 as a unit. Collins suggests that v. 35 "marks a new beginning in the development of Paul's argument,"[16] but this is true only when vv. 29–34 separate vv. 35–58 from vv. 1–28. Without vv. 29–34, v. 35 marks not "a new beginning" but simply a logical continuation of the argument begun in vv. 1–28. The proclamation of Christ's resurrection (vv. 1–11), insistence that denying the resurrection negates Christ's resurrection and thus Christian faith itself (vv. 12–19), and assertion that Christ's resurrection guarantees the future resurrection of believers and the destruction of death (vv. 20–28) is now followed, "in loose diatribe style,"[17] by consideration of the most likely objection that might be raised (vv. 35–53)—namely, an objection regarding the nature of the resurrection body. Consideration of this objection would quite appropriately be introduced with the adversative conjunction ἀλλά; indeed, the objection itself would most likely have begun with ἀλλά. The objection, however, would have been directed not against v. 34 or even vv. 29–34 as a whole but rather against Paul's line of reasoning in vv. 1–28. Thus, the ἀλλά of v. 35 would be understandable following v. 28, but not following v. 34. This, again, suggests that vv. 29–34 represent an intrusion into the text of 1 Corinthians 15.

Finally, the literary style of 1 Cor 15:29–34 is strikingly different from that of chap. 15 as a whole. This difference was noted by Robert Martyr Hawkins more than six decades ago: "Coming between two passages which move in stately periods [vv. 1–28 and 35–58], verses 29–34 immediately impress one with their difference in style."[18] Similarly, N. T. Wright characterizes the style of vv. 29–34 as "something of an interlude, a brief respite from dense and involved argumentation":

> Jerky writing; short sentences; swift subject-changes; a quotation from pagan poetry. The flavor is both *ad hoc* and *ad*

---

16. Collins, *First Corinthians*, 562.
17. Conzelmann, *1 Corinthians: A Commentary*, 280.
18. Hawkins, *Recovery of the Historical Paul*, 198.

hominem, a quick, improvised, scattergun approach . . . Four different subjects in five verses . . ."[19]

This stands in sharp contrast to "the rhythmic sentences" and "stately language" of the "majestic anthem" that comprises chap. 15 as a whole.[20] Such a contrast also suggests that vv. 29–34 were not originally a part of chap. 15.

In short, it is my judgment that 1 Cor 15:29–34 did not originally appear at its present location, separating vv. 35–58 from vv. 1–28. Indeed, one can only wonder how it got there! Assuming that Paul himself put it there, Wright suggests, no doubt with tongue in cheek, that he did so "to make sure the listener [was] still awake."[21] I regard it as much more likely, however, that the verses were placed there by some later interpolator. This does not necessarily mean, of course, that Paul was not the author of 1 Cor 15:29–34. It is possible that some or all of the passage was composed by Paul as part of a different letter, now no longer extant, and later inserted into the Corinthian letter. It is also possible that the verses were written by Paul but originally appeared elsewhere in 1 Corinthians—possibly even after 15:19. Thus, any decision regarding actual authorship must depend upon considerations other than those of context.

Vocabulary

1 Corinthians 15:29–34 contains a total of eighty-one words.[22] Eleven of these words, however, appear to be quotations from Isa 22:13b[23] and the Greek playwright Menander.[24] In addition,

---

19. Wright, *Resurrection of the Son of God*, 338.
20. Orr and Walther, *I Corinthians: A New Translation*, 319. The reference is to the KJV translation, but the description would apply at least equally well to the original Greek.
21. Wright, *Resurrection of the Son of God*, 338.
22. This includes ἀδελφοί (v. 31), for which the textual evidence is divided.
23. Φάγωμεν καὶ πίωμεν αὔριον γὰρ ἀποθνήσκομεν (v. 32b).
24. Φθείρουσιν ἤθη χρηστὰ ὁμιλίαι κακαί (v. 33b), from Menander, *Thais*, fragment 218 in Kock, *Comicorum Atticorum Fragmenta*.

thirty-five are simply common pronouns,[25] prepositions,[26] conjunctions,[27] interrogatives,[28] articles,[29] or negatives.[30] Finally, four are the nouns Χριστός ("Christ"), Ἰησοῦς ("Jesus"), κύριος ("Lord"), and Θεός ("God"). Thus, of the eighty-one words that comprise vv. 29–34, fifty would appear to shed little if any light on the question of authorship.[31] The remaining thirty-one words actually represent only twenty-six *different* words, however, because βαπτίζεσθαι ("to be baptized"), ἐγείρεσθαι ("to be raised"), and ἀποθνῄσκειν ("to die") appear twice and νεκροί ("dead ones") three times. Of these twenty-six different words, six (i.e., 23.08 percent) are *hapax legomena* in the Pauline corpus: κινδυνεύειν ("to be in danger," v. 30),[32] νή ("by," v. 31),[33] θηριομαχεῖν ("to fight with animals," v. 32),[34] ὄφελος ("benefit," v. 32),[35] ἐκνήφειν ("to come to one's senses," v. 34)[36] and ἀγνωσία ("ignorance," v. 34).[37] In addition, δικαίως ("correctly" or "rightly," v. 34) appears only once elsewhere in the authentic Pauline letters,[38] ἐντροπή ("shame," v. 34) only once,[39] ὅλως ("at all," v. 29) only twice,[40] and πλανᾶν ("to mislead" or "deceive," v. 33) only twice.[41] In short, ten of the twenty-six words (i.e., 38.46 percent) appear to be not typically Pauline. This alone, in my judgment, is sufficient to raise serious questions regarding Pauline authorship of 1 Cor 15:29–34.

---

25. Αὐτῶν, ἡμεῖς, ἥν, ἡμῶν, μοι, τινες, and ὑμῖν.
26. Ὑπέρ (twice), καθ᾽, ἐν (twice), κατά, and πρός.
27. Ἐπεί, εἰ (three times) καί (three times), and γάρ.
28. Τι (four times).
29. Οἱ, τῶν, τήν, τῷ, and τό.
30. Οὐκ (twice) and μή (twice).
31. See, e.g., Leppä, *Making of Colossians*, 56.
32. Elsewhere in the NT only at Luke 8:23; Acts 19:27, 40.
33. Only here in the NT.
34. Only here in the NT.
35. Elsewhere in the NT only at Jas 2:14, 16.
36. Only here in the NT.
37. Elsewhere in the NT only at 1 Pet 2:15.
38. 1 Thess 2:10; elsewhere in the NT only at Luke 23:41; Titus 2:12; 1 Pet 2:23.
39. 1 Cor 6:5; nowhere else in the NT.
40. 1 Cor 5:1; 6:7; elsewhere in the NT only at Matt 5:34.
41. 1 Cor 6:9; Gal 6:7; frequently elsewhere in the NT.

In addition, however, five phrases or clauses in 1 Cor 15:29–34 are not otherwise Pauline: (1) Πᾶσαν ὥραν ("every hour," v. 30) appears nowhere else in the entire New Testament. (2) Καθ' ἡμέραν ("daily," v. 31) appears nowhere else in the Pauline corpus.[42] (3) Μὴ ἁμαρτάνετε ("do not sin," v. 34) appears elsewhere in the New Testament only in the pseudonymous Eph 4:26. (4) It has already been noted that ὄφελος (v. 32) is a *hapax legomenon* in the Pauline corpus, but it is also significant that Paul elsewhere (Rom 3:1) poses a question similar to that in v. 32 using the word ὠφέλεια("advantage") rather than ὄφελος.[43] This, together with the fact that Paul uses the verb ὠφελεῖν ("to be of benefit") either three or four times[44] but never uses the verb ὀφέλλειν ("to be of advantage"), suggests that the question in v. 32 is non-Pauline. (5) Τὴν ὑμετέραν καύχησιν (literally, "your boasting," v. 31) presents a special problem. The language of "boasting"—καυκᾶσθαι, καύχημα, and καύχησις—is common in Paul's letters[45] and rare elsewhere in the New Testament,[46] and this might suggest that the phrase is Pauline. The peculiar construction, τὴν ὑμετέραν καύχησιν, however, is otherwise unattested. Normally, the phrase would mean "your boasting," but the words that immediately follow—ἣν ἔχω ἐν Χριστῷ Ἰησοῦ τῷ κυρίῳ ἡμῶν ("which I have in Christ Jesus our Lord")—appear to indicate that the reference is rather to "my boasting about you." Elsewhere, however, when Paul speaks of his own boasting on behalf of other people, he uses the wording καύχησις ὑπὲρ ὑμῶν ("boasting on your behalf" [2

---

42. Elsewhere in the NT at Matt 26:55; Mark 14:49; Luke 9:23; 11:3; 16:19; 19:47; 22:53; Acts 2:46, 47; 3:2; 16:5; 17:11; 19:9.

43. Τίς ἡ ὠφέλεια τῆς περιτομῆς;

44. Rom 2:25; 1 Cor 13:3; 14:6; Gal 5:2. 1 Cor 13:3 may, however, be part of a non-Pauline interpolation; see Walker, *Interpolations*, 147–65.

45. Καυκᾶσθαι: Rom 2:17, 23; 5:2, 3, 11; 1 Cor 1:29, 31 (twice); 3:21; 4:7; 13:3; 2 Cor 5:12; 7:14; 9:2; 10:8, 13, 15, 16, 17 (twice); 11:12, 16, 18 (twice), 30 (twice); 12:1, 5 (twice), 6, 9; Gal 6:13, 14; Phlm 3:3; καύχημα: Rom 4:2; 1 Cor 5:6; 9:15, 16; 2 Cor 1:14; 5:12; 9:3; Gal 6:4; Phil 1:26; 2:16; καύχησις: Rom 3:27; 15:17; 2 Cor 1:12; 7:4, 14; 8:24; 9:4; 11:10, 17; 1 Thess 2:19. See, e.g., Fee, *First Epistle to the Corinthians*, 84, 417–18.

46. Καυκᾶσθαι: only at Eph 3:3; Jas 1:9; 4:16; καύχημα: only at Heb 3:6; καύχησις: only at Jas 4:16.

Cor 7:4; 8:24]) or τὸ καύχημα ἡμῶν τὸ ὑπὲρ ὑμῶν ("our boasting on your behalf" [2 Cor 9:3]).⁴⁷ To be sure, Thucydides employs the phrase αἱ ὑμετέραι ἐλπίδες to mean "the hopes they have placed in you" (*History* 1.69.5), and this has been cited as a precedent for τὴν ὑμετέραν καύχησιν in 1 Cor 15:31.⁴⁸ Moreover, Fee cites εἰς τὴν ἐμὴν ἀνάμνησιν ("in memory of me") in 1 Cor 11:24, 25 as an analogous "objective use" of the possessive adjectival pronoun by Paul.⁴⁹ The example from Thucydides, however, demonstrates that such a construction was possible but sheds no light on the question of whether Paul employed it. Regarding the example from 1 Corinthians 11, it must be noted that Paul is here almost certainly quoting the tradition as he had received it (see 1 Cor 11:23). Thus, the wording is presumably not his own but rather comes from the tradition, and therefore carries little if any weight so far as establishing Paul's own vocabulary is concerned. In short, τὴν ὑμετέραν καύχησιν appears to be non-Pauline. Indeed, a few witnesses, apparently recognizing the problem, changed ὑμετέραν to ἡμετέραν ("our"), thus bringing the wording more closely into line with characteristic Pauline phraseology.⁵⁰ To be sure, Dennis Ronald MacDonald has argued (a) that the words ἣν ἔχω ἐν Χριστῷ Ἰησοῦ τῷ κυρίῳ ἡμῶν represent a later, non-Pauline, interpolation; (b) that τὴν ὑμετέραν καύχησιν does, in fact, mean "your boasting" or "your boast"; (c) that the content of the "boast" was Paul's struggle with beasts in Ephesus; but (d) that it was the Corinthians, not Paul, who made this boast.⁵¹ If correct, MacDonald's argument would support Pauline authorship of τὴν ὑμετέραν καύχησιν but not of ἣν ἔχω ἐν Χριστῷ Ἰησοῦ τῷ κυρίῳ ἡμῶν. The argument is attractive, but it becomes both unnecessary and improbable if, as I am persuaded, vv. 29–34 as a whole are an interpolation.

---

47. Cf. 2 Cor 5:12: καύχημα ὑπὲρ ἡμῶν.
48. E.g., Conzelmann, *1 Corinthians: A Commentary*, 277 n. 126; Fee, *First Epistle to the Corinthians*, 769 n. 44.
49. Fee, *First Epistle to the Corinthians*, 769 n. 44.
50. Of the early witnesses, only A (fifth century) made this change.
51. MacDonald, "Conjectural Emendation of 1 Cor 15:31–32."

It is possible that the vocative ἀδελφοί ("brothers") in v. 31b constitutes an additional argument against Pauline authorship of 1 Cor 15:29–34. Ἀδελφοί appears in a number of important early witnesses, including Sinaiticus (fourth century), A (fifth century), and B (fourth century), but it is missing in others, including P[46] (ca. 200 CE) and D (fifth century). Noting that its insertion "is so much easier to explain than its omission" and that it is omitted in both the earliest witness (P[46]) and the Western text (D), Anthony C. Thiselton concludes that ἀδελφοί is a later addition.[52] It is included in brackets, however, in both the twenty-eighth edition of Nestle-Aland and the third edition of the United Bible Societies' critical text[53] and is accepted by both the RSV and the NRSV. Thus, ἀδελφοί may well be original in 1 Cor 15:31. According to Ellingworth and Hatton, however, "it is unusual for Paul to use the word . . . in the middle of a sentence" and "in other parts of 1 Corinthians the word has always introduced a new theme."[54] The appearance of ἀδελφοί in the middle of a sentence (v. 31) may, therefore, be an indication of non-Pauline authorship. Indeed, it is possible that ἀδελφοί was deleted from the text by some scribes precisely because it violated their own observation of Paul's customary use of the word.

A possible argument supporting Pauline authorship of 1 Cor 15:29–34 might be the presence of the phrase κατὰ ἄνθρωπον (literally, "according to a human being," v. 32). This phrase appears five times elsewhere in the authentic Pauline letters (Rom 3:5; 1 Cor 3:3; 9:8; Gal 1:11; 3:15) and nowhere in the remainder of the New Testament. In all of the other instances, however, the phrase

---

52. Thiselton, *First Epistle to the Corinthians*, 1249.

53. See *TCGNT* 568.

54. Ellingworth and Hatton, *Translator's Handbook*, 309. See 1 Cor 1:10, 11, 26; 2:1; 3:1; 4:6; 7:24, 29; 10:1; 11:33; 12:1; 14:6, 20, 26, 39; 15:1, 50, 58; 16:15. In every case except 1:11; 7:24, 29; and 14:39, the NRSV has its translation of ἀδελφοί at the beginning of a new paragraph; and the 28th edition of the Nestle-Aland text also has a break before 7:29 and 14:39. Thus, except for 1:11 and 7:24, the observation of Ellingworth and Hatton regarding Paul's use of ἀδελφοί in 1 Corinthians appears to be accurate.

is related, either directly or indirectly, to the act of *speaking* and appears to mean "speaking in a purely human manner" or "speaking with purely human authority."[55] In 1 Cor 15:32, however, the meaning of κατὰ ἄνθρωπον is far from clear. Referring to "the much debated prepositional phrase," Fee notes that suggested interpretations "are many and varied."[56] While it is possible that the phrase refers here, as elsewhere, to a merely "human" manner of speaking with the verb of speaking simply to be understood, there is no explicit reference to "speaking," as in the other occurrences of the phrase, and the most natural reading of the text associates κατὰ ἄνθρωπον with the only verb that does occur, namely ἐθηριομάχησα ("I fought with beasts").[57] Such a usage of κατὰ ἄνθρωπον is, of course, significantly different from that found elsewhere in Paul's letters, and this suggests that the phrase here is likely non-Pauline in origin. The author would likely have been familiar with Paul's own use of the phrase, however, and may have deliberately, albeit differently, imitated this usage.[58] In short, it is my judgment that the presence of κατὰ ἄνθρωπον in v. 32 provides little if any support for Pauline authorship and probably constitutes evidence against such authorship.

---

55. Rom 3:5: κατὰ ἄνθρωπον λέγω; 1 Cor 9:8: μὴ κατὰ ἄνθρωπον ταῦτα λαλῶ; Gal 1:11: τὸ εὐαγγέλιον τὸ εὐαγγελισθὲν ὑπ᾽ ἐμοῦ . . . οὐκ ἔστιν κατὰ ἄνθρωπον; Gal 3:15: κατὰ ἄνθρωπον λέγω. 1 Cor 3:3 is somewhat different, because κατὰ ἄνθρωπον is here related directly to the act of *walking* (περιπατεῖτε) and apparently equated with being "fleshly" (σαρκικοί ἐστε) and being "human" (ἄνθρωποι in v. 4). Nevertheless, the behavior being criticized by Paul is what the readers are *saying* (ὅταν γὰρ λέγῃ τις . . . in v. 4).

56. Fee, *First Epistle to the Corinthians*, 771 n. 55: "'in the nature of man' (= seeking the rewards for which people risk their lives); 'humanly speaking' (= to use a figure); 'as far as the will of man is concerned' (= those trying to execute Paul acted contrary to God's will); 'according to human folly' . . . ; 'in human form' (= contending with wild beasts in human form . . ."

57. To be sure, MacDonald ("Conjectural Emendation of 1 Cor 15:31–32") argues that κατὰ ἄνθρωπον in 1 Cor 15:32 also refers to *speaking* and is intended by Paul "to indicate that the story of his fight with the wild beast(s) is not true."

58. The phrase does occur earlier in 1 Corinthians, in 1 Cor 9:8.

Another possible argument supporting Pauline authorship of 1 Cor 15:29–34 would be the presence of two clauses that occur elsewhere in the New Testament *only* in the authentic Pauline letters: μὴ πλανᾶσθε ("do not be misled") in v. 33[59] and πρὸς ἐντροπὴν ὑμῖν λαλῶ ("to your shame I speak") in v. 34.[60] It is important to note, however, that μὴ πλανᾶσθε appears only twice and πρὸς ἐντροπὴν ὑμῖν λαλῶ only once elsewhere in the Pauline letters. Moreover, the two clauses are found in very close proximity earlier in 1 Corinthians — πρὸς ἐντροπὴν ὑμῖν λέγω in 6:5 and μὴ πλανᾶσθε in 6:9. It is quite possible, therefore, that an interpolator, who obviously knew at least some parts of the Corinthian letter, introduced the admonitions of 15:33–34 with the Pauline wording of 6:9 and concluded them with that of 6:5.

In short, it is my judgment that the peculiarities of the vocabulary of 1 Cor 15:29–34 are such as to raise serious questions regarding Pauline authorship of the verses. It may be the case, however, that the author of these verses deliberately imitated Paul's phraseology with the μὴ πλανᾶσθε introduction to v. 33, the πρὸς ἐντροπὴν ὑμῖν λαλῶ conclusion to v. 34, and perhaps with the κατὰ ἄνθρωπον of v. 31.

Content

Two items in the content of 1 Cor 15:29–34 are both surprising and perplexing and appear to constitute strong arguments against Pauline authorship. These are the references to baptism on behalf of the dead (v. 29) and to fighting with beasts in Ephesus (v. 32a). In addition, it is my judgment that the quotations from Hebrew Scripture (v. 32b) and from pagan literature (v. 33) point to likely non-Pauline authorship.

---

59. Elsewhere in 1 Cor 6:9 and Gal 6:7, the only other occurrences of πλανᾶν in the authentic Pauline Letters.

60. Elsewhere, either verbatim or almost verbatim in 1 Cor 6:5, the only other occurrence of ἐντροπή in the NT. Most witnesses read λέγω rather than λαλῶ in 6:5, but B (fourth century) has λαλῶ. In 15:34, most witnesses read λαλῶ, but A (fifth century) has λέγω.

Baptism on Behalf of the Dead

1 Corinthians 15:29 refers to οἱ βαπτιζόμενοι ὑπὲρ τῶν νεκρῶν ("those being baptized on behalf of the dead") and asks, εἰ ὅλως νεκροὶ οὐκ ἐγείρονται, τί καὶ βαπτίζονται ὑπὲρ αὐτῶν; ("If dead ones are not raised at all, why also are they being baptized on their behalf?").[61] As Fee notes, "The normal reading of [the verse] is that some Corinthians are being baptized, apparently vicariously, on behalf of some people who have already died." Indeed, "this reading is such a plain understanding of the Greek text that no one would ever have imagined the various alternatives were it not for the difficulties involved."[62]

According to Fee, the difficulties are twofold. The first is that "there is no historical or biblical precedent for such baptism."[63] It is mentioned nowhere else in the New Testament and elsewhere is reported to have been practiced only by later Marcionite and, apparently, Montanist and Cerinthian Christians.[64] If the practice had already existed in Paul's time, even among only a small number of Corinthian Christians, one would expect to find some reference to it elsewhere in early Christian literature.

The second difficulty, according to Fee, is that 1 Cor 15:29 appeals, "without apparent disapproval," to a practice that contradicts Paul's own understanding of "justification by grace *through faith*" and of "baptism as personal response to grace received."[65]

---

61. A few witnesses read τῶν νεκρῶν rather than αὐτῶν, and one has αὐτῶν τῶν νεκρῶν.
62. Fee, *First Epistle to the Corinthians*, 763–64.
63. Fee, *First Epistle to the Corinthians*, 764.
64. See, e.g., Conzelmann, *1 Corinthians: A Commentary*, 276 n. 117. References to the practice among Marcionites appear, for example, in John Chrysostom, *Hom. I Cor.* 40, and perhaps in Tertullian, *Adversus Marcionem* 5.10, and *De resurrectione carnis* 48. Didymus the Blind (fourth century) said that "the Marcionites baptize the living in behalf of dead unbelievers, not knowing that baptism saves only the person who receives it" (Bray, *1–2 Corinthians*, 166). Apparently, the Montanists and Cerinthians also practiced baptism on behalf of the dead (see, e.g., Harnack, *Marcion: The Gospel of the Alien God*, 168 n. 35.
65. Fee, *First Epistle to the Corinthians*, 764–65.

In this regard, J. Paul Sampley expresses surprise "that Paul did not oppose the practice, which seems to suppose either that grace is transferable or that one can be a surrogate believer for another," and MacDonald states quite bluntly: "Surely Paul himself did not approve of the practice."[66] To be sure, one might argue that Paul did recognize a kind of "vicarious faith" on the part of one person that could serve as a basis for the baptism of others—in other words, that one *could* "be a surrogate believer for another."[67] Paul speaks, for example, of having baptized "the household of Stephanas" (τὸν Στεφανᾶ οἶκον), not Stephanas alone (1 Cor 1:16), and Acts reports the baptism of Lydia "and her household" (καὶ ὁ οἶκος αὐτῆς), presumably by Paul himself (Acts 16:15). Such baptism of entire households might undercut the notion that, for Paul, baptism is necessarily and always a "personal response to grace received" and thereby open the way for possible recognition of vicarious baptism. Three points are to be noted, however:

1. It is not clear that "vicarious faith" was involved in the baptism of the household of Stephanas. 1 Corinthians 16:15 refers to "the household of Stephanas" (τὴν οἰκίαν Στεφανᾶ) as "ἀπαρχή of Achaia," and ἀπαρχή, which literally means "first fruits," is translated by both the RSV and the NRSV as "first converts." This suggests that the entire household, not just Stephanas, was "converted" prior to their baptism.
2. Although the Acts narrative mentions the opening only of Lydia's heart (Acts 16:14b), this should not be seen as ruling out the opening of other hearts in the household as well. Moreover, Acts should be used only with great caution as a source for Paul's own understanding of baptism or even of his own baptizing activity.
3. Elsewhere in Acts where a group baptism is reported, the narrative explicitly states that, prior to their baptism, "the

---

66. Sampley, "First Letter to the Corinthians," 982; MacDonald, "Conjectural Emendation of 1 Cor 15:31–32," 270.
67. Compare the practice of infant baptism.

Holy Spirit fell upon *all* who heard the word" (emphasis mine), not just upon Cornelius, the head of the household (Acts 10:44–48).

Thus, it is far from clear that Paul recognized any kind of "vicarious faith" that could serve as a basis for the baptism of others. Even if he did recognize such "vicarious faith," however, this by no means implies his approval of vicarious baptism. The two are simply not the same! In short, apart from 1 Cor 15:29, there is no evidence that Paul would have approved vicarious baptism of the living on behalf of the dead. Certainly, apart from 1 Cor 15:29, the idea of such vicarious baptism could never be inferred from the references to baptism elsewhere in Paul's letters (1 Cor 1:13–17; 12:13; Gal 3:27; Rom 6:3–4).

Because of these difficulties, numerous attempts have been made to interpret 1 Cor 15:29 as speaking of something other than baptism on behalf of the dead.[68] Indeed, according to Conzelmann, "the ingenuity of the exegetes has run riot."[69] The apparent logic underlying these interpretations is the following: (a) the text appears to speak, without disapproval, of vicarious baptism on behalf of the dead; (b) it is highly unlikely, however, that Paul would have approved of such a practice. Therefore, (c) the text must be speaking of something other than vicarious baptism on behalf of the dead. Conzelmann insists, however, that "the wording [of 1 Cor 15:29] demands the interpretation in terms of vicarious baptism,"[70] and C. F. G. Heinrici observed many years ago that other interpretations appear to be little more than "example[s] of exegetical distress and caprice." In my judgment, they are correct. I propose, therefore, to base the understanding of 1 Cor 15:29 upon the following logic:

---

68. For a discussion of various interpretations, see, e.g., Thiselton, *First Epistle to the Corinthians*, 1242–48.
69. Conzelmann, *1 Corinthians: A Commentary*, 276.
70. Conzelmann, *1 Corinthians: A Commentary*, 276; Heinrici, *Der erste Brief an die Korinther*, quoted by Conzelmann, *1 Corinthians: A Commentary*, 276 n. 122.

1. The text speaks, without disapproval, of vicarious baptism on behalf of the dead.
2. It is highly unlikely, however, that Paul would have approved of such a practice.
3. Therefore, the text is most likely non-Pauline in origin.

In short, it is my judgment that the reference to baptism on behalf of the dead constitutes a very strong argument against Pauline authorship of 1 Cor 15:29–34.

Fighting with Beasts in Ephesus

The second problematic feature of 1 Cor 15:29–34, insofar as content is concerned, is the reference to fighting with beasts in Ephesus (v. 32a),[71] which, as Abraham J. Malherbe notes, "has long been a notorious *crux interpretum*."[72] Scholars disagree on whether the reference to "beasts" is to be understood literally or figuratively[73] and, if literally, whether the construction is a simple condition or a contrary-to-fact condition—that is, whether "I" is or is not said to have *actually* fought with beasts.[74] It is clear, how-

---

71. The English phrase reflects a single Greek verb, θηριομαχεῖν, and could refer to fighting either with one or with more than one beast. The verb occurs only here in the NT, but it appears four times in the Apostolic Fathers—three times used literally (Ign. *Eph.* 1.2; Ign. *Trall.* 10; *Mart. Pol.* 3.1) and once figuratively (Ign. *Rom.* 5.1). The verb θηριομαχεῖν, the noun θηριομαχίον, and the adjective θηριομάχος also appear in *Acts of Paul*—the verb in 3,9; 4,8; 5,13; the noun in 2,11; 36,3 and 17; the adjective in 5,30.

72. Malherbe, "Beasts at Ephesus," 71.

73. For a summary of the arguments, see, e.g., Osborne, "Paul and the Wild Beasts," 225–30. See also, e.g., Malherbe, "Beasts at Ephesus," 71–80, for examples of fighting with beasts in a figurative sense. At least in part, the debate focuses on the meaning of the phrase κατὰ ἄνθρωπον.

74. Because there is neither a verb nor the particle ἄν in the *apodosis*, it is impossible to be certain regarding the nature of the conditional sentence. Citing only 1 Cor 2:8; 11:31; 12:19; Gal 1:10; 3:21; 4:15, BDF (188) observes: "Unreal periods [i.e., contrary-to-fact conditional sentences] are remarkably scarce in Paul." Only in 1 Cor 12:19 are ἄν and the verb omitted as in 1 Cor 15:32a, but it is clear from the context that this is a contrary-to-fact condition.

ever, that "fighting with beasts" is related to "being in danger every hour" (κινδυνεύομεν πᾶσαν ὥραν, v. 30) and "dying daily" (καθ᾽ ἡμέραν ἀποθνῄσκω, v. 31)—that is, to life-threatening peril of some sort. Moreover, as Malherbe notes, "if Paul is here referring [simply] to his struggle with opponents of his ministry, he is using a very unusual expression for what was to him a very usual experience." Indeed, "despite the fact that the figurative use elsewhere is not unknown, such a use of the verb [θηριομαχεῖν] without any further qualification sounds unusual."[75] Finally, as MacDonald observes, "Surely the author of the list of sufferings in 2 Cor 11:23–33 could have selected a better example of mortal perils than his philosophical diatribes in Ephesus, no matter how vitriolic the debate or how obstreperous the opponents."[76] Thus, the reference must be to some sort of actual life-threatening physical danger, and, despite uncertainty regarding the phrase κατὰ ἄνθρωπον, I am inclined to interpret the verb literally. The question at issue, however, is not how the reference is to be interpreted but rather whether it is to be attributed to Paul. My own judgment is that it is not.

To be sure, as Fee notes, there are "hints" in both 1 and 2 Corinthians "that [Paul's] stay in Ephesus was anything but an Aegean holiday."[77] Paul indicates that there were "many adversaries" (ἀντικείμενοι πολλοί) in Ephesus (1 Cor 16:9); he speaks of what he clearly regarded as a life-threatening ordeal in Asia (2 Cor 1:8–10); he refers to being "afflicted," "perplexed," "persecuted," "struck down," and "given up to death" (2 Cor 4:8–12); and he provides a general catalogue of his sufferings and hardships (2 Cor 11:23–28). In none of these passages, however, does Paul mention fighting with beasts. Moreover, although his reference to "Asia" in 2 Cor 1:8–10 may have Ephesus in mind (it was the most important city in Asia, and 1 Cor 16:9 makes it clear that

---

75. Malherbe, "Beasts at Ephesus," 71; see also, e.g., Bowen, "I Fought with Beasts at Ephesus," 66–67.
76. MacDonald, "Conjectural Emendation of 1 Cor 15:31–32," 269.
77. Fee, *First Epistle to the Corinthians*, 769.

Paul faced opposition there), it makes no explicit mention of the city. Finally, although Paul's catalogue of sufferings and hardships in 2 Cor 11:23–28 "probably was written after 1 Cor 15:32 and to the same audience," it makes no mention of "fighting with beasts"[78] and says nothing about Ephesus as the locale for any of the sufferings or hardships.

It is true, of course, that Acts 19:23–41 reports an incident in Ephesus in which Paul faced possible bodily injury or even death in "the theater" (τὸ θέατρον).[79] As MacDonald notes, however, the account "does not speak of wild beasts, and in fact, Paul does not even enter the arena"; moreover, at least in MacDonald's view, "Paul wrote 1 Corinthians *before* this ordeal in Ephesus."[80] Thus, on the face of it, the reference in 1 Cor 15:32a to fighting with beasts in Ephesus would appear to have nothing to do with the narrative in Acts 19:23–41.

Finally, the pseudo-Pauline 2 Tim 4:17b refers to Paul being "rescued from the lion's mouth" (ἐρρύσθην ἐκ στόματος λέοντος). It is unclear whether the words are to be interpreted literally or figuratively, but it is important to note that the (fictive) setting is not in Ephesus but rather in Rome.[81]

In short: 1 Cor 16:9 speaks of "many adversaries" in Ephesus but provides no details; 2 Cor 1:8–10 refers to a life-threatening ordeal in Asia but provides little detail, does not mention beasts, and does not explicitly identify Ephesus as the locale for the ordeal; both 2 Cor 4:8–12 and 2 Cor 11:23–28 — the former rather generally and the latter more specifically — mention various sufferings and hardships but say nothing about locale and do not mention

---

78. MacDonald, "Conjectural Emendation of 1 Cor 15:31–32," 268.

79. Latinized as *theatrum* and applied to arenas in which, *inter alia*, people fought with beasts. On the theater in Ephesus, see, e.g., Trebilco, "Asia," 348–50.

80. MacDonald, "Conjectural Emendation of 1 Cor 15:31–32," 268. It is generally agreed that 1 Corinthians was written from Ephesus (see 1 Cor 16:8), and, according to Acts 20:1, Paul left Ephesus shortly after the "uproar."

81. See the reference to Rome in 2 Tim 1:17 and the references to Ephesus in 1:18 and 4:12.

beasts; Acts 19:23–41 speaks of a dangerous incident in Ephesus that could have proven fatal for Paul but does not mention beasts and explicitly notes that Paul did not enter the theater;[82] and 2 Tim 4:17b speaks of Paul being "rescued from the lion's mouth" but indirectly indicates that this did not occur in Ephesus.

It is only in the second-century *Acts of Paul* that all of this comes together in a narrative about Paul being condemned to the arena in Ephesus and delivered from a lion and other beasts that were expected to kill and eat him.[83] It is noteworthy, however, that 1 Cor 15:32a goes beyond even the narrative in the *Acts of Paul*, because it speaks of actually *fighting* with beasts in Ephesus, not simply "standing like a statue in prayer" in the presence of the beasts.

My own suggestion is that the author of 1 Cor 15:32a was familiar with some or all of the following: (1) Paul's reference in 1 Cor 16:9 to "adversaries" in Ephesus, (2) his reference in 2 Cor 1:8–10 to a life-threatening ordeal in Asia, (3) his reference to sufferings and hardships in 2 Cor 4:8–12 and 2 Cor 11:23–28, (4) the report in Acts 19:23–41 of the mob scene in Ephesus, (5) the statement of Pseudo-Paul in 2 Tim 4:17 about being "rescued from the lion's mouth," and probably (6) some form of the story now preserved in the *Acts of Paul* about Paul in the arena in Ephesus with the beasts. I strongly suspect that the notion of Paul fighting with beasts in Ephesus developed after the death of the Apostle[84] and that the reference in 1 Cor 15:32a was intended to provide a dramatic illustration of the "danger" and "death" mentioned in vv. 30–31a. If so, then Paul was clearly not the author of v. 32a.

---

82. See n. 79 above on use of the "theater" as the arena for fights between humans and beasts.

83. See Schneemelcher, *New Testament Apocrypha*, vol. 2, 251–53. As MacDonald ("Conjectural Emendation of 1 Cor 15:31–32," 271, 272–74) notes, this story was also known by Hippolytus of Rome (ca. 202) and perhaps by Ignatius (ca. 107), and probably originated in oral tradition as a variant of the well-known story of Androcles and the lion.

84. *Pace* MacDonald ("Conjectural Emendation of 1 Cor 15:31–32," 272–75) who argues that the tradition developed during Paul's own lifetime.

Quotation from Hebrew Scripture

The slogan in 1 Cor 15:32b, φάγωμεν καὶ πίωμεν, αὔριον γὰρ ἀποθνήσκομεν ("Let us eat and drink, for tomorrow we die"), appears to be a quotation from Isa 22:13b.[85] Given Paul's numerous quotations from the Hebrew Scriptures, such a quotation, in and of itself, would by no means be surprising.[86] What is surprising, however, is the fact that although Paul elsewhere quotes the Scriptures only approvingly, to provide "proof texts" for his own argument,[87] the words of Scripture are employed in 1 Cor 15:32b to epitomize a position that the author strongly opposes. To be sure, the slogan φάγωμεν καὶ πίωμεν, αὔριον γὰρ ἀποθνήσκομεν is also a quotation in Isa 22:13b, and the author of Isa 22:13b, like the author of 1 Cor 15:32b, rejects this slogan. This becomes clear, however, only when one reads the entire pericope, Isa 22:12–14. Thus, while it is true that the author of 1 Cor 15:32b is in agreement with the overall sentiment of Isa 22:12–14, it is also the case that this author strongly opposes the perspective expressed in the words that are actually quoted. This is without parallel elsewhere in the Pauline letters, where Paul quotes only words with which he is quite unambiguously in agreement.

Moreover, as Fee observes, the quotation from Isa 22:13b may "point simultaneously in two directions"—not only to the passage in Isaiah but also to the Epicurean philosophy.[88] This suggestion is developed more fully by Malherbe, who notes that the Epicureans denied any afterlife and maintained that one's "moral life should therefore be lived totally within the perspective of the present life." Moreover, "the libertinistic life popularly, if unjustly, associated with the philosophy of Epicurus is frequently summarized [in Hellenistic literature] as ἐσθίειν καὶ πίνειν." Thus, the

---

85. The wording is verbatim the same as that in the LXX version of Isa 22:13b and is a literal translation of the Hebrew.
86. For a list of generally recognized quotations, see Silva, "Old Testament in Paul," 631.
87. Clearly, this is the case elsewhere in 1 Corinthians; see 1 Cor 1:19, 31; 2:9, 16; 3:19, 20; 5:13; 6:16; 9:9; 10:7, 26; 14:21; 15:25, 27, 45, 54, 55.
88. Fee, *First Epistle to the Corinthians*, 772.

quotation from Isa 22:13b "would be reminiscent of the slogan attributed to the Epicureans and reflects the contemporary anti-Epicurean bias." Supporting this interpretation, Malherbe notes that the admonition ἐκνήψατε δικαίως ("Come rightly to your senses") in v. 34 contains Epicurean terminology and "may come from an ironic demand made of Epicureans that they sober up in a just manner."[89] If Malherbe is correct—and I am inclined to think that he is—then the scriptural words of Isa 22:13b are employed in 1 Cor 15:32b not only to epitomize a position that the author strongly opposes but also to summarize what was believed to be one of the tenets of a particular Hellenistic philosophy. Such a use of the Hebrew Scriptures is quite without parallel elsewhere in the letters of Paul.

In short, it is my judgment that the quotation from Isa 22:13b in 1 Cor 15:32b constitutes a rather strong argument against Pauline authorship of the passage.

Quotation from Pagan Literature

As already noted, the epigram, φθείρουσιν ἤθη χρηστὰ ὁμιλίαι κακαί ("evil associations [or "conversations"] corrupt good customs," v. 33) is apparently a quotation from the Greek playwright Menander.[90] This appears to be the only quotation from classical literature in any of the authentic Pauline letters. Indeed, according to Edwin M. Yamauchi, it is one of only "three certain citations of classical literature in the [entire] NT."[91] Although the other two—Acts 17:28 and Titus 1:12[92]—are also attributed to Paul, this suggests simply that later Paulinists thought it appropriate to attribute such classical quotations to their hero, not necessarily that

---

89. Malherbe, "'Beasts at Ephesus,'" 76, 77, 78; see the entire discussion, 74–78.

90. See, e.g., Conzelmann, *1 Corinthians: A Commentary*, 278–79 n. 139: "This saying was widely known as a familiar quotation." See also, e.g., Malherbe, "Beasts at Ephesus," 73.

91. Yamauchi, "Hellenism," 386.

92. Quoting from Aratus, *Phaenomena* 5, and Epimenedes, *De Oraculis*, respectively.

Paul himself quoted from the classics. In fact, with this one possible exception, Paul did not do so.

Initially, it might appear that an additional argument could be mounted against Paul's use of the epigram from Menander, because, at least explicitly, it has nothing to do with the question of resurrection, which is the topic of 1 Corinthians 15. As Fee observes, it "comes into the argument as something of a jolt":

> As countless generations in every culture and clime have experienced, this epigram is independently true. . . . Keeping company with evil companions can have a corrosive influence on one's own attitudes and behavior. *But why that word here, in the middle of an argument against their denial of the resurrection of the dead?* (Emphasis added)

Fee goes on to suggest, however, that the admonition is probably related directly to the situation at hand in Corinth: namely, the presence and corrupting influence of those who deny the resurrection.[93] As will be clarified below, my own judgment is that the epigram is indeed related to the question of resurrection, but in a somewhat different way. In either case, its lack of explicit reference to resurrection should not necessarily be viewed as evidence against Pauline authorship.

Nevertheless, for the reasons already noted, I regard the quotation from pagan literature in 1 Cor 15:33 as an argument against Pauline authorship of 1 Cor 15:33 and perhaps of vv. 29–34 as a whole.

Conclusion

It is my judgment that the reference to baptism on behalf of the dead (v. 29), the allusion to fighting with beasts in Ephesus (v. 32a), the use of the quotation from the Hebrew Scriptures (v. 32b), and the quotation from pagan literature (v. 33) argue against Pauline authorship of 1 Cor 15:29–34.

---

93. Fee, *First Epistle to the Corinthians*, 773.

The Self-Contained Unity of Verses 29–34

If 1 Cor 15:29–34 is removed from its present context, any unifying logic to the verses is not immediately apparent. Vv. 29–32 suggest that baptism on behalf of the dead and facing danger for the sake of the gospel are pointless if there is no resurrection, culminating with the words, "If dead people are not raised, let us eat and drink, for tomorrow we die." Verse 33, however, appears to be simply a rather general moral maxim, and v. 34 to be simply an admonition to right thinking and sinless conduct coupled with the observation that certain (unnamed) people "have an ignorance of God." Neither verse appears to address the question of resurrection.

I suggest, however, that vv. 29–34 do in fact constitute a logically coherent unit and that the key to interpreting vv. 33–34 is to be found in v. 32b: "If dead people are not raised, let us eat and drink, for tomorrow we die" (v. 32b). As noted above, the last part of this sentence would almost inevitably have been viewed in antiquity as the slogan of the Epicureans. Thus, the real thrust of v. 32b is, "If dead people are not raised, then the Epicureans are right, and we might as well join their ranks." The lifestyle of the Epicureans, however, was popularly assumed to be immoral and licentious. Moreover, as the quotation from Menander (v. 33) makes clear, associating with such people will inevitably have a corrupting influence upon one's own behavior. Thus, in v. 34, the author appeals to the readers to "sober up rightly" (ἐκνήψατε δικαίως)—that is, to "get their heads together," to think correctly about the implications of a denial of the resurrection—and thereby avoid the sinful life (μὴ ἁμαρτάνε) that will inevitably result if they join the ranks of the Epicureans, who "are ignorant about God" (ἀγνωσίαν γὰρ Θεοῦ τινες ἔχουσιν).[94] Finally,

---

94. This probably refers to the Epicurean belief that the gods were totally uninvolved in human affairs.

v. 34c acknowledges that the author wishes to "shame" the readers (πρὸς ἐντροπὴν ὑμῖν λαλῶ) into maintaining their belief in the resurrection and thereby disassociating themselves from the Epicureans.

In short, vv. 29–32a point out the futility of baptism on behalf of the dead and risking one's life for the sake of the gospel if there is no resurrection, and v. 32b suggests that the readers might as well become Epicureans if there is no resurrection. This latter, however, is unthinkable to the author, who, in vv. 33–34 points out the pitfalls of associating with the Epicureans. Thus, the entire pericope, 1 Cor 15:29–34, constitutes a statement of certain *practical* and the *ethical* implications of denying the resurrection. Such a statement could stand alone, quite independently of its present location in 1 Corinthians 15. This, of course, does not prove that the passage *is* an interpolation, but it does provide additional evidence that it very well *may be*.

The Absence of Text-Critical Evidence for Interpolation

Some scholars have insisted that any interpolation hypothesis, to be credible, must be supported by direct text-critical evidence,[95] and it is clear that no such evidence exists in the case of 1 Cor 15:29–34. As Christopher Mount notes, however, "unqualified confidence in the manuscript tradition of Paul's Corinthian correspondence is unwarranted":

> Virtually no trace is left in the manuscript tradition of the complex redaction of this correspondence to produce the archetype or archetypes that have come to be known as 1 Corinthians and 2 Corinthians in the NT collection of Pauline letters. Despite a lack of evidence in the manuscript tradition, there is a measure of consensus about some of the redac-

---

95. E.g., Wisse, "Textual Limits to Redactional Theory," 177–78; and Ellis, "Silenced Wives of Corinth," 220.

tion—for example, the letter fragment 2 Corinthians 10–13. On the other hand, is 2 Cor 6:14–7:1 an anti-Pauline fragment? Is 1 Cor 13:33b–36 non-Pauline? In each case, appeals to the manuscript tradition are of little value for reconstructing the redaction of the Corinthian correspondence.[96]

Three points are particularly relevant in this regard: (1) The absence of direct text-critical evidence for interpolation is nothing more than "the *absence* of evidence, which, in the face of otherwise compelling evidence for interpolation, should not be allowed to decide the issue."[97] (2) Paul's letters "would have been most susceptible to textual alteration, including interpolation, precisely during the period prior to the date of the oldest surviving manuscript."[98] (3) There are "plausible answers to the question of why no manuscripts not containing presumed interpolations have survived."[99] These include (a) the likelihood that the text of the letters was deliberately "standardized" by the emerging "orthodox" leadership of the churches and that "deviant" versions were deliberately destroyed[100] and (b) the simple probability that copyists, "being unwilling to lose anything precious," would almost inevitably follow longer rather than shorter texts and that shorter texts "would be regarded as incomplete or defective and therefore either destroyed or allowed to fall into disuse and thus disrepair and eventual disintegration."[101]

In short, the absence of direct text-critical evidence should not be regarded as in any way decisive in determining whether 1 Cor 15:29–34 is a later, non-Pauline interpolation. The matter must be decided upon other grounds.

---

96. Mount, "1 Corinthians 11:3–16: Spirit Possession and Authority," 315–16.
97. Walker, *Interpolations*, 55; cf. the discussion, 44–47.
98. Walker, *Interpolations*, 55–56; see the discussion, 47–50.
99. Walker, *Interpolations*, 56; see the discussion, 50–55.
100. Walker, *Interpolations*, 53; cf. the discussion, 51–54.
101. Walker, *Interpolations*, 54–55.

The Cumulative Nature of the Argument for Interpolation

As noted by Winsome Munro, the determination that a particular passage is an interpolation "depends on no one infallible criterion"; rather, "it is a matter of taking into account the cumulative effect of converging lines of evidence."[102] 1 Corinthians 15:29–34 appears to interrupt its context, both substantively and stylistically; certain features of the vocabulary of 1 Cor 15:29–34 appear to be distinctively different from those normally associated with Paul; some of the content of 1 Cor 15:29–34 appears to be un-Pauline; 1 Cor 15:29–34 makes use of a quotation from the Hebrew Scriptures in a way not found elsewhere in the Pauline letters; unlike other parts of the authentically Pauline corpus, 1 Cor 15:29–34 contains a quotation from a classical author; 1 Cor 15:29–34 appears to be a self-contained unit that could stand alone, apart from its present context; and the absence of text-critical evidence for interpolation in the case of 1 Cor 15:29–34 cannot be determinative in deciding the issue. No one of these considerations, in and of itself, proves that 1 Cor 15:29–34 is an interpolation, nor, perhaps, does a combination of two or three. Cumulatively, however, they constitute what I regard as a persuasive argument that 1 Cor 15:29–34 is a later, non-Pauline interpolation.

Possible Origin of the Interpolation

If 1 Cor 15:29–34 is in fact a non-Pauline interpolation, as I have argued, questions immediately arise as to when the interpolation was made, by whom, why, and why at this particular place in the Pauline correspondence? The short answer to each of these questions, of course, is that we simply do not know. In my own judgment, however, a possible—and, I suggest, plausible—scenario can be sketched, focusing on the reference to baptism on behalf of the dead in v. 29.

---

102. Munro, *Authority in Paul and Peter*, 24–25.

According to Adolf von Harnack, 1 Cor 15:29–34 was included in Marcion's version of 1 Corinthians.[103] Moreover, according to Harnack, Marcion noted the silence of the gospel regarding baptism for the dead and maintained that "Paul's acknowledgment of this custom proves his position as one who can lay down law for the church."[104] This suggests that vv. 29–34 were a part of 1 Corinthians 15 no later than the middle of the second century and that Marcion himself approved of baptism on behalf of the dead. Further, as already noted, it appears that baptism on behalf of the dead was practiced by at least some Marcionite Christians. Indeed, such baptism was consistent with their view that salvation became possible only *after* the advent of Christ. This raises the possibility that the practice itself originated in Marcionite or proto-Marcionite circles, as a means of salvation for people who had died before the time of Christ. If so, 1 Cor 15:29–34 may have been inserted into Paul's Corinthian letter by a Marcionite or proto-Marcionite interpolator in order to provide apostolic warrant for the practice. Moreover, vv. 30–34 also contain Marcionite themes: i.e., the exaltation of Paul (vv. 30–32a) and the emphasis upon moral purity (vv. 32b–34). This suggests that the entire unit, vv. 29–34, may have originated in Marcionite or proto-Marcionite circles.

Why was the insertion made at this particular point in the Pauline letters? 1 Corinthians 15:29–34 deals with the resurrection (vv. 29–32 directly and vv. 33–34 less so), and 1 Corinthians 15 is the place where Paul most fully, in any of his letters, discusses the resurrection. Thus, the most natural place for the interpolation is somewhere within this chapter. Within the chap. 15, as already noted, the most logical place for the interpolation would appear to be after vv. 12–19, where Paul discusses *theological* and *soteriological* implications of denying the resurrection. This might well have been followed by vv. 29–34, which suggest *practical* and

---

103. Harnack, *Marcion. Das Evangelium vom Fremden Gott*, "Beilagen," 92–93.
104. Harnack, *Marcion: The Gospel of the Alien God*, 112.

ethical implications of such denial. Further, the reference to "those who have died in Christ" (vv. 18–19) might lead logically to mention of baptism on behalf of the dead (v. 29). Why, then, were vv. 29–34 inserted later, after vv. 20–28? It may be that the interpolator was hesitant to break the obvious connection between the theological and soteriological features of vv. 12–19 and the soteriological and eschatological features of vv. 20–28. If so, this would leave insertion of the interpolation after vv. 20–28 as the only other reasonable option. In either case, however, vv. 29–34 would interrupt the underlying logic of Paul's argument in chap. 15 as a whole.

Chapter 9

Second Corinthians 3:7–18 as a Non-Pauline Interpolation

As Paul B. Duff observes, 2 Cor 3:6–18 has typically been interpreted as a "polemic against Judaism"—either "setting the Gospel over against the Law or [setting] the scriptural reading of the ἐκκλησία over against that of the synagogue." Thus, Paul is seen as "argu[ing] against Judaism, whether its adherence to the Torah or its manner of reading the scriptures."[1] Duff also notes, however, that this sort of interpretation poses a number of problems, including: (a) "why . . . Paul [would] mount an argument against Judaism" in a letter "to a gentile church . . . that seems not to have been troubled by Judaizing issues like some of his other churches"; (b) "the seeming poor fit of this text" within "its larger context" in 2 Corinthians; (c) "the significant number of *haplax legomena* found in this section"; (d) "the fact that its subject matter, at least as it is typically interpreted, appears nowhere else in the Corinthian correspondence;" and (e) "the difficulty of reconciling Paul's logic with the structure of his argument in verses 3–7."[2]

"Second Corinthians 3:7–18 as a Non-Pauline Interpolation." *JSPL* 3,2 (Fall 2013) 67–89. Copyright © 2013 Eisenbrauns, Inc. Reprinted with permission.

1. Duff, "Glory in the Ministry of Death," 313, 314.
2. Duff, "Glory in the Ministry of Death," 314–17. On point b, see especially Windisch, *Der zweite Korintherbrief*, 112. On point c, see especially Schulz, "Die Decke des Moses," 11; Lambrecht, *Second Corinthians*, 59–60. On point d, Duff ("Glory in the Ministry of Death," 316 n. 10) notes that many scholars have assumed "that Paul's adversaries (in Corinth) were advocating Torah observance," and one (Lambrecht, *Second Corinthians*, 62) "suggests the possibility of 'non-Christian Jewish opposition in Corinth.'" Duff concludes, correctly in my judgment: "Although both of these suggestions are possible, neither is likely." I would add that there is no evidence for either suggestion elsewhere in 2 Corinthians or, for that matter, in 1 Corinthians. Regarding point e, the reference to "verses

Duff points out that "various solutions have been proposed to deal with these problems," including the following:

1. Paul's opponents in Corinth originally appealed to Exodus 34 and, as a result, Paul constructed this midrash on that passage in response.[3]
2. Paul previously wrote 2 Cor 3:7–18 for a different occasion and inserted it here when he addressed the Corinthians.[4]
3. Paul did not write this piece but rather, it was a Jewish-Christian midrash that Paul emended and inserted here.[5]
4. Paul revised a midrash that had previously been constructed by his opponents in Corinth. In the original the opponents had compared themselves favorably to Moses. Paul emended the text in an attempt to undermine their claim.[6]

Duff's own judgment, however, is that "there are problems with using any of these theories to explain the oddities of 2 Cor 3:7–18" and that, as a matter of fact, "Paul was not arguing about Judaism at all" in these verses.[7] Rather, "Paul sets up a contrast between the old covenant (3:14) and the new (3:6) in order to illustrate first, his belief that the status of gentiles has fundamentally changed because of the saving act of Christ and second, how that change should affect the Corinthian view of Paul."[8]

3–7" appears to be a typographical error, because in what follows Duff analyzes the structure of the argument in vv. 7–11, not that in vv. 3–7.

3. See, e.g., Windisch, *Der zweite Korintherbrief*, 112.

4. See, e.g., Lietzmann, *An die Korinther II*, 111.

5. See, e.g., Schulz, "Die Decke des Moses" (this is the point of the entire article).

6. Duff, "Glory in the Ministry of Death," 316–17. On the fourth point, see Georgi, *Opponents of Paul in Second Corinthians*, esp. 264–71.

7. Duff, "Glory in the Ministry of Death," 317, 314–15.

8. Duff, "Glory in the Ministry of Death," 315. Hafemann ("Paul's Use of the Old Testament in 2 Corinthians," 246–47) maintains "that [2 Cor] 2:14–3:18 is the theological heart of the epistle, providing the framework for understanding the rest of Paul's discussion in chapters 4–9, and perhaps also chapters 10–13." In his view, "The significance of 2:14–3:18 thus reflects the central role scripture played in Paul's self-understanding,

It is not my purpose in the present study to assess Duff's interpretation of 2 Cor 3:6–18, although it will soon become evident that I find his analysis problematic. Rather, I shall offer yet another solution to the problems posed by the passage—one that is, in fact, suggested by Duff's own listing of these problems. I shall propose that vv. 7–18 were neither composed by Paul nor inserted by him at their present location in 2 Corinthians—that they are, in fact, a later, non-Pauline interpolation.[9] More specifically, I shall argue (a) that the relation of vv. 7–18 both to their immediate context between 2 Cor 3:6 and 2 Cor 4:1 and to their larger context in 2 Corinthians as a whole points to secondary insertion of the passage at its present location, (b) that distinctive vocabulary and ideas in vv. 7–18 indicate composition of the passage by someone other than Paul, and (c) that, nevertheless, apparent verbal and/or ideational links between vv. 7–18 and their immediate context suggest that the verses were composed (by someone other than Paul!) precisely for the purpose of insertion at their present location in 2 Corinthians.

Before presenting my argument, however, I must acknowledge an objection that would be raised by many scholars, some of whom are quite willing to agree, at least in principle, that there are interpolations in the Pauline letters: there is no *text-critical evidence* for identifying 2 Cor 3:7–18 as an interpolation. It appears—between 3:6 and 4:1—in all of the extant early manuscripts, and there are no textual irregularities at its beginning or end that would suggest a disruption of the text. In response to this objection, I can only note "that the absence of direct text-critical evidence for interpolation must be seen as precisely what it is: the *absence* of evidence, which, in the face of otherwise compelling evidence for interpolation, should not be allowed to decide the

---

since Paul develops his theological concepts in 3:1–18 by offering the most extended interpretation of an Old Testament text found anywhere in his epistles." See also Hafemann, *Suffering and Ministry in the Spirit*; and Hafemann, *Paul, Moses, and the History of Israel*.

9. For reasons that will become apparent as I proceed, I do not include v. 6 in the proposed interpolation.

issue."[10] I am persuaded that there is, in the case of 2 Cor 3:7-18, this sort of "compelling evidence," and it is to this evidence that I now turn.

Relation to Context
An Indication of Secondary Insertion

Before analyzing the relation between 2 Cor 3:7-18 and its context, both immediate and larger, it is necessary to recognize that most scholars regard 2 Corinthians as a "composite" letter, composed of parts of at least two originally separate letters (chaps. 1-9 and chaps. 10-13), or perhaps even as many as six (1:1-2:13 and 7:5-16; 2:14-6:13; 6:14-7:1;[11] 8; 9; 10-13).[12] This would appear to make problematic any attempt to analyze the relation between 2 Cor 3:7-18 and its context as an indication that the passage is a secondary insertion. It is important to note, however, that all parts of the letter except 6:14-7:1 are generally regarded as (a) Pauline in origin, (b) addressed to the Corinthian church, and, (c) except for chaps. 8 and 9, dealing with various stages in essentially the same problem in the relation between Paul and this church. Moreover, all of the major partition theories include 3:7-18 as part of a letter that includes, at least, 2:14-6:13. Thus, it would appear appropriate to analyze 3:7-18 both within the immediate context of 2:14-6:13 and within the larger context of 2 Corinthians as a whole.

As has already been noted, Duff points out several respects in which 2 Cor 3:7-18 appears not to "fit" either in its immediate context or in the larger context of 2 Corinthians as a whole: (a) the argument against Judaism in a letter to a gentile church that appears not to have been troubled by Judaizing issues, (b) the fact that its subject matter appears nowhere else in the Corinthian correspondence, and (c) "the difficulty of reconciling Paul's logic

---

10. Walker, *Interpolations*, 55 (see the entire discussion, 44-56).
11. Some scholars regard 6:14-7:1 as a later non-Pauline interpolation; see, e.g., Walker, *Interpolations*, 199-209.
12. For a brief discussion, see, e.g., Betz, "Corinthians, Second Epistle to the," 1148-49 and the literature cited there.

with the structure of his argument in verses 3–7."[13] Noting these and other difficulties, "Hans Windisch, whose influence on the subsequent interpretations of this passage has been enormous, pointed out many years ago that 2 Cor 3:7–18 could easily be extracted from its current location without disturbing the surrounding text's argument."[14] I would go further. In my judgment, these verses actually interrupt the context in which they now appear. Moreover, if removed from this context, they could easily stand alone as an independent literary unit.

Victor Paul Furnish suggests that the overriding theme of 2 Cor 2:14–5:19 is Paul's apostleship, "and specifically . . . its authenticity and meaning."[15] It should be noted, however, that the terms "apostle" (ἀπόστολος) and "apostleship" (ἀποστολή) do not appear in the passage.[16] Rather, the operative terms are "minister" (διάκονος), "ministry" (διακονία), and "to minister" (διακονέω).[17] Thus, it would be more accurate to say that the overriding theme of 2 Cor 2:14–5:19 is Paul's ministry (διακονία), not his apostleship (ἀποστολή). According to Furnish, 2:14–3:6 "is best regarded as introductory to the discussion proper, which takes place in 3:7–5:19," and he divides this introduction into "an affirmation . . . in doxological form . . . of the apostolic vocation in general (2:14–16a)" and "Paul's formulation and brief explication of the question he regards as fundamental: Who is adequate to

---

13. Duff, "Glory in the Ministry of Death," 314, 316, 317.
14. Duff, "Glory in the Ministry of Death," 315; see Windisch, *Der zweite Korintherbrief*, 112.
15. Furnish, *II Corinthians*, 185.
16. Ἀπόστλος appears in 2 Corinthians only at 1:1; 8:23; 11:5, 13; 12:11, 12, and only at 1:1 and 12:12 does it apply to Paul; ἀποστολή does not appear in 2 Corinthians at all.
17. Διάκονος: 2 Cor 3:6. Elsewhere in 2 Corinthians at 6:4; 11:15 *bis*, 23, but applied to Paul only at 6:4. Διακονία: 2 Cor 4:1. Elsewhere in 2 Corinthians at 5:18; 6:3; 8:4; 9:1, 12, 13; 11:8, but applied specifically to Paul's activity only at 5:18; 6:3; 11:8. Not included here are 2 Cor 3:7, 8, 9 *bis*, which will be discussed below. Διακονέω: 2 Cor 3:3. Elsewhere in 2 Corinthians only at 8:19, 20, where it refers to the role of Paul and his associates in collecting money for the Christians in Jerusalem.

fulfill the responsibilities of apostleship? (2:16b–3:6)."[18] Changing "apostolic vocation" to "ministerial vocation" and "apostleship" to "ministry," I accept this analysis. In other words, the principal motif in 2 Cor 2:14–3:6 is Paul's "adequacy" as a "minister" (διάκονος) of the Gospel. In 2:16b, he asks, "Who is adequate (ἱκανός) for these things?" Then, in 3:5–6, having acknowledged that this kind of adequacy is not self-generated, he declares that it is God "who has made us adequate (ὁ . . . ἱκάνωσεν ἡμᾶς) to be ministers of a new covenant."

Following 3:7–18, the motif of Paul's ministry reappears in 4:1, where Paul speaks of "having this ministry as we have received mercy" (ἔχοντες τὴν διακονίαν ταύτην καθὼς ἠλεήθημεν). The verbal connection between this and 3:6 is obvious and unmistakable (that is, διακόνους in 3:6 and διακονία in 4:1), and the conceptual link is only slightly less so (that is, God "made us adequate to be ministers" and "having this ministry as we have received mercy"). Indeed, 4:1 could easily, without any break in the logic of Paul's argument, follow immediately after 3:6.

Between 3:6 and 4:1, however, is 3:7–18, which has nothing whatsoever to do with Paul's adequacy as a minister. Indeed, these verses say nothing at all about Paul's ministry *per se*. To be sure, the word διακονία does appear four times (vv. 7, 8, and 9 *bis*). It refers, however, not to *Paul's* ministry as such but rather to "the ministry of death" (ἡ διακονία τοῦ θανάτου), "the ministry of the Spirit" (ἡ διακονία τοῦ πνεύματος), "the ministry of condemnation" (ἡ διακονία τῆς κατακρίσεως), and "the ministry of righteousness" (ἡ διακονία τῆς δικαιοσύνης). Moreover, it is by no means clear that "ministry" is even the appropriate translation of διακονία in these verses. Although this is the rendition favored by most versions, including the NRSV, others prefer "ministration" (e.g., ASV), "administering" (e.g., NJB), or even "dispensation" (e.g., RSV). Indeed, Furnish appears to suggest that the only rationale for the translation "ministry" in 3:7–9 is simply the fact that

---

18. Furnish, *II Corinthians*, 185.

διάκονοι clearly means "ministers" in 3:6 and διακονία clearly means "ministry" in 4:1.[19] This rationale, however, obviously begs the question of whether 3:7–18 might be an interpolation in which διακονία carries a somewhat different meaning. Indeed, it might well have been precisely the presence of διάκονος in 3:6 and of διακονία in 4:1 that led an interpolator to insert between these two verses a passage (i.e., 3:7–18) that employs διακονία but in a different sense. In any case, 3:7–18 breaks the clear and logical connection between what would, in its absence, be regarded as the introduction to the discussion of Paul's ministry (2:14–3:6) and the discussion proper (4:1–5:19).

Moreover, as Windisch noted many years ago, both 2:16b–3:6 and the material beginning at 4:1 are characterized by a "special apologetic motif," whereby Paul argues for the legitimacy of his own ministry, but this motif "completely disappears" in 3:7–18. Thus, 3:7–18 "could easily be removed without the literary connection suffering."[20]

In addition, it is clear that 3:7–18, unlike the material immediately preceding and immediately following, exhibits midrashic features.[21] Indeed, Windisch regarded it purely and simply as a "Christian midrash" on Exod 34:29–35,[22] and other scholars have suggested that it was originally a synagogue sermon, preached either by Paul himself or by someone else, that Paul adapted for inclusion in his letter to the Corinthians.[23] Midrashic features of this sort by no means make these verses distinctive within the Pauline corpus, because other passages have also been identified

---

19. Furnish, *II Corinthians*, 202.
20. "Literary" = *brieflich*. Windisch, *Der zweite Korintherbrief*, 112 (my translation).
21. E.g., Windisch, *Der zweite Korintherbrief*, 112; Hanson, "Midrash in 2 Corinthians 3"; Barnett, *Second Epistle to the Corinthians*, 178–209.
22. Windisch, *Der zweite Korintherbrief*, 112; see also, e.g., Fitzmyer, "Glory Reflected on the Face of Christ," 631–32.
23. E.g., Moule, *Birth of the New Testament*, 70 n. 1; and Martin, *2 Corinthians*, 59.

as possessing such features.²⁴ These features do, however, set vv. 7–18 apart from their immediate context in 2 Corinthians.²⁵

Further, a rather striking difference in terminology is to be noted between 3:7–18 and its immediate context. On the one hand, both the material immediately preceding and that immediately following refer repeatedly to "Christ" and "God,"²⁶ but 3:7–18 never speaks of "God" and mentions "Christ" only once (3:14). On the other hand, 3:7–18 mentions the "Lord" (κύριος) five times, but the term is absent altogether from 2:14–3:6²⁷ and appears only once in 4:1–6 (in v. 5), where it is used not independently as in 3:16–18 but rather to characterize "Jesus Christ" (οὐ γὰρ ἑαυτοὺς κηρύσσομεν ἀλλὰ Ἰησοῦν Χριστὸν κύριον). Moreover, it is noteworthy that, while Paul typically uses κύριος to refer to Jesus (as in 2 Cor 3:5) "except when [he] is quoting scripture or working closely with a scriptural text,"²⁸ the references in 2 Cor 3:16–18 appear to be *theological* rather than *Christological*—i.e., references to *God*.²⁹ In addition, the statement in v. 17 that "the Lord is the Spirit" (ὁ . . . κύριος τὸ πνεῦμά ἐστιν)³⁰ is without parallel not only elsewhere in 2 Corinthians, but in the undisputed Pauline letters as a whole.³¹ All of this, in my judgment, constitutes additional grounds for regarding 3:7–18 as a secondary insertion at its present location in 2 Corinthians.

---

24. E.g., Rom 9:6–29; 1 Cor 10:1–5; and Gal 5:21–31.

25. As has already been noted (n. 8 above), vv. 1–18 have also been characterized as "the most extended interpretation of an Old Testament text found anywhere in [Paul's] epistles," and this alone might be sufficient to call into question its Pauline authorship.

26. 3:3, 4; 4:4, 5, 6 refer to Christ. 3:3, 4, 5; 4:2 *bis*, 4 *bis*, 6 *bis* refer to God.

27. Furnish (*II Corinthians*, 173) identifies 2:14–3:6 as the "introduction" to Paul's "Comments on Apostolic Service" (2:14–5:19).

28. Furnish, *II Corinthians*, 211.

29. To be sure, this point is debated, but I am persuaded by the arguments of Furnish (*II Corinthians*, 211–12, 234–35) and others that the reference here is *theological*.

30. Cf. also v. 18, where πνεύματος may be an appositional genitive expressing essentially the same idea; for discussion, see, e.g., Furnish, *II Corinthians*, 216.

31. The closest NT parallel is John 4:24 (πνεῦμα ὁ Θεός).

Finally, if removed from its present context, 2 Cor 3:7–18 could easily stand alone as a complete and self-contained literary unit. Verses 7–11 contrast the "splendor" (δόξα) of "the διακονία of death"/"the διακονία of condemnation" with "the διακονία of the Spirit"/"the διακονία of righteousness." Verses 12–18 contrast the "veil" that conceals with the "unveiling" that reveals, and the entire pericope is unified by the notion of the "splendor" or "glory" (δόξα) of the Lord.

In short, despite the arguments of Duff and others to the contrary, 2 Cor 3:7–18 simply does not fit within its present context. If it was in fact Paul who composed it for inclusion at its present location in 2 Corinthians, then it clearly must be regarded as something of an excursus—a digression perhaps triggered by his reference in v. 6 to "a new covenant, not of letter but of Spirit" (καινῆς διαθήκης οὐ γράμματος ἀλλὰ πνεύματος). In my judgment, however, it is much more likely that the verses represent a secondary insertion. In and of itself, of course, this judgment by no means rules out Pauline authorship of the passage—perhaps as part of a different letter. The question of authorship must be decided on the basis of other considerations.

Distinctive Vocabulary
An Indication of Non-Pauline Authorship

Before analyzing the vocabulary of 2 Cor 3:7–18 as an indication of non-Pauline authorship, it is necessary to acknowledge once again the likely "composite" nature of 2 Corinthians.[32] This would appear to suggest that the vocabulary of 2 Cor 3:7–18 should, in the first instance, be compared not with that of 2 Corinthians as a whole but rather with the particular letter fragment in which the passage is located—e.g., 2 Corinthians 1–9 or 2 Cor 2:14–6:13. Because there is considerable uncertainty regarding the component parts of 2 Corinthians, however, and because all of the parts appear to have been addressed to the Corinthian church and,

---

32. See above under "Relation to Context: An Indication of Secondary Insertion."

with the exception of chaps. 8 and 9, to address various stages of the same essential difficulty in the relation between Paul and this church, I regard it as appropriate to consider 2 Corinthians as a whole in analyzing the vocabulary of 2 Cor 3:7–18 as an indication of non-Pauline authorship. Particular attention should be paid, however, to 2 Cor 2:14–6:13, which, by any of the major partition theories, is where 3:7–18 belongs.

It is also important to recognize that Paul himself, like all creative authors, may well have used the same word with a somewhat different meaning at different places in his correspondence (perhaps even in the same letter). This means that the argument for non-Pauline authorship based upon vocabulary must (a) demonstrate that there is a *significant* difference in meaning rather than only a difference in nuance and (b) rest its case upon the *cumulative* weight of a number of individual examples.

2 Corinthians 3:7–18 contains a total of 193 words. Of these 193 words, however, at least 116 would appear to be essentially irrelevant for the purpose of determining Pauline or non-Pauline authorship of the passage.[33] Moreover, of the remaining seventy-seven words, δόξα appears eleven times, διακονία four times, πρόσωπον four times, κατεργέω four times, κάλυμμα four times, μᾶλλον three times, ἀτενίζω twice, δοξάζω twice, μένω twice, καθάπερ twice, σήμερον twice, ἀνακαλύπτω twice, and ἡνίκα twice. Thus, the passage contains only forty-six *different* words that might be relevant for determining Pauline or non-Pauline authorship.

Of these forty-six different words that might be relevant for determining Pauline or non-Pauline authorship, nine (i.e., 19.6 percent) appear nowhere else in the undisputed Pauline letters: ἐντυπόω (v. 7), ἀτενίζω (vv. 7, 13), εἵνεκεν (v. 10), κάλυμμα (vv. 13, 14, 15, 16), ἀνάγνωσις (v. 14), ἀνακαλύπτω (vv. 14, 18),

---

33. These include: (a) quite ordinary definite articles, prepositions, conjunctions, personal pronouns, demonstratives, negatives, particles, and the like; (b) certain widely used nouns (υἱός, Ἰσραήλ, Μωυσῆς, ἡμέρα, Χριστός, κύριος, and πνεῦμα), (c) certain widely used verbs (γίνομαι, δύναμαι, εἰμί, and ἔχω), and (d) the adjectives πολύς and πᾶς.

ἡνίκα (vv. 15, 16), περιαιρέω (v. 16), and κατοπτρίζομαι (v. 18).³⁴ In addition, five of the forty-six (i.e., 10.9 percent) appear only once elsewhere in the undisputed Pauline letters: κατάκρισις (v. 9), ὑπερβάλλω (v. 10), πωρόω (v. 14), σήμερον (vv. 14, 15), and μεταμορφόω (v. 18).³⁵ Beyond this, ἐπιστρέφω (v. 16) appears only twice elsewhere in the undisputed Pauline letters, λίθος (v. 7) appear only three times including twice in successive verses based upon a quotation from the LXX; παρρησία (v. 12) appears only four times, παλαιός (v. 14) appears only three times, ἀναγινώσκω (v. 15) appears only three times; and κεῖμαι (v. 15) appears only three times.³⁶ In short, twenty of the forty-six

---

34. Ἐντυπόω: Nowhere else in the NT. Ἀτενίζω: Elsewhere in the NT only in Luke-Acts (Luke 4:20; 22:56; Acts 1:10; 3:4, 12; 6:15; 7:55; 10:4; 11:6; 13:9; 14:9; 23:1). Εἵνεκεν: Elsewhere in the NT only at Luke 4:18. The alternate spelling ἕνεκεν appears at Matt 5:10, 11; 10:18, 39; 16:25; 19:29; Mark 8:35; 10:7, 29 bis; 13:9; Luke 9:24; 18:29; 21:12; Rom 8:36; 14:20; 2 Cor 7:12 tris, and the alternate spelling ἕνεκα appears at Matt 19:5; Luke 6:22; Acts 19:32; 26:21. Particularly significant is the fact that, elsewhere in the undisputed Pauline letters (Rom 8:36; 14:20; 2 Cor 7:12), including elsewhere in 2 Corinthians, the spelling is ἕνεκεν rather than εἵνεκεν as in 2 Cor 3:10. Κάλυμμα: Nowhere else in the NT. Ἀνάγνωσις: Elsewhere in the NT only at Acts 13:15; 1 Tim 4:13. Ἀνακαλύπτω: Nowhere else in the NT. Ἡνίκα: Nowhere else in the NT. Περιαιρέω: Elsewhere in the NT only at Acts 27:20, 40; 28:13; Heb 10:11. Κατοπτρίζομαι: Nowhere else in the NT.

35. Κατάκρισις: 2 Cor 7:3; nowhere else in the NT. Note, however that κατάκρισις in 2 Cor 7:3 refers to Paul's motivation in speaking as he does to his readers, while it refers in 3:9 in a much more generalized sense to the "ministry of condemnation." Ὑπερβάλλω: 2 Cor 9:14; elsewhere in the NT only at the pseudo-Pauline Eph 1:19; 2:7; 3:19. Πωρόω: Rom 11:7 (cf., however, πώρωσις at Rom 11:25); elsewhere in the NT only at Mark 6:52; 8:17; John 12:40. Σήμερον: Rom 11:8 (quotation from Isa 29:10); fairly frequently elsewhere in the NT. Μεταμορφόω: Rom 12:2; elsewhere in the NT only at Matt 17:2; Mark 9:2.

36. Ἐπιστρέφω: Gal 4:9; 1 Thess 1:9; fairly frequently elsewhere in the NT. Λίθος: Rom 9:32, 33 (quotation from Isa 8:14; cf. Isa 28:16); 1 Cor 3:12; fairly frequently elsewhere in the NT. In Rom 9:32, 33, the reference is to "a stone of stumbling" (λίθος προσκόμματος); in 1 Cor 3:12, it is to "precious stones" (λίθοι τίμιοι). In 2 Cor 3:7, however, λίθοι apparently refers to the stones on which the Ten Commandments were inscribed. Thus, the usage here is different from that elsewhere in the undisputed

different words that might be relevant for determining Pauline or non-Pauline authorship of 2 Cor 3:7-18 (i.e., 43.5 percent) either do not appear at all or appear fewer than four times elsewhere in the undisputed Pauline letters.[37] These twenty words would appear, therefore, not to be typically Pauline. It may be significant, too, that four of the twenty-nine words appear more than once in the passage: κάλυμμα (four times), ἀνακαλύπτω (twice), ἡνίκα (twice), and σήμερον (twice). In my judgment, these data alone are sufficient to raise serious questions regarding Pauline authorship of 2 Cor 3:7-18.

There are four words that appear both in 2 Cor 3:7-18 and elsewhere in the undisputed Pauline letters but nowhere else in 2 Corinthians. It may well be that such words were not a part of Paul's *operative* vocabulary as he wrote 2 Corinthians and that they, too, therefore point to non-Pauline authorship of 3:7-18. Most notable of these words is καταργέω, which appears four times in

---

Pauline letters. Παρρησία: 2 Cor 7:4; Phil 1:20; Phlm 8; elsewhere in the NT at Mark 8:32; John 7:4, 13, 26; 10:24; 11:14, 54; 16:25, 29; 18:20; Acts 2:29; 4:13, 29, 31; 28:31; Eph 3:12; 6:19; Col 2:15; 1 Tim 3:13; Heb 3:6; 4:16; 10:19, 35; 1 John 2:28; 3:21; 4:17; 5:14. In 2 Cor 7:4, πολλὴ παρρησία refers to *Paul's* "great confidence" in his readers; in Phil 1:20, πᾶσα παρρησία refers to *Paul's* "full courage" as he faces the alternatives of life or death; in Phlm 8, πολλὴ παρρησία refers to *Paul's* "great boldness" in addressing Philemon. In 2 Cor 3:12, however, the subject of the phrase πολλῇ παρρησίᾳ χρώμεθα, which appears nowhere else in the undisputed Pauline letters or in the NT as a whole, is not Paul alone but rather the "we" who "have such hope" (ἔχοντες . . . τοιαύτην ἐλπίδα). Thus, the usage here is different from that elsewhere in the undisputed Pauline letters. Παλαιός: Rom 6:6; 1 Cor 5:7, 8; fifteen times elsewhere in the NT (in Matthew, Mark, Luke, Ephesians, Colossians, and 1 John). Ἀναγινώσκω: 2 Cor 1:13; 3:2; 1 Thess 5:27; fairly frequently elsewhere in the NT. Κεῖμαι: 1 Cor 3:11; Phil 1:16; 1 Thess 3:3; twenty times elsewhere in the NT (in Matthew, Luke, John, 1 Timothy, 1 John, and Revelation).

37. Beyond this, νόημα (v. 14) appears only five times elsewhere in the undisputed Pauline letters (2 Cor 2:11; 4:4; 10:5; 11:3; Phil 4:7), χράομαι (v. 12) appears only six times (1 Cor 7:21, 31; 9:12, 15; 2 Cor 1:17; 13:10), γράμμα (v. 7) appears only six times (Rom 2:27, 29; 7:6; 2 Cor 3:6 *bis*; Gal 6:11), and ἐλευθερία appears only six times (Rom 8:21; 1 Cor 10:29; Gal 2:4; 5:1, 13 *bis*). This comes to a total of twenty-four words (i.e., 52.2 percent of the different words that might be relevant for determining Pauline or non-Pauline authorship) that appear to be not typically Pauline.

2 Cor 3:7–18[38] and eighteen times elsewhere in the undisputed Pauline letters[39] but nowhere else in 2 Corinthians. Of particular significance, however, is the fact that the reference and meaning of καταργέω in 3:7–18 appear to be distinctively different from the reference and meaning elsewhere in the undisputed Pauline letters. Elsewhere, it means (a) "to nullify," "invalidate," "make powerless," or "make ineffective"; (b) "to abolish," "wipe out," or "set aside"; or (c) "to discharge" or "release."[40] In 2 Cor 3:7–18, however, καταργέω refers to the "fading" of the brightness (δόξα) of Moses' face (vv. 7, 13), the "fading" of the "splendor" (δόξα) of "the ministry of condemnation" (v. 11), and the "removal" of the veil (κάλυμμα) that obscures the reading of Moses (v. 14).[41] Thus, although the fourfold appearance of καταργέω in 2 Cor 3:7–18 might initially appear to constitute an argument for Pauline authorship, it actually turns out to be an argument against such authorship.

Other words that appear both in 2 Cor 3:7–18 and elsewhere in the undisputed Pauline letters but not elsewhere in 2 Corinthians are πῶς, ἐλευθερία, and οὗ. Πῶς appears once in 2 Cor 3:7–18 and twenty-one times elsewhere in the undisputed Pauline letters,[42] but nowhere else in 2 Corinthians. Ἐλευθερία appears once

---

38. 2 Cor 3:7, 11, 13, 14.

39. Rom 3:3, 31; 4:14; 6:6; 7:2, 6; 1 Cor 1:28; 2:6; 6:13; 13:8 *bis*, 10, 11; 15:24, 26; Gal 3:17; 5:4, 11. Elsewhere in the NT, it appears only at Luke 13:7; Eph 2:15; 2 Thess 2:8; 2 Tim 1:10; Heb 2:14.

40. (A) Rom 3:3, 31; 4:14; 1 Cor 1:28; Gal 3:17; (b) Rom 6:6; 1 Cor 2:6; 6:13; 13:8 *bis*, 10, 11; 15:24, 26; Gal 5:11; (c) Rom 7:2, 6; Gal 5:4.

41. Hafemann ("Paul's Use of the Old Testament in 2 Corinthians," 256 n. 5) maintains that the meaning of καταργέω in 2 Cor 3:7, 11, 13, 14 is the same as elsewhere in the Pauline corpus. His argument is circular, however, inasmuch as the only evidence he presents is the meaning of καταργέω elsewhere in the letters. Obviously, this begs the question of whether a different writer (i.e., an interpolator) might use the word with a somewhat different meaning.

42. 2 Cor 3:8 and in Rom 3:6; 4:10; 6:2; 8:32; 10:14 *tris*, 15; 1 Cor 3:10; 7:32, 33, 34; 14:7, 9, 16; 15:12, 35; Gal 2:14; 4:9; 1 Thess 1:9; 4:1. Elsewhere in the NT, it appears eighty-three times: fourteen times in Matthew, fifteen times in Mark, sixteen times in Luke, twenty times in John, nine times in Acts, once in Ephesians, once in Colossians, once in 2 Thessalonians, twice in 1 Timothy, once in Hebrews, twice in 1 John, and once in Revelation.

in 2 Cor 3:7–18 and six times elsewhere in the undisputed Pauline letters[43] but nowhere else in 2 Corinthians. Οὗ appears once in 2 Cor 3:7–18 and four times elsewhere in the undisputed Pauline letters[44] but nowhere else in 2 Corinthians.

Beyond this, there are four words that appear both in 2 Cor 3:7–18 and elsewhere in the undisputed Pauline letters but only once elsewhere in 2 Corinthians. Δοξάζω appears twice in 2 Cor 3:7–18 (both times in v. 10) and nine times elsewhere in the undisputed Pauline letters[45] but only once elsewhere in 2 Corinthians (9:13). In 3:10, however, it refers to the "glorification" of the old and new "ministries" or "dispensations" (διακονίαι), while in 9:13 it refers to glorifying God. Εἰκών appears once in 2 Cor 3:7–18 (v. 18) and six times elsewhere in the undisputed Pauline letters[46] but only once elsewhere in 2 Corinthians (4:4). In 3:18, however, it refers to the "image" of the Lord (κύριος) into which believers are being transformed, while in 4:4 (just four verses later) it refers to Christ as the "image" of God. Μένω appears twice in 2 Cor 3:7–18 (vv. 11, 14) and eleven times elsewhere in the undisputed Pauline letters[47] but only once elsewhere in 2 Corinthians (9:9). The appearance in 9:9, however, is in a quotation from Ps

---

43. 2 Cor 3:17 and in Rom 8:21; 1 Cor 10:29; Gal 2:4; 5:1, 13 *bis*; Elsewhere in the NT, it appears only four times: Jas 1:25; 2:12; 1 Pet 2:16; 2 Pet 2:19

44. 2 Cor 3:17 and in Rom 4:15; 5:20; 9:26; 1 Cor 16:6; twenty times elsewhere in the NT: three times in Matthew, five times in Luke, nine times in Acts, once in Colossians, once in Hebrews, and once in Revelation.

45. Rom 1:21; 8:30; 11:13; 15:6, 9; 1 Cor 6:20; 12:26; 2 Cor 9:13; Gal 1:24. Elsewhere in the NT, it occurs fifty times: four times in Matthew, once in Mark, nine times in Luke, twenty-three times in John, five times in Acts, once in 2 Thessalonians, once in Hebrews, four times in 1 Peter, and twice in Revelation.

46. Rom 1:23; 8:29; 1 Cor 11:7; 15:49 *bis*; 2 Cor 4:4. Elsewhere in the NT, it appears sixteen times: Matt 22:20; Mark 12:16; Luke 20:24; Col 1:15; 3:10; Heb 10:1; Rev 13:14, 15 *tris*; 14:9, 11; 15:2; 16:2; 19:20; 20:4.

47. Rom 9:11; 1 Cor 3:14; 7:8, 11, 20, 24, 40; 13:13; 15:6; 2 Cor 9:9; Phil 1:25. Elsewhere in the NT, it appears 106 times: three times in Matthew, twice in Mark, seven times in Luke, forty times in John, fourteen times in Acts, once in 1 Timothy, three times in 2 Timothy, six times in Hebrews, twice in 1 Peter, twenty-four times in 1 John, three times in 2 John, and once in Revelation.

111:9 and would appear, therefore, to shed little if any light on the question of Pauline authorship of 3:7–18. Τίθημι appears once in 2 Cor 3:7–18 (v. 13) and twelve times elsewhere in the undisputed Pauline letters[48] but only once elsewhere in 2 Corinthians (5:19). In 3:13, however, it refers to the physical act of Moses "placing" a veil over his face, while in 5:19 it refers to God having "placed in us" the word of reconciliation.

In short, 2 Cor 3:7–18 contains nine words that appear nowhere else in the undisputed Pauline letters, five words that appear only once, one word that appears only twice, and five words that appear only three times. This makes a total of twenty words that appear not to be typically Pauline. In addition, the passage contains eight words that appear elsewhere in the undisputed Pauline letters but either not at all or only once elsewhere in 2 Corinthians. All of this, in my judgment, raises serious questions regarding Pauline authorship of the verses in question.

But there is more! 2 Corinthians 3:7–18 also contains twelve distinctive phrases that appear not to be typically Pauline. Four of these phrases—none of which appears elsewhere in the undisputed Pauline letters or, for that matter, in the entire New Testament—include the word διακονία ("ministry," "ministration," "administering," "mediation," "service," or "dispensation"): ἡ διακονία τοῦ θανάτου (v. 7), ἡ διακονία τοῦ πνεύματος (v. 8), ἡ διακονία τῆς κατακρίσεως (v. 9), and ἡ διακονία τῆς δικαιοσύνης (v. 9).[49] Beyond this, ἐν τούτῳ τῷ μέρει (v. 10),[50]

---

48. Rom 4:17; 9:33; 14:13; 1 Cor 2:10, 11; 9:18; 12:18, 28; 15:25; 16:2; 2 Cor 5:19; 1 Thess 5:9. Elsewhere in the NT, it appears eighty-eight times: five times in Matthew, twelve times in Mark, sixteen times in Luke, eighteen times in John, twenty-three times in Acts, twice in 1 Timothy, once in 2 Timothy, three times in Hebrews, twice in 1 Peter, once in 2 Peter, twice in 1 John, and three times in Revelation.

49. The only similar phrase is ἡ διακονία τῆς καταλλαγῆς in 2 Cor 5:18.

50. Elsewhere, Paul has ἀπὸ μέρους (Rom 11:25; 15:15, 24; 2 Cor 1:13; 2:5), ἐκ μέρους (1 Cor 12:27; 13:9 *bis*, 10, 12), ἀνὰ μέρος (1 Cor 14:27), and μέρος τι (1 Cor 11:18). In 2 Cor 9:3, Paul has ἐν τῷ μέρει τούτῳ, which both the RSV and the NRSV translate as "in this case." The RSV also

πολλῇ παρρησίᾳ χρώμεθα (v. 12), ἄχρι τῆς σήμερον ἡμέρας (v. 14),[51] ἡ παλαιὰ διαθήκη (v. 14), ἕως σήμερον (v. 15),[52] ἐπιστρέφω πρὸς κύριον (v. 16), and ἀπὸ δόξης εἰς δόξαν (v. 18) appear nowhere else in the undisputed Pauline letters or in the New Testament as a whole. Πῶς οὐχί appears only at Rom 8:32,[53] and οἱ υἱοὶ Ἰσραήλ (vv. 7, 13) appears only at Rom 9:27, which is a quotation from or paraphrase of Isa 10:22.[54] In my judgment, the appearance of these twelve distinctive phrases provides additional evidence that 2 Cor 3:7–18 was composed by someone other than Paul.

By way of summary to this point: the relation of 2 Cor 3:7–18 to its context suggests that it is a secondary insertion, and the distinctive vocabulary of the verses points to non-Pauline authorship. What remains to be determined, if possible, is whether it was composed specifically for insertion at its present location in 2 Corinthians or whether it was composed for some other purpose and secondarily inserted into the Corinthian letter.

Indication of (Non-Pauline) Composition for Insertion at Present Location

There are at least eight apparent verbal and/or conceptual links between 2 Cor 3:7–18 and the material immediately preceding and/or immediately following. On the face of it, such links would appear to constitute rather convincing evidence not only that the verses were composed precisely for inclusion at their present location in 2 Corinthians but also that they are integrally related to

---

translates ἐν τούτῳ τῷ μέρει in 2 Cor 3:10 as "in this case," while the NRSV simply ignores the phrase. In any case, however, the word order is different in 3:10 from that in 9:3.

51. Cf. ἕως τῆς σήμερον ἡμέρας in Rom 11:8, which is a quotation from Isa 29:10.

52. Cf. n. 35 and n. 51 above.

53. Nowhere else in the NT.

54. The LXX reads ὁ λαὸς Ἰσραηλ ("the people Israel" or "the people of Israel"). "The sons of Israel" may come from Hos 2:1, where the LXX reads "Sons of Israel" (τῶν υἱῶν Ἰσραηλ).

the context in which they appear. Upon close examination, however, it becomes clear that the links are, at least for the most part, only apparent and perhaps even artificial or contrived. Thus, it is my own judgment that, although the author of 2 Cor 3:7–18 deliberately composed the verses with the intention of making them "fit" within their present context, the apparent links with the surrounding material actually strengthen the case not only for secondary insertion of the passage but also for its non-Pauline authorship. In other words, as an examination of the following apparent links will indicate, 2 Cor 3:7–18 represents the work of a rather *good* but by no means *perfect* interpolator.

Διακονία

The noun διακονία appears four times in 2 Cor 3:7–9 and fourteen times elsewhere in the undisputed Pauline letters, including eighteen times elsewhere in 2 Corinthians.[55] More to the point, διακονία appears at 4:1, the verse immediately following 3:7–18. Moreover, the related noun διάκονος appears at 3:6, the verse immediately preceding 3:7–18,[56] and the related verb διακονέω appears at 3:3, which is only four verses before 3:7–18.[57] Thus, the fourfold appearance of διακονία in 3:7–18 would appear to link the passage both with what immediately precedes and with what immediately follows in 2 Corinthians.

---

55. Rom 11:13; 12:7 *bis*; 15:31; 1 Cor 12:5; 16:15; 2 Cor 4:1; 5:18; 6:3; 8:4; 9:1, 12, 13; 11:8. Elsewhere in the NT, it appears sixteen times: Luke 10:40; Acts 1:17, 25; 6:1, 4; 11:29; 12:25; 20:24; 21:19; Eph 4:12; Col 4:17; 1 Tim 1:12; 2 Tim 4:5, 11; Heb 1:14; Rev 2:19. It may be significant that, except for Heb 1:14 and Rev 2:19, διακονία appears only in Luke (once), Acts (eight times), the undisputed Pauline letters (eighteen times), and the pseudo-Pauline letters (five times). This may suggest that the term was in vogue primarily in Pauline circles.

56. Διάκονος appears twelve times elsewhere in the undisputed Pauline letters, including four times elsewhere in 2 Corinthians: Rom 13:4 *bis*; 15:8; 16:1; 1 Cor 3:5; 2 Cor 6:4; 11:15 *bis*, 23; Gal 2:17; Phil 1:1; 1 Thess 3:2.

57. Διακονέω appears four times elsewhere in the undisputed Pauline letters, including twice elsewhere in 2 Corinthians: Rom 15:25; 2 Cor 8:19, 20; Phlm 13.

It should be noted, however, that διακονία in 4:1, διάκονος in 3:6, and διακονέω in 3:3 all refer explicitly to *Paul's* ministry. Moreover, elsewhere in the undisputed Pauline letters, including elsewhere in 2 Corinthians, διακονία consistently refers either to Paul's ministry, to Christian ministry in general, or to the monetary contribution Paul was collecting for the Christians in Jerusalem.[58] The one possible exception is 2 Cor 5:18, which speaks of "the ministry of reconciliation" (ἡ διακονία τῆς καταλλαγῆς). Even here, however, Paul speaks of God "having given *us* the ministry of reconciliation" (τοῦ Θεοῦ ... δόντος ἡμῖν τὴν διακονίαν τῆς καταλλαγῆς), thus making it clear that he is referring to his own ministry. In 2 Cor 3:7–9, however, διακονία refers neither specifically to Paul's ministry, nor to Christian ministry in general, nor to the monetary collection. Rather, it indicates successively "the ministry of death" (ἡ διακονία τοῦ θανάτου), "the ministry of the Spirit" (ἡ διακονία τοῦ πνεύματος), "the ministry of condemnation" (ἡ διακονία τῆς κατακρίσεως), and "the ministry of righteousness" (ἡ διακονία τῆς δικαιοσύνης). Structurally, to be sure, these phrases parallel "the ministry of reconciliation" (τὴν διακονίαν τῆς καταλλαγῆς) in 5:18. Moreover, "the ministry of the Spirit" (ἡ διακονία τοῦ πνεύματος) and "the ministry of righteousness" (ἡ διακονία τῆς δικαιοσύνης) might be seen as virtually synonymous in meaning with "the ministry of reconciliation" (τὴν διακονίαν τῆς καταλλαγῆς), and Paul might easily have used either or both phrases to characterize his own ministry or Christian ministry in general. Clearly, however, "the ministry of death" (ἡ διακονία τοῦ θανάτου) and "the ministry of condemnation" (ἡ διακονία τῆς κατακρίσεως) are different. They *cannot* refer to Paul's ministry or to Christian ministry in general. Thus, the use of διακονία in these phrases is quite without parallel elsewhere in the undisputed Pauline letters and, in particular, is quite different from that in the material immediately before and imme-

---

58. *Paul's ministry*: Rom 11:13; 2 Cor 4:1; 6:3; 11:8. *Christian ministry*: Rom 12:7 *bis*; 1 Cor 12:5; 16:15. *Monetary contribution*: Rom 15:31; 2 Cor 8:4; 9:1, 12, 13.

diately after 2 Cor 3:7–18. Moreover, as has already been noted, it is by no means clear that "ministry" is the most appropriate translation of διακονία in vv. 7, 8, and 9. In any case, the meaning of διακονία in 3:7–9 is somewhat different from that in 4:1 and elsewhere in the undisputed Pauline letters.

In short, far from providing evidence *for* Pauline authorship of 2 Cor 3:7–18, the apparent link between διακονία (3:7–9) and διάκονος/διακονία/διακονέω (3:6; 4:1; 3:3) would appear to constitute an argument *against* such authorship. Nevertheless, it may well have been Paul's reference in 3:3 to "a letter of Christ *administered* by us" (ἐπιστολὴ Χριστοῦ διακονηθεῖσα ὑφ᾽ ἡμῶν), followed by that in 3:6 to "*ministers* of a new covenant, not of letter but of Spirit" (διακόνους καινῆς διαθήκης, οὐ γράμματος ἀλλὰ πνεύματος), and that in 4:1 to "having this *ministry*" (ἔχοντες τὴν διακονίαν ταύτην) that provided the occasion and impetus for composition and insertion of a passage explicitly contrasting two opposing διακονίαι and, by implication, of two opposing διαθῆκαι: "the old covenant" (τῆς παλαιᾶς διαθήκης) in v. 14 and "the new covenant" (καινῆς διαθήκης) in v. 6.

Γράμμα

Γράμμα appears once in 2 Cor 3:7 and six times elsewhere in the undisputed Pauline letters including twice elsewhere in 2 Corinthians.[59] More to the point, both of the other occurrences in 2 Corinthians are at 3:6, which is the verse immediately preceding 3:7. Thus, the presence of γράμμα in 3:7 would appear to link 3:7–18 with what immediately precedes in 2 Corinthians. In addition, the following points are to be noted:

1. Both v. 3 and v. 7 speak of something—clearly an allusion to the "old covenant" implied by the reference to a "new covenant" in v. 6—as "having been inscribed" on "stone tablets" or on "stones" (v. 3: ἐγγεγραμμένη . . . ἐν πλαξὶν λιθίναις; v. 7: ἐντετυπωμένη λίθοις), and each

---

59. Rom 2:27, 29; 7:6; 2 Cor 3:6 *bis*; Gal 6:11. Elsewhere in the NT, it appears at Luke 16:6, 7; John 5:47; 7:15; Acts 26:24; 28:21; 2 Tim 3:15.

employs the passive perfect tense to characterize the "inscription."
2. Both v. 6 and v. 7 associate γράμμα or γράμματα with death: v. 6 asserts that τὸ γράμμα kills (ἀποκτέννει), and v. 7 refers to "the ministry of death" (ἡ διακονία τοῦ θανάτου) as "having been carved in letters on stones" (ἐν γράμμασιν ἐντετυπωμένη λίθοις).
3. Both v. 6 and vv. 7–8 — although in different ways — contrast γράμμα or γράμματα with πνεῦμα: in v. 6, τὸ γράμμα, which "kills" (ἀποκτέννει), is the opposite of τὸ πνεῦμα, which "gives life" (ζῳοποιεῖ); in vv. 7–8, "the ministry of death" (ἡ διακονία τοῦ θανάτου) is the antithesis of "the ministry of the Spirit" (ἡ διακονία τοῦ πνεύματος).

All of this would appear to suggest that vv. 7–18 "fits" in its present context in 2 Corinthians.

It should be noted, however, that, while the appearance of γράμμα in 3:7 is in the *plural* (γράμμασιν), both appearances in 3:6 are in the *singular* (γράμματος and γράμμα). Moreover, three of the four other appearances in the undisputed Pauline letters are in the singular.[60] As in 3:7, however, the seven other appearances in the New Testament — including the pseudo-Pauline 2 Tim 3:15 — are all in the *plural*. It would appear, therefore, that Paul characteristically refers to the law as γράμμα in the singular while the author of 2 Cor 3:7–18 refers to it with the plural.[61] It should further be noted that v. 3 employs the verb ἐγγράφω

---

60. The exception is Gal 6:11, where the singular would be inappropriate because Paul is referring to the "large letters" (πηλίκοις . . . γράμμασιν) with which he is writing.

61. Note that some witnesses, including B (fourth century) and the original of D (fifth century) read γράμματι (singular) rather than γράμμασιν (plural) at 3:7. P[46] (ca. 200), Sinaiticus (fourth century), A (fifth century), C (fifth century), and most other witnesses, however, have the plural. Apparently, some scribes, noting the difference between 3:7 and Paul's usage elsewhere, changed the plural to the singular for the sake of consistency.

to characterize the "inscribing" on "stone tablets," while v. 7 has ἐντυτόω to describe the "carving" on "stones." This, again, may suggest a different author for vv. 7 and following. Finally to be noted is the distinction between "stone tablets" (πλαξὶν λιθίναις) in v. 3 and simply "stones" (λίθοις) in v. 7.

Considered separately, none of these differences would be sufficient to call into question Pauline authorship of vv. 7–18. Considered cumulatively, however, they do, in my judgment, cast serious doubt on such authorship. At the same time, however, Paul's twofold reference to γράμμα in v. 6, together with his contrast in v. 5 between "ink" and "stone tablets" on the one hand and "the Spirit of the living God" on the other hand, may well have prompted an interpolator to begin a passage contrasting two διακονίαι and, by implication, two διαθῆκαι with the indication that one of the διακονίαι was "inscribed in letters (γράμμασιν) on stones (λίθοις)."

Δόξα

Δόξα appears eleven times in 2 Cor 3:7–18 and forty-six times elsewhere in the undisputed Pauline letters including eight times elsewhere in 2 Corinthians.[62] More to the point, four of the other appearances in 2 Corinthians are in the chapter immediately following 3:7–18. Furthermore, two of the references to δόξα in 3:7–18 are similar to those in chap. 4: δόξα in 4:4, 6, 15, 17 refers respectively to "the glory of Christ," "the glory of God," "the glory of God," and "glory being prepared for us" (δόξης κατεργάζεται ἡμῖν); similarly, δόξα in 3:18 refers to the "glory of the Lord" (τὴν

---

62. 2 Cor 3:7 *bis*, 8, 9 *bis*, 10, 11 *bis*, 18 *tris*. Also in Rom 1:23; 2:7, 10; 3:7, 23; 4:20; 5:2; 6:4; 8:18, 21; 9:4, 23 *bis*; 11:36; 15:7; 16:27; 1 Cor 2:7, 8; 10:31; 11:7 *bis*, 15; 15:40, 41 (four times), 43; 2 Cor 1:20; 4:4, 6, 15, 17; 6:8; 8:19, 23; Gal 1:5; Phil 1:11; 2:11; 3:19, 21; 4:19, 20; 1 Thess 2:6, 12, 20. Elsewhere in the NT, it appears 111 times: eight times in Matthew, three times in Mark, thirteen times in Luke, nineteen times in John, four times in Acts, eight times in Ephesians, four times in Colossians, twice in 2 Thessalonians, three times in 1 Timothy, twice in 2 Timothy, once in Titus, seven times in Hebrews, once in James, eleven times in 1 Peter, five times in 2 Peter, three times in Jude, and seventeen times in Revelation.

δόξαν κυρίου) and to the transformation "from glory to glory" (ἀπὸ δόξης εἰς δόξαν) being experienced by those who behold the glory of the Lord.[63] All of this might point to Pauline authorship of these verses and their original inclusion at their present location in 2 Corinthians.

It should be noted, however, that the other eight occurrences of δόξα in 3:7–18 refer either to the "splendor" or "brightness" of one or the other διακονίαι or to the "splendor" or "brightness" of Moses' face (3:7).[64] Thus, for the most part, the meaning of δόξα in 3:7–18 is distinctively different from that in chap. 4,[65] and this may be an indication of different authorship. At the same time, however, the references to "glory" (δόξα) in chap. 4 may well have prompted an interpolator to compose a passage in which the same word—though with a different meaning for the most part—figures rather prominently.

Πρόσωπον

Πρόσωπον appears four times in 2 Cor 3:7–18 and seventeen times elsewhere in the undisputed Pauline letters including eight times elsewhere in 2 Corinthians.[66] More to the point, one of the other appearances in 2 Corinthians is at 2:10, in the chapter immediately preceding 3:7–18, and another is at 4:6, the chapter immediately following. In both cases, however, πρόσωπον appears in the phrase "in the face of (Jesus) Christ" (ἐν προσώπῳ [Ἰησοῦ] Χριστοῦ). In 3:7–18, by way of contrast, πρόσωπον refers either to the face of Moses (vv. 7, 13) or to the "unveiled face" of those

---

63. Elsewhere in 2 Corinthians, δόξα refers either to the "glory" of God (1:20), "the glory of the Lord" (8:19), the "glory of Christ" (8:23), or the "honor" experienced by Paul and his associates (6:8).

64. *One or the other διακονία*: 3:7, 8, 9 bis, 10, 11 bis. *Moses' face*: 3:7.

65. And elsewhere in 2 Corinthians; see n. 63 above.

66. 2 Cor 3:7 bis, 13, 18 and in 1 Cor 13:12 bis; 14:25; 2 Cor 1:11; 2:10; 4:6; 5:12; 8:25; 10:1, 7; 11:20; Gal 1:22; 2:6, 11; 1 Thess 2:17 bis; 3:10. Elsewhere in the NT, it appears fifty-six times: ten times in Matthew, three times in Mark, fourteen times in Luke, twelve times in Acts, once in Colossians, once in 2 Thessalonians, once in Hebrews, twice in James, once in 1 Peter, once in Jude, and ten times in Revelation.

who behold the glory of the Lord (v. 18). Thus, the reference of πρόσωπον is different in 3:7–18 from those in chaps. 2 and 4. Nevertheless, the appearance of πρόσωπον both in 2:10 and in 4:6 may have prompted an interpolator to compose a passage in which the same word figures rather prominently.

Νόημα

Νόημα occurs once in 2 Cor 3:14 and five times elsewhere in the undisputed Pauline letters including four times in 2 Corinthians[67] but nowhere else in the New Testament. Thus, it would appear to be a characteristically or even distinctively Pauline word. One of the other appearances in 2 Corinthians is at 2:11, in the chapter immediately preceding 2 Cor 3:7–18. Here, however, the reference is to the "thoughts" or "designs" (νοήματα) of Satan, and it would be difficult to see any relation between this and 3:14, which states that "their [i.e., the Israelites'] minds were hardened" (ἐπωρώθη τὰ νοήματα αὐτῶν).

The word also appears, however, at 4:4—just four verses after 3:7–18. Here, Paul asserts that "the god of this age blinded the minds of the unbelieving ones" (ὁ θεὸς τοῦ αἰῶνος τούτου ἐτύφλωσεν τὰ νοήματα τῶν ἀπίστων). Initially, it might be assumed that the same author was responsible for the statements in both 3:14 and 4:4, both of which speak of a "hardening" or "blinding" of τὰ νοήματα. A closer examination, however, reveals significant differences between the two statements. In the first place, different verbs are employed: 3:14 has "hardened" (ἐπωρώθη), while 4:4 has "blinded" (ἐτύφλωσεν). In the second place, 3:14 uses the passive voice, suggesting that the subject of the verb is God,[68] while 4:4 has the active voice, and the stated subject is not God but rather "the god of this age" (ὁ θεὸς τοῦ αἰῶνος τούτου). In the third place, in 3:14 it is "the sons of Israel" (v. 13) whose minds are hardened, while in 4:4 it is "the unbelieving ones"— that is, the non-Christians—whose minds are blinded. Thus, once

---

67. 2 Cor 2:11; 4:4; 10:5; 11:3; Phil 4:7.
68. See, e.g., BDF 72 on the so-called divine passive.

again, what appears to be a similarity between 3:7–18 and the surrounding material turns out to be a difference. The apparent similarity of wording and ideas, however, suggests that an interpolator designed 2 Cor 3:7–18 specifically for inclusion between 3:6 and 4:1.

Διαθήκη

Διαθήκη appears once in 2 Cor 3:14 and seven times elsewhere in the undisputed Pauline letters including once elsewhere in 2 Corinthians.[69] More to the point, the other appearance in 2 Corinthians is at 3:6, which is the verse immediately preceding 3:7–18. Furthermore, 3:6 refers to a "new covenant" (καινὴ διαθήκη),[70] thereby implying the existence of an "old covenant," and 3:14 refers explicitly to "the old covenant" (ἡ παλαιὰ διαθήκη). Thus, the reference to "the old covenant" in 3:14 would appear simply to build on that to "a new covenant" in 3:6.

It should be noted, however, that 3:14 is the *only* reference to "the old covenant," not only in the letters of the Pauline corpus but in the New Testament as a whole.[71] By way of contrast, "a new covenant" is mentioned not only in the Eucharistic traditions but also in Hebrews.[72] It may be significant, as well, that 3:14 speaks of "the *reading* of the old covenant" (ἡ ἀνάγνωσις τῆς παλαιᾶς διαθήκης), and v. 15 refers explicitly to "whenever Moses is *read*" (ἡνίκα ἂν ἀναγινώσκηται Μωυσῆς). This suggests that, despite

---

69. Rom 9:4; 11:17; 1 Cor 11:25; 2 Cor 3:6; Gal 3:15, 17; 4:24. Elsewhere in the NT, it appears twenty-five times: once in Matthew, once in Mark, twice in Luke, twice in Acts, once in Ephesians, seventeen times in Hebrews, and once in Revelation.

70. Paul also refers to "the new covenant" (ἡ καινὴ διαθήκη) in 1 Cor 11:25, but this is part of the Eucharistic tradition.

71. Heb 9:15 refers to "the first covenant" (ἡ πρώτη διαθήκη); cf. 8:13, where it is characterized as "growing old" (παλαιούμενον). Furnish (*II Corinthians*, 208) observes that 2 Cor 3:14 "is the first known use of the phrase *hē palaia diathēkē*" and suggests that Paul may have been "the first to employ it." If 3:14 is part of a later interpolation, however, then it might be the interpolator, not Paul, who was the first to use the phrase.

72. 1 Cor 11:25; Luke 22:20; variant in Matt 26:28 and Mark 14:24. Also in Heb 8:8; 9:15; 12:24.

Chapter 9 ❦ *2 Cor 3:7–18 as a Non-Pauline Interpolation* 147

the apparent allusion specifically to the Decalogue in v. 7,[73] "the old covenant" in v. 14 may be simply a synonym for the written Torah. If so, this may reflect at least the beginning of a movement toward the eventual distinction between "the Old Testament" and "the New Testament" as two different collections of written documents, both of which are regarded as Scripture. Such a movement would appear to postdate the lifetime of Paul and therefore to suggest a later date for the composition of 2 Cor 3:7–18.[74] In any case, it may well have been Paul's reference to "a new covenant" in 3:6 that prompted an interpolator to speak of "the old covenant" in 3:14.

Τοιοῦτος

Τοιοῦτος appears once in 2 Cor 3:12 and twenty-eight times elsewhere in the undisputed Pauline letters including nine times elsewhere in 2 Corinthians.[75] One of the other appearances in 2 Corinthians is at 3:4, just three verses before 3:7–18, and, indeed, both the construction and the meaning are similar in vv. 4 and 12. The former reads, πεποίθησιν δὲ τοιαύτην ἔχομεν, and the latter reads, ἔχοντες οὖν τοιαύτην ἐλπίδα. This might constitute an argument *for* Pauline authorship of 3:7–18. It should be noted, however, that v. 4 speaks of having such "confidence" (πεποίθησις) while v. 12 refers to having such "hope" (ἐλπίς). Moreover, the verb ἔχω appears as a finite verb in v. 4 and as a participle in v. 12.

---

73. "Engraved in letters on stones" (ἐν γράμμασιν ἐντετυπωμένη λίθοις).

74. See, e.g., Furnish, *II Corinthians*, 209: "Melito, Bishop of Sardis (late second century), is the first writer known to have applied the phrase ['old covenant'] to the books of the Jewish scripture in general ('the books of the Old Covenant,' cited in Eusebius, *Eccles. Hist*. IV.xxvi.13–14), but even then an equivalent list of Christian writings is not presumed."

75. Rom 1:32; 2:2, 3; 16:18; 1 Cor 5:1, 5, 11; 7:15, 28; 11:16; 15:48 *bis*; 16:16, 18; 2 Cor 2:6, 7; 3:4, 12; 10:11 *bis*; 11:13; 12:2, 3, 5; Gal 5:21, 23; 6:1 Phil 2:29; Phlm 2:29. Elsewhere in the NT, it appears twenty-nine times: three times in Matthew, six times in Mark, twice in Luke, three times in John, five times in Acts, once in Ephesians, once in 2 Thessalonians, once in Titus, five times in Hebrews, once in James, and once in 3 John.

Finally, the word order is different in the two verses; in particular, τοιαύτην *follows* the noun it modifies in v. 4 but *precedes* it in v. 12. These differences may provide some evidence *against* common authorship of the two verses.

Καρδία

Καρδία appears once in 2 Cor 3:15 and thirty-six times elsewhere in the undisputed Pauline letters including ten times elsewhere in 2 Corinthians.[76] Two of the other appearances in 2 Corinthians are in 3:2 and 3:3, just a few verses before 3:7–18, and one is in 4:6, just a few verses after 2 Cor 3:7–18. Thus, the appearance of καρδία in 3:15 would appear to constitute a link with the material immediately preceding and following 3:7–18. This may suggest, of course, that that the same author wrote both 3:7–18 and the material immediately preceding and following. It should be noted, however, that καρδία in 3:2–3 refers metaphorically to the "tablets of human hearts" upon which Paul's "letter of recommendation" is inscribed and is contrasted with the "stone tablets" upon which the Decalogue was written. In 3:15, however, καρδία refers to the seat of knowledge or understanding and is synonymous with νοήματα in v. 14. To be sure, καρδία *may* also refer to the seat of knowledge or understanding in 4:6; thus the appearance of καρδία in 3:15 is, in the final analysis, inconclusive in terms of evidence for or against Pauline authorship of 3:7–18.

Conclusion

Upon close examination, the eight apparent verbal and/or ideational links between 2 Cor 3:7–18 and the surrounding mate-

---

76. Rom 1:21, 24; 2:5, 15, 29; 5:5; 6:17; 8:27; 9:2; 10:1, 6, 8, 9, 10; 16:18; 1 Cor 2:9; 4:5; 7:37 *bis*; 14:25; 2 Cor 1:22; 2:4; 3:2, 3; 4:6; 5:12; 6:11; 7:3; 8:16; 9:7; Gal 4:6; Phil 1:7; 4:7; 1 Thess 2:4, 17; 3:13. Elsewhere in the NT, it appears 120 times: sixteen times in Matthew, eleven times in Mark, twenty-two times in Luke, seven times in John, twenty-one times in Acts, six times in Ephesians, five times in Colossians, twice in 2 Thessalonians, once in 1 Timothy, once in 2 Timothy, eleven times in Hebrews, five times in James, three times in 1 Peter, twice in 2 Peter, four times in 1 John, and three times in Revelation.

rial—διακονία, γράμμα, δόξα, πρόσωπον, νόημα, διαθήκη, τοιοῦτος, and καρδία—would appear, on balance, to argue *for* secondary insertion of the verses and *against* Pauline authorship. Moreover, the very number of such apparent links may well suggest a deliberate attempt on the part of an interpolator to make vv. 7–18 "fit" into the surrounding material.

Conclusion

I have argued (a) that the relation of 2 Cor 3:7–18 to its context points to secondary insertion of the passage between 2 Cor 3:6 and 2 Cor 4:1, (b) that distinctive vocabulary in vv. 7–18 indicates composition of the passage by someone other than Paul, and (c) that apparent verbal and/or conceptual links between vv. 7–18 and their immediate context suggest composition (by someone other than Paul) precisely for the purpose of insertion at their present location in 2 Corinthians. In short, it is my contention that 2 Cor 3:7–18 was neither composed by Paul nor inserted by him at its present location in 2 Corinthians—that the verses are, in fact, a later, non-Pauline interpolation.

This conclusion, of course, poses the question: Why would someone other than Paul compose these verses and insert them at their present location in 2 Corinthians? It is impossible to be certain, but the following would appear to be a plausible scenario: In v. 3, Paul contrasts "a letter from Christ . . . written with [the] spirit of [the] living God . . . on tablets of human hearts" (ἐπιστολὴ Χριστοῦ . . . ἐγγεγραμμένη . . . πνεύματι Θεοῦ ζῶντος . . . ἐν πλαξὶν καρδίαις σαρκίναις) with one written "with ink . . . on stone tablets" (μέλανι . . . ἐν πλαξὶν λιθίναις). In v. 6, his reference to "a new covenant" (καινῆς διαθήκης) suggests a similar contrast between this "new covenant" and "an old covenant." These two contrasts provides an ideal opportunity for an elaboration of the difference between the two "letters" or "covenants," which is precisely what we find in vv. 7–18. As already noted, however, this elaboration interrupts the flow of Paul's argument in 2 Cor 2:14–5:19 and, indeed, presents a much more negative assessment of Judaism than is found elsewhere in the Pauline letters. It can be assumed, therefore, that the author of vv. 7–18 had an "anti-Judaism" agenda and simply saw 2 Cor 3:3, 6 as providing a suitable springboard for the articulation of such an agenda. In order to make vv. 7–18 "fit," however, this author seized upon features of the material immediately preceding and immediately following and used them as building blocks for the new composition. It is for this reason that the terms διακονία, γράμμα, δόξα, πρόσωπον, νόημα, διαθήκη, τοιοῦτος, and καρδία—all of which, as has already been noted, figure rather prominently in the material immediately preceding and/or immediately following 3:7–18—also appear, in some cases rather prominently, in 3:7–18. As has also been noted, however, these terms are not necessarily used in the same ways, but their appearance seems to represent an interpolator's attempt to make the new material "fit" into the context in which it is being inserted. In short, as was suggested earlier, this interpolator was a *good*, but not a *perfect* interpolator.

Afterword

If 2 Cor 3:7–18 is in fact a later non-Pauline interpolation, and if 1 Thess 2:13–16 (or 14–16) is, as some scholars hold, also an interpolation,[77] then Paul himself cannot be accused of any anti-Jewish bias. Rather, his attitude toward Judaism is to be seen primarily in his letter to the Romans, especially in chaps. 11–13. Indeed, although it involves something of a circular argument, the anti-Jewish tone of 2 Cor 3:7–18 might be seen as an argument against its Pauline authorship.

---

77. See, e.g., Walker, *Interpolations*, 210–20.

Chapter 10

Apollos and Timothy as the Unnamed "Brothers" in 2 Corinthians 8:18–24

In 2 Cor 8:18–24, Paul refers to two unnamed "brothers" who are to accompany Titus as the latter collects money for "the ministry to the saints."[1] Verses 18–19 refer to "the brother for whom there is praise throughout all the churches for his proclamation of the good news" (τὸν ἀδελφὸν οὗ ὁ ἔπαινος ἐν τῷ εὐαγγελίῳ διὰ πασῶν τῶν ἐκκλησιῶν), noting that he "has been appointed by the churches as our traveling companion with this gift that is being administered by us for the glory of the Lord [himself] and to show our goodwill" (χειροτονηθεὶς ὑπὸ τῶν ἐκκλησιῶν συνέκδημος ἡμῶν σὺν τῇ χάριτι ταύτῃ τῇ διακονουμένῃ ὑφ᾽ ἡμῶν πρὸς τὴν [αὐτοῦ] τοῦ κυρίου δόξαν καὶ προθυμίαν ἡμῶν).[2] Then, v. 22 speaks of "our brother whom we have often tested and found to be diligent in many things, who is now much more diligent because of his great confidence in you" (τὸν ἀδελφὸν ἡμῶν ὃν ἐδοκιμάσαμεν ἐν πολλοῖς πολλάκις σπουδαῖον ὄντα νυνὶ δὲ πολὺ σπουδαιότερον πεποιθήσει πολλῇ εἰς ὑμᾶς).[3] This second "brother" is to accompany Titus and the "brother" referred to in vv. 18–19. Finally, in a clear reference to both "brothers," v.

"Apollos and Timothy as the Unnamed 'Brothers' in 2 Corinthians 8:18–24." *CBQ* 73,2 (April 2011) 318–38. Copyright © 2011 Catholic Biblical Association of America. Reprinted with permission.

1. Cf. 2 Cor 8:4: τῆς διακονίας τῆς εἰς τοὺς ἁγίους. Clearly, this is a reference to the collection being assembled for the Christians in Jerusalem; see 1 Cor 16:1–4; 2 Corinthians 8–9; Rom 15:25–28a; and probably Gal 2:10. For Titus' role in the collection, see 2 Cor 8:6, 16–17, 23. In the undisputed Pauline letters, Titus is mentioned only in 2 Corinthians (2:13; 7:6–7, 13–14; 8:16–17, 23; 12:18) and in Galatians (2:1–3).

2. Translation mine. Διὰ πασῶν τῶν ἐκκλησιῶν could also be translated as "by all the churches." For the translation/paraphrase of ἐν τῷ εὐαγγελίῳ as "for his proclamation of the good news," see below.

3. Translation mine.

23 speaks in the plural of "our brothers, apostles of churches" (ἀδελφοὶ ἡμῶν, ἀπόστολοι ἐκκλησιῶν).[4]

Three times in chap. 8, Paul refers to Titus by name (vv. 6, 16, and 23). It appears somewhat strange, therefore, that the two "brothers" who are to accompany Titus are not also identified by name.[5] Hans Dieter Betz and others have argued that Paul deliberately omitted the names, perhaps in order to "play down the role of the brothers."[6] Other scholars assume that Paul did name them "but that the names were subsequently deleted by some editor," perhaps because the two had for some reason fallen into disfavor in Corinth.[7] Various names have been proposed for the two "brothers,"[8] but Victor Paul Furnish, in agreement with many commentators, insists that "attempts to identify the *renowned brother* [of 8:18–19] are little more than conjecture" and "it is no easier to pin a name on [the] earnest brother [of 8:22] than on the *renowned brother*."[9]

---

4. In 2 Cor 9:3–5, Paul speaks of sending "the [unnamed] brothers" (τοὺς ἀδελφούς) to Achaia in connection with "the offering for the saints" (τῆς διακονίας τῆς εἰς τοὺς ἁγίους). The reference may or may not be to the "brothers" mentioned in chap. 8; for discussion, see, e.g., Betz, *2 Corinthians 8 and 9*, 93–95. Note, however, that Titus is not mentioned—at least not by name—in chap. 9. In 2 Cor 12:18, Paul states that he "urged Titus [to visit the recipients of his letter] and sent the brother [note the singular] with him" (παρεκάλεσα Τίτον καὶ συναπέστειλα τὸν ἀδελφόν). Although Furnish (*II Corinthians*, 436, 560, 566) and others believe that the reference here is to the "brother" of 8:22, the fact that the person in question is identified simply as "the brother" (as in 8:18) rather than as "our brother" (as in 8:22) may indicate that Paul here has in mind the "brother" of 8:18–19. It should be noted, however, that various partition theories with regard to 2 Corinthians would identify chaps. 8 and 12 as (parts of) different letters, in which case the unnamed "brother" of 12:18 might be someone other than either of the unnamed "brothers" in chap. 8.

5. Betz (*2 Corinthians 8 and 9*, 73) notes that "commentators have long found the omission of the names puzzling."

6. Betz, *2 Corinthians 8 and 9*, 73–74.

7. Furnish, *II Corinthians*, 435 (see references there).

8. See, e.g., Heinrici, *Der zweite Brief an die Korinther*, 287–88, 291–92; Hughes, *Paul's Second Epistle to the Corinthians*, 312–16, 319; and Furnish, *II Corinthians*, 435–37.

9. Furnish, *II Corinthians*, 435, 436–37.

It is my contention, however, that there are plausible grounds for identifying the first of the two unnamed "brothers" as Apollos, whom Paul mentions by name in 1 Corinthians but not in 2 Corinthians,[10] and the second as Timothy, whom Paul mentions by name in Romans, 1 Corinthians, 2 Corinthians, Philippians, 1 Thessalonians, and Philemon.[11] To be sure, the evidence for these identifications is circumstantial and by no means conclusive. Moreover, there are at least two possible objections to what I am proposing. Nevertheless, it is my judgment that a careful examination of the evidence points to Apollos and Timothy as the two who, among all of Paul's known associates, are the most likely candidates for identification as the unnamed "brothers" of 2 Cor 8:18–24.[12]

In this study, I shall argue first that the two unnamed "brothers" are most likely Apollos and Timothy. Then I shall summarize and attempt to refute possible arguments against these identifications. Finally, I shall note some implications of identifying the "brothers" as Apollos and Timothy. The structure of the argument regarding Timothy will differ from that regarding Apollos because the nature of the evidence is somewhat different.

Apollos as the First Unnamed "Brother"

In what follows, I shall: (a) call attention to what Paul actually *says* regarding the first unnamed "brother" of 2 Cor 8:18–24; (b) point out what he appears also to *imply* or *suggest* regarding the

---

10. 1 Cor 1:12; 3:4, 5, 6, 22; 16:12. Apollos also appears at Acts 18:24–9:1a; Titus 3:13.

11. Rom 16:21; 1 Cor 4:17; 16:10; 2 Cor 1:1, 19; Phil 1:1; 2:19; 1 Thess 1:1; 3:2, 6; Phlm 1. Timothy also appears at Acts 16:1; 17:14, 15; 18:5; 19:22; 20:4; Col 1:1; 2 Thess 1:1; 1 Tim 1:2, 18; 6:20; 2 Tim 1:2; Heb 13:23.

12. So far as I can ascertain, neither Apollos nor Timothy has previously been suggested. As Heinrici (*Der zweite Brief an die Korinther*, 287–88) and others have noted, the first "brother" has been identified variously as an actual brother of Titus, an actual brother of Paul, Barnabas, Silas, Luke, Erastus, Mark, Trophimus, and Aristarchus. The second "brother" has occasionally been identified as an actual brother of Paul himself (Heinrici, 291).

"brother"; (c) on the basis of (a) and (b), construct a profile of the "brother" and his relationship to Paul; (d) present what I regard as grounds for identifying the "brother" as Apollos; and (e) draw preliminary conclusions from what I have thus far set forth.

What Paul Says regarding the First "Brother"

1. The "brother" is a Christian.[13]

This could, of course, simply be assumed, but Paul makes it explicit by referring to him as "brother" (ἀδελφός), which is his usual term for a fellow Christian.[14]

2. The "brother" is a preacher of the gospel.

Paul refers to his "proclamation of the good news" (ἐν τῷ εὐαγγελίῳ). To be sure, there is some debate regarding the proper translation of the phrase ἐν τῷ εὐαγγελίῳ. The Greek is cryptic and, as Furnish notes, "has to be paraphrased." Acknowledging that it might mean "because of his preaching of the gospel," Furnish points out, however, that there is no "clear indication that 'preaching' is specifically in mind," and he therefore prefers "to interpret the expression more generally."[15] Thus, he translates the phrase as "because of his work for the gospel."[16] It appears clear,

---

13. The label "Christian" is probably anachronistic at this point, but I use it simply for convenience.

14. Ellis ("Paul and His Co-Workers," 15, but see the entire discussion, 13–22) maintains that "when used in the plural with an article, 'the brothers' in the Pauline literature fairly consistently refers to a relatively limited group of workers, some of whom have the Christian mission and/or ministry as their primary occupation." Ellis also suggests that "brother" (singular) might refer to a member of this group (p. 14). It is possible, therefore, that both "the brother" (v. 18) and "our brother" (v. 22) fall into this category (cf. "our brothers" in v. 23). See, however, the critique of Ellis' suggestion by Ollrog (*Paul und Seiner Mitarbeiter*, 78 n. 93). My own judgment is that "the brother" in 2 Cor 8:18 most likely refers simply to a fellow Christian.

15. Furnish, *II Corinthians*, 422.

16. Furnish, *II Corinthians*, 420; cf., e.g., Barrett, *Commentary on the Second Epistle to the Corinthians*, 228: "whose praise in the Gospel is current in all the churches."

however, that "work for the gospel" would, at the very least, include proclaiming or preaching the gospel. Moreover, Gerhard Friedrich, appealing to the "derivation of the word from OT and Rabbinic usage," maintains that, at least for the most part, εὐαγγέλιον in the New Testament "is a *nomen actionis*—i.e., that "it describes the act of proclamation." Thus, he translates ἔπαινος ἐν τῷ εὐαγγελίῳ in 2 Cor 8:18 as "praise at the preaching of the Gospel."[17] Along the same lines, Paul Barnett renders ὁ ἔπαινος ἐν τῷ εὐαγγελίῳ διὰ πασῶν τῶν ἐκκλησιῶν as "praise for proclaiming the gospel . . . through all the churches."[18] In my judgment, Friedrich and Barnett are correct, and my own translation/paraphrase of ἐν τῷ εὐαγγελίῳ is "for his proclamation of the good news."

3. The "brother" has a reputation as an outstanding preacher.

Paul speaks of "praise for his proclamation of the good news" (οὗ ὁ ἔπαινος ἐν τῷ εὐαγγελίῳ). As Betz notes, such a characterization "is unique in Paul" and "is a tribute to the reputation and standing of this man in the Christian churches, a fact which Paul simply reported."[19]

4. The "brother's" reputation as an outstanding preacher is widespread.

Paul indicates this by including the phrase, perhaps a bit hyperbolically, διὰ πασῶν τῶν ἐκκλησιῶν. As noted above,[20] this

---

17. Friedrich, "εὐαγγελίζομαι, εὐαγγέλιον, προευαγγελίζομαι, εὐαγγελιστής," 729. To be sure, Friedrich (pp. 729–30) also speaks of a "twofold sense" of the word εὐαγγέλιον whereby it can refer either to the act of preaching or to the content of the preaching or to both. In most instances, however, he views εὐαγγέλιον as a *nomen actionis*. Moreover, the construction in 2 Cor 8:18 would appear to make it clear that εὐαγγέλιον refers here not to the *content* of preaching but rather to some type of *activity*, and the most obvious type of activity would appear to be that of proclaiming the good news.
18. Barnett, *Second Epistle to the Corinthians*, 420
19. Betz, *2 Corinthians 8 and 9*, 74.
20. See n. 2 above.

could mean "by all the churches," in which case τὸν ἀδελφὸν οὗ ὁ ἔπαινος ἐν τῷ εὐαγγελίῳ διὰ πασῶν τῶν ἐκκλησιῶν would mean "the brother for whom there is praise by all the churches for his proclamation of the good news." Most commentators, however, translate the phrase as "throughout all the churches."[21] In either case, Paul characterizes the unnamed "brother" of 2 Cor 8:18–19 as one who is widely praised for his proclamation of the good news.

 5. The "brother" was "appointed by the churches" to participate in the collection and administration of the offering.

As Betz notes, the verb translated as "appointed" (χειροτονεῖν) "is a technical term and describes the process of electing envoys by the raising of hands in the assembly."[22] Thus, the "brother" is a representative of the churches within the delegation that is to collect the offering for the Christians in Jerusalem. This, of course, suggests that he was highly regarded and trusted by the churches.[23]

 6. The "brother" is an "apostle."

In 2 Cor 8:23, Paul refers to both him and the other "brother" who is to accompany Titus as "apostles" (ἀπόστολοι). To be sure, ἀπόστολοι is here qualified as ἀπόστολοι ἐκκλησιῶν ("apostles of churches") and therefore may mean simply messengers or envoys, as it apparently does in Phil 2:25.[24] Typically, however, Paul restricts the term ἀπόστολοι to a small group of leaders in the

---

21. See, e.g., BDAG 224.
22. Betz, *2 Corinthians 8 and 9*, 74. For further discussion, see, e.g., Plummer, *Critical and Exegetical Commentary on the Second Epistle*, 249.
23. Most scholars assume that "all the churches" refers to the churches of Macedonia; for discussion of the options and the conclusion that Macedonia is the most likely option, see, e.g., Barnett, *Second Epistle to the Corinthians*, 420. Nickle (*The Collection*, 19–20) argues, however, that the reference is most likely to the churches of Judea. My own judgment is that Paul has in mind the areas of his own activity, namely, Asia, Macedonia, and Achaia.
24. In Phil 2:25, Paul refers to Epaphroditus as "your envoy and minister to my need" (ὑμῶν ἀπόστολον καὶ λειτουργὸν τῆς χρείας μου).

church, and ἀπόστολος is, of course, the title he so proudly and insistently claims for himself.[25] Thus, Paul's reference to the two unnamed "brothers" of 2 Corinthians 8 as ἀπόστολοι certainly indicates a status more elevated than that simply of ἀδελφοί ("brothers"), and it may at least hint at something more than "messengers." Clearly, the "brothers" are not simply rank-and-file members of the church.

What Paul Appears to Imply or Suggest regarding the First "Brother"

  1. Paul does not feel as close to the first "brother" as he does to the second.

This is indicated by two items in his characterization of the two "brothers." In the first place, he refers to the "brother" of vv. 18–19 as "*the* brother" while designating the "brother" of v. 22 as "*our* brother."[26] To be sure, v. 23 speaks collectively of the two as "*our* brothers," but the initial difference in characterization would appear to be significant.[27] In the second place, Paul characterizes the latter as one "whom we have often proved to be diligent in many things" but says nothing comparable regarding the former. This suggests a close relationship of rather long standing between Paul and the latter but not between Paul and the former. Indeed, Paul makes no mention at all of any past association between himself and the "brother" of 2 Cor 8:18–19.

  2. Paul is somewhat less enthusiastic about the first "brother's" preaching than are the churches.

He does not himself praise the "brother" for his preaching; rather, as Betz observes, he simply reports the fact that there is

---

25. Rom 1:1; 11:13; 1 Cor 1:1; 4:9; 9:1–2; 15:9; 2 Cor 1:1; 12:11–12; Gal 1:1; 1 Thess 2:6.

26. Emphasis mine.

27. Even if Ellis is correct in his view that "brother" means more than simply "fellow Christian" (see n. 14 above), the distinction between "*the* brother" (v. 18) and "*our* brother" (v. 22) would appear to require some explanation.

praise for him throughout all the churches.[28] Further, noting that for Paul it is "God's praise alone" that really counts,[29] Betz suggests that this aspect of Paul's characterization of the "brother" may even be "slightly ironic."[30]

> 3. It was the churches, not Paul, who selected the "brother" of 2 Cor 8:18–19 to participate in the collection of the offering.

To be sure, Paul does in some sense endorse the selection by saying in v. 18 that "we" are sending "the brother" with Titus. At the same time, however, he explicitly states in v. 19 that the "brother" was "appointed by the churches." Moreover, it is noteworthy that he says nothing comparable regarding the "brother" of v. 22. This suggests that the latter was chosen by someone other than the churches—presumably Paul himself.[31] The distinction between a "brother" chosen by the churches and a "brother" chosen by Paul is, of course, quite consistent with Paul's reference to the former as "*the* brother" and to the latter as "*our* brother."

> 4. The "brother" was included in the delegation—or at least his inclusion was endorsed by Paul—for the purpose of forestalling criticism regarding the collection and administration of the offering.

The exact translation of the two verses immediately following Paul's characterization of "the brother" in 2 Cor 8:18–19 is problematic, but the NRSV renders them as follows: "We intend that no one should blame us about this generous gift that we are

---

28. Betz, *2 Corinthians 8 and 9*, 74.
29. See Rom 2:29; 1 Cor 4:5.
30. Betz, *2 Corinthians 8 and 9*.
31. Paul refers to both "brothers" in v. 23 as "apostles of churches" (ἀπόστολοι ἐκκλησιῶν). This entire verse, however, is cryptic and difficult to translate (see, e.g., Betz, *2 Corinthians 8 and 9*, 78: "The unusual statements found in v 23 have been a source of puzzlement to readers ever since they were written"; cf. his entire discussion, 78–82), and it may or may not imply anything regarding the process by which the two "brothers" were selected for inclusion in the delegation.

administering, for we intend to do what is right not only in the Lord's sight but also in the sight of others." As Furnish notes, the concern is to "certify the integrity of the enterprise" or, in other words, "to assure that no impropriety occurs or is even suspected."[32] The desire that "no one should blame us" suggests a degree of defensiveness on Paul's part and perhaps a wish that including the "brother" had not been necessary. Indeed, it is quite possible that Paul originally intended to send only Titus to collect the funds, that the churches insisted on having "*the* brother" (vv. 18–19) accompany Titus, that Paul somewhat reluctantly agreed to this (vv. 20–21), but that he in turn insisted on including "*our* brother" (v. 22) as a way of weighting the delegation in his own favor. In any case, as Betz notes, "the discrepancy between the standing of [the "brother" of vv. 18–19] within the churches and the role he is given to play in Paul's disposition of the collection is remarkable." In short, "There can be no doubt that Paul did all he could to lower the man's profile in the context of the delegation."[33]

> 5. Although the "brother" of 2 Cor 8:18–19 is indeed an "apostle," his apostolic status, like that of the "brother" of v. 22, is different from and somewhat less elevated than the status of Paul himself.

Paul is "an apostle of Christ Jesus,"[34] but, as has already been noted, the "brothers" are "apostles of churches." Paul apparently bases his own apostleship on the fact that he has "seen Jesus our Lord" (1 Cor 9:1), but the designation of the two "brothers" as "apostles" raises the question of whether there might by other "apostles" who have not "seen Jesus our Lord" and, if so, whether the "brothers" of 2 Cor 8:18–19, 22–23 might be among this latter group. In short, it would appear that Paul regards himself as

---

32. Furnish, *II Corinthians*, 434; see also Betz, *2 Corinthians 8 and 9*, 76–78.
33. Betz, *2 Corinthians 8 and 9*, 74. Cf. e.g., Windisch, *Der Zweite Korintherbrief*, 265, where Titus, in contrast to the "brothers," is identified as "the leader of the delegation to Corinth" (translation mine).
34. 1 Cor 1:1; 2 Cor 1:1; cf. 1 Thess 2:6; Gal 1:1.

belonging to what might be regarded as the first tier of apostles and the "brothers" to a subordinate tier. This is supported by the fact Paul is included among those who *send* the "brothers" while the "brothers" are those who are *sent*.

Profile of the First "Brother" and His Relationship to Paul

Combining what Paul appears to imply or suggest regarding the unnamed "brother" of 2 Cor 8:18–24 with what he actually says about the "brother" results in the following profile: On the one hand, Paul (a) regards him as a "brother"—that is, a fellow Christian, (b), acknowledges that he is widely praised for his preaching of the gospel, (c) recognizes that he was appointed by the churches to participate in the collection of the offering, and (d) designates him an "apostle"—however this is to be understood. On the other hand, (a) Paul's relationship to "*the* brother" is less intimate than his relationship to "*our* brother," (b) Paul is somewhat less enthusiastic about the "brother's" preaching than are the churches, (c) it was the churches and not Paul who decided upon the "brother's" involvement in the offering, (d) the reason for including the "brother" was the desire to forestall criticism regarding the collection of the offering, and (e) Paul regards the "brother's" apostolic status as different from and somewhat less elevated than his own.

With this profile of the "brother" before us, the question now to be posed is whether we know of anyone within Paul's circle of acquaintances to whom the profile might apply. I suggest that we do and that this person is Apollos. Indeed, Paul's characterization of the unnamed "brother" of 2 Cor 8:18–19 is remarkably consistent with what we know and/or can surmise regarding Apollos.

Grounds for Identifying the First "Brother" as Apollos

1. Paul's reference to the "brother" as "brother" is consistent with his reference to Apollos in 1 Cor 16:12 as "brother."

As already noted, of course, this is by no means surprising, because "brother" is Paul's usual term for a fellow Christian.

2. Paul's reference to the "brother" as "the" rather than "our" brother as in 2 Cor 8:22 is, however, somewhat unusual but is consistent with his reference to Apollos as "the" brother in 1 Cor 16:12.

Except in salutations at the beginning of three letters and in greetings at the end of one letter,[35] Apollos is the only individual to whom Paul refers by name simply as "the brother" (1 Cor 16:12). Moreover, the only places where Paul refers to an unnamed single individual simply as "the brother" are 2 Cor 8:18 and 2 Cor 12:18.[36] In other words, except in opening salutations and closing greetings, Paul refers to a single individual simply as "*the* brother" only at 1 Cor 16:12 (Apollos), at 2 Cor 8:18 (the first of the two unnamed "brothers" who are to accompany Titus), and at 2 Cor 12:18 (an unnamed "brother" who accompanies Titus). This suggests that the unnamed "brother" of 2 Cor 8:18—and perhaps also of 2 Cor 12:18—may well in fact be none other than Apollos, who is identified by name simply as "*the* brother" in 1 Cor 16:12.

3. Paul's characterization of the "brother" as one "for whom there is praise for his proclamation of the good news" is consistent with we know and/or can surmise regarding Apollos.

Apollos is described in Acts 18:24–28 as "an eloquent man" (ἀνὴρ λόγιος),[37] "fervent in spirit" (ζέων τῷ πνεύματι), who "spoke boldly" (παρρησιάζεσθαι) and "powerfully confuted the Jews in public" (εὐτόνως ... τοῖς Ἰουδαίοις διακατηλέγχετο δημοσίᾳ). To be sure, the portrayal of Apollos in the book of Acts is problematic for at least two reasons. In the first place, it is widely

---

35. Sosthenes in 1 Cor 1:1, Timothy in 2 Cor 1:1 and Phlm 1; Quartus in Rom 16:23.

36. Of course, he often refers collectively to unnamed people as "brothers" (ἀδελφοί).

37. Ἀνὴρ λόγιος could also be translated as "a learned" or "cultured man," but the further description of Apollos would appear to support "eloquent."

acknowledged that there are serious questions regarding the historicity of the book of Acts in general. In the second place, it has recently been argued that the portrayal of Apollos in Acts is based in large measure on what Paul says and/or implies about him in 1 Corinthians.[38] Thus, it may well be the case that the portrayal of Apollos in Acts is of no *direct* relevance for the identification of the unnamed "brother" of 2 Cor 8:18–19. This portrayal may, however, have some *indirect* relevance to the extent that it reflects a general perception in the early church of Apollos as one "for whom there [was] praise throughout all the churches for his proclamation of the good news." Moreover, it is at least possible that the author of Acts—and perhaps other early Christians as well—understood 2 Cor 8:18–19 as a reference to Apollos and that the portrayal of Apollos in Acts is therefore based in part on these verses.[39] In any case, the portrayal of Apollos in Acts is at this point clearly consistent with Paul's characterization of the unnamed "brother" of 2 Cor 8:18–19 as one "for whom there is praise throughout all the churches for his proclamation of the good news."

Moreover, quite apart from the portrayal of Apollos in Acts, the characterization of the "brother" as one "for whom there is praise for his proclamation of the good news" would appear to be consistent with what Paul himself says and/or implies about Apollos in 1 Corinthians. In 1 Cor 1:17b; 2:1–5, Paul acknowledges his own shortcomings as an orator, implicitly contrasting himself with others who are presumably more gifted in this regard.[40] Because references to Apollos both precede and follow Paul's comments regarding his own oratorical deficiencies,[41] it requires no major

---

38. Walker, "Portrayal of Aquila and Priscilla in Acts," 486–87 (chapter 16 in this volume).

39. If I, in the twenty-first century, can see Apollos as the unnamed "brother" of 2 Cor 8:18–19, the same identification might well have been made in the second century (for a second-century dating of Acts, see most recently and comprehensively, Pervo, *Dating Acts*). Indeed, it is even possible that the author of Acts might have *known* the unnamed "brother" to be Apollos.

40. See the entire passage, 1 Cor 1:17–2:5; see also 2 Cor 10:10.

41. 1 Cor 1:12; 3:4, 5, 6, 22; 4:6.

leap of the imagination to conclude that it is Apollos—or at least Apollos among others—with whom he is comparing himself. In short, Paul appears—at least by implication—to portray Apollos as a skilled and eloquent orator—indeed, as one "for whom there [would be] praise for his proclamation of the good news."

4. Paul's indication that praise for the "brother's" preaching is found "throughout all the churches" is consistent with what we know and/or can surmise regarding Apollos.

The phrase "all the churches" is surely hyperbolic, and its precise geographical scope is by no means clear. It could refer simply to the churches in the immediate vicinity of Paul's current activity and/or that of the recipients of his letter, but my own judgment is that a somewhat broader arena is intended and that what Paul intends to convey is that the "brother" is *widely* praised for his preaching of the gospel. Both Acts and Paul's Corinthian correspondence locate Apollos not only in Asia but also in Achaia. According to Acts 18:24–28, Apollos was active first in Corinth (a major city of Achaia) and then in Ephesus (the major city of Asia). To be sure, as noted above, the historical reliability of Acts is suspect, but Paul's references to Apollos in 1 Corinthians associate him with both Ephesus and Corinth.[42] Thus, Apollos would have been known both in Asia and in Achaia, and, for Paul, διὰ πασῶν τῶν ἐκκλησιῶν might well have been shorthand for such geographical latitude. In short, Paul apparently recognizes that Apollos is widely known and presumably widely praised for his preaching, and this is consistent with his characterization of the unnamed "brother" of 2 Cor 8:18–19 as one "for whom there is praise throughout all the churches for his proclamation of the good news." Moreover, we know of no other associate of Paul who fits this characterization.

5. Paul's reference to the "brother" as an "apostle" (ἀπόστολος) is consistent with what he says and/or implies regarding Apollos in 1 Corinthians.

---

42. 1 Cor 1:12; 3:4–8, 22; 4:6; 16:12 (cf. v. 8).

In 1 Cor 3:21, Paul refers jointly to himself, Apollos, and Cephas. Just two verses later, in 4:1, he speaks of "us" (presumably himself, Apollos, and Cephas) as "servants of Christ and stewards of the mysteries of God" (ὑπηρέτας Χριστοῦ καὶ οἰκονόμους μυστηρίων Θεοῦ). Then, in 4:6, he states that what he has been saying applies to himself and Apollos. Finally, in 4:9, he refers to "us the apostles" (ἡμᾶς τοὺς ἀποστόλους). Clearly, Paul regards both himself and Cephas as ἀπόστολοι, and the preceding references to Apollos almost certainly indicate that ἡμᾶς here includes Apollos as well. In short, Paul regards Apollos as, like himself and Cephas, an "apostle." This by no means makes Apollos unique, of course, because Paul clearly recognizes other early Christian leaders as apostles. It may be significant, however, that he refers to no one else *by name* as an apostle other than Cephas and James (Gal 1:18–19), almost certainly Junia and Andronicus,[43] and possibly Epaphroditus.[44] In short, Paul apparently regards Apollos as an ἀπόστολος, and this is consistent with Paul's reference in v. 23 to the unnamed "brother" of 2 Cor 8:18–19 as an ἀπόστολος.

6. The fact that Paul refers to praise for the "brother's" preaching "throughout all the churches" without himself uttering such praise is consistent with what he implies and/or suggests regarding Apollos in 1 Corinthians.

It has already been noted that Paul acknowledged his own oratorical limitations as compared with the skills of others, almost certainly including Apollos. It should also be noted, however, that Paul apparently did not regard this as a shortcoming. Indeed, he appears to go out of his way to denigrate the preaching of the gospel "in eloquent wisdom" (ἐν σοφίᾳ λόγου) or "in superiority of speech or wisdom" (ἐν ὑπεροχὴν λόγου ἢ σοφίας) or "in plausible words of wisdom" (ἐν πειθοῖς σοφίας λόγοις), contrasting all of this with his own preaching "in demonstration of the Spirit

---

43. Rom 16:7; see Epp, *Junia*.
44. See n. 24 above.

and of power" (ἐν ἀποδείξει πνεύματος καὶ δυνάμεως).[45] Thus, the way in which Paul refers in 2 Cor 8:18 to the praise for the "brother's" preaching "throughout all the churches" without himself uttering such praise would appear to be in keeping both with his general attitude toward preaching and with his relationship with Apollos.

> 7. The fact that Paul suggests some degree of "distance" between himself and the first "brother" is consistent with what he says and/or implies regarding Apollos in 1 Corinthians.

In 1 Cor 1:11–12, Paul speaks of factions in the church that claim allegiance, respectively, to Paul, Apollos, Cephas, and Christ. This is reiterated in 1 Cor 3:4–6 and in 4:6 with reference specifically to Paul and Apollos as well as in 1 Cor 3:22 with reference to Paul, Apollos, and Cephas. Moreover, in 1 Cor 4:15, Paul says, "For though you have countless guides (παιδαγωγούς) in Christ, you do not have many fathers; for I became your father in Christ Jesus through the gospel." This suggests some degree of tension between Paul and other leaders, almost certainly including Apollos. It may also suggest that Paul's apostolic status somehow surpasses that of Apollos, even though the latter can appropriately be called an "apostle." Finally, in 1 Cor 16:12, Paul indicates that he had "strongly urged" (πολλὰ παρεκάλεσα)[46] Apollos to visit the readers of his letter and that Apollos had been unwilling to do so at the present time (καὶ πάντως οὐκ ἦν θέλημα ἵνα νῦν ἔλθῃ) but would come when the time was right.[47] In other words, Paul had no control over the actions of Apollos; indeed, Apollos

---

45. 1 Cor 1:17; 2:1, 4–5; see the entire passage, 1 Cor 1:17–2:5.

46. The Greek could also be translated as "often urged," but the phrase "with the brothers" (μετὰ τῶν ἀδελφῶν) suggests that Paul has in mind one particular occasion.

47. The verb εὐκαιρεῖν means "to experience a favorable time or occasion for some activity" (BDAG 406).

resisted Paul's strong urging that he accompany the "brothers."[48] Such indications of distance and even tension between Paul and Apollos may indeed indicate that "the conflict in Corinth was at its core a debate between Paul and the Apollos party."[49] This, coupled with the somewhat impersonal reference to Apollos in 1 Cor 16:12 as "*the* brother" may suggest that the even more impersonal reference to the unnamed "brother" in 2 Cor 8:18–19 as "*the* brother" who "has been appointed by the churches" has Apollos in mind. In any case, intimations in 1 Corinthians of "distance" between Paul and Apollos are consistent with similar intimations of a certain degree of distance between Paul and the unnamed "brother" of 2 Cor 8:18–19.

Preliminary Conclusion regarding the First "Brother"

It is true that the evidence for identifying the "brother" of 2 Cor 8:18–24 as Apollos is circumstantial and by no means conclusive, but, as has been indicated, the various features of Paul's characterization of the "brother" are remarkably consistent with what we know and/or can surmise regarding Apollos. Furthermore, on the basis of the available source materials, this cannot be said regarding any of Paul's other known associates. This suggests rather strongly, in my judgment, that the "brother" was, in fact, none other than Apollos.

Timothy as the Second Unnamed "Brother"

Some of what Paul says regarding the first unnamed "brother" of 2 Cor 8:18–24, as well as some of what he appears to imply or suggest regarding this "brother," also applies to the second unnamed

---

48. The word πάντως suggests that Apollos *strongly* objected to Paul's request. To be sure, the statement καὶ πάντως οὐκ ἦν θέλημα ἵνα νῦν ἔλθῃ could be interpreted as meaning that it was not God's will for Apollos to come at the present time. In any case, however, Apollos did not do what Paul wished him to do.

49. Wolter, "Apollos und die ephesinischen Johannesjünger," 66 (translation mine); see references in n. 80 in Wolter.

"brother": he is a Christian ("brother"), he is an "apostle" (in some sense of the word), but his apostolic status is different from and somewhat less elevated than the status of Paul himself. Although all three of these characteristics can, as I have argued, be applied to Apollos, only the first can, on the basis of what we otherwise know about Timothy, be applied to him. Thus, the argument for identifying the second "brother" as Timothy must proceed differently than that for identifying the first "brother" as Apollos. In what follows, therefore, I shall introduce six independent lines of evidence, which, in my judgment, point to Timothy as the second unnamed "brother" of 2 Cor 8:18–24. This will be followed by a seventh, which, however, depends on the prior identification of the first "brother" as Apollos.

First Line of Evidence

Paul refers to both the second "brother" of 2 Cor 8:18–24 and Timothy—but only to them—as "*our* brother" (ὁ ἀδελφὸς ἡμῶν).[50] Paul frequently uses the word ἀδελφός, both in the singular and, more often, in the plural, but he rarely refers to a particular named individual as ἀδελφός. Only Timothy, Quartus, Sosthenes, Apollos, Titus, and Epaphroditus are so designated.[51] Of the six, however, only Timothy is referred to (once) as "*our* brother" (ὁ ἀδελφός ἡμῶν).[52] Elsewhere, the term is "*the* brother (ὁ ἀδελφός)[53] or "*my* brother" (τὸν ἀδελφόν μου).[54] In short,

---

50. As already noted, Paul refers to the first "brother" simply as "*the* brother" (τὸν ἀδελφόν).

51. Timothy: 1 Thess 3:2; 2 Cor 1:1; Phlm 1. Quartus: Rom 16:23. Sosthenes: 1 Cor 1:1. Apollos: 1 Cor 16:12. Titus: 2 Cor 2:13; cf. v. 23. Epaphroditus: Phil 2:25.

52. 1 Thess 3:2. Elsewhere, Timothy is "the brother" (2 Cor 1:1; Phlm 1).

53. 1 Cor 1:1 (Sosthenes); 1 Cor 16:12 (Apollos); 2 Cor 1:1 (Timothy); Rom 16:23 (Quartus); Phlm 1 (Timothy).

54. 2 Cor 2:13 (Titus); Phil 2:25 (Epaphroditus). Note: in Phil 2:25, the entire phrase is τὸν ἀδελφὸν καὶ συνεργὸν καὶ συστρατιώτην μου, and it is unclear whether the μου is intended to modify all three nouns or only συστρατιώτην.

Paul refers to a particular individual as "*our* brother" (ὁ ἀδελφὸς ἡμῶν) only twice—in 1 Thess 3:2, where Timothy is named, and in 2 Cor 8:22, where no name is given. This suggests at least the possibility that the unnamed "our brother" (ὁ ἀδελφὸς ἡμῶν) of 2 Cor 8:22 is none other than Timothy.[55]

Paul does refer to the two unnamed brothers of 2 Cor 8:18–24, in the plural, as "our brothers" (ἀδελφοὶ ἡμῶν) in v. 23. Also, one might argue that the plural "our" (ἡμῶν) in both 2 Cor 8:22 and 1 Thess 3:2 is dictated by the two plural verbs (συνεπέμψαμεν and ἐπέμψαμεν). For these reasons, the significance of "our" (ἡμῶν) should not be overestimated. Nevertheless, the contrast between "*the* brother" (τὸν ἀδελφόν) in 2 Cor 8:18 and "our brother" (τὸν ἀδελφὸν ἡμῶν) in 2 Cor 8:22 is noteworthy, as is, perhaps, also the absence of the article (οἱ) before ἀδελφοὶ ἡμῶν in v. 23. Thus, when seen in conjunction with the other lines of evidence yet to be introduced, Paul's reference to both the unnamed "brother" of 2 Cor 8:22 and Timothy—but to no one else—as "our brother" (τὸν ἀδελφὸν ἡμῶν) may constitute evidence that the two are one and the same.[56]

Second Line of Evidence

Both the second unnamed "brother" of 2 Cor 8:18–24 and Timothy were with Paul when the latter composed at least some of his Corinthian correspondence.[57] Timothy's presence with Paul is probably indicated in 1 Cor 4:17, where Paul speaks of "send-

---

55. It would be interesting to speculate regarding a possible difference in significance between "*our* brother" and "*my* brother," but that is beyond the scope of the present study.

56. It would also be interesting to speculate regarding the difference between Paul's reference to Titus as "*my* associate and fellow worker for you" (κοινωνὸς ἐμὸς καὶ εἰς ὑμᾶς συνεργός) and to the two unnamed "brothers" as "*our* brothers" (ἀδελφοὶ ἡμῶν).

57. Also with Paul when some of the Corinthian correspondence was written were Sosthenes (1 Cor 1:1), Apollos (1 Cor 16:12), probably Stephanus and Fortunatus (1 Cor 16:17–18), Aquila and Prisca (1 Cor 16:19), and Titus (2 Cor 7:6–7, 13–15; 8:6, 16–24).

ing" Timothy to Corinth,[58] and it is clearly stated in the salutation of 2 Corinthians (2 Cor 1:1), where Paul and Timothy are identified as the authors of the letter. To be sure, many scholars believe that 2 Corinthians is a composite letter, with chap. 8 representing (part of) an originally separate letter;[59] thus, Timothy's name in the salutation (2 Cor 1:1) does not necessarily mean that he was with Paul when the latter composed chap. 8. Nevertheless, the fact that the two were together when Paul composed at least one, and probably two, of his letters to the Corinthians suggests that Timothy may very well have been with Paul when 2 Corinthians 8 was written. If so, he clearly could be one of the two unnamed "brothers" who are to accompany Titus.

Third Line of Evidence

Paul speaks of "sending" (συμπέμπειν) the unnamed "brother" of 2 Cor 8:22 along with Titus and the unnamed "brother" of v. 18, and, with the possible exception of Titus, Timothy appears to be the person whom Paul most frequently "sends" (πέμπειν) on missions to churches from which he himself is separated. Apart from 2 Cor 8:18–24, Paul speaks eight times of "sending" (πέμπειν, ἀποστέλλειν, or συναποστέλλειν) one or more people. In four instances, the people are not named (1 Cor 16:3; 2 Cor 9:3; 12:17, 18). Epaphroditus is named once (Phil 2:25–30), but here Paul is simply sending Epaphroditus back to Philippi, from which he had come bringing aid for Paul. Timothy, however, is named three times (1 Cor 4:17; Phil 2:19–24; 1 Thess 3:2, 6), and, in addition, 1 Cor 16:10–11 speaks of Timothy's expected arrival in Corinth and of his return to Paul. Furthermore, Timothy is sent to three different churches: Thessalonica, Corinth, and Philippi. Such references to Timothy serving as Paul's representative, coupled with the fact, already noted, that Timothy was with Paul when at least some of

---

58. The verb ἔπεμψα is in the *aorist* tense, but it is most likely to be understood as an *epistolary* aorist (cf. 1 Cor 16:10).

59. See, e.g., Betz, *2 Corinthians 8 and 9*.

the Corinthian correspondence was written, suggest that Timothy might well be the person selected by Paul to accompany Titus and the other unnamed "brother" as they collected money for the "offering."

Fourth Line of Evidence

The most important line of evidence may well be the fact that what Paul says about the second "brother" in 2 Cor 8:18–24 is completely consistent with—and, at one point, strikingly similar to—what he says elsewhere about Timothy. The unnamed "brother" is characterized as one "whom we have often tested and found to be diligent in many matters" (ὃν ἐδοκιμάσαμεν ἐν πολλοῖς πολλάκις σπουδαῖον ὄντα). Such a characterization suggests (a) that the "brother" has been intimately associated with Paul over a rather long period of time, (b) that he has been involved in a variety of activities in association with and/or on behalf of Paul, and (c) that Paul has developed a high degree of confidence in him.

This is completely consistent with the following data: (1) Of all Paul's associates, Timothy and Titus are the ones whom he mentions most often—eleven times each.[60] Moreover, Timothy's name appears in all of the undisputed letters except Galatians (Titus appears only in 2 Corinthians). By way of contrast, Apollos appears only seven times (in one letter: 1 Cor 1:12; 3:4, 5, 6, 22; 4:6; 16:12) and Barnabas appears only four times (in two letters: 1 Cor 9:6; Gal 2:1, 9, 13).[61] This suggests a long and intimate relationship between Timothy and Paul and the plausibility of Paul's selecting Timothy to accompany Titus and the other unnamed "brother" in collecting money for the offering. (2) Timothy is associated with

---

60. Timothy: Rom 16:21; 1 Cor 4:17; 16:10; 2 Cor 1:1, 19; Phil 1:1; 2:19; 1 Thess 1:1; 3;2, 6; Phlm 1. He appears also in the pseudo-Pauline Col 1:1; 2 Thess 1:1; 1 Tim 1:2, 18; 6:20; 2 Tim 1:2. Cf. also Acts 16:1; 17:14, 15; 18:5; 19:22; 20:4, where he is associated with Paul; and Heb 13:23. Titus: 2 Cor 2:13; 7:6, 13, 14; 8:6, 16, 23; 12:18 *bis*; Gal 2:1, 3. He appears also in the pseudo-Pauline 2 Tim 4:10; Titus 1:4.

61. Cf. the pseudo-Pauline Col 4:19. In the Book of Acts, on the other hand, Barnabas' name appears some twenty-three times.

Paul in the salutations of four of the seven undisputed Pauline letters (1 Thess 1:1; 2 Cor 1:1; Phil 1:1; Phlm 1). Otherwise, only Silvanus and Sosthenes are named (once each) in the salutations.[62] Again, this points to a rather lengthy and intimate association. (3) Paul tells the Thessalonians (1 Thess 3:2) that he has sent Timothy, whom he characterizes as "our brother and God's fellow-worker" (τὸν ἀδελφὸν ἡμῶν καὶ συνεργὸν τοῦ Θεοῦ)[63] "to establish you and to comfort you in your faith" (εἰς τὸ στηρίξαι ὑμᾶς καὶ παρακαλέσαι ὑπὲρ τῆς πίστεως ὑμῶν). This indicates that Paul trusts Timothy to fulfill important tasks. (4) Similarly, Paul tells the Corinthians (1 Cor 4:17) that he has sent Timothy, whom he characterizes as "my beloved and faithful child in the Lord" (μου τέκνον ἀγαπητὸν καὶ πιστὸν ἐν κυρίῳ), "to remind you of my ways in Christ" (ὃς ἀναμνήσει τὰς ὁδούς μου τὰς ἐν Χριστῷ Ἰησοῦ). (5) Paul also tells the Corinthians (1 Cor 16:10) that Timothy is "doing the work of the Lord, as I am" (τὸ . . . ἔργον κυρίου ἐργάζεται ὡς κἀγώ). (5) Perhaps most significant of all, Paul tells the Philippians (Phil 2:19–22) that he hopes to send Timothy to them soon and adds these words regarding Timothy:

> I have no one like him, who will be genuinely anxious for your welfare. They all look after their own interests, not those of Jesus Christ. But his proven worth (δοκιμή) you know, how as a son with a father he has served with me in the gospel.

Particularly noteworthy here is Paul's use of the noun δοκιμή (translated above as "proven worth") with reference to Timothy. The word means "a testing process" or "test" and, by extension, "the experience of going through a test with special ref[erence] to the result."[64] In other words, Paul is saying that Timothy has been tested and has passed the test. This is precisely what Paul

---

62. Silvanus: 1 Thess 1:1. Sosthenes: 1 Cor 1:1. Gal 1:1 refers to "all the brothers who are with me" (οἱ σὺν ἐμοὶ πάντες ἀδελφοί).

63. Cf. also Rom 16:21: "my fellow worker" (ὁ συνεργός μου) and Phil 1:1, where Paul characterizes himself and Timothy as "slaves of Christ Jesus" (δοῦλοι Χριστοῦ Ἰησοῦ).

64. BDAG 256.

says when he refers to the unnamed "brother" in 2 Cor 8:22 as "our brother whom we have often tested and found to be diligent in many matters" (τὸν ἀδελφὸν ἡμῶν ὃν ἐδοκιμάσαμεν ἐν πολλοῖς πολλάκις σπουδαῖον ὄντα). Indeed, the same root is used: δοκιμή in Phil 2:22 and ἐδοκιμάσαμεν in 2 Cor 8:22. Also to be noted is the fact that Paul refers to such "testing" with reference to both Timothy and the unnamed "brother" of 2 Cor 8:22 but to no one else. Again, this suggests that the two are likely one and the same.

Fifth Line of Evidence

Paul has such glowing words of praise for none of his associates other than the unnamed "brother" of 2 Cor 8:22 and Timothy—not even for Titus, who apparently is the leader of the group involved in collecting the money for "the ministry to the saints" and whom Paul refers to as "my brother" (ὁ ἀδελφός μου [2 Cor 2:13]) and "my associate and fellow worker on your behalf" (κοινωνὸς ἐμὸς καὶ εἰς ὑμᾶς συνεργός [2 Cor 8:23]). Perhaps the closest parallel is what Paul says about Prisca and Aquila, whom he describes as "my fellow workers in Christ Jesus, who risked their necks for my life, to whom not only I but also all the churches of the Gentiles give thanks" (Rom 16:3–4). This, too, suggests that the unnamed "brother" of 2 Cor 8:22 and Timothy are likely one and the same.

Sixth Line of Evidence

We have pseudo-Pauline letters to "Timothy" and "Titus" but none to any of Paul's other associates. This suggests that post-Pauline Christians were aware of Paul's close relationship with both Timothy and Titus, and such an awareness might well have been based, at least in part, on the two's known involvement in the collection of money for the offering.

Seventh (Possible) Line of Evidence

As already noted, the first unnamed "brother" of 2 Cor 8:18–24 was apparently selected to accompany Titus not by Paul but rather by "the churches" (cf. v. 19). I have argued that this first unnamed "brother" was Apollos and that relations between Paul and Apollos were somewhat strained. If I am correct, it would be only natural for Paul to wish to "balance"—or even "weight"—the makeup of the delegation by selecting one of his most trusted associates as its third member. Based on the information we have, Timothy would appear to be the most likely candidate for this role.

Preliminary Conclusion regarding the Second "Brother"

By way of summary:

1. Paul refers to both the second unnamed "brother" of 2 Cor 8:18–24 and Timothy—but *only* to them—as "*our* brother" (ὁ ἀδελφὸς ἡμῶν).
2. Both the unnamed "brother" and Timothy were with Paul when at least some of the Corinthian correspondence was composed.
3. Timothy appears to be the person whom Paul most frequently "sends" (πέμπειν) on missions to churches from which he himself is separated.
4. What Paul says about Timothy is completely consistent with—and, at one point, strikingly similar to— what he says about the unnamed "brother."
5. It is *only* for the unnamed "brother" and Timothy that Paul has such glowing words of praise.
6. We have pseudo-Pauline letters addressed only to Timothy and Titus—a likely indication that the two were associated in the minds of early Christians as Paul's most trusted associates.
7. Finally, given what we know about both Apollos and Timothy and their relationship to Paul, it is reasonable to infer, if Apollos was in fact, the first "brother" of 2 Cor 8:18–24, that Paul would have selected Timothy as the second "brother" as a way of "balancing" or "weighting" the delegation headed by Titus.

As in the case of the first "brother," the evidence for identifying the second unnamed "brother" of 2 Cor 8:18–24 as Timothy is circumstantial and by no means conclusive, but the cumulative force of the seven lines of evidence would appear to make Timothy the most likely candidate. At the very least, none of Paul's other known associates has a stronger claim.

Possible Objections to Identifying the Unnamed "Brothers" as Apollos and Timothy

There are at least two possible objections to identifying the unnamed "brothers" of 2 Cor 8:18-24 as Apollos and Timothy, and these must now be considered.

> 1. When Paul refers to Apollos and Timothy elsewhere, he calls them by name,[65] and this suggests that he would be unlikely to omit their names in 2 Cor 8:18-24.

I suggest, however, that there are plausible reasons why Paul would omit the names in 2 Cor 8:18-24. Because the reasons differ regarding Apollos and Timothy, it will be necessary to consider the matter separately for each.

Apollos. As has been noted, the conflict in Corinth may well have been essentially a split between Paul and the Apollos party. If so, this would account for the references to Apollos by name in chaps. 1, 3, and 4 of 1 Corinthians: it is necessary for Paul to mention his name in order to make the point he wishes to make regarding the role of and relation among various specified leaders in the Christian churches. No such necessity would exist, however, with regard to 2 Cor 8:18-19.

Paul also refers to Apollos by name at 1 Cor 16:12 (περὶ δὲ Ἀπολλῶ τοῦ ἀδελφοῦ), however, and this cannot be explained in the same manner. Nevertheless, a plausible explanation is possible. Noting that the reference to Apollos in 1 Cor 16:12 is introduced by the words περὶ δέ, Gordon D. Fee and others suggest that v. 12 is the beginning of Paul's response to "one final item" in the letter from the Corinthians to Paul.[66] "Apparently they

---

65. Apollos: 1 Cor 1:12; 3:4, 5, 6, 22; 4:6; 16:12. Timothy: Rom 16:21; 1 Cor 4:17; 16:10; 2 Cor 1:1, 19; Phil 1:1; 2:19; 1 Thess 1:1; 3:2, 6; Phlm 1.

66. Other such instances of περὶ δέ are at 7:1; 7:25; 8:1; 12:1; and 16:1. Note that περὶ δὲ Ἀπολλῶ τοῦ ἀδελφοῦ ("and concerning Apollos the

have requested him to ask Apollos to return and minister among them."[67] In order to make it clear that he was in fact responding to their request regarding Apollos, Paul almost necessarily would refer to him by name.

At 2 Cor 8:18–19, however, Paul is neither addressing the problem of the roles of and relations among various leaders in the Christian movement nor responding to any specific request or question regarding a particular individual. Rather, he simply indicates that he is sending this "brother" with Titus as the latter carries out the task of collecting money for the offering (cf. 2 Cor 8:1–6). Thus, there would be no necessity to provide a name for the "brother." Indeed, it is quite possible that Paul's reference to "the brother for whom there is praise throughout all the churches for his proclamation of the good news" and "who has been chosen by the churches as our traveling companion" would itself have been sufficient to identify this "brother."

Moreover, it is my judgment that Hans Dieter Betz is moving in the right direction in his suggestion that Paul deliberately omitted the names both in v. 18 and in v. 22 because "he intend[ed] to play down the role of the brothers." According to Betz, Paul omitted their names in order to avoid "giving them more status than was due."

> By neglecting to mention their names, in effect, Paul created two levels of authorization within the delegation. Titus alone was authorized in the full sense, while the brothers derived their authority from him. The brothers were not authorized as individuals. Their role could be played by any suitable person, while without Titus the letter had no legal force at all.[68]

---

brother") in 1 Cor 16:12 comes shortly after vv. 1–4, which begin with περὶ δὲ λογείας τῆς εἰς τοὺς ἁγίους ("and concerning the collection for the saints")—only a brief excursus regarding Paul's travel plans (vv. 5–9) and instructions regarding Timothy (vv. 10–11) intervene. This would appear to suggest that, in Paul's mind, Apollos was associated with the collection.

67. Fee, *First Epistle to the Corinthians*, 823.
68. Betz, *2 Corinthians 8 and 9*, 73.

As has already been suggested, Paul may well have less than enthusiastic about including the first "brother" in the delegation to collect the offering, and this might account, at least in part, for the omission of his name.

In short, there are plausible reasons why Paul might refer to Apollos by name in 1 Corinthians but not in 2 Cor 2:18–19. Thus, the first possible argument against identifying "the brother" of 2 Cor 8:18–19 as Apollos would appear to be far from compelling.

Timothy. The reasons suggested for the omission of Apollos' name in 2 Cor 8:18–19 do not apply, of course, to the omission of Timothy's name in v. 22. My own suggestion, however, is that Paul omits Timothy's name precisely *because* he has omitted Apollos' name. The inclusion of Timothy's name would have called attention to the omission of Apollos' name and thus to Apollos himself and thereby elevated him, with Timothy, to a status within the delegation more nearly approximating that of Titus. In short, Paul may well have diverted attention away from Timothy as a way of doing the same with regard to Apollos.

In addition, just as the characterization of the first "brother" as the one "for whom there is praise throughout all the churches for his proclamation of the good news" and "who has been chosen by the churches as our traveling companion" might have been sufficient to identify him, so, too, the characterization of the second "brother" as the one "whom we have often tested and found to be diligent in many things" might have been sufficient to identify him.

2. Apollos and Timothy were so well known in Corinth that Paul would almost certainly have identified them by name if it was indeed they whom he had in mind in 2 Cor 8:18–24.[69]

---

69. Furnish (*II Corinthians*, 437) asserts that Apollos cannot be the unnamed "brother" of 2 Cor 8:22 "since he was so well known in Corinth (see 1 Cor 1:12; 3:5, 6; 16:12) as to make the comments of 8:22 seem quite patronizing as well as unnecessary" (cf. Windisch, *Der zweite Korintherbrief*, 266; Hughes, *Paul's Second Epistle to the Corinthians*, 319).

It is quite possible, however, that Paul would have thought it unnecessary to name them precisely because they were so well known. As has already been suggested, simply characterizing the first "brother" as "the brother for whom there is praise throughout all the churches for his proclamation of the good news" and who "has been chosen by the churches as our traveling companion" might very well, in and of itself, have been sufficient to identify him as Apollos. By the same token, characterizing the second "brother" as "our brother whom we have often tested and found diligent in many things" might have been sufficient to identify him as Timothy. Moreover, as has also been noted, there are quite plausible reasons why Paul might not identify Apollos and Timothy by name in 2 Cor 8:18–24 even though he does so elsewhere. Thus, the second possible argument against identifying "the brothers" as Apollos and Timothy, like the first, is considerably less than persuasive.

Implications of Identifying the Unnamed Brothers as Apollos and Timothy

In what precedes, I have presented evidence suggesting that the two unnamed "brothers" of 2 Cor 8:18–24 are most likely Apollos and Timothy and have attempted to answer two possible arguments against so identifying them. I have by no means *proved* that the "brothers" are Apollos and Timothy, but it is my judgment that, among all the people we know to have been associated with Paul, they are the most likely candidate for the roles.

What now remains is to note what I regard as the most important implications of identifying the two "brothers" of 2 Cor 8:18–24 as Apollos and Timothy.

1. If the first "brother" is Apollos, we now have some additional information regarding Apollos.

With some modification, this judgment might apply equally well to the unnamed "brother" of 8:18–19, where the comments would probably not be regarded as "patronizing," but, if they refer to Apollos, they might well be seen as unnecessary in a letter to the Christians of Corinth.

We know that he was widely praised for his proclamation of the gospel, that he was trusted by the churches, and that he played a role in the collection and administration of the offering for Christians in Judea. The first point is consistent with the portrayal of Apollos in Acts 18:24–28, and it may provide confirmation that Paul has Apollos at least partially in mind when, by implication, he contrasts his own oratorical deficiencies with the rhetorical skills of others in 1 Corinthians. The second point, however, goes beyond anything said elsewhere about Apollos, and the third point is entirely new. Apollos has always been something of an enigmatic character in the story of the early Christian movement, but identifying him as the unnamed "brother" of 2 Cor 8:18–19 enables us to understand him and his role in the church somewhat more fully.

2. If the second "brother" is Timothy, we now some additional information regarding Timothy.

Specifically, we know that he was involved in collecting money for the offering to Jerusalem and that Paul regarded him as, in some sense, an "apostle."

3. If the first "brother" is Apollos, we now have further evidence of the complexity of the relationship between Apollos and Paul.

On the one hand, Paul did not feel as close to Apollos as he did to some of his other associates,[70] he appears to have had some reservations regarding both Apollos' preaching of the gospel and his inclusion in the delegation to collect the offering, and he viewed his own apostolic status as somewhat more elevated than that of Apollos. On the other hand, there apparently was no open break between them (as there appears to have been at one point, for example, between Paul and Barnabas; see Gal 2:13; cf. Acts 15:36–40), and Paul was willing to endorse the inclusion of Apollos in the delegation named to assemble the collection. Much of this, of

---

70. For example, "our brother" in 2 Cor 8:22.

course, is consistent with references to Apollos in 1 Corinthians, but we now have a bit more by way of detail.

> 4. If the two "brothers" are Apollos and Timothy, we now have more information about the collection of the offering.

We know that the delegation assembled for this purpose included both someone selected by the churches whose own relationship to Paul was somewhat ambiguous (Apollos) and someone apparently selected by Paul himself whose relationship to Paul was longstanding and intimate (Timothy). In other words, the composition of the delegation represented something of a compromise between Paul and the churches.

> 5. If the two "brothers" are Apollos and Timothy, we now know more about the politics at work in the early church.

We know that it involved compromise and perhaps what would today be characterized as "horse-trading." Further, it appears that Paul and others who were involved were amenable to if not enthusiastic about such compromise and "horse-trading."

In short, identifying the two "brothers" of 2 Cor 8:18–24 as Apollos and Timothy enables us to fill in some important gaps in our knowledge regarding (a) Apollos, (b) Timothy, (c) Apollos' relationship to Paul, (d) the offering, and (e) politics in the early church.

Chapter 11

Romans 8:29–30 as a Non-Pauline Interpolation

J. C. O'Neill on Rom 8:28c–30, 33

More than thirty-five years ago, J. C. O'Neill maintained that Rom 8:28c–30 and Rom 8:33 are two parts of a "comment"—or, as I prefer, a non-Pauline "interpolation"[1]—that was added to the text by a later glossator or editor.[2] The material in question reads as follows:

> τοῖς κατὰ πρόθεσιν κλητοῖς οὖσιν. ὅτι οὓς προέγνω καὶ προώρισεν συμμόρφους τῆς εἰκόνος τοῦ υἱοῦ αὐτοῦ εἰς τὸ εἶναι αὐτὸν πρωτότοκον ἐν πολλοῖς ἀδελφοῖς. οὓς δὲ προώρισεν τούτους καὶ ἐκάλεσεν, καὶ οὓς ἐκάλεσεν τούτους καὶ ἐδικαίωσεν, οὓς δὲ ἐδικαίωσεν τούτους καὶ ἐδόξασεν. . . . τίς ἐγκαλέσει κατὰ ἐκλεκτῶν Θεοῦ; Θεὸς ὁ δικαιῶν.

O'Neill viewed v. 28c (τοῖς κατὰ πρόθεσιν κλητοῖς οὖσιν) as the interpolator's expansion and clarification of the authentically Pauline v. 28a (τοῖς ἀγαπῶσιν τὸν Θεόν),[3] and, although he did not say so, he apparently regarded vv. 29–30 as simply a fuller development of v. 28c (τοῖς κατὰ πρόθεσιν κλητοῖς οὖσιν). Labeling v. 33 (τίς ἐγκαλέσει κατὰ ἐκλεκτῶν Θεοῦ; Θεὸς ὁ δικαιῶν), then, as an "addition of the predestinarian commentator responsible

---

"Romans 8:29–30 as a Non-Pauline Interpolation." *JSPL* 2,1 (Spring 2012) 27–40. Copyright © 2012 Eisenbrauns, Inc. Reprinted with permission.

1. By "non-Pauline" I mean neither composed by Paul nor included at this point in the Roman letter by Paul.
2. O'Neill, *Paul's Letter to the Romans*, 126, 142–43.
3. O'Neill, *Paul's Letter to the Romans*, 142: "this is a definition of those who love God from God's point of view, as it were."

for vv. 28c–30," he saw v. 34a (τίς ὁ κατακρινῶν;) as "the original [authentically Pauline] rhetorical question," which "takes up v. 1 (οὐδὲν ἄρα νῦν κατάκριμα τοῖς ἐν Χριστῷ Ἰησοῦ), with which the argument began."[4] O'Neill offered no explanation, however, as to why the interpolation was divided into two parts (vv. 28c–30 and v. 33), separated by vv. 31–32, or, indeed, why the second part of the interpolation was needed at all.

O'Neill presented little by way of evidence for viewing Rom 8:28c–30, 33 as a non-Pauline interpolation, simply asserting that "there is a logical contradiction between the first part of v. 28 and [the] comment in vv. 28c–30 that is so great that we can scarcely believe that one man was responsible for both."[5] According to O'Neill, Rom 8:28c–30 "says Christians are predestined from the beginning" while the remainder of chap. 8 "assumes that men may choose whether or not they will receive the Spirit by faith (cf. Gal. 3.1–5) and that those the Apostle is addressing have so chosen."[6] More specifically:

> To love God [τοῖς ἀγαπῶσιν τὸν Θεόν in v. 28c] implies a free choice of God that could have gone the other way, but the election of some men and not others by God implies that they had no choice. . . . Love knows that it is called by God and is unworthy of God, but if love knows that it had no choice it could not go on being love. . . . The commentator got a foothold in Paul's argument because Paul is emphasizing the great hope of which Christians can be assured. The commentator took this certainty for his sort of certainty, the certainty of what could never possibly have been otherwise.[7]

---

4. O'Neill, *Paul's Letter to the Romans*, 143.
5. O'Neill, *Paul's Letter to the Romans*, 142.
6. O'Neill, *Paul's Letter to the Romans*, 136.
7. O'Neill, *Paul's Letter to the Romans*, 142–43. See also p. 136: "Paul's emphasis on the certainty of the Spirit's witness that they are in fact children of God (v. 16) has provided the commentator with some grounds for introducing the doctrine of predestination, which leaves no room for genuine human choice."

So far as I am aware, no one has agreed with O'Neill in print, nor, however, has anyone attempted to refute his argument.[8] My own judgment is that, strictly speaking, he was correct in seeing a "logical contradiction" between vv. 28c–30, 33, and the surrounding material. It would be difficult to argue, however, that Paul does not elsewhere espouse some form of a doctrine of election[9] or that he does not elsewhere alternate between divine and human agency.[10] In any case, the imposition of a theological or logical "straightjacket" on Paul is risky at best. Thus, in my view, O'Neill has by no means provided adequate grounds for labeling the material in question a non-Pauline interpolation. His observations do, however, raise a legitimate question as to whether this material "fits" either at its present location in Paul's Roman letter or, for that matter, anywhere within the corpus of Paul's authentic writings. This, in turn, leads to the more general question regarding the origin of the material.

In the present study, it is my intention to argue that O'Neill was, for the most part,[11] correct in viewing Rom 8:28c–30, 33 as a non-Pauline interpolation and to present additional evidence to support a slightly revised version of his view. I cannot, of course, *prove* that the material in question is an interpolation. It is my judgment, however, that the evidence to be presented, when weighed

---

8. To be sure, more than three decades earlier, Hawkins (*Recovery of the Historical Paul*, 114–15), had included Rom 8:29–30 as part of a larger interpolation, but he provided very little by way of evidence to support his argument. Jewett (*Romans: A Commentary*, 985–1011) finds only two interpolations in Romans (16:17–20a and 16:25–27). In discussing Rom 8:28–30 (pp. 526–41), he makes no mention of the possibility of interpolation.

9. See, e.g., 1 Thess 1:4; 1 Cor 1:24, 26–29; Gal 1:15–16; Rom 9:11. It should be noted, however, that O'Neill (*Paul's Letter to the Romans*, 154–55, see also 148–51) regards Rom 9:11 as part of a non-Pauline interpolation.

10. E.g., 1 Cor 8:2–3; 13:12 (which may, however, be part of a non-Pauline interpolation; see Walker, *Interpolations*, 147–65); Phil 2:12–13.

11. See directly below for my own modification of O'Neill's position.

carefully and *cumulatively*, is sufficient to establish this as, at the very least, a plausible possibility.

The Extent of the Interpolation

As already noted, O'Neill saw the proposed interpolation as consisting of two parts: vv. 28c–30 and v. 33, separated by vv. 31–32. In my own judgment, however, the evidence for interpolation is less clear for vv. 28c and 33 than it is for vv. 29–30.

Verse 28c speaks of "those being called according to [God's] purpose" (τοῖς κατὰ πρόθεσιν κλητοῖς οὖσιν). In the very next chapter of Romans (9:11), Paul refers to the purpose of God [that works] according to election" (ἡ κατ᾽ ἐκλογὴν πρόθεσις τοῦ Θεοῦ). The word πρόθεσις appears both in 8:28c and in 9:11, and, although 8:28c apparently refers to individuals while 9:11 has Israel in mind, the basic idea is essentially the same in both verses.[12] Moreover, κλητός appears six times elsewhere in the undisputed Pauline letters (Rom 1:1, 6, 7; 1 Cor 1:1, 2, 24),[13] including four times in the plural (Rom 1:6, 7; 1 Cor 1:2, 24) and once in the plural with the article (1 Cor 1:24) as in Rom 8:28c. Thus it might appear difficult to argue that either the vocabulary or the theology of Rom 8:28c is non-Pauline.

The following points, however, should be noted: (1) Πρόθεσις appears *only* at Rom 8:28c and 9:11 in the undisputed Pauline letters,[14] but it appears *four times* in the pseudo-Pauline letters (Eph 1:11; 3:11; 2 Tim 1:9; 3:10) including twice in the phrase κατὰ πρόθεσιν (Eph 1:11 and 3:11; see also κατὰ ἰδίαν πρόθεσιν in 2 Tim 1:9). In addition, the phrase κατὰ πρόθεσιν is associ-

---

12. As has already been noted (in n. 9), however, O'Neill (*Paul's Letter to the Romans*, 154–55, see also 148–51) regards Rom 9:11 as part of a non-Pauline interpolation.

13. For purposes of the present study, I am assuming that the undisputed Pauline letters are 1 Thessalonians, 1 Corinthians, 2 Corinthians, Galatians, Philippians, Philemon, and Romans (the authenticity of Philippians has, however, occasionally been questioned).

14. As has already been noted (in n. 9 above), O'Neill (*Paul's Letter to the Romans*, 154–55, see also 148–51) regards Rom 9:11 as part of a non-Pauline interpolation.

ated with the verb προορίζειν both in Rom 8:28c–30 (κατὰ πρόθεσιν in v. 28c and προώρισεν in vv. 29 and 30) and in Eph 1:11 (προορισθέντες κατὰ πρόθεσιν). Thus, the word πρόθεσις and the phrase κατὰ πρόθεσιν, particularly in association with the verb προορίζειν, would appear to be more typically pseudo-Pauline than Pauline. (2) In the undisputed Pauline letters, *only* Rom 8:28c and 1 Cor 1:24 use κλητός absolutely, without some indication of the nature of the calling; elsewhere, it is κλητὸς ἀπόστολος (Rom 1:1; 1 Cor 1:1), κλητοὶ Ἰησοῦ Χριστοῦ (Rom 1:6), or κλητοῖς ἁγίοις (Rom 1:7; 1 Cor 1:2). (3) As already indicated, τοῖς κατὰ πρόθεσιν κλητοῖς οὖσιν is apparently intended to expand and clarify the τοῖς ἀγαπῶσιν τὸ Θεόν of v. 28a, but it can also be seen as a bridge, created by an interpolator, between the Pauline v. 28ab and the non-Pauline vv. 29–30.

On balance, therefore, the evidence appears to point against Pauline authorship of v. 28c. Nevertheless, because the evidence is somewhat ambiguous, I have decided not to include v. 28c in the present study.

The situation is somewhat different regarding v. 33, which poses the rhetorical question τίς ἐγκαλέσει κατὰ ἐκλεκτῶν Θεοῦ; and answers the question Θεὸς ὁ δικαιῶν. The verb ἐγκαλεῖν is a *hapax legomenon* in the Pauline corpus,[15] and ἐκλεκτός appears elsewhere in the undisputed Pauline letters only at Rom 16:13, where it refers to Rufus as "the elect one in the Lord" (τὸν ἐκλεκτὸν ἐν κυρίῳ). Moreover, ἐκλεκτός appears four times in the pseudo-Pauline writings (Col 3:12; 1 Tim 5:21; 2 Tim 2:10; Titus 1:1), and the phrase ἐκλεκτοὶ τοῦ Θεοῦ appears in the pseudo-Pauline Col 3:12 and Titus 1:1. Thus the vocabulary of v. 33a would appear not to be typically Pauline. In addition, v. 33a is redundant in light of v. 34a, which asks essentially the same rhetorical question: τίς ὁ κατακρινῶν; Clearly, however, both the vocabulary and the theology of v. 33b (Θεὸς ὁ δικαιῶν) are characteristically Pauline.

---

15. Elsewhere in the NT, it appears only at Acts 19:38, 40; 23:28, 29; 26:2, 7. In all except the first two instances, it refers to charges brought against Paul.

Therefore, I am strongly tempted to include v. 33a but not v. 33b in the proposed interpolation and to link v. 33b to v. 34a: Θεὸς ὁ δικαιῶν. τίς ὁ κατακρινῶν; Nevertheless, because the evidence is divided and because v. 33 is separated from vv. 29–30 by the intervening vv. 31–32, I have decided not to include any of v. 33 in the present study.

The Absence of Direct Text-Critical Evidence for Interpolation

The strongest possible evidence for interpolation, of course, would be direct text-critical evidence—i.e., the absence of a passage from one or more of the ancient manuscripts or perhaps the location of the verses at different places in the text. It must be acknowledged that such evidence is lacking in the case of Rom 8:29–30, which appears in all of the extant manuscripts and, indeed, at the same location in all of the manuscripts. It is far from clear, however, that text-critical considerations such as this should finally be decisive in determining whether a particular passage is or is not an interpolation. The presence of a passage in all extant manuscripts means only that the passage was a part of the text by around the end of the second century;[16] it says nothing about whether it was included earlier or, if so, how much earlier. Indeed, the fact that a passage appears in *all* of the surviving manuscripts may mean simply (a) that, once the passage had been introduced as an interpolation, subsequent scribes would have been unwilling to omit it because to do so would have meant overlooking something that might, indeed, have come from Paul and (b) that manuscripts lacking the passage would then have been regarded as defective and therefore discarded or even destroyed. Moreover, the period between the composition of the Pauline letters (mid-first century) and the latter part of the second century was a time of considerable controversy within the church, some of which involved Paul and his letters, and would appear, therefore, to be precisely the

---

16. P[46], which is generally regarded as the earliest extant manuscript of the Pauline letters, is most often dated ca. 200 CE.

period during which the letters would have been most susceptible to textual alteration.[17] Thus, "the absence of direct text-critical evidence for interpolation must be seen as precisely what it is: the *absence* of evidence, which, in the face of otherwise compelling evidence *for* interpolation, should not be allowed to decide the issue."[18] It is my judgment that there is in fact "otherwise compelling evidence" for regarding Rom 8:29–30 as a non-Pauline interpolation, and it is to this evidence that I now turn.

Contextual Evidence for Interpolation

Romans 8:29–30 stands out from its immediate context in at least six respects. In the first place, as has already been noted, there appears to be something of a "logical contradiction" between these verses, which speak of God's predestination, and the surrounding material, which appears to assume human freedom.[19]

In the second place, the "person" and "number" indicated in the verbs and pronouns of vv. 29–30 are different from those in the surrounding material. Verse 28 begins with the *first-person plural* verb οἴδαμεν, and v. 31 begins with τί οὖν ἐροῦμεν (also a *first-person plural* verb) πρὸς ταῦτα; Moreover, most of the language in vv. 1–27 and much of that in vv. 31–39 is in the *first-person plural*—"we" and "us."[20] All of the finite verbs in vv. 29–30, however, are in the *third-person singular* ("he"), with God as the implied subject. It is quite possible, of course, that Paul himself might have moved from first-person plural to third-person singular and then back to first-person plural. Indeed, the fact that v. 28ab (presumably Pauline in origin) shifts from the first-person plural to the third-

---

17. We know, for example, that the second-century "heretic" Marcion used a collection of Pauline letters that differed significantly from the one accepted by his opponents.

18. Walker, *Interpolations*, 55; for a full discussion of the issue, see 44–56.

19. This would be particularly the case if vv. 28c and 33 were included in the proposed interpolation.

20. Verses 9–11, however, employ the second-person plural.

person singular would appear to argue against such a shift as evidence for interpolation. Nevertheless, the overall difference in this regard between vv. 29–30 and the surrounding material, particularly when viewed in conjunction with other evidence pointing in the same direction, at least suggests that these verses may be an insertion into the text of Paul's Roman letter.

In the third place, the systematic, linear, repetitive, formalized, and one might almost say "scholastic" manner in which vv. 29–30 spell out the progression from foreknowledge to predestination to calling to justification to glorification differs markedly from the style of the surrounding material,[21] which is much less formal and repetitive and much more free-flowing.[22] Moreover, it is without parallel elsewhere in the undisputed Pauline letters.[23] Again, this may be an indication that vv. 29–30 represent a secondary insertion into the text.

In the fourth place, there appears to be something of a disjunction between vv. 29–30 and their context in terms of subject matter. It is difficult to assemble the somewhat disparate parts of Romans 8 under a single topic, but frequent references to the Spirit in vv. 1–27 have led various scholars to identify the overriding theme of chap. 8 as "a life characterized by the indwelling of God's Spirit"[24] or simply "life in the Spirit."[25] There are, however, no references whatsoever to the Spirit in vv. 29–30, and this would appear to indicate a disjunction between these verses and the remainder of the chapter in terms of subject matter. It must be noted, however,

---

21. Cranfield (*Critical and Exegetical Commentary on Romans*, 1.431–33) refers to "links" in a "fivefold chain." Similarly, Byrne (*Romans*, 268) speaks of "a step-by-step sequence." Fitzmyer (*Romans: A New Translation*, 524–25) refers to "five steps" but cautions that Paul's "anthropomorphic language should not be too facilely transposed into the *signa rationis* of later theological systems of predestination."

22. A possible exception is vv. 35, 38–39.

23. Byrne (*Romans*, 268) suggests, however, that the "step-by-step sequence" is "reminiscent of [Rom] 5:3–4."

24. Cranfield, *Critical and Exegetical Commentary on Romans*, 1.370–444.

25. Sanday and Headlam, *Critical and Exegetical Commentary on Romans*, 189; Myers, "Romans," 823.

that the Spirit is also not mentioned in the verses immediately following 29–30 (vv. 31–39). Thus, the absence of such references in vv. 29–30 indicates a disjunction between these verses and the immediately preceding verses (vv. 1–27) but not between these verses and the remainder of the chapter (vv. 31–39). It would be impossible to argue on the basis of subject matter *alone* that Rom 8:29–30 is an interpolation, but the shift in subject matter between vv. 1–28 and vv. 29–30 is nevertheless worthy of note.

In the fifth place, the removal of vv. 29–30 would leave a smooth transition from v. 28—οἴδαμεν δὲ ὅτι τοῖς ἀγαπῶσιν τὸν Θεὸν πάντα συνεργεῖ [ὁ Θεὸς] εἰς ἀγαθόν, τοῖς κατὰ πρόθεσιν κλητοῖς οὖσιν, either with or without the last five words—to v. 31— τί οὖν ἐροῦμεν πρὸς ταῦτα; εἰ Θεὸς ὑπὲρ ἡμῶν, τίς κατ' ἡμῶν;

In the sixth place, and finally, except for the opening word, ὅτι, vv. 29–30 can stand alone as a complete, self-contained, and meaningful theological statement that sets forth, in systematic fashion, a logical progression from foreknowledge to predestination to calling to justification to glorification.

In short, a number of features of Rom 8:29–30 suggest that it does not "fit" at its present location in Paul's Roman letter. Viewed separately, each of these features can perhaps be explained without recourse to an interpolation hypothesis. It is my judgment, however, that their *cumulative* weight makes such an explanation highly problematic. It might also be possible to explain some or even all of these features by arguing that the verses represent a "digression" on the part of Paul or that he is here citing a pre-Pauline creedal formula—perhaps one with which he himself was not necessarily in full agreement.[26] This appears unlikely, however, because there is no apparent reason for such a digression or citation at this point in the Roman letter—i.e., the subject matter of the verses has little if any apparent relation to that of the surrounding material.[27]

---

26. See, e.g., Rom 1:3–4 and perhaps Phil 2:6–11.
27. This would be particularly the case if v. 28c were also regarded as part of the proposed interpolation.

My own conclusion, therefore, is that vv. 29–30 most likely represent a later addition to the text. This conclusion, however, does not answer the question of authorship, because the material could have been Pauline in origin but composed for a different setting and later inserted at its present location in Romans. To decide the question of authorship, it is necessary to examine the vocabulary of the verses and, at the same time, some of the ideas associated with this vocabulary.

Linguistic Evidence for Interpolation
Statistics

Romans 8:29–30 contains a total of thirty-seven words, but twenty-three of these are either conjunctions, relative pronouns, definite articles, personal pronouns, demonstrative pronouns, prepositions, or a form of the verb "to be."[28] In addition, one of the thirty-seven words is the quite-ordinary noun υἱός (in the genitive singular), and one is the very common adjective πολύς (in the masculine dative plural). This leaves only twelve words—nouns, adjectives, and verbs—that might be relevant for determining whether the vocabulary of Rom 8:29–30 is Pauline or non-Pauline. Of these twelve words, however, three (προορίζειν, καλεῖν, and δικαιοῦν) appear twice. Thus, there are only nine *different* words in Rom 8:29–30 that might indicate Pauline or non-Pauline vocabulary.

Of the nine words in Rom 8:29–30 that might indicate Pauline or non-Pauline vocabulary, one (πρωτότοκος) appears nowhere else in the undisputed Pauline letters, and three (προγινώσκειν, προορίζειν, and σύμμορφος) appear only once elsewhere in the undisputed letters.[29] Moreover, as will be demonstrated below, two of the nine (ἀδελφός and δοξάζειν) are used in ways that

---

28. Conjunctions: ὅτι, καί (five times), and δέ (twice). Relative pronouns: οὕς (four times). Definite articles: τῆς, τοῦ, and τό. Personal pronouns: αὐτοῦ and αὐτόν. Demonstrative pronouns: τούτους (three times). Prepositions: εἰς and ἐν. Verb of being: εἶναι.

29. Προγινώσκειν: Rom 11:2. προορίζειν: 1 Cor 2:7. σύμμορφος: Phil 3:21.

appear not to be typically Pauline. Thus, only three of the nine different words that might indicate Pauline or non-Pauline vocabulary (εἰκών, καλεῖν, and δικαιοῦν) can be regarded as *characteristically* Pauline. Moreover, as will also be demonstrated below, none of these is *distinctively* Pauline. In short, *there is no distinctively Pauline vocabulary in Rom 8:29–30, very little characteristically Pauline vocabulary, and a preponderance of what would appear to be non-Pauline vocabulary.*

These bare statistics alone, in my judgment, are sufficient to call into serious question the Pauline authorship of Rom 8:29–30. A detailed examination of each of the nine relevant words, however, would appear virtually to rule out such authorship. I now turn, therefore, to this examination.

Linguistic Evidence for Interpolation
Individual Words

The word προγινώσκειν appears only once elsewhere in the undisputed Pauline letters. Rom 11:2 declares that "God has not rejected his people whom he foreknew (προέγνω)." There is a significant difference, however, between Rom 8:29–30 and Romans 9–11: the latter is speaking of the nation Israel, while the former appears to be speaking of individuals. Thus, the single appearance of προγινώσκειν elsewhere in the undisputed Pauline letters would appear to have little relevance for the question of whether Rom 8:29–30 is non-Pauline in origin. In addition, it should be noted that *all* of the other occurrences of the words in the New Testament are in non-Pauline and, indeed, post-Pauline writings.[30]

The word προορίζειν, like προγινώσκειν, appears only once elsewhere in the undisputed Pauline letters. In 1 Cor 2:7, it refers to "a secret and hidden wisdom of God, which God decreed (προώρισεν) before the ages." This verse may, however, be part of a non-Pauline interpolation (1 Cor 2:6–16) and thus not relevant

---

30. 1 Pet 1:20 (Christ was "foreknown before the foundation of the world"); 2 Pet 3:17 (the readers, having been warned, "foreknow"); Acts 26:5 (the Jews "foreknew" Paul's piety as a practicing Jew).

in terms of identifying Pauline vocabulary.[31] In any case, the reference here is to "wisdom," not to people as in Rom 8:29. Thus, as in the case of προγινώσκειν, the single appearance of προορίζειν elsewhere in the undisputed Pauline letters would seem to have little relevance for the question of whether Rom 8:29–30 is non-Pauline in origin. Moreover, it is noteworthy that the word appears elsewhere in the New Testament only in post-Pauline writings.[32]

Particularly significant, however, is the fact that προορίζειν appears in the pseudo-Pauline Eph 1:11. Here, the author states that he and his readers "were appointed and predestined (προορισθέντες) according to the purpose" (κατὰ πρόθεσιν) of God.[33] Earlier, in Eph 1:5, the author declares that God has "predestined" him and his readers "unto sonship" (προορίσας ἡμᾶς εἰς υἱοθεσίαν). This, of course, is reminiscent of the reference in Rom 8:29 to "firstborn among many brothers" (πρωτότοκον ἐν πολλοῖς ἀδελφοῖς). Thus, the vocabulary—and with it the thought world—of Rom 8:29–30 appears at this point to be related to that of Ephesians and, like προγινώσκειν, to point to a post-Pauline point of view.

The word σύμμορφος, like προγινώσκειν and προορίζειν, appears only once elsewhere in the undisputed Pauline letters and not at all elsewhere in the New Testament. In Phil 3:10, σύμμορφος refers to "our lowly body" (τὸ σῶμα τῆς ταπεινώσεως ἡμῶν) being transformed "to be similar in form" (σύμμορφον) to Jesus Christ's "glorious body" (τῷ σώματι τῆς δόξης αὐτοῦ).[34] This, of course, is somewhat akin to what is said in Rom 8:29. It should be noted, however, that the syntactical construction is different in Rom 8:29, where συμμόρφους is followed by the *genitive* of that to which people are to be made "similar in form"; in Phil 3:10, how-

---

31. See Walker, *Interpolations*, 127–46.
32. Eph 1:5, 11; Acts 4:28.
33. Here, προορίζειν and πρόθεσις are juxtaposed as in Rom 8:28c–29; moreover, the same prepositional phrase, κατὰ πρόθεσιν, appears in both Eph 1:11 and Rom 8:28c. This may lend support to O'Neill's view that Rom 8:28c is part of the proposed interpolation.
34. See also Phil 3:10, where the verb συμμορφίζειν ("to make similar in form") refers to becoming like Christ in his death.

ever, σύμμορφον is followed by the *dative* of that to which "our lowly body" is to be "similar in form." This raises the question of why Paul would use two different syntactical constructions to express the same idea and suggests that there may actually be two different authors involved.[35] Thus, the appearance of σύμμορφος both in Rom 8:29 and in Phil 3:10 may have little relevance in terms of identifying Pauline vocabulary, and the word does not appear elsewhere in the undisputed Pauline letters.

The word εἰκών appears six times elsewhere in the undisputed Pauline letters. It refers in Rom 1:23 to an "image of a corruptible human" (εἰκόνος φθαρτοῦ ἀνθρώπου); in 1 Cor 11:7 to the male (ἀνήρ) as the "image and glory of God" (εἰκὼν καὶ δόξα Θεοῦ); and in 2 Cor 4:4 to Christ as the "image of God" (εἰκὼν τοῦ Θεοῦ).[36] None of these three references parallels the use of εἰκών in Rom 8:29, which speaks of "the image of his [God's] son" (τῆς εἰκόνος τοῦ υἱοῦ αὐτοῦ). In 1 Cor 15:49, however, Paul says that "just as we have borne the image (τὴν εἰκόνα) of the earthly one ["the first Adam"], we shall also bear the image (τὴν εἰκόνα) of the heavenly one" ["the last Adam" or Christ]. Moreover, 2 Cor 3:18 speaks of Christians "being changed into the same image" (τὴν αὐτὴν εἰκόνα), presumably meaning the image of the Lord. Thus, the appearance of εἰκών in Rom 8:29 might serve as an argument for Pauline authorship.

It should be noted, however, that εἰκών appears sixteen times elsewhere in the New Testament—once in Matthew, once in Mark, once in Luke, twice in Colossians, once in Hebrews, and ten times in Revelation.[37] Thus, while it may be regarded as, at least to some degree, a *characteristically* Pauline word, it is by no means *distinctively* Pauline. Moreover, the appearance of εἰκών in the pseudo-Pauline Col 1:15 may provide some evidence of a post-Pauline

---

35. It should be noted, however, that Pauline authorship of Philippians—either in whole or in part—has occasionally been questioned; for a brief discussion, see, e.g., Fitzgerald, "Philippians," 319–20.

36. 1 Cor 11:7 may, however, be part of a non-Pauline interpolation (11:3–16); see Walker, *Interpolations*, 90–126.

37. Matt 22:20; Mark 12:16; Luke 20:24 (synoptic parallels); Col 1:15; 3:30; Heb 10:1; Rev 13:14, 15 (three times); 14:9, 11; 15:2; 16:2; 19:20; 20:4.

milieu. Colossians 1:15 speaks of Christ as the "image of the invisible God" (εἰκὼν τοῦ Θεοῦ ἀοράτου) and the "firstborn of all creation" (πρωτότοκος πάσης κτίσεως). Here, the appearance of both εἰκών and πρωτότοκος is, of course, reminiscent of Rom 8:29, where both terms also appear. To be sure, the genitives following the terms are different—"image of his son" in Rom 8:29 and "image of the invisible God" in Col 1:15 and "firstborn among many brothers" in Rom 8:29 and "firstborn of all creation" in Col 1:15. Nevertheless, the appearance of both εἰκών and πρωτότοκος in both Rom 8:29 and Col 1:15 suggests that the vocabulary of Rom 8:29 and that of Col 1:15 are in some sense related.

The word πρωτότοκος appears nowhere else in the undisputed Pauline letters, but it does appear, with essentially the same signification, in the post-Pauline Col 1:15, 18;[38] Heb 1:6; and Rev 1:5.[39] In Col 1:15, 18, God's "beloved son" (v. 13: ὁ υἱὸς τῆς ἀγάπης αὐτοῦ) is referred to as "firstborn of all creation" (πρωτότοκος πάσης κτίσεως) and "firstborn from the dead" (πρωτότοκος ἐκ τῶν νεκρῶν). More succinctly, Heb 1:6 refers to God's "son" (υἱός in vv. 2, 5) simply as "the firstborn" (ὁ πρωτότοκος). Finally, in Rev 1:5, Jesus Christ is spoken of as "the firstborn of the dead" (πρωτότοκος τῶν νεκρῶν). It may be significant that in Rom 8:29, Col 1:15, 18, and Heb 1:6—but not in Rev 1:5—it is specifically God's "son" (υἱός) who is referred to as πρωτότοκος. This may suggest some connection among the passages.[40] Particularly noteworthy is the fact, already noted, that the vocabulary—and thus the thought world—of Rom 8:29–30 appears at this point to be related to the vocabulary—and thus the thought world—of pseudo-Pauline Colossians.

---

38. Although some debate continues regarding the authorship of Colossians, it is widely regarded, correctly in my judgment, as pseudo-Pauline.

39. Elsewhere in the NT, πρωτότοκος occurs only at Luke 2:7 (with reference to Jesus as the firstborn son of Mary), Heb 11:28 (with reference to the firstborn humans and animals in Egypt at the time of the Exodus), and Heb 12:23 (with reference to an "assembly of the firstborn enrolled in heaven" (ἐκκλησίᾳ πρωτοτόκων ἀπογεγραμμένων ἐν οὐρανοῖς).

40. Jewett (*Romans: A Commentary*, 529) refers to "liturgical parallels" among Rom 8:29; Col 1:15, 18; and Heb 1:1–6.

Not only, however, does πρωτότοκος not appear elsewhere in the undisputed Pauline letters, but Paul himself, in one of the undisputed letters, expresses essentially the same idea with a quite-different word: ἀπαρχή ("first fruits"). In 1 Cor 15:20, 23, Christ, having been raised from the dead, is characterized as the "first fruits of those who have fallen asleep" (ἀπαρχὴ τῶν κεκοιμένων) and the "first fruits" (ἀπαρχή) of those who "shall be made alive" (ζωοποιηθήσονται). It is possible, of course, that Paul used ἀπαρχή in 1 Cor 15:20, 23 and πρωτότοκος in Rom 8:29 to express essentially the same idea, but, given the fact that he elsewhere uses ἀπαρχή four times—three of them in Romans[41]— and πρωτότοκος not at all, it is at least equally possible that πρωτότοκος in Rom 8:29 is to be attributed to someone other than Paul. Moreover, the fact that post-Pauline writings—Colossians, Hebrews, and Revelation—express essentially the same idea with πρωτότοκος, not ἀπαρχή, suggests a post-Pauline hand also at Rom 8:29. In short, it may well be the case that the notion of Christ as "firstborn" (πρωτότοκος) is a post-Pauline notion that appears at Rom 8:29 only because a later interpolator placed it there.

The word ἀδελφός appears in Rom 8:29, which refers to God's son as "firstborn among many brothers" (πρωτότοκον ἐν πολλοῖς ἀδελφοῖς). The word is found a total of 113 times in the undisputed Pauline letters—thirty-one times in the singular and eighty-two times in the plural. In the singular, it refers once to James as "the brother of the Lord," seven times to some other named member of the Christian community, six times to a particular member of the community whose name is not stated, and seventeen times simply to any member of the community.[42] In the plural, it overwhelmingly appears in the vocative case indi-

---

41. Not, however, with reference to Christ: Rom 8:23; 11:16; 16:5; 1 Cor 16:15.

42. *James*: Gal 1:19. *Named Christians*: Quartus (Rom 16:23), Sosthenes (1 Cor 1:1), Apollos (1 Cor 16:12), Titus (2 Cor 2:13), Timothy (2 Cor 1:1; 1 Thess 3:2; Phlm 1), Epaphroditus (Phil 2:25). *Unnamed member of the community*: 2 Cor 8:18, 22; 12:18; Phlm 7 (Philemon), 16 (Onesimus), 20 (Philemon). *Any member of the community*: Rom 14:10 (twice), 13, 15, 21; 1 Cor 5:11; 6:5, 6 (twice); 7:12, 14, 15; 8:11, 13 (twice); 2 Cor 2:13; 1 Thess 4:6.

cating the people whom Paul is addressing—that is, members of the Christian community.[43] Otherwise, it refers once to "the brothers of the Lord," once to Paul's fellow Jews, and seventeen times simply to unnamed members of the community.[44] Apart from Rom 8:29, however, the Pauline writings *never* speak of Christians believers as "brothers" *of Christ* but only as "brothers" *of one another*. Thus, the reference in Rom 8:29 to God's "son" as "firstborn among many brothers" (πρωτότοκον ἐν πολλοῖς ἀδελφοῖς) would appear to be non-Pauline. It should be noted, further, that Heb 2:11–17—clearly non-Pauline—does refer to Christians as "brothers" (ἀδελφόι) of Jesus. In short, the idea of Christians as "brothers" of Jesus/Christ appears to be a post-Pauline notion.

The word καλεῖν appears twice in Rom 8:30 and twenty-five times elsewhere in the undisputed Pauline letters—six times in Romans, twelve times in 1 Corinthians, four times in Galatians, and three times in 1 Thessalonians,[45] but, interestingly, not at all in 2 Corinthians, Philippians, or Philemon. It must, therefore, be regarded as a *characteristically* Pauline word. Because, however, it also occurs very frequently elsewhere in the New Testament,[46] it can by no means be seen as a *distinctively* Pauline term.

Of the six occurrences of καλεῖν in Romans, five are clustered in chap. 9, which is part of Paul's discussion of Israel and the gos-

---

43. Rom 1:13; 7:1, 4; 8:12; 10:1; 11:25; 12:1; 15:14, 30; 16:17; 1 Cor 1:10, 11, 26; 2:1; 3:1; 4:6; 7:24, 29; 10:1; 11:33; 12:1; 14:6, 20, 26, 39; 15:1, 31, 50, 58; 16:15; 2 Cor 1:8; 8:1; 13:11; Gal 1:11; 3:15; 4:12, 28, 31; 5:11, 13; 6:1, 18; Phil 1:12; 3:1, 13, 17; 4:1, 8; 1 Thess 1:4; 2:1, 9, 14, 17; 3:7; 4:1, 10, 13; 5:1, 4, 12, 14, 25.

44. *Brothers of the Lord*: 1 Cor 9:5. *Fellow Jews*: Rom 9:3. *Unnamed members of the community*: Rom 16:14; 1 Cor 6:8; 8:12; 15:6; 16:11, 12, 20; 2 Cor 8:23; 9:3, 5; 11:9; Gal 1:2; Phil 1:14; 4:21; 1 Thess 4:10; 5:26, 27.

45. Rom 4:17; 9:7, 12, 24, 25, 26; 1 Cor 1:9; 7:15, 17, 18 (twice), 20, 21, 22 (twice), 24; 10:27; 15:9; Gal 1:6, 15; 5:8, 13; 1 Thess 2:12; 4:7; 5:24.

46. Twenty-six times in Matthew, four times in Mark, forty-three times in Luke, twice in John, eighteen times in Acts, twice in Ephesians, twice in Colossians, once in 2 Thessalonians, once in 1 Timothy, once in 2 Timothy, six times in Hebrews, once in James, six times in 1 Peter, once in 2 Peter, once in 1 John, and seven times in Revelation. The only non-Pauline writings in which it does not appear are Titus, 2 John, 3 John, and Jude.

pel.[47] Otherwise, apart from Rom 8:30, καλεῖν appears in Romans only at 4:17, where it refers to God as the one who "calls into existence the things that do not exist" (τοῦ . . . καλοῦντος τὰ μὴ ὄντα ὡς ὄντα). Thus, it would appear that the use of καλεῖν in Rom 8:30 with reference to God's "calling" of individuals may not be typically Pauline, at least so far as the Roman letter is concerned. In almost all appearances of καλεῖν elsewhere in the undisputed Pauline letters, however, it does refer to God's "calling" of individuals, either to Christian faith or to special service within the church.[48]

In short, the appearance of καλεῖν in Rom 8:30 provides little if any evidence *against* Pauline authorship, but nor, because of its widespread occurrence elsewhere in the New Testament, does it provide evidence *for* Pauline authorship.

The word δικαιοῦν appears in Rom 8:30 and twenty-four times elsewhere in the undisputed Pauline letters—fourteen times in Romans, twice in 1 Corinthians, and eight times in Galatians,[49] but, interestingly, not at all in 2 Corinthians, Philippians, 1 Thessalonians, or Philemon. Like καλεῖν, therefore it must be regarded as a *characteristically* Pauline word. Unlike καλεῖν, however, it occurs relatively infrequently elsewhere in the New Testament—a total of only fourteen times.[50] Thus, its appearance in Rom 8:30 might be regarded as an argument *for* Pauline authorship or at least for Pauline influence.

The word δοξάζειν appears in Rom 8:30 and eight times elsewhere in the undisputed Pauline letters—four times in Romans, twice in 1 Corinthians, three times in 2 Corinthians, and once

---

47. It should be noted that O'Neill (*Paul's Letter to the Romans*, 145–91) regards much of Romans 9–11 as non-Pauline.

48. Exceptions are 1 Cor 10:27, where it refers to being "invited" to dinner, and perhaps Gal 1:6, where it refers either to God or to Paul as the one who "called" the Galatian Christians.

49. Rom 2:13; 3:4, 20, 24, 26, 28, 30; 4:2, 5; 5:1, 9; 6:7; 8:33; 1 Cor 4:4; 6:11; Gal 2:16 (three times), 17; 3:8, 11, 24; 5:4.

50. Twice in Matthew, five times in Luke, twice in Acts, once in 1 Timothy, once in Titus, and three times in James.

in Galatians,⁵¹ but, interestingly, not at all in Philippians, 1 Thessalonians, or Philemon. Like καλεῖν and δικαιοῦν, therefore, it must be regarded as a *characteristically* Pauline word. Like καλεῖν and unlike δικαιοῦν, however it also occurs rather frequently elsewhere in the New Testament⁵² and can, therefore, by no means be seen as a *distinctively* Pauline term.

Within the undisputed Pauline letters, δοξάζειν refers six times to humans "glorifying" God, once to Paul "glorifying" or "exalting" his own ministry, and once to one member of the body being "glorified" or "honored" — presumably by other members of the body.⁵³ In 2 Cor 3:10, the verb appears twice contrasting the "glory" of the "dispensation of death"/"dispensation of condemnation" with that of the "dispensation of the Spirit"/"dispensation of righteousness." Apart from Rom 8:30, however, Paul *never* uses δοξάζειν to speak of the "glorification" of humans by God. Thus, on the face of it, the reference in Rom 8:30 to God's having "glorified" humans would appear to be non-Pauline.

Further, it is significant that the verb appears here in the *aorist* tense: he *glorified* them.⁵⁴ By way of contrast, Rom 5:2 speaks of the (*future*) "hope of the glory of God" (ἐλπίδι τῆς δοξῆς τοῦ Θεοῦ). Moreover, elsewhere in chap. 8, Paul refers to being "glorified with" (συνδοξασθῶμεν) Christ *in the future* (v. 17), to "the glory that *is to be* revealed to us" (v. 18: τὴν μέλλουσαν δόξαν ἀποκαλυφθῆναι εἰς ἡμᾶς), and to the (*future*) "freedom of the glory of the children of God" (v. 21: τὴν ἐλευθερίαν τῆς δόξας

---

51. Rom 1:21; 11:13; 15:6, 9; 1 Cor 6:20; 12:26; 2 Cor 3:10 (twice); 9:13; Gal 1:24.

52. Four times in Matthew, once in Mark, nine times in Luke, twenty-three times in John, five times in Acts, once in 2 Thessalonians, once in Hebrews, four times in 1 Peter, and twice in Revelation. It does not appear in Ephesians, Colossians, James, 2 Peter, 1 John, 2 John, 3 John, or Jude.

53. *Humans glorifying God*: Rom 1:21; 15:6, 9; 1 Cor 6:20; 2 Cor 9:13; Gal 1:24. *Paul exalting his own ministry*: Rom 11:13. *Someone being honored*: 1 Cor 12:26.

54. See, e.g., Jewett, *Romans: A Commentary*, 530: "exegetes have struggled to explain the past tense verb in v. 30."

τῶν τέκνων τοῦ Θεοῦ). Thus, again, the reference in Rom 8:30 to God's *having* "glorified" humans would appear to be non-Pauline and, indeed, to represent a kind of "realized eschatology" that appears in the post-Pauline era.

Conclusion

Romans 8:29–30 stands out from its immediate context in terms of literary style and subject matter. In addition, the removal of these verses would in no way interrupt or disturb this context. Further, vv. 29–30 can stand alone as a complete, self-contained, and meaningful theological statement. Most importantly, however, the vocabulary and much of the theology expressed in this vocabulary argue strongly against Pauline authorship of Rom 8:29–30 and, indeed, would appear to fit better within the milieu of the pseudo-Pauline and other post-Pauline writings. None of these data, considered separately, would be adequate to show that these verses are a non-Pauline interpolation. Indeed, as I indicated at the outset, I can by no means prove this to be the case. It is my judgment, however, that the cumulative weight of the evidence, considered carefully and in detail, points to the conclusion that Rom 8:29–30 is most likely a non-Pauline interpolation—inserted by a later hand to spell out in systematic fashion the implications of Paul's own affirmation of a positive future for those who love God.

The most immediately apparent implication of this, so far as an understanding of Paul is concerned, is to separate him from the type of systematic, linear, formalized, and even "scholastic" thinking that moves in orderly stages from foreknowledge to predestination to calling to justification to glorification of individual Christians. Paul's own understanding of the purpose and activity of God, as reflected elsewhere in his letters, would appear to be much more flexible and nuanced than this.

Part Three

The Book of Acts and the Letters of Paul

Chapter 12

The Timothy-Titus Problem Reconsidered

Some years ago, Kirsopp Lake and Henry J. Cadbury suggested that the account of Timothy's circumcision in Acts 16:1-3 "is a confused and perhaps erroneous memory" of the episode referred to in Gal 2:3-5, which involves the possible circumcision of Titus.[1] This suggestion has not been widely accepted; indeed, C. K. Barrett simply dismisses it with the comment that it "does not afford a convincing explanation of what is certainly a puzzling narrative."[2] It seems to me, however, that the suggestion by Lake and Cadbury should not be so easily dismissed. I propose, therefore, to present as strong a case as possible for the suggestion, with the conviction that it is consistent with certain significant features of the book of Acts.

The first point to be noted in this connection—and it often has been noted with some surprise—is that Titus, who figures rather prominently in two of Paul's letters, Galatians and 2 Corinthians, is never mentioned in the book of Acts.[3] Sit William M. Ramsay, among others, has spoken of "the enigmatic silence of Acts about Titus," suggesting that anyone "who solves that enigma will throw a flood of light on the early history of Christianity in the Aegean lands."[4] This total absence of Titus from the narrative of Acts is particularly surprising in the light of the fact that Acts refers to a number of people who, at various times and in various places, were associated with Paul as helpers or co-workers,

---

"The Timothy-Titus Problem Reconsidered." *ExpT* 92,8 (May 1981) 231–35. Copyright © 1981 Sage Publications. Reprinted with permission.

1. Lake and Cadbury, *Acts of the Apostles*, vol. 4, 184.
2. Barrett, "Titus," 3.
3. Isolated attempts, by various scholars, to detect references to Titus in Acts 13:1 and 18:7 have proved to be quite inconclusive.
4. Ramsay, *Luke the Physician*, 17.

and, in the case of some of these people, such as Barnabas, Silas, Timothy, Apollos, and Priscilla and Aquila, Acts supplies a fair amount of information.

Various possible explanations for this silence about Titus have been offered. Bishop J. B. Lightfoot, for example, suggested that Titus simply was not well enough known to be mentioned in Acts.[5] Ramsay and others have conjectured that Titus may have been a relative (brother or perhaps cousin) of Luke and Luke "thought it right to omit his relative's name, as he did his own name, from his history."[6] Similarly, it has been proposed that Luke and Titus were very close friends.[7] Another suggestion is that Titus may have been Luke's eye-witness source for parts of the book of Acts.[8] It is even possible, although to my knowledge no one has suggested it, that Titus might have been the actual author of the "We-Passages" in Acts or even of the book of Acts as a whole. It is also possible, of course, that the author of Acts was simply not interested in reporting the events in which Titus played a part.[9] None of these possible explanations, however, moves beyond the realm of pure conjecture. The only established fact at this point is that, for whatever reason, Acts does not mention Titus.

The second point to be noted is that the author of Acts almost certainly would have known at least something about Titus. Against Lightfoot's suggestion that Titus simply was not well enough known to be mentioned in Acts, it must be pointed out that Titus apparently had been known earlier to the recipients of both Galatians and 2 Corinthians and that he was later well enough known to be designated as the addressee of a pseudo-

---

5. Lightfoot, *Biblical Essays*, 281.
6. Ramsay, *St. Paul the Traveller*, 390; cf. Ramsay, *Luke the Physician*, 17–18; cf. also Souter, "Suggested Relationship," 285; Souter, "Relationship between Titus and Luke," 335–36; and Boys-Smith, "Titus and Luke," 380–81.
7. Bartlet, "Titus the Friend of Luke," 367–75.
8. Oakley, "Contributions and Comments," 564; Souter, "Suggested Relationship," 335.
9. Edmundson, "Enigma of Titus," 321–34.

Pauline letter that is now part of the canon, to be mentioned in the apocryphal Acts of Paul, to become the hero of an apocryphal Acts of Titus, and to be pressed into service as the alleged author of a pseudepigraphical epistle extolling the virtues of chastity. Furthermore, it can plausibly be argued that the author of Acts knew at least some of Paul's letters, including the two that mention Titus. It is true that Acts never refers to any of the letters, nor does it even indicate that Paul ever wrote any letters, and that most modern scholars have denied that the author knew any of the letters. John Knox and a few others, however, have maintained that the author of Acts did know, or at least know of, letters of Paul but chose not to make any significant use of them or even to mention them, perhaps because to have done so would inevitably have called attention to the controversies reflected in the letters (a matter that he preferred not to mention) and possibly because of what he regarded as a misuse of the letters by pre-Marcionite or even Marcionite Christians.[10] Going further, Morton Scott Enslin has suggested that the author of Acts not only knew Paul's letters but also used them as the principal source for his narrative. However, he refrained from mentioning them for the reasons proposed by Knox.[11] This issue has not been resolved, but it is surely worth observing that there are significant verbal parallels between Acts and Galatians (one of the two letters that mention Titus) and that Paul's escape from Damascus is reported both in Acts (9:23–25) and in 2 Corinthians (11:32–33) with some significant verbal parallels (2 Corinthians, of course, is the other letter that mentions Titus). On the basis, then, of parallels between Acts and the letters, pointed out by Enslin, and of the inherent improbability that the author of Acts would have been ignorant of the Pauline letters, observed by Knox,[12] it is my own at least tentative

---

10. Knox, "Acts and the Pauline Letter Corpus," 279–87.
11. Enslin, "'Luke' and Paul," 81–91; and Enslin, "Once Again, Luke and Paul," 253–71.
12. Enslin, "'Luke' and Paul," 81–91; Enslin, "Once Again, Luke and Paul," 253–71; and Knox, "Acts and the Pauline Letter Corpus."

judgment that the author of Acts probably did know at least some of the letters of Paul, including Galatians and 2 Corinthians, and thus was aware of the existence and some of the activities of Titus. This does not necessarily mean that the author of Acts had direct access to the texts of the letters as he composed his narrative; he may simply have read them in the past or heard them read. In any case, however, it is highly unlikely that he would have been completely ignorant about Titus; thus, the total silence of Acts regarding Titus would seem to have been deliberate on the part of the author.

The third point to be noted is that there appear to be good reasons why the author of Acts might have avoided mentioning Titus in his account of the early church. Barrett has suggested "that Titus was closely bound up with Paul's collection and with Corinth, and that Luke—no doubt for the good reason that both provided insights into the life of the early church that would not have proved edifying for the church of his own day—gives abridged and edited versions of them."[13] On the one hand, the generally irenic perspective and perhaps purpose of the author of Acts have often been noted: "For whatever reason Luke does almost completely omit from his account of the Early Church the controversial element, which the Pauline letters prove to have been very considerable."[14] On the other hand, the references to Titus in Paul's letters, without exception, identify him with the more controversial aspects and events of the Apostle's life and activity. These include Paul's collection for the Jerusalem church and the stormy situation in Corinth (2 Cor 2:12–13; 7:5–15; 8:6, 16–23; 12:17–18), mentioned by Barrett, but also the controversy over circumcision (Gal 2:1–5). Furthermore, we must confess our almost total ignorance regarding the outcome of these three situations, and thus we cannot be certain whether or to what extent reference to them by the author of Acts would still have caused problems when he wrote his narrative. In the case of the collection, we simply do not know whether

---

13. Barrett, "Titus," 2.
14. Barrett, "Acts and the Pauline Corpus," 3.

it accomplished its intended purpose; indeed, it is possible not only that the Jerusalem Christians refused to accept Paul's collection, but also that the church in Jerusalem made no attempt to save Paul from his near death and subsequent imprisonment and perhaps even instigated or contributed to these developments, either directly or indirectly. In any event, it appears that the collection had been the occasion of some misunderstanding and perhaps resentment in Corinth (2 Cor 8–9, esp. 8:8, 13–14, 20–21; cf. 12:16–18). Except for one oblique reference in Acts 24:17, however, and a possibly misplaced reference in Acts 11:27–30 and 12:25, the book of Acts is, for whatever reason, completely silent regarding the collection. Similarly, in the case of the situation in Corinth, we simply do not know how things eventually turned out. Although parts of 2 Corinthians suggest a happy resolution of the problems, other parts of the letter point to continuing and even increasing difficulties. F. F. Bruce observes that "there never came a time during Paul's life, so far as can be known, when he could feel that the cause of gospel liberty had finally triumphed at Corinth."[15] It is perhaps instructive, too, to recall that, a full generation after Paul's death, the author of *1 Clement* found it necessary to rebuke certain members of the Corinthian church for their factious spirit, based perhaps upon charismatic claims, that was producing dissension within the church. Again, however, as in the case of the collection, Acts gives no indication at all of any such problems within the church at Corinth, although it does speak of difficulties at the hands of "the Jews" (Acts 18:1–18; 20:2–3). Finally, in the case of the controversy over circumcision, we cannot be certain whether the controversy was ever really resolved in Paul's lifetime, and, indeed, it is by no means clear whether Titus himself was or was not circumcised or, if he was, whether this was or was not done as an act of "subjection" on the part of Paul.[16] Acts, of course, is not silent regarding the circumcision issue, as it is regarding the collection and the intra-church problems in Corinth,

---

15. Bruce, *Paul: Apostle of the Heart Set Free*, 278–79.
16. See, e.g., Lake and Cadbury, *Acts of the Apostles*, vol. 5, 196–99.

but, as Barrett observes, "The question about circumcision and other requirements of the Law is settled [in Acts] almost as soon as it is raised,"[17] and it certainly does not disturb the internal tranquility of the church for any extended period of time.

Thus, in summary, it may well be that the complete silence of Acts regarding Titus is related to and stems from its general avoidance of the more controversial aspects and events of early Christian history, since even to have mentioned the name of one who was known largely (or perhaps exclusively) because of his involvement in such controversies would, almost inevitably, have called attention to the controversies themselves. Such silence, of course, could have been more or less unconscious and unintended on the part of the author, but I strongly suspect that it was, at least to some extent, deliberate and conscious.

The fourth point to be noted is that there are no necessary chronological or geographical discrepancies between the account of Timothy's circumcision in Acts 16:1–3 and the reference to Titus in Gal 2:3–5, nor is there necessarily any discrepancy as to whether a circumcision did, in fact, occur. According to the usual readings, the circumcision of Timothy took place in Asia Minor after the Conference in Jerusalem, while the episode involving Titus came at the time of the Conference in Jerusalem.[18] It is possible, of course, that the author of Acts has simply misplaced his account, either intentionally or accidentally, but the possibility of another solution to this problem has been suggested by T. W. Manson and J. B. Orchard. They propose that Gal 2:3–5 (or, according to Manson, only vv. 4 and 5) is a "parenthesis" in Paul's account of the Conference in Jerusalem, that it refers to a subsequent development (presumably known to his Galatian readers), and that it is introduced at this point because of the reference to Titus in v. 1 (and perhaps because the subject of circumcision related both

---

17. Barrett, *New Testament Essays*, 87.
18. It is here assumed that the Conference described in Acts 15:1–29 and that reported in Gal 2:1–10 are the same.

to the Conference and to the Titus situation).[19] If Manson and Orchard are correct, and their arguments are cogently presented, then there is no necessary chronological discrepancy between the Acts narrative about Timothy and Paul's reference to Titus, since both now come at some point after the Conference in Jerusalem. Furthermore, there is no geographical discrepancy between the two passages if the so-called "South Galatia" theory regarding the destination of Galatians is valid; indeed, it would be natural to assume that Paul is referring to an occurrence that is known to his Galatian readers, and it is clear in Acts that Timothy's circumcision took place in the Roman province of Galatia.

Regarding the matter of Titus' possible circumcision, it has already been indicated that it is impossible to be certain whether Gal 2:3–5 means that Titus was circumcised or that he was not circumcised or, if he was, whether this was or was not done as an act of "subjection" on the part of Paul. The more relevant question at this point, however, is whether Paul's text (or possibly some other version of the same episode) could have been interpreted by the author of Acts as meaning that Titus was circumcised, and here the answer must surely be in the affirmative. If the author of Acts knew Gal 2:3–5, he clearly could have understood it to mean that Titus was circumcised. Thus, just as there is no necessary chronological or geographical discrepancy between the Acts account of Timothy's circumcision and the Galatian reference to Titus, neither is there necessarily any discrepancy as to whether a circumcision actually took place: Acts 16:1–3 states clearly that it did, and Gal 2:3–5 can and often has been interpreted to mean that it did.

Thus far, of course, no positive evidence has been presented to show that Acts 16:1–3 is, in fact, based upon the episode referred to in Gal 2:3–5. All that has been done is to remove some possible

---

19. Manson, *Studies in the Gospels and Epistles*, 175–76; Orchard, "New Solution," 154–74; Orchard, "Ellipsis between Galatians 2,3 and 2,4," 469–81; and Orchard, "Once Again the Ellipsis," 254–55.

objections to such a view and, in other ways, to lay a groundwork for whatever positive evidence there may be. It must be granted that the positive evidence is minimal, as would be expected in such a situation, but a careful comparison of the two passages in question, with particular attention to certain verbal, structural, and substantive parallels, in the context of some general observations regarding the overall "tendencies" of Acts, does suggest some such positive evidence.

The fifth point to be noted, then, is that there are such significant verbal, structural, and substantive parallels between Gal 2:3–5 and Acts 16:1–3 as to suggest some type of literary relationship between the two passages. In the first place, Gal 2:3 describes Titus as "the one with me" (*ho sun emoi*), and Acts 16:3 says that Paul wishes Timothy "to go away with him" (*sun autō exelthein*). In the second place, both Gal 2:3 and Acts 16:1, 3 use the term "Hellene" (*Hellēn*) with reference to the person under discussion, Galatians indicating that Titus was a "Hellene" and Acts speaking of Timothy as the son of a "Hellene," and both passages indicate that the question of circumcision arose precisely because of this "Hellenic" or "semi-Hellenic" identity. In the third place, both Gal 2:4 and Acts 16:3 state that the circumcision (or possibly only the suggestion of circumcision in the case of Titus) was somehow "because of" certain individuals (*dia tous*). In the fourth place, both Gal 2:4 and Acts 16:3 stress what might be termed the "presence" or "location" of these individuals, Galatians by referring to them as ones "who came in beside" (*hoitines pareisēlthon*) and Acts by describing them as ones "who were in those places" (*tous ontas en tois topois ekeinois*). In the fifth place, Acts 16:3 says that Paul, "having taken" (*labōn*) Timothy, circumcised him, and Gal 2:1b earlier has Paul speak of "having taken along" (*sumparalabōn*) Titus. I doubt that so many and such specific verbal, structural, and substantive parallels between two such brief passages, particularly passages that deal with the same general topic, could be completely coincidental; rather, they seem to suggest some type of literary relationship between the two.

The sixth, and final, point to be noted is that the major differences between Gal 2:3–5 and Acts 16:1–3 can all be accounted for on the basis of what appear to be certain general "tendencies" of the author of Acts. In the first place, if this author interpreted Gal 2:3–5 as indicating that Titus was, in fact, circumcised, as I believe he did, and if there were other reasons for the supposition that Paul had advocated or permitted circumcision on at least one occasion, as I believe there are,[20] then the author of Acts would wish to make it completely clear that this circumcision occurred, not in the case of a gentile convert, but rather in the case of a half-Jewish convert. Such an insistence would be of a piece with his overall portrayal of Paul and the other early Christians as going out of their way to avoid any break with Judaism or any act that would give Jews any legitimate grounds for offence against Christians. For Paul to circumcise a gentile would violate this author's understanding of Paul's position in the circumcision controversy; for him to circumcise the son of a Jewish mother and a Greek father, however, would be completely consistent. Thus, in Acts, the gentile who apparently was believed to have been circumcised becomes the half-Jew who was circumcised.

In the second place, the author of Acts would wish to make it clear that those who insisted upon circumcision and thus created the problem were non-Christian Jews, not Jewish Christians. This, too, is consistent with his general tendency to trace the problems in the early church to extramural rather than intramural disagreements and, in particular, to blame the Jews for such problems.[21] Thus, the "false brethren secretly brought in, who slipped in to spy out our freedom which we have in Christ Jesus, that they might bring us into bondage" (Gal 2:4) become simply "the Jews that were in those places" (Acts 16:3), making it clear that the problem exists because of non-Christian Jews, not, as Galatians seems to imply, because of Jewish Christians.

In the third place, as has already been noted, the author of Acts would not wish to mention Titus by name in this anecdote

---

20. See, e.g., Gal 5:11.
21. See, e.g., Sandmel, *Anti-Semitism in the New Testament?*, 99: "It was the Jews, whether in Judea or in the Greek world, who had caused the troubles for the blameless and faithful Christians."

because Titus appears to have been known primarily in connection with the more controversial aspects of Paul's life and career. Furthermore, it may have been known in the churches that Titus was a Greek, not a half-Jew. Thus, Timothy, who probably was even better known than Titus and who was not associated primarily with controversial situations and events,[22] is substituted for Titus in Acts 16:1–3. It may even be that the similarity between the two names played some part, either consciously or unconsciously, in the substitution.

In conclusion, I suggest that, while the six points that have been noted by no means prove the account of Timothy's circumcision in Acts 16:1–3 to be an altered version of the Titus reference in Gal 2:3–5, they do render such a view highly plausible.

---

22. Note that Timothy, unlike Titus, is associated with Paul in the salutations of some of the Pauline letters.

Chapter 13

Acts and the Pauline Corpus Reconsidered

Introduction

It is the "nearly universal judgment" of contemporary New Testament scholarship, according to Werner Georg Kümmel, that the author of Acts did not know the letters of Paul.[1] The reasoning that supports this judgment is relatively simple and straightforward: If this author (hereafter to be referred to as "Luke")[2] had known Paul's letters, he surely would have used them in the composition of his own narrative about Paul (Paul is, after all, the hero of the entire second half of Acts), or, at the very least, he would have given some indication that Paul wrote letters. There is very little, if any, evidence, however, that Luke did make use of the letters,[3] and, although he mentions and even "quotes" letters attrib-

---

"Acts and the Pauline Corpus Reconsidered." JSNT 24,1 (Sept 1985) 3–23, reprinted in Porter and Evans, *Pauline Writings*, 55–74. Copyright © 1985 Sage Publications. Reprinted with permission.

1. Kümmel, *Introduction to the New Testament*, 186; cf., e.g., Mitton, *Epistle to the Ephesians*, 216: "Those who have tried to demonstrate that the author of Acts was acquainted with Paul's epistles as a whole have failed to prove their case because of the almost complete absence of similarities of thought and phrase"; and Mitton, *Formation of the Pauline Corpus*, 24–28.

2. I very much doubt that Luke was the actual author, but I use the name simply for the sake of convenience.

3. Luke fails to include a great deal of important information about Paul that, in the judgment of many, he surely would have included had he been aware of it: e.g., the episode involving the question of Titus' circumcision (Gal 2:1–5), the confrontation with Cephas in Antioch (Gal 2:11–14), the problems of the church in Corinth, Paul's catalogue of his own sufferings (2 Cor 11:23–33), the story of Onesimus (Philemon), and Paul's reference to having "fought with beasts at Ephesus" (1 Cor 15:32); for other examples, see, e.g., Zahn, *Introduction to the New Testament*,

uted to others,[4] nowhere does he so much as hint that Paul ever wrote letters. It follows, therefore, that Luke cannot have known Paul's letters. Such, apparently, has been the reasoning of most recent scholarship.

This consensus, however, "is a relatively recent conclusion, not shared by earlier scholars." Moreover, it appears to have emerged "with almost no examination of the evidence," as part of a more general reaction against the Tübingen school, which had simply assumed that Luke knew the Pauline letters[5] and, indeed, "that one of his strongest motives was to contradict and neutralize them wherever they did not confirm his own conception of early Christian solidarity and order."[6] Noting this fact, Morton S. Enslin proposed, in 1938, "that a new and completely fresh examination of this whole question be made," indicating, at the same time, "a few points that would appear to merit consideration in such a study."[7] Subsequently, John Knox took up the matter in a brief essay,[8] Enslin contributed a second article on the subject, largely in response to Knox's essay,[9] and C. K. Barrett entered the discussion.[10]

III.119–21. Moreover, the portrayal of Paul in Acts, as regards his thought, his activities, and his situation, is, in many respects, significantly different from and even contradictory to the portrayal in Paul's own letters; on this point, see, e.g., Haenchen, *Acts of the Apostles*, 112–16; and Vielhauer, "On the 'Paulinism' of Acts." Finally, in the judgment of many, very few, if any, significant verbal parallels have been found between Acts and the Pauline letters.

4. Acts 15:23b–29; 23:26–30.

5. Enslin, "Once Again, Luke and Paul," 254–55; cf. his "'Luke' and Paul," 81–82. Despite Enslin's assertion, there were, as he acknowledged, at least two treatments of the evidence resulting in the conclusion that Luke did know Paul's letters: Sabatier, "L'auteur du livre des Actes des Apôtres?"; and Zahn, *Introduction to the New Testament*, III.118–26. More recently, Barrett has suggested that Luke "simply did not know" Paul's letters; see his "Acts and the Pauline Corpus," esp. 4–5.

6. Knox, "Acts and the Pauline Letter Corpus," 281.

7. Enslin, "'Luke' and Paul," 84.

8. Knox, "Acts and the Pauline Letter Corpus."

9. Enslin, "Once Again, Luke and Paul." It should be noted, at this point, that this second article is essentially an expansion of the 1938 article, done primarily in the light of the intervening essay by Knox. Thus, much of the content of the two articles is identical.

10. Barrett, "Acts and the Pauline Corpus."

Thus far, at least to my knowledge, the "new and completely fresh examination" of the matter, called for by Enslin, has not been made, nor is this the purpose of the present paper. What I intend is simply to summarize and evaluate the views of Enslin, Knox, and Barrett and, insofar as is possible at the present time, to advance the discussion somewhat by the introduction of some additional considerations.

Most of the debate (to the extent that the matter has been debated) has centered around three questions:

1. Did Luke know any of Paul's letters?
2. Did he make any use of these letters in the composition of his own work?
3. If he did know about the letters, and particularly if he made use of them, why did he fail to mention them or even to hint that Paul ever wrote letters?[11]

Thus, my own discussion will be structured in terms of these three questions, although I shall reverse the order of the second and the third.

Did Luke Know Paul's Letters?

To the first question (Did Luke know any of the letters of Paul?), Enslin responded with an unequivocal affirmative: "He may not have had copies of them, may not have had them, so to speak, open on the desk as he wrote, but that he had heard them, some at least, read in church services, and knew at least imperfectly their content appears to me inescapable."[12] Enslin's conclusion, at this point, was based almost entirely upon what he regarded as the

---

11. Actually, the relevant questions are at least five in number: (1) Was Luke even aware that Paul wrote letters at all? (2) Was he aware of particular letters written by Paul? (3) Was he familiar with the contents of any or all of Paul's letters, and, if so, to what extent? (4) Did he have access to the actual text of any or all of the letters? (5) Did he make use of any or all of the letters (either their general contents or their actual text) in the composition of his own narrative? If the answer to even the first of these questions is affirmative, a sixth question then necessarily follows: (6) Why does Luke never so much as hint that Paul wrote letters?

12. Enslin, "Once Again, Luke and Paul," 257; cf. "'Luke' and Paul," 84.

a priori improbability that an admirer of Paul, writing no earlier than the end of the first century[13] (at a time when other Paulinists certainly knew Paul's letters),[14] would have been ignorant of these letters. Speaking to the same point, Knox strongly agreed:

> This case is strong, indeed almost unanswerable. . . . He must have known letters of Paul. How could he have escaped knowing them? I agree with Enslin that it is all but incredible that such a man as Luke, writing in any one of the later decades of the first century about Paul and his career, should have been "totally unaware that this hero of his had ever written letters" and quite as hard to believe that he would have found it impossible, or even difficult, to get access to these letters if he had wanted to.[15]

In the past, various scholars had anticipated and challenged this type of *a priori* argument,[16] but the strongest and most plausible dissent, to date, has come from Barrett, who suggested five points "not as a conclusive answer to the question—it may prove to be one to which no final answer is possible—but as possibly worthy of consideration and further discussion":[17]

> 1. At the time when Acts was written, the letters of Paul were not yet regarded as "canon," some of them had certainly been lost (in some cases, perhaps, only temporarily), and some of them may have been intentionally suppressed because of "remarks that were uncomplimentary" to particular individuals or groups.

---

13. If Acts was written earlier, and particularly if it was written by an associate of Paul, it would be even less likely that the author would be unaware of Paul's activity as a letter-writer.

14. This point, not specifically noted by Enslin, was made by Barrett ("Acts and the Pauline Corpus," 2).

15. Knox, "Acts and the Pauline Letter Corpus," 282–83.

16. For summaries and responses, see, e.g., Enslin, "'Luke' and Paul," 83–84; "Once Again, Luke and Paul," 253–54, 256–57; and Knox, "Acts and the Pauline Letter Corpus," 283.

17. Barrett, "Acts and the Pauline Corpus," 4.

2. Inasmuch as "it scarcely shows any traces of the development of Frühkatholizismus, as this term is commonly understood,"[18] Acts may well have been written earlier than is sometimes supposed, perhaps earlier even than any of the pseudo-Pauline writings (and, by implication, before Paul's letters became widely known).
3. It is highly unlikely that the author of Acts knew Paul personally; thus he cannot be assumed to have had personal knowledge regarding Paul's letters.
4. The so-called "We Document," which is to be regarded as a simple itinerary rather than a journal, probably would not have made reference to letters of Paul.
5. Luke apparently reconstructed his story of Paul almost entirely upon the basis of this "We Document" and "traces that he could not overlook" (i.e., "local recollections") of Paul, discovered "again and again" by him in the course of "his travels and study of the mission field"; thus, it is Luke's own "non-Pauline (but not anti-Pauline)" theology, not that of Paul himself, that finds expression in the book of Acts (the implication being that this would be unlikely if Luke had actually known Paul's letters).[19]

Barrett's points are, to be sure, interesting and suggestive, but, in my own judgment, they are not finally convincing. In particular, if Luke did, as Barrett suggests, "again and again" discover "traces" of Paul, he almost certainly would have learned that Paul wrote letters, he very likely would have encountered at least some of these letters, and he might reasonably be expected to have looked for others. Thus, it is my own conclusion that Enslin and Knox are correct as regards this first question: Luke surely knew, in some sense, at least some of the letters of Paul.[20] At this point,

---

18. Barrett, "Acts and the Pauline Corpus," 4.
19. Barrett, "Acts and the Pauline Corpus," 4–5.
20. Barrett ("Acts and the Pauline Corpus," 2–3) acknowledges that "there appears to be a growing tendency" to accept this view, citing, as examples, the following: Klein, *Die zwölf Apostel*, 191; and Burchard, *Der dreizehnte Zeuge*, 157.

however, it would be premature to raise the further question of just how well or in what way he knew them; this can only be dealt with in connection with the later question, whether he made any use of the letters in the composition of his own narrative.[21]

Why Did Luke Not Mention Paul's Letters?

Regarding the second question (Why, if he knew them, did Luke not mention Paul's letters or, at least, the fact that Paul wrote letters?),[22] there is a basic agreement between Enslin and Knox, although it is Enslin who has dealt most comprehensively with the matter. Enslin suggested three lines of approach to the question:[23] (1) Inasmuch as Paul's letters contain very little narrative material, consisting primarily of "reproofs, corrections, and long-winded theological arguments" that Luke perhaps failed to understand, there is little in these letters that would lend itself to direct use by the author of a narrative such as Acts. Rather, Luke, as a "creative writer," apparently "preferred to write his own story, utilizing as suggestions hints which he chose to write up, not to copy."[24] Thus, there was no real reason, Enslin implied, for Luke to mention Paul's letters, because his purpose was quite different from that of the letters and he used them only indirectly and sparingly. (2) "One of the most evident qualities of Acts is the attempt to tone down or omit mentions of clashes between Christian groups."[25]

---

21. See the first two paragraphs of my "Conclusion" below.
22. This question becomes even more pressing, of course, if it is concluded that Luke not only knew but also used Paul's letters.
23. Enslin, "Once Again, Luke and Paul," 268–71.
24. Enslin, "Once Again, Luke and Paul," 268–69.
25. Enslin, "Once Again, Luke and Paul," 269; cf. 269–79. See also, e.g., Talbert, *Luke and the Gnostics*, 88: "The author of Acts wanted to portray the church of the apostolic age as free from internal conflicts, possessing an inner unity. Because of this overall aim in Acts, the author omitted any reference to Paul's controversies in Galatia, in Corinth, in Philippi, and in Colossae. Moreover, it is almost certainly for the same reason that there is no reference in Acts to Paul as a letter writer. To have referred to Paul's letters to Corinth or Colossae would have necessitated a reference to the

It is not surprising, therefore, that Luke would not wish to call attention to such episodes as Paul's controversy with the church in Corinth and the collection for Jerusalem (which, according to Enslin, "failed lamentably to accomplish what Paul had hoped that it would" and, indeed, was regarded by the Jerusalem Christians as an attempt by Paul to "buy his way" into the inner circle), both of which figure prominently in Paul's correspondence. Even so much as a reference to the letters, it was implied, might well remind readers of such episodes or send them to the letters, where they would learn of the episodes. In short, Luke would not wish to call attention to Paul's letters because his own picture of early Christian history is so different from that implied in the letters. Thus, there may well have been a very positive reason for not mentioning the letters. (3) A strong case can be made, as Knox had suggested earlier,[26] that one of the principal reasons for the writing of Acts, with Paul as its chief character, was that Paul's letters had been "appropriated" by "pre-Marcionite, perhaps even Marcionite, Christians," who threatened "to take exclusive possession of Paul himself as 'the Apostle'." Thus, it was implied, Luke would wish, on the one hand, to avoid reference to Paul's letters, which, in his view, lent themselves to misunderstanding and misuse,[27] but he would also be eager, on the other hand, to re-present the great apostle, whose reputation and stature were such that he could not be overlooked or belittled, in a light more congenial and sympathetic to the emerging concerns of Christian "orthodoxy." Here, then, would be a second reason for not mentioning the letters of Paul.

Again, Barrett, while acknowledging that there is much truth in Enslin's arguments, has attempted to show that these arguments

---

controversies out of which the letters sprang and to the solution of which they were directed. . . . This silence is a part of Luke's purpose. It is part of his overall aim to idealize the apostolic age, portraying it as a period of almost absolute inner unity."

26. Knox, "Acts and the Pauline Letter Corpus," 284–86.
27. See, e.g., 2 Pet 3:15b–17.

are not finally persuasive.[28] Barrett maintained, in the first place, that a great deal of material in Paul's letters would not have been at all problematic for Luke and that he, if he had known the letters, could have used such material, simply omitting any reference to the more controversial aspects. It would not have been necessary for him to ignore the entire corpus of letters. The problem, however, is that any direct use of or explicit reference to the letters at all might have served to call attention to the letters and thus to matters that, in the view of Luke, would better be left to sink into obscurity. In the second place, Barrett, quoting Philipp Vielhauer, suggested that it would be "an undertaking as hopeless as it is improbable" to "attempt to discredit Paul's letters by setting Paul himself in high esteem."[29] Here, too, however, Barrett appears to have missed the real thrust of Enslin's argument. Luke is not attempting to "discredit" Paul's letters; rather, he is seeking to "rehabilitate" Paul as a spokesman for and a champion of "orthodox" Christianity. In order to do this, he must direct attention away from Paul's letters, with their often controversial and problematic contents, in the direction of the apostle's activities as missionary and martyr. He is, in fact, attempting to build up the reputation of Paul for Christians who are suspicious of his theology and ethics, but he does this, not by "discrediting" Paul's letters, but rather by setting Paul (and his letters insofar as they are known) within the larger context of early Christian history and faith, as he understands them, where Paul (and the letters) can be seen, not in isolation, but as an integral expression of apostolic Christianity.[30] In the final analysis, therefore, it cannot be said that

---

28. Barrett, "Acts and the Pauline Corpus," 3–4.

29. Barrett, "Acts and the Pauline Corpus," 3–4; cf. Vielhauer, *Geschichte der urchristlichen Literatur*, 407.

30. I am even tempted, at times, to suggest that it was Luke (not the author of Ephesians, as Edgar J. Goodspeed and others have held) who "published" the first collection of Paul's letters and that he intended Acts (and perhaps his Gospel as well) as the "introduction" to this collection — an "introduction," that is, that would set the letters in the proper context.

Barrett has successfully refuted Enslin on the matter of why Luke fails to mention Paul's letters. Enslin's arguments are, at the very least, highly plausible: There was no real need or reason for Luke to mention the letters of Paul, and he apparently had very strong reasons for choosing not to mention them.[31]

Did Luke Make Use of Paul's Letters?

Thus far, I have indicated my own basic agreement with Enslin and Knox, as over against Barrett, so far as the first two questions are concerned: I believe that Luke did know the letters of Paul, some of them at least, and that it is possible to show, with a high degree of plausibility, why he chose not to mention these letters. The crucial question, however, is whether Luke made any use of the Pauline letters in his own composition. If it can be shown that he did, then it necessarily follows that he must have known the letters, even if no satisfactory answer could be given as to why he never mentioned them. If, on the other hand, it cannot be shown that Luke used the letters, then any discussion of the other two questions necessarily remains highly speculative and inconclusive.

---

31. The apparently liberal use of Paul's letters in the almost certainly pseudonymous Pastoral Letters, written to combat certain "heretical" teachings perhaps promoted in the name of Paul, might be taken as evidence against such an attempt to "rehabilitate" Paul without mention or overt use of the letters. The following points must, however, be noted: (1) Different writers may operate quite differently, even when dealing with essentially the same problem. (2) We do not know enough about the situation faced either by Luke or by the author of the Pastorals to say just how similar their situations (or purposes) were. (3) Even the Pastorals make no direct *mention* of the authentic Pauline letters. (4) Someone writing a *letter* in Paul's name would understandably seek to pattern the letter after other letters known or believed to have been written by Paul; such would not necessarily be the case, however, with someone writing a *narrative* about Paul, particularly if the principal motivation for writing the narrative was to put to rest certain apprehensions about Paul that could find support in the letters, by directing attention away from the letters or at least setting them in the "proper" context.

Before considering the third question, however, attention must be called to what Knox has termed "the hidden major premise" in most discussions of the matter, namely: "If Luke knew the letters of Paul, he must have used them." Here, two distinct but related questions are confused: (1) Did Luke *know* Paul's letters? and (2) Did Luke *use* Paul's letters? As Knox insisted, the possibility must at least be kept open that Luke "knew, or at least knew of, letters of Paul—even *the* (collected) letters of Paul—and quite consciously and deliberately made little or no use of them."[32] Knox, in fact, argued that this apparently was the case: Luke knew but chose not to use the letters of Paul. Thus, the question of Luke's use of the Pauline letters must be considered separately from that of his knowledge of the letters.[33]

Enslin, in dealing with the question, whether Luke made any use of the letters of Paul, acknowledged that "the evidence is very fragmentary" and scarcely conclusive but maintained, nevertheless, that there are "a few cases which appear . . . easier of explanation on the assumption that Luke not only did know but made occasional use of at least some of these letters."[34] Noting that "many other passages would have to be considered in a complete study," he cited eleven points, which, he asserted, were "chosen as examples, not as an all-inclusive list":[35]

---

32. Knox, "Acts and the Pauline Letter Corpus," 284.
33. If Luke did not know the letters of Paul, then, of course, the question of his use of them becomes meaningless.
34. Enslin, "Once Again, Luke and Paul," 257. Indeed, in a slightly later work (*Reapproaching Paul*, 26–27), Enslin went further: "In my judgment Luke used them [Paul's letters] very fully. Back of almost every incident he paints is a statement or basis for inference in one or more of the letters quite sufficient for a writer who was an author, not a copyist or restricted editor. . . . Far from being unknown or unused, the letters of Paul . . . would appear to have been the principal source used by Luke in reconstructing the activities of the man who brought to reality the Gentile mission."
35. Enslin, "Once Again, Luke and Paul," 267; cf. Enslin, "'Luke' and Paul," 90. The eleventh point is not actually numbered in Enslin's articles, but it might well have been. As other possible examples, he mentioned

1. Paul's missionary travels, as set forth in Acts, carry him to precisely those places, and only those places, to which we have Pauline letters or which could easily be inferred from references in these letters.
2. The perplexing statement in Luke 24:34, "The Lord is risen indeed, and hath appeared to Simon," which has no corresponding narrative, is best explained as based upon Paul's catalogue of resurrection appearances in 1 Cor 15:5.[36]
3. The idea that Jesus was seen "for many days" (Acts 13:31), that is, for forty days (Acts 1:3), after his resurrection, representing, as it does, a revision of Luke's earlier notion that the ascension occurred shortly after the resurrection (Luke 24:50–53), is best understood as based upon Paul's repeated "then . . . then . . . then . . ." in his catalogue of resurrection appearances (1 Cor 15:5–7).
4. There are several striking verbal similarities between Acts (or the Gospel according to Luke) and Paul's letters, coupled, in some instances, with remarkable parallels in concept, that suggest dependence of the former upon the latter.[37]
5. A strong case can be made that the report of Paul's escape from Damascus "through" the wall (Acts 9:23–25) represents Luke's modification of Paul's own reference to the same occurrence (2 Cor 11:32–33).

---

the reference to Paul and Barnabas as "apostles" (Acts 14:4, 14; cf. 1 Cor 9:6) and the insistence that only those who have seen the Lord are eligible to be apostles (Acts 1:21; cf. 1 Cor 9:1). An additional possible example, not mentioned by Enslin, is Paul's statement, before leaving Ephesus, that, after visits to Macedonia and Achaia, he intends to go to Jerusalem and then to Rome (Acts 19:21; cf. similar indications in the Corinthian correspondence and in Romans); see Knox, "Acts and the Pauline Letter Corpus," 281–82.

36. Enslin assumed, of course, as do I, that the same author wrote Luke and Acts.

37. For a discussion of these, together with other examples, see below.

6. The several differences between Acts 15:1–29 and Gal 2:1–10 (accounts of the so-called "Jerusalem Conference")[38] are most easily explained by assuming that Luke has altered Paul's material in order to soften or eliminate the references to internal dissension among Christians.
7. The references to Paul having studied at the feet of Gamaliel (Acts 22:3), his involvement in the stoning of Stephen (Acts 7:58; 8:1), and his trip to Damascus (Acts 9:1–2) may well have been suggested by comments in Paul's own letters regarding his Pharisaic background, his zeal for the law, his persecution of Christians, and his conversion in or near Damascus (Phil 3:5–6; Gal 1:13–14, 17).
8. Various obscurities in the brief account of Paul's eighteen months in Corinth (Acts 18:1–17) are easily explained on the assumption that the source for the account is Paul's own letter to the Corinthians (i.e., 1 Corinthians), and virtually all of the details in this passage could be inferred from the letter.
9. It is at least possible that the reversal of the order of the cup and the bread in Luke 22:17–19a is based upon the same order in 1 Cor 10:16, 21 (this order occurs elsewhere only at *Did.* 9.1–5).
10. The reference to Paul's last-minute change in plans regarding his route from Corinth to Jerusalem (Acts 20:3) may well have been prompted by an inexact recollection of Paul's words in 2 Cor 1:15–2:12 and Rom 15:31.
11. So far as the sometimes-noted argument from silence is concerned (Why, if he knew the letters of Paul, would Luke have omitted such items as Paul's catalogue of sufferings [2 Cor 11:23–33], the story of Onesimus

---

38. Whether the gathering described in Acts 15:1–29 and that reported in Gal 2:1–10 are the same continues to be a matter of some debate among scholars; for a commentary based upon the assumption that they are the same, see, e.g., Haenchen, *Acts of the Apostles*, 440–72; cf. also, e.g., Lake, "Note XVI. The Apostolic Council of Jerusalem."

> [Philemon], or Paul's reference to having "fought with beasts at Ephesus" [1 Cor 15:32]?), there may, in fact, be reminiscences or suggestions of some of these items in Acts,[39] and, "after all, authors can omit what they do not want or what they feel unable to use for lack of space."[40]

In short, it was the contention of Enslin, although he acknowledged that he saw no way of proving it, that Luke did make use of the letters of Paul in reconstructing his own narrative about Paul.

Responding to Enslin, Knox asserted "that the effort to demonstrate Luke's use of Paul with actual evidence fails, as all efforts to do this have previously failed, because every instance of his alleged dependence on the letters can be explained almost, if not quite, as plausibly by the hypothesis of his access to some independent tradition."[41] Indeed, according to Knox, while it cannot be demonstrated that Luke did not use Paul's letters, "so long as only a meager use is claimed," neither "can one demonstrate that he did."[42] The most interesting and potentially damaging aspect of Knox's critique, however, is his suggestion that "the absence of adequate evidence of *verbal* dependence" may actually have the effect of reversing Enslin's argument, for, in effect, Enslin has asked one to believe "that Luke used the letters of Paul as sources for *facts* or *data* but succeeded in avoiding . . . any trace of their actual language." Thus, Knox concluded, in the absence of verbal parallels, "every possible piece of evidence of Luke's having used the letters increases the probability that he did not use them."[43]

---

39. See Enslin, "Once Again, Luke and Paul," 267–68, for the suggestion (1) that Luke did, in fact, make "a very fair epitome" of Paul's catalogue of sufferings "in his catena of trials and hardships encountered by his hero" and (2) that Luke understood Paul's reference to having "fought with beasts in Ephesus" as "a figurative reference to Paul's clash with the infuriated Ephesian mob." Cf. Enslin, "'Luke' and Paul," 90–91.

40. Enslin, "Once Again, Luke and Paul," 267; cf. Enslin, "'Luke' and Paul," 90.

41. Knox, "Acts and the Pauline Letter Corpus," 281.

42. Knox, "Acts and the Pauline Letter Corpus," 284.

43. Knox, "Acts and the Pauline Letter Corpus," 282.

In reply to Knox, five general points are to be noted; then, some additional evidence will be cited to support Enslin's contention that Luke did make use of Paul's letters; finally, specific attention will be devoted to Knox's suggestion regarding the absence of verbal parallels between Acts and the letters of Paul. The first general point is that, while it may appear unlikely that an author would make use of a source for facts or data and yet avoid any trace of this source's actual language, this can by no means be accepted as an absolute principle of literary criticism. An author may, for whatever reason, simply prefer a vocabulary more compatible with his/her own style, situation, or purpose, or she/he may also be using another source or sources whose vocabulary is viewed as more suitable. The second general point is that any "independent tradition" used by Luke that would account adequately for the various similarities between Acts and Paul's letters would, itself, almost necessarily be dependent, at least to some extent, upon these letters. Thus, Luke would still be at least *indirectly* dependent upon the letters of Paul. The third general point is that, as Knox himself apparently recognized, the hypothesis of an independent tradition explains the instances of alleged dependence upon the letters "almost, if not quite, as plausibly" as the hypothesis that Luke actually used the letters; in other words, the latter hypothesis would appear, on the face of it, somewhat stronger, all other things being equal. The fourth general point, worthy, at least, of consideration, is that an application of "Ockham's razor" to this matter would require a serious attempt to account for the similarities between Acts and Paul's letters without appealing to unknown, hypothetical sources, allowing for the introduction of such sources only if the matter could not be adequately resolved otherwise.[44] The fifth general point is that it would be

---

44. For a similar argument regarding, e.g., the Synoptic Problem, see Frye, "Synoptic Problem and Analogies," 285–86; cf. Farmer, *The Synoptic Problem*, 209. For a critique of the application of "Ockham's Razor" to such literary-historical problems, see Tyson, "Literary Criticism and the Gospels," 325–27.

virtually impossible for any author who is familiar with materials directly related to the subject matter of his/her own composition not to make at least some use of these materials, either directly or indirectly, intentionally or unintentionally, consciously or unconsciously, in her/his own work. Even if such an author intends to correct these materials, is writing in direct opposition to them, or wishes to conceal the very fact of their existence, they remain in his/her mind and influence both what she/he says and how it is said. Thus, if Luke knew the letters of Paul, as both Enslin and Knox agree that he did, he almost inevitably would have made some use of them (perhaps even unintentionally and unconsciously) in the writing of Acts.

So far as additional evidence supporting Enslin's contention that Luke used Paul's letters is concerned, two points are to be noted. The first is this: As I have argued elsewhere, a rather strong case can be made that the account of the circumcision of Timothy in Acts 16:1–3 represents an altered version of Paul's reference to the question of the circumcision of Titus in Gal 2:3–5. This case is based upon, among others, the following considerations:

1. Titus, who figures rather prominently in two of Paul's letters, is never mentioned in Acts.
2. Luke almost certainly would have known at least something about Titus.
3. There appear to be good reasons why Luke might have avoided mentioning Titus in his account of the early church.
4. The major differences between Gal 2:3–5 and Acts 16:1–3 can all be accounted for on the basis of the general "tendencies" of Luke.
5. There are such significant verbal, structural and substantive similarities between Gal 2:3–5 and Acts 16:1–3 as to suggest some type of literary relationship between the two passages.[45]

---

45. Walker, "Timothy-Titus Problem Reconsidered" (chapter 12 in this volume).

The second point, then, is this: It can plausibly be argued, not only that the account of the so-called Jerusalem Conference in Acts 15 depends on Paul's reference to the same gathering in Galatians 2,[46] but also that, at least to some extent, the account in Acts is intended to correct impressions that might be conveyed by Paul's material.[47] For example, Paul claims that *he* has "been entrusted with the gospel to the uncircumcised" and Peter with that "to the circumcised" (Gal 2:7-9), while in Acts, Peter claims it as God's choice that by *his* mouth "the Gentiles should hear the word of the gospel and believe" (Acts 15:7). In the same context, *Paul* insists that "God shows no partiality" (Gal 2:6), while, in Acts, it is *Peter* who asserts that God "made no distinction between us and them" (Acts 15:9). Moreover, a few verses later, Paul claims that *he* accused Peter of seeking to "compel the Gentiles to live like Jews," even though he, Peter, being a Jew, lived "like a Gentile and not like a Jew" (Gal 2:14), while in Acts, it is *Peter* who accuses others of "putting a yoke upon the neck of the disciples which neither our fathers nor we have been able to bear" (Acts 15:10). Furthermore, in Galatians, it is *Paul* who insists, "We ... know that a person is not justified by works of the law but through faith in Jesus Christ" (Gal 2:16), while, in Acts, it is *Peter* who says, "But we believe that we shall be saved through the grace of the Lord Jesus, just as they will" (Acts 15:11). In short, Luke has Peter "utter the same opinions about law and gospel as Paul, according to the epistle, expressed in Antioch."[48] This is particularly remarkable in light of the fact that, in Galatians, it is precisely Peter to whom or about whom these views are expressed. Finally, where Paul has spoken of "certain ones" (*tinas*) who came from (*apo*) James and

---

46. See n. 38 above.

47. Cf., however, Knox, "Acts and the Pauline Letter Corpus," 282: "Actually, it would be more accurate to say that Galatians is correcting Acts—not Acts itself, of course, but that understanding of Paul's relation to the Jerusalem apostolate which happens to reach us in Acts but which was obviously prevalent in Paul's own time (since he is concerned in Galatians to deny its truth) and which undoubtedly left its traces in records to which Luke a generation or so later had access."

48. Von Weizsäcker, *Apostolic Age of the Christian Church*, 1.211.

created dissension in Antioch (Gal 2:12), Acts refers to "certain ones" (*tines*) who came from (*apo*) Judea for the same purpose, thus eliminating Paul's clear implication that there was dissension within the leadership of the church (Acts 15:1). Thus, there are a number of indications that Luke's material in Acts 15 is, to some extent, based upon that of Paul in Galatians 2 and is intended, at least in part, to correct certain impressions that might otherwise be conveyed by the latter.

We move now to the question of verbal parallels. As was noted above, Knox was particularly impressed by what he took to be the absence of verbal parallels between Acts and the letters of Paul, regarding this as the most serious obstacle to any hypothesis that Luke actually made use of the letters in the composition of his own work. It is not really correct, however, as Knox suggested,[49] that the absence of verbal parallels is total. Enslin had already, in his first article on the subject, noted several instances of "similarity of phrase," most striking of which is the use of the same rather unusual term, *porthein*, to describe Paul's activities in opposing the Christian movement (Gal 1:13; Acts 9:21). Other examples included the somewhat unconventional idea, expressed in similar terminology in the two passages, that the law was given through the instrumentality of angels (Gal 3:19–20; Acts 7:53), the phrase *zēlotēs hyparchōn* (Gal 1:14; Acts 22:3), the verbal similarity between Gal 2:10 and Acts 11:30 (both apparently referring to the sending of aid), and certain similarities of vocabulary and concept between 1 Cor 7:32–35 and Luke 10:40–42 (both referring to the advantage of freedom from all "cares" that would "distract" attention from the Lord). In two of these instances (i.e., *porthein* and a word stem in 1 Cor 7:32–35 and Luke 10:40–42), the distinctive terminology occurs nowhere else in the New Testament.[50] In a different context, Enslin had also noted two verbal parallels in the reports of Paul's escape from Damascus (2 Cor 11:33; Acts 9:25):

---

49. Knox, "Acts and the Pauline Letter Corpus," 282.
50. Enslin, "'Luke' and Paul," 87–88; cf. Enslin, "Once Again, Luke and Paul," 262–63.

both passages include the phrase, "through the wall" (*dia tou teichous*), and both have a form of the verb "to let down" (*chalan*) with the preposition "in" (*en*).[51]

In addition to these examples of verbal parallels already noted by Enslin, it can also be argued, again on the basis of striking verbal parallels, that, in at least two instances, the Lukan version of a saying of Jesus is dependent upon a Pauline saying.[52] For example, Matt 5:44 has Jesus say, "Love your enemies and pray for those who persecute you," while Luke 6:27–28 has "Love your enemies, do good to those who hate you, bless those who curse you, pray for those who abuse you" (there is no Markan parallel). The first clause in Luke's version is identical to that in Matthew's version, and Luke's final clause is similar to Matthew's second (final) clause. Luke's second and third clauses have no parallel in the Matthean version, but it is to be noted that the third clause ("bless those who curse you") has striking verbal similarities to Rom 12:14 ("Bless those who persecute you; bless and do not curse them"), with the same word for "bless" (*eulogein*) and the same word for "curse" (*katarasthai*). (Elsewhere in the New Testament, *eulogein* and *katarasthai* are juxtaposed in this way only at Jas 3:9–10.) It is surely at least possible that Luke's third clause was suggested by Rom 12:14. A second example is seen when Luke 10:8b ("eat what is set before you"), missing from the Matthean parallel, is compared with 1 Cor 10:27b ("eat whatever is set before you"), where the same word is used for "eat" (*esthiein*) and the same word for "set before" (*paratithenai*) and, in both cases, *paratithenai* is followed by *hymin* ("you"). Much more work needs to be done by way of comparing the Lukan version of dominical sayings with similar materials in the Pauline letters, and these two examples suggest that such work may prove extremely fruitful.[53]

---

51. Enslin, "'Luke' and Paul," 88–89; Enslin, "Once Again, Luke and Paul," 263.

52. See n. 36 above.

53. It could be argued, of course, that verbal parallels indicate, rather, Paul's knowledge of the Jesus tradition in its Lukan form, and, indeed, this is the usual approach; see, e.g., Dungan, *Sayings of Jesus in the Churches of Paul*.

On the basis, then, of the evidence cited by Enslin, the five general points noted above in response to Knox, the additional evidence brought in to support Enslin's view, and a number of specific verbal parallels between Luke-Acts and the letters of Paul, it is my own conclusion that Luke not only knew at least some of Paul's letters but also made some use of these letters in the composition of his own narrative.[54]

Conclusion

As I have already indicated, I am in basic agreement with Enslin as over against Barrett and, to some extent, Knox, regarding the three questions at issue: Luke almost certainly knew, in some sense, at least some of the letter of Paul, he made some use of these letters in the writing of his own work, and there are plausible reasons why he, nevertheless, did not mention the letters or even indicate that Paul ever wrote letters. What now remains is to say something more about the nature and extent of Luke's knowledge and use of the letters, about his general purpose in writing Acts, and about specific ways in which his familiarity with the letters may have influenced the presentation in Acts.

I very much doubt that Luke had the text of Paul's letters before him as he wrote. He had read, or heard read, at least some of these letters, perhaps on numerous occasions, he was familiar with their basic content, and he had even absorbed some of their terminology. In writing his own work, it was almost inevitable that what he knew from the letters would influence what he wrote, even to the extent of affecting his vocabulary and the structuring of his

---

54. When speaking of the letters of Paul in this discussion, I have had in mind only those letters generally agreed to be authentically Pauline, namely, Romans, 1 and 2 Corinthians, Galatians, Philippians, 1 Thessalonians, and Philemon. Mitton, among others, has noted a special relation between Acts and Ephesians, suggesting that the author of Ephesians was familiar with Acts; see his *Epistle to the Ephesians*, 220; and *Formation of the Pauline Corpus*, 27–28. For various theories regarding the relation between Acts and the Pastoral Letters, see, e.g., Moule, "Problem of the Pastoral Epistles"; Strobel, "Schreiben des Lukas?"; Quinn, "The Last Volume of Luke"; and Wilson, *Luke and the Pastoral Epistles*.

materials. It may very well be that he was unaware of the extent to which he made use of the writings of Paul.

At certain points, however, it appears to me that he must have been writing in some sort of conscious dialogue with the letters (e.g., in his account of the Jerusalem Conference). At such points, I judge that he was not so much concerned to disagree with or to correct Paul as to reassure others who were inclined to reject the apostle because of his popularity among Christians whose "orthodoxy" and perhaps morality were suspect. What Luke sought to do was to reclaim Paul for the mainstream of the Christian movement, by showing that Paul did, in fact, stand in the same apostolic tradition as Peter, James, and John (a point that Paul, himself, had somewhat contentiously attempted to make in his own letters) and that he, like they, also stood in the same tradition as did authentic Judaism. Paul, in other words, despite appearances to the contrary, was neither a Marcionite, a Gnostic, nor any other type of "maverick." In his own mind, Luke no doubt believed that he was, in a sense, rescuing Paul from himself (that is from some of the hasty and provocative *ad hoc* statements in his letters) and from those who would misuse Paul in the service of their own "heresies" and "lawlessness."[55] To the success of this endeavor, the acceptance of Paul's letters into the canon of Christian scripture and the longstanding regard for Paul as apostle *par excellence* bear eloquent testimony. With Acts as an "introduction," Paul's letters could become truly "catholic"; without such an "introduction," they might well have remained purely "sectarian." When read with Acts as a "preface," Paul's letters can be seen as "orthodox"; standing alone, they risk the charge of "heresy" or, at least, eccentricity.

It is not enough, however, merely to see Acts as providing the proper context in which the Pauline letters are to be read and understood. If Enslin is correct, as I believe him to be, regarding

---

55. This is not necessarily to imply that Acts was written as late as the middle of the second century, although this can by no means be ruled out. There were certainly "proto-Gnostic" and "pre-Marcionite" tendencies within the Christian movement before the end of the first century.

Luke's knowledge and use of the letters, then the influence of the letters on the narrative of Acts can be seen in various ways and at different levels. At one level, it appears simply in more-or-less unconscious echoes of Pauline terminology and thought: for example the use of *porthein* in Acts 9:21 to describe Paul's activities in opposing the Christian movement (cf. Gal 1:13) or the notion in Acts 7:23 of the law being given through the instrumentality of angels (cf. Gal 3:19–20). At a more substantive level, it would determine the actual content of the story in Acts, particularly if, as Enslin suggests, the letters of Paul constitute "the principal source used by Luke in reconstructing the activities of the man who brought to reality the Gentile mission."[56] Examples here might include the account in Acts 9:23–25 of Paul escaping from Damascus in a basket (cf. 2 Cor 11:32–33) and perhaps even the itineraries of Paul's various journeys in Acts. (This content would be somewhat modified, of course, to reflect Luke's own particular interests and concerns in writing his narrative.)

At the deepest level, however, the influence of the letters is to be seen in a strangely paradoxical way. As has already been noted, Paul strongly suggests in his letters that he is the real leader (and perhaps even the founder) of the Gentile mission (e.g., Gal 2:6–9). He also insists that he is to be regarded as an "apostle" (e.g., Gal 1:1; Rom 1:1–6). Furthermore, at least in Galatians and Romans, the doctrine of "justification through faith" is an essential feature of Paul's gospel. In Acts, however, as has also been noted, it is Peter who is the real founder of the Gentile mission and the chief spokesman for the doctrine of justification through faith (although in a somewhat muted form); furthermore, except at Acts 14:4, 14, Luke never refers to Paul as an "apostle." Thus, it would appear that, while the Pauline letters have, at certain points, influenced the language and thought of Acts, as well as some of its actual content, this influence does not extend to the basic features of the Pauline message. In short, the external course of events in Acts may well reflect the influence of the letters of Paul, but

---

56. See n. 34 above.

apparently not the portrayal of Paul's theology and message; here, the influence seems to disappear. Such a conclusion is premature, however, for Luke does refer to Paul as an "apostle" in the one passage already cited, thus indicating his familiarity with the notion, and he does, at one point (Acts 13:39), betray his awareness of the doctrine of justification through faith and, indeed associate this doctrine with Paul. It is far from clear, from this passage, that Luke really understands the doctrine, and it is evident that the doctrine holds little real interest for him.[57] Nevertheless, there are clear, though distorted, echoes of Galatians and Romans in the passage. Luke is aware of Paul's doctrine of justification through faith. What is significant, however, is the fact that, according to Acts, it is Peter, not Paul, who first gives practical expression to this doctrine in the conversion of the Gentile Cornelius (Acts 10:1–11:18), and it is Peter who alone articulates the doctrine (although in diluted form) at the Jerusalem Conference—indeed, in language strikingly reminiscent of Paul's own language in Gal 2:7–9,

---

57. The verse reads in the RSV: "and by him every one that believes is freed from everything from which you could not be freed by the law of Moses." The NEB has: "It is through him that everyone who has faith is acquitted of everything for which there was no acquittal under the Law of Moses." The Greek word translated as "freed" in the RSV and as "acquitted"/"acquittal" in the NEB is the passive of *dikaioun*, normally meaning "to justify" (as it is, indeed translated in the KJV). Haenchen observes that the verse is "evidently intended to reproduce Pauline theology," noting that "Luke's contemporaries were still aware that Paul had preached 'justification through faith'" (*Acts of the Apostles*, 412). Cf. also Foakes-Jackson and Lake, *Acts of the Apostles*, part I, vol. 4, 157: "Critics advocate two interpretations: (i) the ὧν οὐκ ἠδυνήθητε, etc., means that by the Law of Moses acquittal of some things was possible, but not of others, and Paul was announcing this possible method of going beyond what the Law could do; (ii) ὧν, etc., merely qualify πάντων, 'forgiveness for everything—which the Law never offered'. The former view is possible, but the latter seems more natural. Nor can I resist the belief that this verse is an attempt to express Pauline doctrine. Whatever hypothesis be adopted, it is incredible that the author of Acts was ignorant of the main outlines of Paul's teaching, and it was surely a part of his message that salvation is open to everyone who believes, in a way which was not given by the Law, even though he may have been unfair to Judaism in so presenting it."

14–16 (Acts 15:7–11), and this despite the fact that Paul portrays Peter as precisely the one who fails to understand fully and follow the implications of the doctrine (Gal 2:11–14).[58]

At this point, then, it might appear that the purpose of Luke here is to "rehabilitate" Peter as a champion of the Gentile mission and of freedom from the law. Shortly after the conversion of Cornelius, however, Peter simply disappears from the narrative of Acts (12:17b: "Then he departed and went to another place"), to reappear only for a moment at the Jerusalem Conference, where he emphasizes his own pioneering role as apostle to the Gentiles and endorses the work of Paul (Acts 15:7–11). It is clear, therefore, that the real object of Luke's interest is not Peter but rather Paul, who, for the remainder of the narrative, is the principal character. Indeed, it could even be said that, for Luke, Peter (like Stephen) serves as a kind of "forerunner" for Paul. Thus, Paul is seen not as an innovator and certainly not as a rebel (as might be suggested by some passages in the letters) but rather as the legitimate successor of Peter as missionary to the Gentiles. Paul belongs to the "church" (founded by Peter and the other apostles), not to some heretical or schismatic faction.

In short, the primary influence of Pauline theology as reflected in the letters is to be seen, not in Luke's portrayal of Paul's message, but rather in his portrayal of Peter's message and activity. Pauline language and ideas are placed on the lips of Peter, not (except at Acts 13:39) on the lips of Paul. This is done, however, for the sake of Paul. One can only surmise that Luke (like many others, both then and since) poorly understood and little appreciated Paul's doctrine of justification through faith, but he had great respect for Paul's activity as missionary to the Gentiles. The association of the doctrine, however, was too well known (from the letters?) to be denied or completely ignored, as was its relation

---

58. Particularly if the second interpretation suggested by Foakes-Jackson and Lake is followed, the verse clearly echoes authentic Pauline theology as seen in Galatians and Romans (see, e.g., Gal 2:16; 3:11, 21; Rom 3:20). In either case, as both Haenchen and Foakes-Jackson/Lake observe, it is intended to "reproduce" or "express" Pauline thought.

to the Gentile mission. Unable, then, to deny or ignore the fact that Paul had preached justification through faith, the next best expedient for Luke was to attribute the doctrine (in muted form) initially and primarily to the one great rival of Paul for preeminence in the church, namely, Peter, thus making it impossible to reject Paul because of his espousal of the doctrine without, at the same time, rejecting Peter for the same reason. Similarly, by portraying Peter as the real founder of the Gentile mission, Luke set the missionary activities of Paul in the larger context of the primitive apostolic mission, thus legitimizing both the work of Paul and the churches founded by him. Finally, by virtually ignoring Paul's claim to apostleship, Luke emphasized the continuity and concord that, in his view, marked (or should have marked) the progress of the Christian movement in the apostolic age. The achievement of Luke was, indeed remarkable: he succeeded in painting a picture of early Christianity that survived until the rise of modern critical scholarship.

Chapter 14

Acts and the Pauline Corpus Revisited
Peter's Speech at the
Jerusalem Conference

In a 1985 article entitled "Acts and the Pauline Corpus Reconsidered,"[1] I argued that the author of Acts "almost certainly knew, in some sense, at least some of the letters of Paul, [that] he made some use of these letters in the writing of his own work, and [that] there are plausible reasons why he, nevertheless, did not mention the letters or even indicate that Paul ever wrote letters."[2] As a part of the argument, I suggested "not only that the account of the so-called Jerusalem Conference in Acts 15 depends on Paul's reference to the same gathering in Galatians 2[3] but also that, at least to

---

"Acts and the Pauline Corpus Revisited: Peter's Speech at the Jerusalem Conference," pp. 77–86 in Thompson and Phillips, *Literary Studies in Luke-Acts*. Copyright © 1998 Mercer University Press. Reprinted with permission.

1. Walker, "Acts and the Pauline Corpus Reconsidered," reprinted in Porter and Evans, *The Pauline Writings*. All references will be to the initial publication in *JSNT*. See also chapter 13 in this volume.

2. Walker, "Acts and the Pauline Corpus Reconsidered," 14 (chapter 13, p. 231 in this volume).

3. Scholars have long debated whether the Jerusalem gathering described in Acts 15:1–29 and that reported by Paul in Gal 2:1–10 are the same. On the positive side, the location, the central issue, and at least some of the principal characters are identical. On the negative side, the reported outcome is radically different: in Acts, it is the "apostolic decree" (Acts 15:22–29); according to Paul, it is "only that they would have us remember the poor" (Gal 2:10). For a brief treatment of the issues involved, see, e.g., Cousar, "Jerusalem, Council of." For commentaries based upon the assumption that Acts and Galatians do in fact report the same gathering, see, e.g., Haenchen, *Acts of the Apostles*, esp. 440–73; and Conzelmann, *Acts of the Apostles*, esp. 114–22. For reasons not to be discussed here, I assumed when I wrote the 1985 article, and indeed still assume, that Acts 15:1–29 and Gal 2:1–10 do refer to the same gathering.

some extent, the account in Acts is intended to correct impressions that might be conveyed by Paul's material."[4] The purpose of the present study is to treat more fully this suggestion regarding the relation between Acts 15 and Galatians 2, with particular reference to Peter's speech in Acts 15:7–11.

At the outset, one feature of Paul's material must be noted. According to most interpretations, Gal 2:11–21[5] describes an occurrence that was later in time than the Jerusalem Conference reported in Gal 2:1–10.[6] My own judgment, however, is that, in something of a "flashback" fashion, Gal 2:11–21[7] represents simply Paul's further elaboration of the controversy in Antioch that led to the Conference in Jerusalem.[8] Indeed, I would suggest that the "false brethren secretly brought in, who slipped in to spy out our freedom which we have in Christ Jesus" (Gal 2:4) and the "certain men [who] came from James" (Gal 2:11) are the same people.[9] They came from Jerusalem to Antioch and instigated a controversy there that involved both Peter (Gal 2:11–12) and, at least temporarily, Barnabas (Gal 2:13) in opposition to Paul. As a result, Paul, Barnabas, and Titus went to Jerusalem (Gal 2:1), and the conference followed.[10] Thus, in my view, it is the entire chapter in Galatians that represents Paul's account of the Jerusalem

---

4. Walker, "Acts and the Pauline Corpus Reconsidered," 11 (chapter 13, p. 228 in this volume).

5. Or perhaps only vv. 11–14.

6. See, e.g., Bruce, *Epistle of Paul to the Galatians*, 128: "it is most natural to take this as an incident that followed the conference of vv 1–10." For a defense of this view, see, e.g., Ogg, *Chronology of the Life of Paul*, 89–98.

7. Or at least vv. 11–14.

8. For a cogent defense of this view, see, e.g., Munck, *Paul and the Salvation of Mankind*, 100–103.

9. Biblical quotations in this essay are from the RSV unless otherwise noted.

10. For the argument that the *twofold* reason for the trip to Jerusalem was divine revelation and the appearance of the "false brethren," see Walker, "Why Paul Went to Jerusalem" (chapter 1 in this volume).

Conference, not just vv. 1–10.[11] Even if this is not correct, however, the author of Acts, if he knew (and used?) Galatians in constructing his own account of the Conference, almost certainly knew (and used?) all of chap. 2, not just vv. 1–10. Thus, in what follows, I shall treat the entire chapter as a unit.

With this point clarified, I now return to the question of the relation between Peter's speech in Acts 15:7–11 and Paul's material in Galatians 2. Scholars have occasionally noted that "the argument of [Peter's] speech is remarkably Pauline,"[12] with particular attention to Acts 15:11: "But we believe that we shall be saved through the grace of the Lord Jesus, just as they will."[13] What has not been noted, however, at least to my knowledge, is the remarkable similarity, both ideational and verbal, between *Peter's speech as a whole* (Acts 15:7–11) and *Paul's report regarding the Jerusalem Conference* (Galatians 2). Also unnoticed or at least not emphasized, so far as I can ascertain, has been what can be termed the surprising "transfer of roles" from Paul to Peter that appears when one moves from Galatians 2 to Acts 15:7–11.

First, regarding the transfer of roles: In Galatians, *Paul* claims not only that it is he, Paul, who has "been entrusted with the gospel to the uncircumcised" and Peter with that "to the circumcised" but also that this division of responsibility was recognized and approved by the reputed "pillars" of the Jerusalem church: James, Cephas,[14] and John (Gal 2:7–9). Here, *Paul* is the apostle *par excellence* to the Gentiles and Peter is the apostle to the Jews.[15] In Acts

---

11. It may be, to be sure, that some or all of vv. 15–21 represents Paul's later reflection on the issues and not what he actually said to Peter in Antioch. Nevertheless, it is my own judgment that the entire chapter has in mind the controversy in Antioch and the conference in Jerusalem.

12. Foakes-Jackson, *Acts of the Apostles*, 137.

13. See, e.g., Haenchen, *Acts of the Apostles*, 446: "Peter speaks in terms familiar to us from Paul."

14. Regarded by most scholars, correctly in my judgment, as simply the Aramaic equivalent of the Greek Πέτρος.

15. In Gal 2:9, to be sure, James and John are also included in the mission to the Jews. Nevertheless, the emphasis clearly is on Peter (cf. v. 7).

15:7, however, *Peter* alludes to the conversion of the Gentile centurion Cornelius (Acts 10:1–11:18) as evidence of God's decision "in the early days" that it was to be by his, Peter's, mouth that "the Gentiles should hear the word of the gospel and believe." Here, *Peter* is the apostle *par excellence* to the Gentiles, and, at least by implication, others are responsible for the mission to the Jews.[16] To be sure, it might be argued that the division of responsibility mentioned by Paul represents a *later* development[17] and that Peter was indeed the original pioneer in the mission to the Gentiles. Taken simply at face value, however, the two passages appear to be in direct conflict. The role claimed by *Paul* in Galatians is claimed by *Peter* in Acts.

Perhaps even more surprising, however, is the fact that, in articulating his claim to this role in Acts 15:7–11, Peter employs ideas and even words that are remarkably reminiscent of Paul's ideas and words in Galatians 2, where the latter claims the same role for himself. Thus, not only is there a transfer of *roles* from Paul to Peter when one moves from Galatians 2 to Acts 15:7–11; there is also a transfer from Paul to Peter of essentially the same *ideas* and many of the same *words*. Indeed, as the following examples indicate, virtually everything in Peter's speech at the Jerusalem Conference (Acts 15:7–11) has parallels either in Paul's report regarding the same gathering (Galatians 2) or in other passages in Galatians:

1. In Gal 2:7, *Paul* refers to his message to the Gentiles as "gospel."[18] Similarly, in Acts 15:7, *Peter* speaks of his message to the Gentiles as "gospel."[19]
2. In Gal 2:7, as already noted, *Paul* speaks of a division of responsibility whereby he is to be the missionary to the

---

16. This latter point, I believe, is implied in Acts 15:7: "Brothers, you know that in the early days *God made choice among you* . . ." (emphasis added).
17. Perhaps even an agreement made at the Jerusalem Conference.
18. "The gospel to the uncircumcised."
19. "The word of the gospel."

Gentiles and Peter to the Jews. In Acts 15:7, *Peter* at least suggests a similar division of responsibility,[20] but here he is to go the Gentiles and others to the Jews.

3. In Gal 2:7–8, *Paul*, somewhat obliquely to be sure, attributes to divine decree his own selection as missionary to the Gentiles and that of Peter as missionary to the Jews.[21] In Acts 15:7, *Peter* appeals to God's "choice" as the basis for his selection as missionary to the Gentiles.[22]

4. In Gal. 2:6, *Paul* insists that "God shows no partiality." In Acts 15:9, *Peter* asserts that God "made no distinction." To be sure, Peter has in mind a distinction between Jews and Gentiles, while Paul refers to himself and the leaders of the Jerusalem church. Nevertheless, the basic point appears to be essentially the same: God does not play favorites so far as the life and mission of the church are concerned.

5. In Acts 15:8, *Peter* cites the Gentiles' reception of the Holy Spirit as proof that his mission to the Gentiles was approved by God.[23] This has no parallel, to be sure, in Paul's report regarding the Jerusalem Conference; in the passage immediately following this report, however, *Paul* cites reception of the Spirit by the Galatian Christians (presumably Gentiles) as evidence of the validity of his "gospel" and thus of his mission to the Gentiles (Gal 3:2–5).

6. In Acts 15:10, *Peter* refers to the Law as a "yoke" (ζυγός). Again, there is no parallel to this in Paul's report regarding

---

20. As already suggested (n. 16 above), this appears to be implied in the words, "God made choice among you."

21. Paul's use of the passive, "I had been entrusted . . . Peter had been entrusted . . ." (Gal 2:7), surely implies that it was God who had done the entrusting, and this is made more explicit by his statement that "he who worked through Peter for the mission to the circumcised worked through me also for the Gentiles" (Gal 2:8).

22. "Brothers, you know that in the early days God made choice among you, that by my mouth the Gentiles should hear the word of the gospel and believe."

23. "God . . . bore witness to [the Gentiles], giving them the Holy Spirit just as he did to us."

the Jerusalem Conference; in Gal 5:1, however, *Paul* refers specifically to the Law as "a yoke (ζυγός) of slavery."[24]

7. More fully, in Acts 15:10, *Peter* speaks of the Law as a "yoke upon the neck of the disciples which neither our fathers nor we have been able to bear" and accuses certain others of attempting to impose this "yoke" upon the Gentiles believers. In Gal 2:14, *Paul* is critical of none other than Peter, who, though himself a Jew, "live[s] like a Gentile and not like a Jew" but would "compel the Gentiles to live like Jews." The idea is at least similar to that in Acts: even Jews do not keep the Law, and yet some would compel the Gentiles to do so.

8. In Acts 15:10–11, *Peter* rejects the Law as a means of salvation and declares that both Jews and Gentiles are "saved through the grace of the Lord Jesus." In Gal 2:16,[25] *Paul* asserts (to Peter of all people) "that a person is not justified by works of the law but through faith in Jesus Christ . . . because by works of the law shall no one be justified."[26] Thus, Acts has *Peter* express precisely the same view about law and gospel as *Paul*, according to Galatians, expressed *to Peter*.[27]

9. In Acts 15:9, *Peter* asserts that God "cleansed [the] hearts" of both Gentiles and Jews "by faith."[28] As already noted, *Paul* insists in Gal 2:16[29] that "justification" is based not

---

24. According to Conzelmann (*Acts of the Apostles*, 117), however, "The concept of the Law as an unbearable burden is neither the common Jewish view . . . nor is it Pauline."

25. And elsewhere!

26. Adaptation of RSV. Many would translate διὰ πίστεως Ἰησοῦ Χριστοῦ as "through the faith/faithfulness of Jesus Christ"; see, e.g., Hays, *Faith of Jesus Christ*, passim; and Howard, *Paul: Crisis in Galatia*, passim.

27. Von Weizsäcker, *Apostolic Age of the Christian Church*, 1.211.

28. Cf. also Acts 15:11: "we believe that we shall be saved through the grace of the Lord Jesus, just as they will."

29. And elsewhere!

upon "works of the law" but rather upon "faith in Jesus Christ."[30]

10. In Acts 15:11, *Peter* declares that salvation comes "through the grace (χάρις) of the Lord Jesus." In Paul's report of the Jerusalem Conference, to be sure, "grace" (χάρις) appears only in a rather general sense, "the grace that was given to me" (Gal 2:9). Earlier in the letter, however, *Paul* refers specifically to the "grace of Christ" (χάρις Χριστοῦ) and to "his [i.e., God's] grace" (ἡ χάρις αὐτοῦ; Gal 1:6, 15).[31] Moreover, as F. J. Foakes-Jackson has noted, "Salvation by the grace of the Lord Jesus is . . . a characteristically Pauline doctrine."[32]

In short, virtually every idea and much of the actual wording of Peter's speech in Acts 15:7–11 have parallels either in Paul's report regarding the Jerusalem Conference (Galatians 2) or elsewhere in the Galatian letter. Indeed, the Acts passage is so remarkably similar to the material in Galatians as to suggest that the author of Acts almost certainly knew this letter and, indeed, used it as a source in constructing Peter's speech at the Jerusalem Conference. It is also surely worthy of note that Acts 15:7–11 is one of only two passages in Acts that articulate what might be called a "Pauline" soteriology[33] and that this soteriology is here attributed not to Paul but rather to Peter.

---

30. Or "Christ's faith/faithfulness."

31. In Gal 1:6, there are textual variants: some mss read "grace of Jesus Christ," some "grace of God," and some only "grace." By far the best attested reading, however, is "grace of Christ."

32. Foakes-Jackson, *Acts of the Apostles*, 137.

33. The other is Paul's speech in Antioch of Pisidia (Acts 13:16–41), where he is represented as saying (vv. 38–39): "Let it be known to you therefore, brethren, that through this man forgiveness of sins is proclaimed to you, and by him every one that believes is freed from everything from which you could not be freed by the law of Moses." For significant differences between this statement and Paul's actual views, however, see, e.g., Vielhauer, "On the 'Paulinism' of Acts," 41–43.

It appears, therefore, that, for some reason, the author of Acts here wishes to have *Peter*, not Paul, express the views more typically associated with *Paul* and, at the same time, to have *Peter* replace *Paul* as the pioneer missionary to the Gentiles. Why would this be? Two theoretical possibilities can almost immediately be rejected: (1) given Paul's dominating role in the following chapters of the book of Acts, it appears most unlikely that the author's goal is a denigration of Paul; and (2) in light of the fact that Peter disappears completely from the narrative immediately following the Jerusalem Conference, it is also unlikely that the goal is to elevate Peter's status and role.

Perhaps a clue to the author's intention is to be found, however, in a comparison of Acts 15:1–2, which introduces the account of the Jerusalem Conference, and Gal 2:11–14, which, according to my interpretation, also refers to events immediately preceding the Conference. Both of these passages speak of the following: (1) a controversy, (2) in Antioch, (3) sparked by "certain people" (τινες),[34] and (4) who came to Antioch "from" (ἀπό) elsewhere. The similarities both in general content and in specific wording suggest the likelihood of some literary relation between the two passages—almost certainly meaning, as already suggested, that the author of Acts knew and used the Galatians passage in constructing his own narrative. Despite the similarities, however, there are three important points at which the passages differ:[35]

---

34. Personal translation. See also Acts 15:24: "certain people (τινες) from us" (my translation). In Gal 2:12, the reading τινα ("a certain person") appears in P[46]. See, e.g., Matera, *Galatians*, 85: "This is an interesting reading in light of 5:10, which could be interpreted as referring to an individual disturbing the Galatian community. The reading of P[46], however, is not supported by any of the other important manuscripts, and it probably arose because of the well attested variant ἦλθεν (3rd sing.) in the same verse."

35. Indeed, there might appear to be a fourth. According to Acts, the subject of controversy was, at least initially, whether Gentile believers must be circumcised in order to be saved (Acts 15:1); according to Paul, however, the specific point at issue in Antioch was whether Jewish Christians should eat with Gentile Christians (Gal 2:12). This, however, is probably not a real contradiction. Acts refers to circumcision as "the

1. According to Paul, the people who created the controversy in Antioch came specifically from *James*, the leader of the church in Jerusalem; according to Acts, however, they came simply from *Judea*.[36] In other words, Paul suggests that James was involved, even if only indirectly, in instigating the controversy in Antioch, while Acts here suggests and later insists that the controversy was sparked only by certain persons from Judea who acted on their own initiative, without authorization from the leaders in Jerusalem.[37]

2. According to Paul, *Peter* (another of the leaders of the church) became directly involved (on the wrong side!) in the controversy in Antioch; in Acts, however, there is no mention of Peter even being in Antioch or of his involvement in the opposition to Paul.

3. According to Paul, "even *Barnabas* was carried away" by the insincerity of "the circumcision party"; in Acts, however, there is no reference to Barnabas' involvement in the controversy except as an ally of Paul.[38]

These three differences between Acts 15:1–2 and Paul's report in Gal 2:11–14 can actually be reduced to one: whether Barnabas

---

custom of Moses" (Acts 15:1), thus pointing to the Law as the basic issue. Moreover, Paul identified the opposition as "the circumcision party" (Gal 2:12) and, in his ensuing discussion, refers repeatedly to the Law as the real point at issue (Gal 2:16, 19, 21). If, as most interpreters hold, Gal 2:11–21 refers to events subsequent to the Jerusalem Conference, another important difference emerges: Paul reports that controversy in Antioch continued and perhaps even intensified after the Conference, while Acts suggests that all outstanding differences were, in fact, resolved at the Conference. As already indicated, however, I do not accept this interpretation of the sequence of events.

36. Indeed, the reference in Acts 15:1 is so vague as to allow the possible interpretation that the people were not even Christians; they might have been non-Christian Jews. Later in the chapter, however, it is made clear that they were, in fact, Christians (v. 24).

37. See Acts 15:24: "Since we have heard that certain people from us have troubled you with words, unsettling your minds, although we gave them no instructions . . ." (adaptation of RSV).

38. Later, to be sure, Acts does report "a sharp contention" between Paul and Barnabas, but the subject of debate is simply whether to take John Mark along on "the second missionary journey" (Acts 15:36–40).

and particularly Peter and James were involved in the controversy in Antioch in opposition to Paul. According to Paul, they were. According to Acts, they were not so involved, and, indeed, at the Jerusalem Conference, all three were in basic agreement with Paul.[39] In light of both the similarities and the differences between the two passages, it is my own judgment that the author of Acts almost certainly was familiar with and made use of Paul's material in Galatians, but that he deliberately altered this material in such a way as to remove James, Peter, and Barnabas from any type of involvement in the opposition to Paul. This alteration of the material includes the following:

1. The author of Acts omits any reference to James (and, indeed, any reference specifically to Jerusalem) in his depiction of the people who instigated the controversy in Antioch (Acts 15:1; cf. Gal 2:12). Ernst Haenchen suggests that he here "wishes to avoid creating the impression that the τινες are a Jerusalem delegation."[40] Even more to the point, I believe, he wishes to avoid any involvement of the *leadership* of the Jerusalem church (e.g., James) in the controversy in Antioch.
2. As already noted, the author omits any reference to *Peter* even being in Antioch (cf. Gal 2:11), thus removing him from any involvement in the controversy there.
3. The author also omits any reference to *Barnabas* except as an ally of Paul.[41]
4. At the Jerusalem Conference, the author attributes to none other than *James* the resolution of the controversy—a resolution that, as he portrays it, was accepted and endorsed

---

39. The position of James, according to Acts, might be regarded as something of a "mediating" one, but James is by no means portrayed as an "opponent" of the Pauline position.

40. Haenchen, *Acts of the Apostles*, 442–43. Note that the more general "Judea" appears, not the more specific "Jerusalem."

41. As already noted (see n. 38 above), the author of Acts does later describe a controversy between Paul and Barnabas, but the issue is totally unrelated to that of the Jerusalem Conference.

by all parties involved, including Paul (Acts 15:13–21, cf. 22–31).
5. Also at the Jerusalem Conference, the author attributes precisely to *James* the declaration that the people who instigated the controversy in Antioch had acted without authorization from the Jerusalem leadership (Acts 15:24).
6. In his most brilliant move of all, the author attributes to none other than *Peter* both the pioneering role as missionary to the Gentiles and, at the Jerusalem Conference, essentially the same ideas and indeed much of the actual language used by Paul in his own report regarding the gathering. Thus, he succeeds in portraying Peter as not only the chief spokesperson for the "Pauline" position but also as the one who, by divine decree, anticipated Paul as missionary *par excellence* to the Gentiles. There is, of course, real irony in this: in Galatians, it is precisely Peter who is the object of Paul's scathing criticism for being led astray by "the circumcision party"; in Acts, however, it is Peter who, more than anyone else, articulates Paul's vision of the Gentile mission.

Again, the question must be raised: What is the purpose of the author of Acts in thus altering Paul's account of the controversy in Antioch and the Conference in Jerusalem that followed? Although this cannot here be worked out in any detail, my own view is that the author's purpose is neither to exalt Peter nor to denigrate Paul but rather to "rehabilitate" Paul in the minds of those Christians who, for whatever reason, look upon him with suspicion.[42] He does this by indicating that Paul's activities as missionary to the Gentiles and his views regarding soteriology are neither idiosyncratic nor novel; rather, they were anticipated and articulated by none other than Peter, supported by James, and endorsed by the assembled "apostles" and "elders" who led the early church in

---

42. For further detail, see Walker, "Acts and the Pauline Corpus Reconsidered," esp. 14–17 (chapter 13, pp. 231–36 in this volume).

Jerusalem. In other words, Paul was not a "maverick" as some might suspect; both his activities and his ideology were squarely within the mainstream of "apostolic" Christianity.[43]

A final word: If this interpretation of the relation between the two accounts of the Jerusalem Conference is correct, two of the three points of my 1985 article are thereby substantiated: the author of Acts "almost certainly knew, in some sense, at least some of the letters of Paul, [and] he made use of these letters in the writing of his own work."[44]

---

43. To be sure, except at 14:4, 14, the author of Acts never refers to Paul as an "apostle," the title Paul so insistently claims for himself in his letters (and particularly in Galatians!).

44. Walker, "Acts and the Pauline Corpus Reconsidered," 14–17 (chapter 13, pp. 231–36 in this volume).

Chapter 15

The Story of Peter and Cornelius as a Corrective to Galatians 2:11–14

The story of Peter's encounter with Cornelius and its aftermath fills almost two entire chapters in the book of Acts (Acts 10:1–11:18). The narrative includes a number of apparently extraneous details,[1] and a significant portion of it is repetitious and unnecessary for acquainting the reader with what transpired.[2] Moreover, later at the Jerusalem Council, the incident is alluded to by both Peter (Acts 15:7–9) and, more briefly, James (Acts 15:14). Obviously, then, as Martin Dibelius notes, the story of Peter and Cornelius "has a special importance in the book of Acts."[3]

The narrative goes as follows: A God-fearing Gentile centurion named Cornelius, living in Caesarea, has a vision instructing him to send for Peter, who is in Joppa at the time. As a result of both a vision from heaven and an explicit command by "the Spirit," Peter goes to Caesarea, where he preaches to Cornelius and his gathered relatives and friends. While Peter is speaking, they receive the Holy Spirit and speak in tongues, whereupon Peter commands that they be baptized in the name of Jesus Christ. When this becomes known in Jerusalem, however, Peter is criticized by "the circumcision party" (οἱ ἐκ περιτομῆς) because he "went to uncircumcised men and ate with them" (εἰσῆλθες πρὸς ἄνδρας

---

1. E.g., "about the ninth hour of the day" (Acts 10:3), "about the sixth hour" (Acts 10:9), "about this hour" (Acts 10:30), and "these six brothers" (Acts 11:12).
2. 10:30–32, on the lips of Cornelius, repeats 10:3–6 almost *verbatim*, and 11:4–17, on the lips of Peter, summarizes 10:9–48.
3. Dibelius, "Conversion of Cornelius," 140. Cf. e.g., vanThanh Nguyen, *Peter and Cornelius*, 123 n. 63, who speaks of "the enormous effort Luke put into the Cornelius sequence"; and Gaventa, *From Darkness to Light*, 123–24.

ἀκροβυστίαν ἔχοντας καὶ συνέφαγες αὐτοῖς). Peter vigorously defends his actions, citing the vision from heaven in which he was commanded three times to eat "unclean food," recounting the details of his encounter with Cornelius, and noting that the Gentiles to whom he preached, like they themselves at an earlier time, received the Holy Spirit. The conclusion of the episode is that Peter's critics are silenced and they glorify God, saying, "Then to the Gentiles also God has given repentance unto life" (ἄρα καὶ τοῖς ἔθνεσιν ὁ θεὸς τὴν μετάνοιαν εἰς ζωὴν ἔδωκεν).

Problems in the Narrative

The story, ending as it does with this final statement on the lips of Peter's erstwhile critics, appears to be a rather straightforward account of how the gospel has now, for the first time, been carried to Gentiles, they have received the Holy Spirit and been baptized, members of "the circumcision party" (οἱ ἐκ περιτομῆς) in Jerusalem have objected, and Peter has persuaded them to change their mind, thus ending the controversy over inclusion of Gentiles in the Christian community. A close reading, however, reveals a number of problems in the narrative and suggests that the author may have more in mind than simply reporting and justifying the evangelizing of Gentiles. I note the following items, each of which is in some way problematic and/or hints that the author's agenda goes beyond the immediately apparent point of the story:[4]

1. The hero of the story is *Peter*; it is he who, despite his initial reluctance, is the first—in Caesarea—to carry the gospel to Gentiles, and it is he who bears the brunt of the initial criticism for having done so. Later in Acts, however, it would appear that *"men of Cyprus and Cyrene"* are the first—not in Caesarea but rather in Antioch—to carry the gospel to Gentiles (Acts 11:19–26)[5] and that

---

4. As Dibelius ("Conversion of Cornelius," 141) notes, "Peter's account [in Acts 11:4–17] differs in various details from the account in Acts 10"; for a discussion of these differences, Dibelius cites Bauernfeind in *Kommentar und Studien zur Apostelgeschichte*.

5. See esp. v. 19: ". . . speaking the word to none except Jews"; and vv. 20–21: "But there were some of them, men of Cyprus and Cyrene,

this is a matter of some concern to "the church in Jerusalem" (see v. 22).[6] Both the intimation that "men of Cyprus and Cyrene" are the first to carry the gospel to Gentiles and the apparent concern on the part of "the church in Jerusalem" are surprising, coming, as they do, *after* the story of Peter and Cornelius, in which the issue of Gentile inclusion appears to have been settled. Still later, Acts 13:45–47, if read in isolation from the earlier materials, appears to suggest that *Paul and Barnabas* are the first—in Antioch of Pisidia—to preach to Gentiles.[7] Finally, in Galatians 2:7–9, Paul reports an agreement whereby he, *Paul* (together with Barnabas), is to go to the Gentiles while James, Cephas/Peter,[8] and John are

---

who on coming to Antioch spoke to the Greeks also, preaching the Lord Jesus. And the hand of the Lord was with them, and a great number that believed turned to the Lord." To be sure, the best witnesses read "Hellenists" (Ἑλληνιστάς) rather than "Greeks" (Ἕλληνάς) in v. 20, and this is in fact the reading adopted by NA[28] and the NRSV. The RSV, however, reads "Greeks." Moreover, the precise meaning of Ἑλληνιστάς is far from clear, and, as Pervo (*Acts: A Commentary*, 291) points out: "Verses 19 and 20 contain parallel constructions, stylistically varied: 'speak the *message to x*.' Since the *x* in v. 19 is (exclusively) 'Jews,' the parallel evidently must include 'non-Jews,' that is, gentiles." For discussion, see, e.g., Pervo, *Acts: A Commentary*, 291; and Metzger, *Textual Commentary*, 2nd ed., 340–42.

6. See v. 22: "News of this came to the ears of the church in Jerusalem, and they sent Barnabas to Antioch." Sending Barnabas to Antioch is reminiscent of sending Peter and John to Samaria following Philip's preaching there (Acts 8:4–17, esp. v. 14).

7. See also Acts 14:27 and 15:4. Is it mere coincidence that both Acts 11:19–21 and Acts 13:45–47 are set in *Antioch* (to be sure, the former is Antioch of Syria and the latter is Antioch of Pisidia), or does it reflect a tradition that it was in fact *Antioch*, not Caesarea, where the gospel was first preached to Gentiles? If the latter, it might suggest that the story of Peter and Cornelius—or at least its setting in Caesarea—has been fabricated by the author of Acts in order to promote some particular item in his or her literary/theological/apologetic agenda. The author would appear to be saying three things: (1) It was not *Paul* who first carried the gospel to the Gentiles; it was *Peter*. (2) This occurred *before* Paul began his missionary work. (3) It happened in *Caesarea*, not in *Antioch*.

8. Κηφᾶς is the Greek transliteration of the Aramaic word meaning "craig," "stone," or "rock"," while Πέτρος is the Greek word for "stone" or "rock"; thus, the two are roughly synonymous (see, e.g., Fitzmyer,

to go to the Jews. This appears to be at odds with the role of Peter in the story of Peter and Cornelius. Thus, there is some degree of tension at this point not only between the story of Peter and Cornelius in Acts and Paul's account in Galatians but also within the book of Acts itself. This suggests that the story of Peter and Cornelius is, at least to some extent, contrived and that there is more to the author's agenda than simply reporting and justifying the initial inclusion of Gentiles in the Christian community.

2. It is "the circumcision party" (οἱ ἐκ περιτομῆς) in Jerusalem who criticize Peter for what he has done. As Richard I. Pervo points out, however, this is an anachronism because "such a faction could have existed only if there were 'a circumcision-free' party,"[9] and the question of Gentile circumcision is not raised in Acts until 15:1. Thus, like the emphasis on Peter as the first to carry the gospel to Gentiles, the reference to "the circumcision party" appears to be artificial and contrived.

3. As just noted, Peter's critics are identified in 11:2 as "the circumcision party" (οἱ ἐκ περιτομῆς); moreover, the criticism is that he "went to *uncircumcised men* (ἄνδρας ἀκροβυστίαν ἔχοντας) and ate with them." This would appear to suggest that the issue was that of *circumcision*. The criticism, however, focuses not on the fact that the men were uncircumcised but rather on the fact that Peter went to them and *ate with them*. This is surprising, because the earlier narrative says nothing about him eating with them,[10]

"Aramaic *Kêphā'* and Peter's Name," 114–15). Although a few scholars argue that "Cephas" and "Peter" are different people (see, e.g., Ehrman, "Cephas and Peter"), most agree that the two names refer to the same person (see, e.g., Allison, "Peter and Cephas"). For purposes of the present study, I shall assume that "Cephas" and "Peter" are roughly synonymous names for the same person. It should be noted, however, that, except in Gal 2:7b–8, which may be a later interpolation (see Walker, "Galatians 2:7b–8 as a Non-Pauline Interpolation," chapter 5 in this volume), Paul always uses the name "Cephas" (Gal 1:18; 2:9, 11, 14; 1 Cor 1:12; 3:22; 9:5; 15:5).

9. Pervo, *Acts: A Commentary*, 284. Indeed, Pervo sees this anachronism as an indication "that Galatians 1–2 is the external source of [the] passage."

10. To be sure, the statement that "they asked him to remain for some days" (10:48b) no doubt carries the implication that Peter ate with the

and, in his defense, he makes no reference to this particular accusation. Thus, like the identification of Peter as the first to carry the gospel to the Gentiles and the reference to "the circumcision party," the criticism for eating with Gentiles appears to be artificial and contrived. Indeed, the accusation specifically of *eating with Gentiles* may suggest that the real issue in the mind of the author is neither preaching to Gentiles nor circumcision but rather *eating* with Gentiles.[11]

4. While Peter is still preaching to them, Cornelius and his household receive the Holy Spirit and speak in tongues, whereupon they are baptized. Here, it is important to note the sequence: they receive the Holy Spirit and speak in tongues *before they are baptized*. Only once elsewhere in Acts does receiving the Holy Spirit precede baptism, and this is in the case of Saul/Paul (Acts 9:17–18);[12] elsewhere, baptism comes first.[13] Thus, the sequence in the story of Peter and Cornelius appears to suggest that, for some reason, the author of Acts wishes to emphasize *receiving the Holy Spirit* as the distinguishing mark of a Christian. Further, the fact that the only other instance of receiving the Holy Spirit before baptism involves Paul may suggest *a connection in the author's mind between Paul and receiving the Holy Spirit as the distinguishing mark of a Christian*.

5. The story of Peter and Cornelius is one of only *three* pericopes in Acts that refer to speaking in tongues. The others are the story of Pentecost (Acts 2, see esp. vv. 3–4) and the account of Paul

---

Gentiles, and the earlier statement that Peter "called them in to be his guests" (10:23) may suggest the same thing. Nevertheless, it is noteworthy that, although his critics focused their attention on eating, his actually having done so receives no mention in the narrative.

11. The fact that Peter's vision includes a command to *eat* may suggest the same thing.

12. It is not explicitly stated that Saul received the Holy Spirit *before* he was baptized, but it is strongly implied.

13. Acts 2:38 (Peter's Pentecost audience); 8:15–17 (the Samaritans); and 19:1–7 (the disciples in Ephesus who were re-baptized by Paul). Baptism and the Holy Spirit are also linked at Acts 1:5, which draws a contrast between John's baptism with water and baptism with the Holy Spirit.

and the disciples in Ephesus who had initially been baptized into John's baptism but whom Paul then had baptized into the name of the Lord Jesus (Acts 19:1-7). This may suggest a linkage of some sort among the three, and it may be intended to indicate the importance of each in the spread of the gospel:[14] the Pentecost story reports the "birth" of the church, the story of Peter and Cornelius reports the first addition of Gentiles to the church, and the story of Paul in Ephesus reports the incorporation of a "fringe group" — perhaps actual followers of John the Baptist—into the church.[15] All of this may be a part of a larger twofold agenda on the part of the author: namely, to emphasize the *inclusiveness* of the church and to emphasize the fact that this inclusiveness began with *Peter*.

6. Although the statement of Peter's erstwhile critics in Acts 11:18 would appear to settle once and for all the question of full inclusion of Gentiles in the Christian community, the issue reappears in Acts 15:1 where "certain ones, having come down from Judea, were teaching the brothers, 'Unless you are circumcised according to the custom of Moses, you cannot be saved,'" and another gathering of Christian leaders in Jerusalem is required to settle this issue. This, too, prompts one to wonder whether the story of Peter and Cornelius is included—and is placed *before* the beginning of Paul's missionary activity—for some reason other than simply reporting and justifying the inclusion of Gentiles in the Christian community.

7. Although this is not in the story of Peter and Cornelius, it is important to note that, later in Acts, when Peter is recalling and defending his actions (Acts 15:7-11), he expresses ideas and employs vocabulary that are remarkably similar to certain *statements*

---

14. To be sure, the story of Paul and the Ephesians is much shorter than the other two, but it marks the beginning of Paul's ministry in Ephesus, which, according to Acts 19:18, lasted for three months.

15. See, e.g., Trebilco, *Early Christians in Ephesus*, 127-34, for the argument that these people were actual disciples of John the Baptist. Other scholars (e.g., Haenchen, *Acts of the Apostles*, 557; Barrett, *Critical and Exegetical Commentary on Acts*, vol. 2, 886; and Fitzmyer, *Acts of the Apostles*, 642) see them more broadly as "sects" or "fringe groups".

made by Paul in his letter to the Galatians. Indeed, "virtually everything in Peter's speech at the Jerusalem Conference (Acts 15:7–11) has parallels either in Paul's report regarding the same gathering (Galatians 2) or in other passages in Galatians."[16]

This suggests that a clue to the author's reason—or at least *one* of the author's reasons—for devoting so much attention to the story of Peter and Cornelius might be found in Galatians.

Items to Note in Galatians

I note, therefore, the following items in Galatians, each of which is related in some way to the story of Peter and Cornelius in Acts:

1. As already noted, Paul reports in Gal 2:7–9 the decision of the "pillars" in Jerusalem that *he* and Barnabas will preach to the Gentiles while *they*—James, Cephas /Peter, and John—will preach to the Jews.
2. Then, in Gal 2:11–14, Paul recounts an incident in which Cephas/Peter *ate with Gentiles* in Antioch until "certain people" came from James, at which point "he drew back and separated himself, fearing *the circumcision party*" (ὑπέστελλεν καὶ ἀφώριζεν ἑαυτόν, φοβούμενος τοὺς ἐκ περιτομῆς). Here, Cephas/Peter is portrayed in a highly negative light. Indeed, Paul accuses him of "hypocrisy" (ὑπόκρισις) and says that he, Paul, "opposed him to his face, because he stood condemned" (κατὰ πρόσωπον αὐτῷ ἀνέστην ὅτι κατεγνωσμένος ἦν). Significantly, the point of the controversy is not whether Gentiles can become Christians but rather whether a Jew should *eat with Gentiles*.[17]

---

16. Walker, "Acts and the Pauline Corpus Revisited," 80 (chapter 14, p. 240 in this volume).

17. The fact that the incident involving Cephas eating with Gentiles (Gal 2:11–14) comes *after* the reported division of labor whereby Paul and Barnabas would go to the Gentiles while James, Cephas, and John would go to the Jews (Gal 2:7–9) is problematic. It may suggest that 2:11–14 is a "flashback," reporting something that actually happened *before* the division of labor. Indeed, the incident in Antioch may even have been part of

3. Later, in Gal 3:2-5, Paul suggests that receiving the Holy Spirit marks the beginning of the Christian life.[18]

Similarities between Acts 10–11 and Galatians

The following similarities between the story of Peter and Cornelius in Acts and what Paul says about Cephas/Peter in Gal 2:11-14 are striking: (1) the principal character is *Peter/Cephas*, (2) the primary issue of controversy—explicitly in Galatians and perhaps implicitly in Acts—is *whether Jews may eat with Gentiles*, (3) Peter/Cephas *does in fact eat with Gentiles* in Galatians and is accused of having done so in Acts,[19] (4) he is *criticized* for eating with Gentiles, and (5) his critics are *"the circumcision party"* (οἱ ἐκ περιτομῆς) in or from Jerusalem.[20] In addition, both the story of Peter and Cornelius and Gal 3:2-5 indicate that it is *reception of the Holy Spirit* that marks the beginning of the Christian life. Moreover, the reference in Gal 3:5 to "the one who supplies the Spirit to you and works *miracles* (δυνάμεις) among you" may well be a veiled reference to *speaking in tongues* as one of these "miracles" that mark the beginning of the Christian life; thus, it may associate speaking in tongues with receiving the Holy Spirit.[21]

---

the reason why Paul and Barnabas went to Jerusalem and met with the "pillars" there (Gal 2:1-10). Further, it is at least possible that *both* Paul and Barnabas went to Jerusalem precisely because they had been on opposite sides of the controversy in Antioch and thus could represent both sides of the debate.

18. The verses read as follows: "Did you receive the Spirit by works of the law or by hearing with faith? Are you so foolish? Having begun with the Spirit, are you now ending with the flesh? Did you experience so many things in vain (if, indeed, it is in vain)? Does he who supplies the Spirit to you and works miracles among you do so by works of the law or by hearing with faith"?

19. He may actually have done so in Acts; see n. 9 above.

20. Jerusalem is explicitly mentioned in Acts 11:2, while Gal 2:12 strongly implies Jerusalem by saying that the critics came "from James" (ἀπὸ Ἰακώβου).

21. It is clear from 1 Corinthians 12–14 that Paul regards speaking in tongues as one of the "spiritual gifts" (πνευματικά or χαρίσματα) and

In my judgment, these striking similarities can hardly be coincidental: Peter/Cephas as the principal character in an incident in which he, a Jew, is criticized for eating with Gentiles; "the circumcision party" (the same wording, οἱ ἐκ περιτομῆς, in both Acts and Galatians) in Jerusalem as Peter/Cephas' critics; and reception of the Holy Spirit (and perhaps speaking in tongues) as marking the beginning of the Christian life. Of particular significance, in my judgment, is the fact that, as already noted, the story of Peter and Cornelius has Peter the subject of criticism precisely for *eating with* Gentiles even though the narrative does not actually say that he did so, and the criticism of Peter reported by Paul in Galatians focuses on *eating with Gentiles*. Such striking similarities require some explanation.

Source(s) for the Peter and Cornelius Story

It is generally agreed that Paul's letter to the Galatians was written some decades earlier than Acts.[22] Moreover, there is a growing body of evidence—and there now appears to be a growing consensus—that the author of Acts knew and used at least some of Paul's letters as sources,[23] and much of the attention in this regard has focused specifically on parallels between Acts and Galatians.[24] It is beyond the scope of the present study to explore this issue, but I am persuaded that the author of Acts did, in fact, know at least

---

thus as a quite legitimate, if sometimes problematic, mark of the Christian life. Indeed, he says in 1 Cor 14:5, "I want all of you to speak in tongues," and in 1 Cor 14:18, "I speak in tongues more than all of you."

22. The relative dating of Galatians is a matter of considerable debate, with some scholars viewing it as one of the earliest, if not the earliest, of Paul's letters and others placing it only shortly before Romans. In any case, however, it is to be dated sometime in the sixth decade of the first century CE. Similarly, the dating of Acts is variously dated between the 60s CE and the early part of the second century. Pervo (*Dating Acts*) settles on "a date c. 115, or 110–120" CE, but my own judgment is that Acts may well have been written later, perhaps even as late as mid-second century.

23. See, e.g., Pervo, *Dating Acts*, 51–147, and the literature cited there.

24. See, e.g., Pervo, *Dating Acts*, 73–96, and the literature cited there.

some of Paul's letters, including Galatians, and that this author used them as source material. Thus, in my judgment, the striking similarities between the story of Peter and Cornelius and the material cited in Galatians are most plausibly to be explained, at least for the most part, by assuming that the author of Acts knew the material in Galatians and that this material served as both the stimulus and the primary source for the story.[25]

This is not necessarily to suggest, of course, that Galatians was the *only* source used by the author of Acts. Indeed, I regard it as likely that the story of Peter and Cornelius was patterned in part on Luke 7:2–10, where a centurion (ἑκατονάρχης — the same Greek word as in Acts 10:1) sends people to Jesus with the request that he come and heal his slave. In Luke 7:2–5, the centurion is described by the elders of the Jews, whom he has sent to Jesus, as being "worthy" for Jesus to heed his call, "for he loves our nation, and he built us our synagogue." Similarly, in Acts 10:22, the centurion who sends for Peter is spoken of as "an upright and God-fearing man, who is well spoken of by the whole Jewish nation."[26] Such parallels suggest that this story in Luke likely served as a partial model for the story of Peter and Cornelius.

It is also possible that some tradition, oral and/or written, lies behind the account in Acts. In addition, the author's own fertile imagination undoubtedly played a major role in the construction of the narrative. In my judgment, however, it is only the author's

---

25. As already noted (see n. 9 above), Pervo (*Acts*, 284) sees the anachronistic reference to "the circumcision party" (οἱ ἐκ περιτομῆς) in Acts 11:2 as an indication "that Galatians 1–2 is the external source of this passage [i.e., Acts 11:1–18]."

26. Cf. v. 1, where he is characterized as "devout and God-fearing" (εὐσεβὴς καὶ φοβούμενος τὸν Θεόν). In both Luke 7:3 and Acts 10:7, the centurion sends *others* to, respectively, Jesus and Peter, while in the parallel to Luke 7:2–10 (Matt 8:5–13), it is *the centurion himself* who comes to Jesus with the request. The Greek word ἑκατονάρχης appears three times in Luke (7:2, 6; 23:47) and a number of times in Acts (10:1, 22; 21:32; 22:25, 26; 23:17, 23; 24:23; 27:1, 6, 11, 31, 43; 28:16) but only four times elsewhere in the NT, all of them in Matthew (8:5, 8, 13; 27:54). The transliterated Latin equivalent, κεντυρίων, occurs only in Mark (15:39, 44, 45).

reliance upon the material cited in Galatians that adequately explains the remarkable similarities between this material and the story of Peter and Cornelius. Thus, I conclude (a) that the story of Peter and Cornelius is—largely if not solely—the composition of the author of Acts, (b) that it likely is patterned in part on Luke 7:2–10, but (c) that it is based in large measure upon material in Paul's letter to the Galatians—particularly the encounter between Paul and Cephas/Peter recounted in Gal 2:11–14.

Differences between Acts 10–11 and Galatians

In addition to the similarities between the story of Peter and Cornelius and Paul's statements in Galatians, however, there are also some differences that are at least equally striking. They are as follows:

1. In Acts, *Peter* is the first to carry the gospel to the Gentiles; in Galatians, however, it is *Paul*, along with Barnabas, who is to go to the Gentiles, while Cephas/Peter, along with James and John, is to go to the Jews.
2. In Acts, the place where the incident sparking the criticism of Peter took place is *Caesarea*; in Galatians, however, the location is *Antioch*.
3. In Acts, both a vision from heaven and instructions from "the Spirit" are required to persuade Peter to go to the Gentiles, but, having gone and having noted their response to his preaching, *he vigorously defends his actions* in the face of criticism by "the circumcision party" (οἱ ἐκ περιτομῆς) in Jerusalem; in Galatians, however, Cephas/Peter initially eats with Gentiles but *ceases doing so* when criticized by "the circumcision party" (οἱ ἐκ περιτομῆς) from Jerusalem.
4. In Acts, *Peter is able to persuade his critics that he has acted correctly* in associating with and preaching to Gentiles, and they end up glorifying God and saying, "Then to the Gentiles also God has granted repentance unto life" (ἄρα καὶ τοῖς ἔθνεσιν ὁ Θεὸς τὴν μετάνοιαν εἰς ζωὴν

ἔδωκεν); in Galatians, however, *it is the critics who carry the day*, persuading not only Cephas/Peter but also Barnabas and "the rest of the Jews" (οἱ λοιποὶ Ἰουδαῖοι) to cease their contact with Gentiles.

5. In Acts, Peter is portrayed in a highly *favorable light*; in Galatians, however, Cephas/Peter is portrayed in a quite *negative light*.[27]

If the similarities between the story of Peter and Cornelius in Acts and what Paul says in Galatians are best accounted for by assuming that Galatians was a primary source for the author of Acts, how are we to account for these striking differences between the two? I propose that the differences between Acts and Galatians are best explained by assuming that the story of Peter and Cornelius in Acts was composed—or at least adapted—*for the specific purpose of rebutting—or at least correcting or "sanitizing"—Paul's highly negative portrayal of Cephas/Peter in Galatians*. This proposal, of course, requires some explication.

Author's Agenda in the Story of Peter and Cornelius

Richard I. Pervo suggests that "Acts . . . can blandly but accurately be characterized as 'legitimating narrative'."[28] There is debate, however, regarding exactly what or whom the author wishes to "legitimate." For some scholars, the goal is to legitimate the Christian movement in the eyes of the Roman world and particularly of Roman officialdom.[29] For others, however, it is the exact opposite: to legitimate the Roman Empire in the eyes of Christians.[30] For still others, a primary goal is to oppose "heretical" teachings and to reclaim Paul from the "heretics" for the de-

---

27. Note that 1 Cor 1:11–12 (cf. 3:22; 9:5) also suggests some degree of tension between Paul and Cephas (Peter).
28. Pervo, *Acts: A Commentary*, 21.
29. E.g., Cadbury, *Making of Luke-Acts*, 306–16.
30. E.g., Walasky, *"And so we came to Rome."*

veloping mainstream of Christianity.[31] My own judgment is that some version of this last alternative is surely *one* of the goals of the author of Acts, although I would prefer to say that the aim here is "to 'rehabilitate' Paul in the minds of those Christians who, for whatever reason, look upon him with suspicion"[32] — i.e., to present him in a light that will make him acceptable to *non-Pauline* Christians. One of the ways in which the author attempts to carry out this "rehabilitation" is by portraying Peter, not Paul, as the first to carry the gospel to the Gentiles, thereby legitimating Paul's activity as simply a continuation of what has already been begun by one of the leaders among the original disciples of Jesus. Another is by having Peter express ideas and employ vocabulary that are remarkably similar to Paul's statements in Galatians, thus placing a stamp of approval on Paul's theology (as this theology is "domesticated" in the book of Acts).

I suggest, however, that a secondary and related goal of the author of Acts is to rebut, correct, or "sanitize" the portrayal of Cephas/Peter in Paul's letter to the Galatians[33] and thus in a sense to "rehabilitate" or "legitimate" him — i.e., to present him in a light that will make him acceptable to *Pauline* Christians.[34] By creating — or adapting — the story of Peter and Cornelius, the author suggests that, even though Peter may at one point have "back-slidden," he nevertheless was the first to carry the gospel to the Gentiles, to associate (and perhaps) eat with them, and to defend his action in so doing. Specifically, although Galatians portrays Cephas/Peter as having initially eaten with Gentiles and then, when criticized, having ceased to do so, Acts reverses

---

31. E.g., Tyson, *Marcion and Luke-Acts;* cf. e.g., Goodenough, "Perspective of Acts," 54.

32. Walker, "Acts and the Pauline Corpus Revisited," 85 (chapter 14, p. 247 in this volume).

33. Again, see also 1 Cor 1:11–12 (cf. 3:22; 9:5).

34. See, e.g., Walker, "'Paulinization' of Peter." The "Paulinization" of Peter involves attributing to him the views and vocabulary found in Paul's letter to the Galatians and having him replace Paul as the pioneer missionary to the Gentiles.

the narrative by having Peter at first unwilling to associate with Gentiles but then willing both to do so and to defend what he has done.[35]

I can only speculate as to why the author of Acts chooses Caesarea rather than Antioch as the locale for Peter's controversial activity. It may be because, if Peter is to be the *first* to carry the gospel to Gentiles, he must do so *before* the "men of Cyprus and Cyrene" preach to Greeks in Antioch (Acts 11:20–21)—i.e., *before* the gospel is carried to Antioch and *before* Saul/Paul arrives in Antioch (Acts 11:25–26). This requires a different locale for Peter's activity. In other words, it was not Paul who first carried the gospel to Gentiles; it was Peter. And it was not in Antioch that this occurred; it was in Caesarea. Alternatively, it may be that the author chooses Caesarea simply because the book of Acts never has Peter moving beyond the boundaries of Palestine; indeed, both he and James are needed in Jerusalem for the Jerusalem Conference (Acts 15:1–21). Thus, if it was *Peter* who first carried the gospel to the Gentiles, it could *not* have been in Antioch. I suggest, however, that locating Peter's activity in Caesarea may also be a subtle way of "sanitizing" Paul's account in Gal 2:11–14 without actually contradicting it. The story of Peter and Cornelius (Acts 10:1–11:18) appears in the book of Acts *before* Saul/Paul goes to Antioch (Acts 11:26). Thus, the author may be intimating that, *prior to* his "hypocrisy" in Antioch (reported by Paul but not in Acts), Peter acted correctly in Caesarea. In other words, the author may be intimating, "Even if you accept what Paul says about him, Peter is not all bad! What happened in Antioch was simply an unfortunate lapse on Peter's part."

Both the "rehabilitation" of Paul and the "sanitizing" of Paul's portrayal of Peter are, of course, part of a larger goal on the part of the author of Acts: namely, to present the Christian movement

---

35. Along somewhat similar lines, the author of Acts appears to have used Paul's insistence that Titus, a Greek, was not compelled to be circumcised (Gal 2:1–3) as the basis for a story in which Paul himself did in fact circumcise Timothy, who was half Jewish and half Greek; see Walker, "Timothy-Titus Problem Reconsidered" (chapter 12 in this volume).

as one that was, except for a few minor problems that were easily resolved, basically unified and harmonious from the very beginning.

Conclusion

It is clear from Paul's letters that there was some degree of tension and, upon at least one occasion, outright conflict between him and Cephas/Peter. It is also clear that this tension is completely absent from the book of Acts. What I am proposing is that the author of Acts wishes to downplay, if not completely erase, the tension and, for the specific purpose of rebutting—or at least correcting or "sanitizing"—Paul's highly negative portrayal of Cephas/Peter in Gal 2:11–14, constructs the story of Peter and Cornelius, relying largely upon Paul's letter to the Galatians, perhaps also to a lesser extent upon Luke 7:2–10, possibly upon the tradition of some actual historical occurrence, and certainly quite heavily upon his or her own fertile imagination.

Chapter 16

The Portrayal of Aquila and Priscilla in Acts
The Question of Sources

The author of Acts—hereafter, with no implications regarding actual identity, to be called simply "Luke"—mentions Aquila and Priscilla three times:

1. In 18:1–3, Paul arrives in Corinth from Athens, takes up residence with the couple, and works with them in their trade as σκηνοποιοί.[1] Aquila is identified as a Jewish native of Pontus who, with his wife Priscilla, has recently moved from Italy to Corinth because the Emperor Claudius had banished all Jews from Rome.
2. In 18:18–19, Priscilla and Aquila leave Corinth with Paul, accompanying him as far as Ephesus, where they remain.
3. In 18:24–26, they correct what they regard as a defective version of the gospel being preached by Apollos in Ephesus.[2]

The same couple—known, however, as Aquila and Prisca[3]—appears three times in the Pauline letters:[4]

"The Portrayal of Aquila and Priscilla in Acts: The Question of Sources." NTS 54,4 (Oct 2008) 479–95. Copyright © 2008 Cambridge University Press. Reprinted with permission.

1. Usually translated as "tentmakers" or "leather workers," but see below on pp. 276–77 for a different possibility.
2. Other references to Aquila (but not Priscilla) in various versions of the "Western" text (Acts 18:2, 7, 18, 21) are almost certainly later additions.
3. "Priscilla" is the diminutive form of "Prisca" and clearly refers to the same person.
4. "Pauline letters" here and elsewhere includes the Pastorals, Ephesians, Colossians, and 2 Thessalonians, all of which I regard as pseudonymous.

1. In 1 Cor 16:19b, Paul conveys greetings from Aquila and Prisca[5] and "the church in their house."
2. In Rom 16:3–5a, Paul asks his readers to greet Prisca[6] and Aquila and "the church in their house," identifying the couple as "fellow workers in Christ Jesus who risked their necks for [his] life" and noting that "not only [he] but also the churches of the Gentiles give thanks for [or "to"] them."
3. In 2 Tim 4:19a, the pseudonymous "Paul" asks "Timothy" to greet Prisca and Aquila.

The consistent linking of the two names and the references to 'the church in their house' indicate that Aquila and Prisca are a married couple.[7]

It is obvious that Paul's references to Aquila and Prisca are based on his own acquaintance with them. There is no evidence, however, that Luke knew Aquila and Priscilla, and his references to them are presumably based on source material of some type. Until recently, many if not most scholars assumed that Acts was written in the first century,[8] and almost all have been persuaded that its author did not know—or at least did not use as sources—any of the Pauline letters.[9] Luke must, therefore, have had access to

---

5. Many witnesses (including C and D) have "Priscilla," but the preferred reading is "Prisca"; see, e.g., Metzger, *Textual Commentary*, 2nd ed., 503. A omits the entire clause, ἀσπάζεται ὑμᾶς ἐν κυρίῳ πολλὰ Ἀκύλας καὶ Πρίσκα.

6. Some witnesses have "Priscilla," but the preferred reading is "Prisca"; see, e.g., Metzger, *A Textual Commentary*, 2nd ed., 475.

7. Acts 18:2 and 1 Cor 16:19b name Aquila first, but Priscilla or Prisca appears first in Acts 18:18, 26; Rom 16:3 and 2 Tim 4:19a. Except when referring specifically to one of the latter four passages, however, I shall name Aquila first because (a) he appears first both in the earliest reference in Acts and in what is almost certainly the earliest reference in the letters and (b) alphabetical order places him first.

8. For discussion, see, e.g., Fitzmyer, *Acts of the Apostles*, 51–55.

9. More than a generation ago, Kümmel (*Introduction to the New Testament*, 186) spoke of this as the "nearly universal judgment" of contemporary NT scholarship.

other source material that included information about Aquila and his wife. Thus, Gerd Lüdemann maintains that here, as elsewhere, Luke drew on "traditions"—written and/or oral and, in some cases, reflecting details of the letters—that were accessible in the Pauline mission fields.[10] Lüdemann distinguishes such traditional material from Lukan redaction on the basis of "concrete details, which in themselves show no special Lucan tendency."[11] With this as his criterion, he concludes that most of what Luke says about Aquila and Priscilla "seems to reflect tradition" (i.e., source material other than the Pauline letters).[12]

Clearly, Luke *might* have used sources such as Lüdemann describes, but, if so, these sources no longer exist and anything that might be said regarding their nature, content, provenance, or accessibility is purely hypothetical and speculative. Increasingly, however, scholars are moving to a second-century date for Acts[13]—a time when some if not all of the Pauline letters would already have been written. Moreover, we still have these letters in something at least approximating their original form and can therefore compare their content with that of Acts. Finally, there

---

10. Lüdemann with Hall, *Acts of the Apostles: What Really Happened*, 18; see also, e.g., Barrett, *Critical and Exegetical Commentary on Acts*, vol. 2, 858.

11. Lüdemann with Hall, *Acts of the Apostles: What Really Happened*, 392; cf. Barrett, *Critical and Exegetical Commentary on Acts*, vol. 2, 858.

12. Lüdemann with Hall, *Acts of the Apostles: What Really Happened*, 392, cf. 235, 248; cf. Barrett, *Critical and Exegetical Commentary on Acts*, vol. 2, 858.

13. For arguments and bibliography, see Pervo, *Dating Acts*; cf. also, e.g., Tyson, *Marcion and Luke-Acts*, 1–23. Both Pervo and Tyson date Acts ca. 100–150 CE, but Pervo (343) regards ca. 110–20 or even ca. 115 as most likely, while Tyson (78) prefers ca. 120–25. In my judgment, however, a date as late as ca. 140–50 CE can by no means be ruled out; see, e.g., Townsend, "The Date of Luke-Acts," esp. 58: "Whatever evidence exists [regarding the date of Luke-Acts] is compatible with a date that approaches the middle of the second century." On the reception of Acts in the period before Irenaeus, see Gregory, *Reception of Luke and Acts*, 299–351. Gregory states (353), "I have found no external evidence to demonstrate that *Luke* was used before the middle of the second century, and no evidence to prove the use of *Acts* until somewhat later."

is now a growing consensus that Luke knew at least some of the letters and used them as sources in composing his narrative of Christian origins.[14] Thus, it is now reasonable to assume, simply on *a priori* grounds, that the letters likely served as sources for at least *some* of the details in Luke's portrayal of Aquila and Priscilla. If, however, *virtually everything* Luke says about the couple could either be derived or inferred from the letters or could plausibly be attributed to Luke's own agenda, there would be no need for an appeal to otherwise unknown and purely hypothetical sources as the basis for his references to Aquila and Priscilla. Moreover, this would render suspect any attempt to use these references as an argument for the existence of such sources.

The thesis of the present study is that virtually everything Luke says about Aquila and Priscilla *can* in fact be either (a) derived or inferred from materials in the Pauline letters or (b) plausibly attributed to Luke's own literary, theological, and/or apologetic agenda. The argument supporting this thesis will proceed in three stages: First, I shall note a series of precise agreements between Luke's references to Aquila and Priscilla and the Pauline references to Aquila and Prisca—agreements that, viewed cumulatively, would appear to constitute strong *prime facie* evidence that Luke not only knew the references in the letters but also used them as a (or perhaps even *the*) primary source for his own portrayal of Aquila and Priscilla. Second, I shall identify a number of additional details in Luke's portrayal of Aquila and Priscilla that could reasonably be inferred from materials in the letters. Third, and finally, I shall discuss details in Luke's portrayal of the couple that appear to derive from his own literary, theological, and/or apologetic agenda.

Precise Agreements between the Lukan and Pauline Portrayals

Five points of precise agreement between Luke's portrayal of Aquila and Priscilla and the Pauline portrayal of Aquila and

---

14. For a detailed presentation of the evidence, with bibliographical references, see Pervo, *Dating Acts*, 51–147.

Prisca are immediately evident, and a sixth may well have been intended by Luke.

1. Both in the best witnesses to Acts and in the letters, neither Aquila nor Priscilla/Prisca is ever mentioned apart from the other. This might mean, of course, that the two were so closely associated in the minds of early Christians that reference to one and not the other would have been unthinkable. It might mean, however, that Luke—either consciously or unconsciously—simply followed the example of the letters in always naming the two together. In either case, this point must be noted because it may be part of a larger pattern of agreement that becomes evident only when other such points are brought into the picture.

2. Both in the best witnesses to Acts and in the letters, Aquila and Priscilla/Prisca are mentioned by name exactly three times.[15] There is no apparent reason why Luke would follow the letters at this point, and this agreement may therefore be purely coincidental. Again, however, it may be part of a larger pattern.

3. Both in Acts and in the letters, Aquila and Priscilla/Prisca are located earlier in Corinth and later in Ephesus. Acts locates them in Corinth,[16] reports their move to Ephesus,[17] and narrates something of their activity there.[18] The letters are less explicit, but they clearly imply the same geographical schema. In 1 Cor 16:19b, Paul conveys greetings to the Corinthians from the couple, thereby indicating that they are known in Corinth and strongly implying their previous residence there. In the same verse, Paul sends greetings from "the churches of Asia," and, in v. 8, he indicates that he himself is now in Ephesus, which was the major city in the Roman province of Asia. This almost certainly means that Aquila and Prisca were in Ephesus when Paul wrote the final verses of 1 Corinthians—in other words, that they had moved from Corinth to Ephesus. Finally, in 2 Tim 4:19a, "Paul" asks "Timothy" to greet

---

15. Acts 18:2, 18, 26b; 1 Cor 16:19b; Rom 16:3; 2 Tim 4:19a.
16. Acts 18:1–3 (having moved there from Rome).
17. Acts 18:18–19.
18. Acts 18:24–26.

Prisca and Aquila, and "Timothy" is clearly to be located, fictively, in Ephesus.[19] This agreement between the letters and Acts might reflect common knowledge regarding the couple's successive places of residence. Luke might, however, simply have followed the geographical schema implied in the letters.

4. Both in the best witnesses to Acts and in the letters, Aquila is named first in one reference[20] and Priscilla/Prisca in two.[21] As Jerome Murphy-O'Connor notes, the latter sequence "is most unusual" and indicates that the wife "was more important than her husband"—in terms either of "social status or independent wealth" or of prominence in the life of the Church.[22] It is unclear why either Acts or the letters would independently vary the order of precedence, but the fact that *both do so and by precisely the same ratio* suggests that Luke, knowing the relevant passages in the letters, simply followed the same numerical pattern of varying precedence.

5. Both in Acts and in the letters, Aquila is named first when the locale in mind is Corinth and Priscilla/Prisca first when the locale is elsewhere. Acts names *Aquila* first when the couple is in Corinth,[23] and Paul mentions *Aquila* first when he sends greetings to Corinth.[24] Acts names *Priscilla* first, however, when the couple is in transit from Corinth to Ephesus[25] and when they are in Ephesus;[26] similarly, Paul mentions *Prisca* first when the couple is in Rome,[27] and "Paul" names *Prisca* first when they are fictively

---

19. 2 Tim 1:15–18; 4:12; cf. also 1 Tim 1:3.
20. Acts 18:2; 1 Cor 16:19b.
21. Acts 18:18, 26b; Rom 16:3; 2 Tim 4:19a. The "Western" text has Aquila first in Acts 18:26, but, as Metzger (*Textual Commentary*, 2nd ed., 413–14) notes, "the unusual order, the wife before the husband, must be accepted as original, for there was always a tendency among scribes to change the unusual to the usual."
22. Murphy-O'Connor, "Prisca and Aquila," 40 and 42.
23. Acts 18:1–3.
24. 1 Cor 16:19b.
25. Acts 18:18.
26. Acts 18:26b.
27. Rom 16:3. See below under Item 6 for the possibility that the location might be Ephesus rather than Rome.

in Ephesus.[28] It is possible (a) that Aquila played the leading role in Corinth but Priscilla/Prisca assumed this role later, (b) that the couple was therefore actually known as "Aquila and Priscilla/Prisca" in Corinth and as "Priscilla/Prisca and Aquila" elsewhere, and (c) that Luke was independently aware of the geographical transposition of primacy and chose to reflect it by the order in which he listed the names. In light of other points of agreement between Acts and the letters, however, it appears more likely that Luke simply knew the relevant passages in the letters and followed not only their numerical but also their geographical pattern of varying primacy.

6. Acts 18:2 states that Aquila and Priscilla resided in Rome before moving to Corinth. Rom 16:3–5a appears also to indicate the presence of Prisca and Aquila in Rome. Thus, a sixth point of agreement between Acts and the letters could be the residence of the couple in Rome. Two potential problems, however, make this questionable.

The first is that Romans 16 may originally have been intended for some destination other than Rome—probably Ephesus.[29] If so, then vv. 3–5a would confirm the presence of Prisca and Aquila in Ephesus rather than in Rome. It is clear, however, that chap. 16 was a part of Romans at least as early as ca. 200 CE and perhaps considerably earlier.[30] Thus, whatever its original destination, chap. 16 may well have been known by Luke as a part of Romans and therefore viewed by him as indicating the presence of Prisca and Aquila in Rome when the letter was written.[31]

The second potential problem is that Romans was almost certainly written *later* than 1 Corinthians and thus places Prisca and Aquila in Rome *after* they had been in Corinth and Ephesus, not *before* as indicated in Acts. Luke may well have assumed, how-

---

28. 2 Tim 4:19a.

29. For discussion and the conclusion that the chapter was an original part of Romans, see, e.g., Jewett, *Romans: A Commentary*, 8–9.

30. It is included in P^{46} (typically dated ca. 200 CE, but cf. Comfort and Barrett, *Text of the Earliest New Testament Greek Manuscripts*, 204–7, where it is placed near the middle of the second century.

31. On the date of Acts, see n. 13 above.

ever, that Romans was written *earlier* than 1 Corinthians. Most of the early witnesses, including all of the best ones,[32] place Romans first—that is, *before* the Corinthian correspondence—among the Pauline letters. Moreover, David Trobisch and Jerome Murphy-O'Connor have independently argued that the very earliest collection of Pauline letters—consisting of Romans, 1 Corinthians, 2 Corinthians, and Galatians—placed Romans first.[33] With Romans as the first letter in the collection, it is precisely the *first* Pauline reference to Prisca and Aquila (Rom 16:3–5a) that locates them in Rome. If Luke was working with such a collection, he might easily have assumed that the couple resided in Rome *before* moving to Corinth and constructed his narrative accordingly. If so, then Luke clearly intended his narrative to agree with the letters at this point.

Considered separately, each of the above points might appear coincidental or inconsequential or both. Viewed cumulatively, however, they form a remarkable pattern of precise agreements between the Lukan and Pauline portrayals of the couple in question—even in matters not involving historicity. In my judgment, such a pattern can hardly be coincidental and would appear, therefore, to indicate that Luke knew and was influenced by the Pauline references to Aquila and Prisca. Indeed, in the absence of evidence for other source material used by Luke, this would appear to constitute rather strong *prime facie* evidence that the Pauline references served as a (or perhaps even the) *primary* source for his own portrayal of the couple.

Features in the Lukan Portrayal
Reasonably Inferred from the Letters

In addition to the precise points of agreement just noted, there are six—or perhaps seven—other features of Luke's portrayal of

---

32. Not only the earliest extant MS, P^{46}, but also B (fourth century), Aleph (fourth century), A (fifth century), C (fifth century), and D (sixth century); on the date of P^{46}, see n. 30 above. For discussion of the sequence of the letters in early collections, see, e.g., Lovering, "Collection, Redaction, and Early Circulation," 259–74; Trobisch, *Paul's Letter Collection*, 18–22; and Trobisch, *First Edition of the New Testament*, 21–38.

33. Trobisch, *Paul's Letter Collection*, 54; Murphy-O'Connor, *Paul the Letter-Writer*, 120–30.

Aquila and Priscilla that could reasonably be inferred from materials in the Pauline letters.

1. The location of Paul in Corinth at the same time Aquila and Priscilla were there (Acts 18:1–3) could reasonably be inferred from materials in 1 Corinthians and Romans. 1 Corinthians 16:19b strongly implies that Aquila and Prisca resided in Corinth before moving to Ephesus,[34] the Corinthian correspondence as a whole indicates that Paul himself was in Corinth more than once,[35] and 1 Cor 16:19b and Rom 16:3–4 demonstrate that Paul was well acquainted with Aquila and Prisca. Although the letters nowhere explicitly state that the three were in Corinth at the same time, they do suggest that this was likely. Thus, Luke may simply have assumed it to have been the case and constructed his narrative accordingly.

2. The portrayal of Paul as having "resided" (ἔμενεν) with Aquila and Priscilla in Corinth (Acts 18:3a) could reasonably be inferred from 1 Cor 16:19b and/or Rom 16:3–5a, both of which refer to the "church" in the couple's home. To be sure, Acts does not mention a church in their home in Corinth. Given the fact that a church met in their home both in Ephesus and in Rome,[36] however, it would be natural to assume that this was the case also in Corinth—particularly if Luke thought the couple's residence in Corinth came between that in Rome and in Ephesus.[37] Further, it would be reasonable to suppose that Paul's Corinthian converts would meet in the home where he himself was residing.[38] Thus, on the basis of Paul's references to "the church in their house,"

---

34. See above, p. 269.
35. E.g., 1 Cor 1:14–16; 2:15; 3:1–10; 4:14–15; 9:1–2; 15:1–3; 16:3–7; 2 Cor 1:15–2.1; 11:7–9; 12:14, 20–21; 13:1–2, 10.
36. 1 Cor 16:19b; Rom 16:5a (assuming Romans 16 to be an original part of Paul's Roman letter).
37. See above, pp. 271–72.
38. Several "Western" witnesses add "with whom also I am lodging" after "Aquila and Prisca" in 1 Cor 16:19b, thus explicitly identifying their home (in Ephesus) both as the meeting place for the church and as Paul's place of abode. If Paul could be presumed to reside in the house where the church met in Ephesus, this could reasonably be supposed to have been the case earlier in Corinth.

Luke may simply have assumed that Paul resided (ἔμενεν) in the home of Aquila and Priscilla while he was in Corinth and made this assumption explicit in his narrative.[39]

3. The portrayal of Paul as "working" (ἠργάζετο) with Aquila and Priscilla (Acts 18:3) could reasonably be inferred from 1 Cor 4:12a and Rom 16:3. In 1 Cor 4:12a, using the same verb that appears in Acts 18:3, Paul speaks of "laboring, working with our own hands" (κοπιῶμεν ἐγγαζόμενοι ταῖς ἰδίαις χερσίν),[40] and the plural forms suggest that he engaged in such labor in collaboration with one or more other people. The identification of Aquila and Priscilla as those with whom he worked in Corinth[41] may have been suggested by Rom 16:3, where Paul refers to Prisca and Aquila as his "fellow workers" (συνεργοί). To be sure, Paul adds "in Christ Jesus" (ἐν Χριστῷ Ἰησοῦ), thereby apparently indicating that he has in mind religious activity, not manual labor as in Acts.[42] Nevertheless, Paul's reference — in the plural — to working with his hands (1 Cor 4:12a) and to Prisca and Aquila as his "fellow workers" (Rom 16:3) may have prompted Luke to assume that Paul "was working" (ἠργάζετο) with the couple in Corinth.[43]

4. The portrayal of Priscilla and Aquila as leaving Corinth with Paul and accompanying him to Ephesus, where they remain while he goes on to Caesarea (Acts 18:18–21), could reasonably be inferred from 1 Cor 16:19b. Here, as noted above, Paul suggests the couple's residence earlier in Corinth and later in Ephesus. Acts 18:18–21 may well be simply Luke's narrative device to get them from Corinth to Ephesus, where they will encounter Apollos.

---

39. Acts 18:7 could indicate either (a) that Paul subsequently moved from the home of Aquila and Priscilla to that of Titius Justus or (b) that he moved his preaching activity from the synagogue (v. 4) to the latter's home (which was adjacent to the synagogue) but maintained his residence in the home of Aquila and Priscilla. The latter is perhaps implied by the report that they accompanied him when he left Corinth (v. 18).

40. See also 1 Cor 9:6 and 1 Thess 2:9.

41. Assuming that παρ' αὐτοῖς goes with both ἔμενεν and ἠργάζετο.

42. Note 1 Thess 3:2; 2 Cor 8:23; Phil 2:25; 4:3; Phlm 1, 24; Rom 16:9, 21, where Paul refers to others as his "fellow workers" (συνεργοί).

43. Note the same root (ἐργ-) in all three passages. Some witnesses, including Aleph* (fourth century), read ἠργάζοντο ("they were working") rather than ἠργάζετο ("he was working") in Acts 18:3.

5. Aquila and Priscilla disappear completely from Luke's narrative following their correction of Apollos' defective version of the gospel (Acts 18:24–26), which, therefore, appears to be the real point of their inclusion at all.[44] Thus, Luke's portrayal of Apollos (Acts 18:24–19:1a) is relevant for the present study. A number of the details in this portrayal could reasonably be inferred from materials in the Pauline letters:

   a. In 1 Corinthians, Paul portrays Apollos as an important figure in the church, associating him with both Ephesus and Corinth.[45] Acts 18:24–19:1a has essentially the same picture of Apollos.
   b. In 1 Cor 1:17b; 2:1–5, Paul notes his own deficiencies as an orator, implicitly contrasting himself with other preachers who presumably are more gifted.[46] Acts 18:24–25, 28, in turn, characterizes Apollos as precisely the kind of eloquent speaker implied in Paul's own disavowal.
   c. In 1 Corinthians, Paul suggests some degree of rivalry and even tension between himself and Apollos,[47] noting that he has no control over the latter's activity[48] and intimating that the two are to some extent competitors for leadership in the church.[49] Indeed, a good case can be made that "the conflict in Corinth was at its core a debate between Paul and the Apollos party."[50] All of this may be reflected in Acts 18:24–26, which states that Apollos' initially defective version of the gospel was corrected, and that it was corrected precisely by associates of Paul.[51]

---

44. On this, see pp. 281 and 283 below.
45. 1 Cor 1:12; 3:4–8, 22; 4:6; 16:12 (cf. v. 8).
46. See the entire passage, 1 Cor 1:17–2.5; see also 2 Cor 10:10.
47. 1 Cor 1:12; 3:4–6, 22; 4:6; 16:12.
48. 1 Cor 16:12.
49. E.g., 1 Cor 3:6, 10; 4:15.
50. Wolter, "Apollos und die ephesinischen Johannesjünger," 66 (translation mine); see references in n. 79 in Wolter. Wolter acknowledges (72) "that Luke was informed about the conflict in Corinth" but denies (72 n. 101) that this information came from 1 Corinthians.
51. Luke's awkward contrasting of "accurately" (ἀκριβῶς) in 18:25 and "more accurately" (ἀκριβέστερον) in 18:26 may reflect Paul's own ambivalence regarding Apollos.

d. In Titus 3:13, however, Apollos is pictured quite positively as a trusted associate of Paul.

Such intimations of initial tension followed by close association between Apollos and Paul may well have set the stage for Luke's creation of a narrative in which Apollos preached a defective version of the gospel, was corrected by Paul's associates, and became a respected leader in the Christian movement.[52]

6. The identification of Priscilla and Aquila as those who corrected Apollos' defective version of the gospel and thus brought him into the circle of Pauline Christianity could reasonably be inferred from various materials in the Pauline letters. Apollos, Aquila, and Prisca are the only people Paul mentions by name as residing with him in Ephesus when he wrote 1 Corinthians.[53] Thus, being in Ephesus with Apollos, the couple would have been well situated to correct his defective version of the gospel. Furthermore, Paul suggests that they would have been well qualified for such a task. The Ephesian and Roman churches meet for worship in their home,[54] and the very high—indeed, apparently unique—esteem in which Paul holds the couple is clear in Rom 16:3-4, where he praises them as "my fellow workers in Christ Jesus, who risked their necks for my life, to [or "for"] whom not only I but also all the churches of the Gentiles give thanks."[55] Thus, the question would almost inevitably pose itself to Luke: "Who better than this couple to correct the erroneous views of Apollos?"

7. Acts 18:3 indicates that Paul was, by trade, a σκηνοποιός—usually translated as "tentmaker" or "leather worker." The word, however, is "a *hapax legomenon* in the New Testament" and "is

---

52. Wolter ("Apollos und die ephesinischen Johannesjünger," 71) argues that Luke's goal in Acts 18:24–19:7 is "to express Pauline dominance over Apollos."

53. 1 Cor 16:8, 12, 19b. "Chloe's people" (1:11) and Stephanus, Fortunatus, and Achaicus (16:16–17) were probably residents of Corinth who merely visited Paul in Ephesus.

54. 1 Cor 16:19; Rom 16:5a.

55. In the extant letters, he praises no one else so highly.

also hardly ever used in older or contemporary writings." Thus, "its meaning is obscure."[56] According to Pollux, though, it was used in Old Comedy to signify "a maker of stage properties" or even "a stagehand" (who moved stage properties).[57] Acts portrays Paul as working in urban, not rural, areas, and "one is left with the strong probability that Luke's publics in [such] areas, where theatrical productions were in abundance, would [probably] think of σκηνοποιός in ref[erence] to matters theatrical."[58] Thus, the intended meaning of σκηνοποιός in Acts 18:3 may well be "maker of stage properties" or "stagehand," and, if so, then Luke is linking Paul professionally to the theater.

It is at least possible, moreover, that this was suggested by Paul's own statement in 1 Cor 4:9: δοκῶ γάρ, ὁ Θεὸς ἡμᾶς τοὺς ἀποστόλους ἐσχάτους ἀπέδειξεν ὡς ἐπιθανατίους, ὅτι θέατρον ἐγενήθημεν τῷ κόσμῳ καὶ ἀγγέλοις καὶ ἀνθρώποις. Clearly, Paul's imagery here is "theatrical" in nature: he states that he has become a θέατρον, with "the world and angels and humans" as his audience. Θέατρον can refer either to *a place* for public entertainment—e.g., dramatic performances, gladiatorial contests, or public execution of condemned criminals—or to the *"spectacle" that one sees* in such a place.[59] Paul, of course, here uses the word in the latter sense. Moreover, he most likely has in mind neither dramatic performances nor gladiatorial contests but rather the public execution of convicted criminals.[60] All three, however, were closely associated in the popular mind as forms of public entertainment and, for this reason, each could be labeled as θέατρον.[61] In addition, the distinction between θέατρον as "what

---

56. Szesnat, "What Did the σκηνοποιός Paul Produce?," 394.
57. Pollux, *Onom.* 7.189; see, e.g., Szesnat, "What Did the σκηνοποιός Paul Produce?," 394 n. 2; *TDNT* 7.393; and BAGD 928–29 and the bibliography cited there.
58. BDAG 929.
59. BAGD 446.
60. Nguyen, "Identification of Paul's Spectacle of Death Metaphor."
61. Θέατρον is related to θεάομαι, which means "to look at," "to see," "to behold."

is seen" and θέατρον as "where it is seen" would be somewhat fluid, given the fact that the same word was used for both. In any case, 1 Cor 4:9 indicates that Paul was familiar with the θέατρον. Moreover, his reference to himself *as a θέατρον* might suggest that he was somehow professionally associated with the θέατρον. Hence perhaps the theatrical term σκηνοποιός to designate his trade in Acts 18:3.

In conclusion, whether considered individually or cumulatively, these seven additional features of Luke's portrayal of Aquila and Priscilla by no means prove that the Pauline letters served as a source for this portrayal. They do, however, indicate that a great deal of what Luke says about the couple could reasonably be inferred from materials in the letters. Thus, coupled with the points of precise agreement discussed earlier, they appear to buttress the case for viewing the letters as a (or even *the*) primary source for Luke's portrayal of Aquila and Priscilla.

Details in the Lukan Portrayal Deriving from the Luckan Agenda

Certain details in Luke's portrayal of Aquila and Priscilla cannot easily be traced, either directly or indirectly, to materials in the Pauline letters. In my judgment, however, these details are best accounted for in terms of Luke's own literary, theological, and/or apologetic agenda.

1. Although the best manuscripts of the Pauline letters always refer to Aquila's wife as "Prisca," Luke consistently employs the diminutive form "Priscilla," which is often viewed as "a term of endearment or familiarity."[62] It is clear that Paul was well acquainted with the woman, however, while Luke presumably was not. It is difficult to understand, therefore, why Luke would change Paul's "Prisca" to "Priscilla" if the latter is in fact "a term of endearment or familiarity."[63] Thus, the difference in nomenclature might appear to argue against Luke's use of the letters at this

---

62. Spencer, "Women of 'the Cloth' in Acts," 150 n. 77.
63. Although a number of mss change "Prisca" to "Priscilla" in the letters (see nn. 5 and 6 above), the reverse never occurs, at least to my knowledge, in Acts.

point. In my judgment, however, there is a plausible reason why Luke would change "Prisca" to "Priscilla."

While the diminutive "may express affection, familiarity, [or] daintiness," it can also signify "pity or contempt."[64] Thus, Murphy-O'Connor suggests that Luke's use of "Priscilla" "might be interpreted as a put-down."[65] It is my suggestion, therefore, that Luke changed "Prisca" to "Priscilla" precisely as a way of belittling or disparaging the woman in question and thus downplaying her role as a leader in the church.

This suggestion is supported by two striking indications in Acts 18:2 that Luke intends to subordinate Priscilla to Aquila: (1) the verse says that Paul "found" *Aquila*, not *both Aquila and Priscilla*; and (2) it provides certain biographical details regarding Aquila—he is a Jew, a native of Pontus, and has recently moved from Rome to Corinth—but says of Priscilla *only* that she is "his wife." Clearly, Aquila is the more important of the two in Acts 18:2. The letters, however, make no distinction in their treatment of Aquila and Prisca, always speaking of the couple as a pair. Thus, the name change from "Prisca" to "Priscilla," together with the imbalance in the treatment of Aquila and Priscilla in Acts 18:2, constitutes a significant downplaying of the role of Priscilla in the book of Acts.[66]

This is consistent with the treatment of women elsewhere in Acts.[67] Apart from Priscilla and Aquila, the only Christian mar-

---

64. Smyth, *Greek Grammar*, 235. Swanson ("Diminutives in the Greek New Testament," 146) lists "deteriorative" as one category of diminutives and cites γυναικάριον ("silly woman") as an example. The last Roman emperor to rule from Rome, Romulus Augustus, was often mockingly referred to as "Romulus Augustulus."

65. Murphy-O'Connor, "Prisca and Aquila," 40.

66. This appears to be an early stage in a trajectory that finds fuller expression in the "Western" text of the chapter; see, e.g., Ropes, *Acts of the Apostles*, vol. 3, 161–79; and Metzger, *Textual Commentary*, 2nd ed., 408–9, 410, 412, 465, 413–14. Moreover, the treatment of Priscilla appears to be but one among other indications of "the anti-feminist tendencies of the 'Western' text in Acts" (Witherington, "Anti-Feminist Tendencies," 82–84; cf. Pervo, "Social and Religious Aspects," 235–40; and Metzger, *Text of the New Testament*, 2nd ed., 295–96).

67. On the treatment of women in Acts, see Levine with Blickenstaff, *Feminist Companion to Acts*. On Luke's tendency to diminish the role

ried couple mentioned in Acts is Ananias and Sapphira (5:1–10), and they are portrayed in a highly negative light.[68] Moreover, while other individual women are mentioned in Acts, none except Priscilla is portrayed as a leader in the church.[69] Finally, although Acts refers to unnamed women who are Christians,[70] the overwhelming emphasis is on men. Not only are the leading characters all men[71] but it is "men" (ἄνδρες), not "people" (ἄνθρωποι), who are repeatedly addressed in the speeches.[72]

In short, Luke portrays the early Christian movement as almost completely dominated by men. The only possible exception is Priscilla. As F. Scott Spencer notes, her encounter with Apollos "is as close as we get in Acts to a woman proclaiming the word to a man." Even here, however, "the scene is normalized somewhat by the presence of her husband."[73] Indeed, one can only wonder why Priscilla finds her way into the narrative at all. My suggestion is that, at least in part, she is included because the Pauline letters consistently speak jointly of Aquila and Prisca but that she is, at the same time, belittled by having her name changed to the diminutive form and being subordinated to Aquila.[74] Thus, the

---

of women, see, e.g., D'Angelo, "Women in Luke-Acts"; Seim, *Double Message*; and Reimer, *Women in Acts*.

68. This was pointed out to me by my colleague Rúben R. Dupertuis.

69. Mary the mother of Jesus (1:14), Tabitha or Dorcas (9:36–41), Mary the mother of John Mark (12:12), a maid named Rhoda (12:13–15), the unnamed mother of Timothy (16:1), Lydia (16:14–15, 40), a slave girl in Philippi (16:16–18), and a woman in Athens named Damaris (17:34). Some of these women—Mary the mother of John Mark, Rhoda, Tabitha, and Lydia—play a significant role in the narrative, but none is portrayed as a leader in the church. Indeed, Harrill ("Dramatic Function of the Running Slave Rhoda") following an earlier suggestion by Pervo (*Profit with Delight*, 62–63) views the Rhoda story as "a highly conventionalized sequence of action elaborated not to uplift slaves [or women] but to entertain with humour that dishonours them" (151).

70. Acts 2:17–18; 5:14; 6:1; 8:1, 12; 9:1; 17:4, 12; 21:5, 9; 22:4.

71. E.g., all of the "Apostles" and, specifically, Peter, John, and James; all of the "Seven" and, specifically, Stephen and Philip; and others, including Ananias, Barnabas, James, and especially Paul.

72. E.g., Acts 1:16; 2:14, 22, 29; 3:12; 7:1; 13:16, 26; 15:13; 17:22; 22:1.

73. Spencer, "Women of 'the Cloth' in Acts," 152.

74. Another possible reason for her inclusion is discussed below under numbers 3 and 4.

name change from "Prisca" to "Priscilla" appears to reflect an item in Luke's own theological/apologetic agenda.

2. A second detail in Luke's portrayal of Aquila and Priscilla that appears to derive from his own agenda is the couple's move from Italy to Corinth because of the Emperor Claudius' edict expelling all Jews from Rome (Acts 18:2). Luke probably read Rom 16:3–5a as indicating that the pair lived in Rome *prior* to their residence in Corinth.[75] What he needs for the sake of his narrative, therefore, is simply a literary device to get them from Rome to Corinth, where they can be associated with Paul. He has earlier dealt with a somewhat analogous situation by using the Emperor Augustus' census decree to get Joseph and Mary from Nazareth to Bethlehem for the birth of Jesus (Luke 2:1–4). Now, his identification of Aquila as a "Jew" enables him to use the edict of Claudius to get Aquila and Priscilla from Rome to Corinth (Acts 18:2). This detail of the narrative, therefore, reflects Luke's own literary agenda, which, in turn, is in the service of his theological/apologetic agenda.[76]

3 and 4. Two remaining details in Luke's portrayal of Aquila and Priscilla must be considered together because, in my judgment, they stem from Luke's own theological/apologetic agenda and are interrelated. The first is the apparently irrelevant identification of Aquila in Acts 18:2 as a Jew[77] and a native of Pontus. The second is the encounter of Priscilla and Aquila with Apollos, in which they correct his defective understanding of the gospel (Acts 18:24–26).[78]

---

75. See above, pp. 271–72.

76. As indicated below (pp. 281 and 284), it apparently was important to Luke to have Aquila (and Priscilla) reside at one time in Rome.

77. Paul's statement that "all the churches of the Gentiles give thanks to" (or "for") Prisca and Aquila" (Rom 16:4) might suggest that they were Gentiles.

78. A few witnesses, including the original of Aleph, read "Apelles" rather than "Apollos" at Acts 18:24 and 19:1, and Kilpatrick ("Apollos—Apelles," 77) suggests that this may be the original reading. If so, the reference might be to the "Apelles" mentioned by Paul in Rom 16:10 as "approved (δόκιμος) in Christ." The adjective suggests approval as a result of testing, which might imply some initial question regarding the status of Apelles. This, in turn might give rise to a narrative in which a

Joseph B. Tyson—following the lead of John Knox—has recently argued that Acts was intended in part as a response to the challenge posed by Marcionite Christianity.[79] I find this argument persuasive and now propose to extend it by suggesting that Luke's portrayal of Aquila and Priscilla is a part of his anti-Marcionite agenda.[80]

With the exception of Barnabas,[81] Aquila and Priscilla are the only associates of Paul who play any independent role in the book of Acts. They are mentioned only in chap. 18, but they appear three times in this chapter, and each of the three appearances establishes one or more quite specific details in the portrayal of the couple. The first (18:2-3) identifies Aquila as a Jew from Pontus, introduces Priscilla as his wife, gets the couple from Rome to Corinth, and associates them closely with Paul; the second (18:18-19) gets them from Corinth to Ephesus; and the third (18:24-26) presents these associates of Paul as correctors of "heresy" in

---

change in status (i.e., from "heretical" to "orthodox") is reported (Acts 18:24-26). Perhaps more intriguing, however, is the fact that "Apelles" was the name of a second-century follower of Marcion, who disagreed with the latter on some points of theology and went to Alexandria, the reported birthplace of Apollos (or Apelles) in Acts 18:24 (see Eusebius, *Hist. Eccl.* V.xiii.2, 5-9 and especially Tertullian, *Praescr.* 30). For purposes of the present discussion, however, I shall assume that the correct reading in Acts 18:24; 9:1 is "Apollos" and not "Apelles."

79. Tyson, *Marcion and Luke-Acts*; see Knox, *Marcion and the New Testament*. The date of Marcion's activity is debated. As Clabeaux notes ("Marcion," 514), "Biographical information on Marcion and his early work is scant and . . . often of dubious reliability." He appears to have been in Rome around the middle of the second century, but previous activity in Asia Minor and particularly Ephesus suggests that he became prominent some time earlier. Tyson argues, convincingly in my judgment, that "Marcion's views were [likely] known, at least in part and in some locations, as early as 115-120 CE." (*Marcion and Luke-Acts*, 31). Tyson then proposes that "the Acts of the Apostles was probably written about 120-25 CE, just when Marcion was beginning to attract adherents into what became the most significant heterodox movement of the second century" (78).

80. To my knowledge, this has not previously been suggested.

81. See Acts 9:27; 11:22-26; 15:36-39.

Ephesus (by implication, of course, also portraying Paul as an opponent of "heresy").[82]

Very little is said about the nature of the "heresy" involved,[83] and Acts makes no explicit reference either to Marcion or to Marcionite Christianity. There are, however, four quite striking parallels between Luke's portrayal of Aquila and what is known about Marcion: (1) both are natives of Pontus,[84] (2) both resided at one time in Rome, (3) both also resided at one time in Asia Minor (Ephesus),[85] and (4) both were, in some sense, Pauline Christians. In my judgment, these parallels cannot be merely coincidental. Indeed, if Tyson is correct regarding the date and occasion of the writing of Acts, any reference, however indirect, to a Christian teacher from Pontus who resided both in Rome and in Asia Minor and was somehow associated with Paul would almost inevitably have brought Marcion to the mind of an attentive reader.[86]

There are, however, also four crucial differences between Luke's portrayal of Aquila and what is known about Marcion:

1. Marcion sought to divorce Christianity from Judaism, but Luke identifies Aquila explicitly as a "Jew."

---

82. It is anachronistic to speak of "heresy" (or "orthodoxy") at this point, but Luke clearly regards Apollos' initial preaching as defective and thus erroneous.

83. Acts 18:25 reports that Apollos "knew only the baptism of John"; cf. the reference in Acts 19:1–7 to "disciples" who had been baptized "into John's baptism" but had not received or even heard of the Holy Spirit. Wolter ("Apollos und die ephesinischen Johannesjünger") argues that Acts 18:24–28 and 19:1–7 are to be linked, with the relation between Apollos and Paul as the common theme. For discussion, see, e.g., Barrett, *Critical and Exegetical Commentary on Acts*, vol. 2, 886–88.

84. Aquila is Ποντικός τῷ γένει (Acts 18:2). Ποντικός occurs only here in the NT (Πόντος appears only in Acts 2:9 and 1 Pet 1:1).

85. Luke, however, has Aquila in Rome *before* going to Corinth and then Ephesus, while Marcion was in Rome *after* his time in Asia Minor.

86. Tyson (*Marcion and Luke-Acts*, 77) suggests that the report of Paul's frustrated attempt to go into Bithynia (Acts 16:6–8) "may . . . contain an allusion to Marcion's homeland." According to Tyson, Bithynia and Pontus were generally associated, Pontus was known as Marcion's place of origin, and Luke wanted to disassociate Paul from Marcion by showing that there had been no Pauline mission in the latter's homeland.

2. Marcion presented himself as a "Paulinist" and, indeed, regarded Paul as the only true apostle of Christ, but Luke portrays Aquila as one who was closely associated with Paul and therefore in a better position to understand Pauline Christianity.
3. Marcion required sexual abstinence, but Luke explicitly portrays Aquila as having a wife (indeed, this may explain in part why he included Priscilla in the narrative).
4. Marcion proclaimed a "heretical" version of Christianity, but Acts reports that Aquila corrected the defective version of Christianity proclaimed by Apollos.

In short, Luke pictures Aquila as the married Jew from Pontus, one-time resident of both Rome and Ephesus, and Pauline Christian who corrects an erroneous version of Christianity. Surely, in the minds of second-century Christians, such a portrayal would cast Aquila as the very antithesis of the celibate Marcion who rejected any connection between Christianity and Judaism—who, however, was also from Pontus, also a one-time resident of both Ephesus and Rome, and also in some sense a Pauline Christian. At the same time, by implication, this clearly would portray Paul as an anti-Marcionite.

In portraying Aquila as the parallel/antithesis to Marcion, Luke appears to be suggesting at least two important points: (1) that not only "heretical" and specifically non-Jewish Christianity but also "orthodox" Christianity with links to Judaism has ties both with Rome and with Asia Minor and, indeed, is to be found even in Pontus—i.e., that Marcionite Christianity is an aberration, not only in Rome and Asia Minor but also in Pontus;[87] and (2) that Paul and his associates represent "orthodox" Christianity that is linked to Judaism and thus are the opponents of "heretical" non-Jewish (i.e., Marcionite) Christianity.

---

87. Acts never indicates when or where Aquila became a Christian—whether in Pontus, in Rome, or in Corinth. The absence of any reference to his conversion and the statement that Paul "found" him in Corinth, however, suggests that he was already a Christian when he arrived in Corinth.

In addition, it may be significant that Luke explicitly identifies both Aquila and Apollos as "a certain Jew"[88] and that they are the only people so identified in the entire book of Acts. The use of identical terminology suggests a parallel and/or contrast between the two. The parallel would be the fact that both are Jewish Christians, and the contrast the fact that they initially represent different versions of Jewish Christianity, one of which is acceptable while the other is not. This may suggest that Luke was concerned not only about Marcionite (i.e., non-Jewish) Christianity but also about some form(s) of Jewish Christianity.[89]

Further, it is almost certainly significant that different places of origin are specified for Aquila and Apollos—using, however, the same syntactical construction.[90] Just as identifying Aquila with Pontus appears to suggest a parallel/contrast between him and Marcion, it is possible that identifying Apollos with Alexandria may imply a similar parallel and/or contrast between him and some unknown—to us—person(s) or movement identified with that city.[91]

Finally, the "more accurate" (ἀκριβέστερον) instruction of Apollos by Priscilla and Aquila could be seen as Luke's way of suggesting that heretics can in fact, if properly informed, be brought into the fold of "orthodox" Christianity. This might represent a

---

88. Aquila (Acts 18:2): τινα Ἰουδαῖον. Apollos (Acts 18:24): Ἰουδαῖος . . . τις.

89. Perhaps even some type of Ebionite-like Christianity.

90. Aquila (Acts 18:2): "a native of Pontus" (Ποντικὸν τῷ γένει). Apollos (Acts 18:24): "a native of Alexandria" (Ἀλεξανδρεὺς τῷ γένει).

91. John Mark, who, according to Eusebius (*Hist. Eccl.* II.xvi.1), traveled to Egypt after Peter's death in Rome and who, in early tradition, was closely associated with Alexandria, receives rather negative treatment in Acts (12:12, 25; 13:13; and especially 15:37, 39; note, however, the positive portrayal of Mark in Phlm 24; Col 4:10; 2 Tim 4:11; and 1 Pet 5:13). *The Secret Gospel of Mark*, if authentic, indicates the presence of "heretical" Christianity in Alexandria in the second century and appears to associate it in some way with Mark; for conflicting views on the authenticity of this document, see Brown, *Mark's Other Gospel*; and Carlson, *Gospel Hoax*. Note also, however, the possibility that the original reading in Acts 18:24; 19:1 is "Apelles," not "Apollos," and the fact that a former follower of Marcion named "Apelles" spent some time in Alexandria (n. 78 above).

kind of "olive branch" held out to Marcionite Christians (and perhaps to other "heretics" as well).

Conclusion and Implications

In three stages, I have argued that virtually everything Luke says about Aquila and Priscilla either (a) can be derived or inferred from materials in the Pauline letters or (b) can plausibly be attributed to Luke's own literary, theological, and/or apologetic agenda. To the extent that this argument is persuasive, it provides support for at least four important but still somewhat controversial propositions regarding the book of Acts:

1. Luke knew at least some of the Pauline letters—including the pseudonymous 2 Timothy and perhaps Titus—and used them as sources in composing his narrative of Christian origins.
2. The book of Acts reflects a distinctly anti-feminist bias.
3. Luke's agenda in the composition of Acts included an anti-Marcionite component.
4. The composition of Acts is to be dated relatively late—certainly sometime in the second century and perhaps as late as the middle of the century. This is supported by (a) evidence that Luke's portrayal of Aquila and Priscilla is based on materials not only in 1 Corinthians and Romans but also in the pseudonymous 2 Timothy and perhaps Titus[92] and (b) the apparent anti-Marcionite thrust of Acts seen in this portrayal (and elsewhere).

---

92. Various dates have been proposed for the Pastoral Letters, ranging from the 50s to near the middle of the second century. For a summary of various views, see, e.g., Quinn, "Timothy and Titus," 568–69. The relation between the Pastoral Letters and the book of Acts has also been a matter of considerable discussion; see, e.g., Quinn, "Timothy and Titus," 568–69. As has already been noted (n. 13), there are good reasons for dating Acts in the second century—perhaps even as late as the middle of the second century. The later Acts is dated, of course, and the earlier the Pastorals are dated, the more likely it is that Luke would have known 2 Timothy and Titus.

Addendum

The "Theology of Woman's Place" and the "Paulinist" Tradition

It is well known that certain passages in the New Testament deal with the status, role, attire, and/or general demeanor of women in such a manner as to support the principle of male dominance and female subordination, both in the home and in the church (and by implication in society as well). These passages are seven in number: 1 Cor 11:3–16; 1 Cor 14:34–35; Col 3:18–19; Eph 5:22–33; 1 Tim 2:8–15; Titus 2:5–6; and 1 Pet 3:1–7.

Over the years, there has been considerable discussion regarding the origin or source of the passages in Colossians, Ephesians, 1 Timothy, Titus, and 1 Peter, what their relationship is to the documents in which they now appear, and whether they represent an apostolic or post-apostolic point of view. On the basis of some rather striking similarities in content, vocabulary, and form, many scholars have concluded that they can be traced to a common source or sources, or at least tradition, employed by the authors of the canonical writings.

Edward Gordon Selwyn, for example, argued that such a "common source or sources" consisted of some type of catechetical code governing domestic and social behavior and relationships that was widely known and used in the early church, suggesting further that the earliest stratum of this code represented "a fusion of Jewish and Gentile thought which may well have originated in Hellenistic Judaism, yet is perhaps most easily explained as due to the synthetic genius of the early Christian Mission." Inasmuch as he regarded Colossians and Ephesians (but apparently not the

---

"The 'Theology of Woman's Place' and the 'Paulinist' Tradition." *Trinity University Studies in Religion* 11 (1982) 131–52. Copyright © 1983 Trinity University Department of Religion. Reprinted with permission in *Semeia* 28 (1983) 101–12. Reprinted with permission.

Pastorals) as authentically Pauline and 1 Peter as authentically Petrine, he clearly envisioned this code as having originated no later than the apostolic period.[1] According to this view, although Paul and Peter drew material for their statements about the status and role of women from the catechetical code, they apparently did so deliberately, thereby indicating their own agreement with its views regarding women. Selwyn's position has not gained wide acceptance, however, principally because it appears unlikely that so well developed a catechetical code as he described could have originated and spread so widely as early as he imagined.

Other scholars have identified the passages in Colossians, Ephesians, 1 Timothy, Titus, and 1 Peter as components of the so-called *Haustafeln* ("Household Tables" or "Rules for the Household"), which apparently had their origin in Hellenistic popular philosophy, were adapted for use by Hellenistic Judaism, and ultimately were taken over and Christianized by the early Hellenistic church as it sought to adapt itself to continuing life in the Gentile world.[2] For the most part, these scholars support a growing consensus that Colossians, Ephesians, and the Pastorals are pseudo-Pauline writings and 1 Peter is pseudo-Petrine and that, for this reason, the views expressed in these documents do not necessarily represent the views of the two Apostles.[3]

---

1. Selwyn, *First Epistle of St. Peter*, 419–39 and esp. 432–35. Cf. also, e.g., Carrington, *Primitive Christian Catechism*; and Lohse, "Paränese und Kerygma im 1. Petrusbrief."

2. The *Haustafeln* are found in the NT at Col 3:18–4:1; Eph 5:21–6:9; 1 Tim 2:8–15; 5:1–2; 6:1–2; Titus 2:1–10; 3:1; 1 Pet 2:11–3:12. See, e.g., Seeberg, *Das Katechismus der Urchristenheit*, 37–39; Seeberg, *Das Evangelium Christi*, 125–27; Seeberg, *Die beiden Wege*; Seeberg, *Die Didache des Judentums*; Dibelius, *An die Kolosser, Epheser, und Philemon*, esp. the excursus following Col 4:1; Weidinger, *Die Haustafeln*; Wendland, "Zur sozialethischen Bedeutung der neutestamentlichen Haustafeln"; Lohse, *Colossians and Philemon*, 154–63; Schroeder, "Die Haustafeln des Neuen Testaments"; Crouch, *Origin and Intention of the Colossian Haustafel*. For a recent discussion of the origin and form of the *Haustafeln*, see Balch, *Let Wives Be Submissive*, esp. 1–62.

3. On Colossians, see, e.g., Lohse, *Colossians and Philemon*, 177–83; on Ephesians, the Pastorals, and 1 Peter, see, e.g., Kümmel, *Introduction to the*

Not mentioned, for the most part, in the discussions just summarized are the two passages in 1 Corinthians (11:3–16; 14:34–35), which differ somewhat from those in Colossians, Ephesians, 1 Timothy, Titus, and 1 Peter in both form and content, in the fact that the former, unlike the latter, do not appear in the context of general instructions regarding domestic and social behavior and relationships, and in the fact that 1 Corinthians, unlike the other documents in question, is almost universally regarded as authentically apostolic in authorship. Although 1 Cor 14:34–35 is now regarded by a substantial number of scholars as a post-Pauline interpolation,[4] and the same has recently been argued regarding 1 Cor 11:3–16,[5] there has been little, if any, attempt to relate these passages directly to the passages dealing with women in Colossians, Ephesians, 1 Timothy, Titus, and 1 Peter.[6]

The suggestion of this paper is that it is now possible to identify more precisely the *Sitz im Leben* of all of the New Testament passages supporting the principle of male dominance and female subordination, including the two passages in 1 Corinthians. Specifically, I propose to argue: (1) that all of the passages in question can, in fact, be traced to a common source, origin, or tradition; (2) that this common source, origin, or tradition is to be located, not in the apostolic period or widely spread throughout the early church, but rather within the post-apostolic "Paulinist" wing of the church; and (3) that the passages represent one aspect of a post-Pauline reaction against what can be termed the "radical

---

New Testament, 357–63, 370–87, and 421–24. It should be noted that the *Haustafeln* are completely absent from the undoubtedly authentic Pauline letters (i.e., 1 Thessalonians, 1 Corinthians, 2 Corinthians, Galatians, Romans, Philippians, and Philemon) but are found in all of the pseudo-Pauline letters except 2 Thessalonians and 2 Timothy (i.e., in Colossians, Ephesians, 1 Timothy, and Titus), as well as in 1 Peter.

4. See, e.g., Walker, "1 Corinthians 11:2–16 and Paul's Views regarding Women," 95 n. 6.

5. See, e.g., Walker, "1 Corinthians 11:2–16 and Paul's Views regarding Women," 94–110 and further discussion of the question later in this paper.

6. Cf., however the work of Winsome Munro, cited in n. 20 below.

egalitarianism" of Paul himself. In support of this argument, the following points are offered for consideration.[7]

The first point to be considered is that, taken as a group, the seven passages in question exhibit some rather striking parallels in vocabulary and thought. For example, the term "submissive" or "subordinate" occurs in every passage under consideration except 1 Cor 11:3–16, where the image of man as "head" of woman (v. 3) and the observations that "man is the image and glory of God, but woman is the glory of man" (v. 7) and that "man was not created for woman but woman for man" (v. 9) clearly carry the same general implication. Even more striking, however, is the complete command that wives be "submissive to their (own) husbands," which occurs with essentially the same wording in Col 3:18; Eph 5:21–22; Titus 2:5 and 1 Pet 3:1, 5).[8] Other parallels include references to "learning" (1 Cor 14:35; 1 Tim 2:11), "silence" or "silent" (1 Cor 14:34; 1 Tim 2:11, 12; 1 Pet 3:4), "not permitting" (1 Cor 14:34; 1 Tim 2:12), "pure" or "holy" (Titus 2:5; 1 Pet 3:2), "adornment," "adorned," or "adorning" (1 Tim 2:9; 1 Pet 3:3,5), "clothing" (1 Tim 2:9; 1 Pet 3:3), "gold" (1 Tim 2:9; 1 Pet 3:3), "braided" or "braiding" (1 Tim 2:9; 1 Pet 3:3), "head" (1 Cor 11:3, 4, 5, 7, 10; Eph 5:23), and "disgrace" of "disgraceful" (1 Cor 11:4, 5, 6, 14; 1 Cor 14:35). Elsewhere, essentially the same ideas are expressed in two or more passages but with slightly different wording: for example, "it is not permitted for them to speak" (1 Cor 14:34) and "I do not permit a woman to teach" (1 Tim 2:12).[9] Such parallels in vocabulary and thought, which link all of the passages under consideration in an interrelated network, are sufficiently numer-

---

7. I shall discuss only the passages dealing directly with the status, role, attire, and/or general demeanor of women, not the *Haustafeln* as a whole. My conclusions, however, will have clear implications for an understanding of the *Sitz im Leben* of the *Haustafeln*, and a complete study of the matter will eventually include consideration of the *Haustafeln* as a whole.

8. See Selwyn, *First Epistle of St. Peter*, 434, for the argument that "submissive to their (own) husbands" belongs to the original source.

9. In several of the examples cited above, the Greek vocabulary is not identical, but is close, and the meaning is always similar.

ous and specific to suggest a common origin or source, or at least a common tradition underlying the group.

The second point to be considered is that at least four of the passages in question appeal to the Old Testament, and particularly to the book of Genesis, to support their views regarding women. 1 Corinthians 11:7–9 cites the creation of Adam and Eve, 1 Tim 2:13–14 the temptation and fall of Adam and Eve, 1 Pet 3:6 the story of Sarah and Abraham, and 1 Cor 14:34 simply "the law."[10] This, too, suggests a common origin or source, or at least a common tradition, underlying the various passages in question.

The third point to be considered is that, taken as a group, the passages in question deal generally with the same three aspects of what was apparently viewed as a single overall problem regarding women. These three aspects of the problem are evident from the three major concerns expressed in the passages: (1) the domestic status and role of women in relationship to their husbands, (2) the religious status and role of women in the life and worship of the church, and (3) the proper attire and demeanor of women in general. Except in Colossians and Ephesians, which deal only with the first concern, it appears that the three were interrelated. Thus, the discussion of attire and demeanor in 1 Tim 2:9–10 is "sandwiched" between a restriction of the activity of praying to the men (v. 8) and a prohibition of teaching by women (vv. 11–12), which also refers to the necessity for "submissiveness" on the part of women (v. 11). Similarly, Titus 2:4–5 speaks of the general demeanor of women, concluding with the command that they be "submissive to their husbands." In somewhat the same manner, 1 Pet 3:1–6 begins with an injunction that women be "submissive" to their husbands (v. 1) and ends on the same note (vv. 5b–6), but the major part of the passage (vv. 2–5a) has to do with the attire and demeanor of women in general. The principal concern of 1 Cor 14:34–35 is that women not speak in church, but it also includes directives that they are to be "subordinate" or "submis-

---

10. This reference to "the law" may have in mind Gen 3:16; see, e.g., Boucher, "Some Unexplored Parallels," 50.

sive" and that, "if there is anything they desire to know," they are to "ask their husbands at home."

1 Corinthians 11:3–16 presents a special problem at this point, since the unity of the passage has recently been questioned.[11] If, as has been suggested, the passage actually consists of three originally separate and distinct pericopes, each dealing with a somewhat different aspect of the status, role, and/or attire of women, then there is rather less indication of interrelation here than elsewhere, although the question of attire is still related to that of public worship in what has been labeled Pericope B of the passage.[12] If, however, the unity of the passage is maintained,[13] then here, as elsewhere, the three concerns are clearly interrelated, with vv. 3, 8–9, 11–12 dealing with the domestic status and role of women in relationship to their husbands, vv. 4–7, 10, 13, 16 dealing with the attire of women as they participate in the religious life of the church, and vv. 14–15 dealing with the attire of women in general.

In all of the passages under consideration, the key motif is that women are to be "submissive" or "subordinate." Apparently the problem, as seen by the authors, was that of women not being properly "submissive" or "subordinate" to men. This problem then manifested itself variously in domestic relationships, in re-

---

11. Walker, "1 Corinthians 11:2–16 and Paul's Views regarding Women," 101–4.

12. The proposed Pericope A (vv. 3, 8–9, 11–12) deals with the domestic status of women in relationship to their husbands, Pericope B (vv. 4–7, 10, 13, 16) with the attire of women as they participate in the religious life of the church, and Pericope C (vv. 14–15) with the proper attire of women.

13. See, e.g., Trompf, "On Attitudes toward Women," 197: ". . . a unity I take to be fairly obvious." So far as I am aware, no one has accepted my proposed division of the passage into "three originally separate and distinct pericopes, each dealing with a somewhat different though related topic." Nevertheless, I continue to believe that the very real differences in subject matter, vocabulary, and literary style, as well as the fact that each of the proposed pericopes forms a complete and intelligible unit by itself, are sufficient to establish a presumption of their original independence. Cf., e.g., Murphy-O'Connor, "Non-Pauline Character of 1 Corinthians 11:2–16?," 616, who rejects my division of the passage but speaks, nevertheless, of "the problems of internal logic that all commentators have noticed in 11:3–16."

ligious matters, and in questions regarding attire and demeanor in general, and the passages in question attempt to deal with the various aspects of the problem. This, too, suggests a common origin or source, or at least a common tradition, underlying the passages being considered.

The fourth point to be considered is that, taken as a group, the passages in question exhibit the same three elements of what appears to have been a specific literary form developed for the express purpose of "keeping women in their place." Characteristically, this form would have consisted of the following three elements: (a) a general statement, assertion, or command regarding the proper status, role, attire, and/or demeanor of women; (b) a reason or justification—theological, historical, rational, or pragmatic—for the statement, assertion, or command; and (c) a "mitigation," "softening of the blow," or "saving phrase" to make the statement, assertion, or command less offensive to women.[14] The literary form can be seen most clearly and fully in 1 Tim 2:8–15, where all three of the elements are present and the pattern is a simple *ABC*:

> A. *General Statement, Assertion, or Command (vv. 8–12)*
> I desire then that in every place the men should pray, lifting holy hands without anger or quarreling; also that women should adorn themselves modestly and sensibly in seemly apparel, not with braided hair or gold or pearls or costly attire but by good deeds as befits women who profess religion. Let a woman learn in silence with all submissiveness. I permit no woman to teach or have authority over men; she is to be silent.
> B. *Reason or Justification (vv. 13–14)*
> For Adam was formed first, then Eve; and Adam was not

---

14. I first suggested the possibility of such a literary form in my "1 Corinthians 11:2–16 and Paul's Views regarding Women," 102 n. 35. Cf., more recently, Trompf, "On Attitudes toward Women," 205–6, where, without reference to any specific literary form *per se*, and with somewhat different terminology than that originally suggested by me, essentially the same three formal elements are identified. For the most part, I am now prepared to accept Trompf's terminology in preference to my own.

deceived, but the woman was deceived and became a transgressor.
C. *Mitigation, Softening of the Blow, or Saving Phrase (v. 15)*
Yet woman will be saved through bearing children, if they continue in faith and love and holiness, with modesty.

In some passages, the pattern becomes more complex, and, at times, it is not clear whether element C is present at all. Thus, the pattern of 1 Pet 3:1–6 is *ABAB* (vv. 1a, 1b–2, 3–4a, 4b–6a, respectively), with v. 6b either a continuation of *B* or perhaps a very subtle form of *C*. The pattern of 1 Cor 14:34–35 is *ABAB* (vv. 34a, 34b, 34c, 34d, respectively), followed by *A* or possibly a subtle form of *C* (v. 35a)[15] and *B* (v. 35b). In Titus 2:4–5, the pattern is a simple *AB* (vv. 4–5a, 5b, respectively), with *C* absent altogether. Three of the passages introduce a somewhat modified form of element *C* with a command to husbands that they love their wives. Thus, Col 3:18–19 follows the simple pattern, *ABC* (v. 18a, 18b, 19, respectively), while Eph 5:22–33 has the more complex pattern *ABACA* (vv. 22, 23, 24, 25–33a, 33b, respectively); and 1 Pet 3:1–7 has the pattern *ABA* (vv. 1a, 1b–2, 3–4a, respectively), followed by *B* (vv. 4b–6 or perhaps 4b–6a with 6b a very subtle form of *C*), then *C* (v. 7).

The analysis of 1 Cor 11:3–16 is again complicated by the question of the unity of the passage.[16] If it is a single unit, then the pattern is apparently *ABCB* (vv. 3–6, 7–10, 11–12, 13–16, respectively), although the distinctions are not as clear here as they are elsewhere. If, however, the passage is divided into three pericopes, as has been suggested, the following patterns emerge: Pericope A follows the pattern *ABC* (vv. 3, 8–9, 11–12, respectively); Pericope B the pattern *A* (vv. 4–6), *B* (vv. 7, 10, 13, 16), with no *C*; and Pericope

---

15. This could conceivably be regarded as a "mitigation," "softening of the blow," or "saving phrase," in that it does allow for women having their questions answered; more likely, however, it is simply part of the general command of silence in the assemblies and subordination to one's own husband.
16. See n. 11 above.

C consists almost entirely of element *B*, with *A* only implied and C absent altogether.[17]

The presence of at least traces of the same three formal elements throughout virtually all of the passages in question not only strengthens the case for a common source, origin, or at least a common tradition, underlying the various passages, it seems to me, but also suggests that a common literary form was, in fact, variously employed in different contexts for the purpose of "keeping women in their place."

The fifth point to be considered is that all of the passages in question come from a single tradition within early Christianity, namely, what can be termed the "Paulinist" tradition, which, however, must be carefully distinguished from the authentically "Pauline" tradition. Although these passages are widely associated with Paul himself, inasmuch as all of them except 1 Pet 3:1–7 are found within the corpus of writings attributed to him, there is now, as was observed earlier in this paper, an apparently growing scholarly consensus that the passages originated, not with Paul himself, but rather within the "Paulinist" tradition, that is, with later writers who somehow stood within a tradition begun by Paul and looking back to him as its founder and inspiration. Thus 1 Timothy and Titus are generally regarded today as "pseudo-Pauline," as are Ephesians and Colossians by a somewhat smaller but substantial number of commentators.[18] 1 Corinthians 14:34–35 is viewed by many as a post-Pauline interpolation,[19] and the same

---

17. Whether this analysis of 1 Cor 11:3–16 strengthens or weakens my arguments for dividing the passage into three pericopes is open to debate. My own judgment is that it strengthens the arguments except perhaps in the case of Pericope C, which consists almost entirely of element *B* (it is possible, however, that part of Pericope C was deleted when it was combined with the other pericopes). The pattern of the literary form may, however, explain in part why three originally separate and distinct pericopes would have been conflated in such a way as to produce the present 1 Cor 11:3–16, with its relatively simply conformity to the pattern.

18. See n. 3 above.

19. See n. 4 above.

has recently been suggested regarding 1 Cor 11:3–16.[20] As regards 1 Pet 3:1–7, which, of course, no one has regarded as directly Pauline, it has long been believed by many that the pseudonymous author of 1 Peter "stands in the line of succession of Pauline

---

20. Walker, "1 Corinthians 11:2–16 and Paul's Views regarding Women." Response to my argument has been mixed. Murphy-O'Connor, while recognizing the difficulties involved in the passage, nevertheless asserts that my arguments "are highly questionable on both factual and methodological grounds" and that the hypothesis regarding 1 Cor 11:2–16 as a post-Pauline interpolation must be rejected; see his "Non-Pauline Character of 1 Corinthians 11:2–16?" In a later article, he attempts to clarify the situation in Corinth and Paul's response to it in such a way as to demonstrate the internal coherence of the passage in question and thus to refute my claim that it is non-Pauline; see his "Sex and Logic in 1 Corinthians 11:2–16." Others who have rejected my argument include: Meier, "On the Veiling of Hermeneutics," 218 n. 12; Thiselton, "Realized Eschatology at Corinth," 520–21; Orr and Walther, *I Corinthians: A New Translation*, 259, 261, 262; and apparently Schüssler Fiorenza, "Study of Women in Early Christianity," esp. 36–37, 47, 54 n. 17, 58 n. 43, who treats my hypothesis as an example of the type of "revisionist apologetics" that seeks to formulate a "canon within the canon" by declaring "one string of the tradition as unauthentic and therefore not normative." (Regarding this last point, I must insist that I have not entered at all into the question of canon nor have I dealt in any way whatsoever with the question of what is or is not "normative.") On the other hand, even before the publication of my article and completely unknown to me at the time, Jeanette Piccard had apparently suggested some tampering with the text of 1 Cor 11:2–16, and Winsome Munro had concluded that the passage is one among a rather large number of non-Pauline interpolations in the Pauline corpus, a view she continues to maintain; see her "Two Strata in 1 Cor 10 and 11"; "Authority and Subjection in Early Christian Paideia"; "Patriarchy and Charismatic Community in 'Paul,'" esp. 191–92; and "Post-Pauline Material in 1 Cor 10, 11, and 14," reportedly to be incorporated in her announced but as yet unpublished book, *Authority in Paul and Peter*. [Editor's Note: *Authority in Paul and Peter* was published in 1983.] After the appearance of my article and Murphy-O'Connor's response, Lamar Cope published an article supporting the non-Pauline character of the passage in question, suggesting only that the interpolation consists of 1 Cor 11:3–16, not 11:2–16, a suggestion that I am now prepared to accept; see his "1 Cor 11:2–16: One Step Further." In my judgment, however the most significant and impressive support for the non-Pauline character of 1 Cor 11:3–16 has come from Trompf, who has not only substantially strengthened the case against Pauline authorship of the passage as a

theology"[21] and thus quite properly can be seen as a representative of the "Paulinist" tradition.[22]

This suggests, as Francis X. Cleary and others have recognized, that attitudes toward women in Pauline (or rather "Paulinist") Christianity must be approached on more than one level. Cleary suggests a distinction that would include "authentic Paul" (Gal 3:28; 1 Cor 7:2–5, 10–16; 11:2–16), "re-written Paul" (Eph 5:22–33), "ghostwritten Paul" (1 Tim 2:9–15), and "interpolated Paul" (1 Cor 14:33b–35).[23] I prefer to speak of "authentic Paul" (Gal 3:27–28; 1 Corinthians 7), "pseudo-Paul" Col 3:18–19; Eph 5:22–33; 1 Tim 2:8–15; Titus 2:4–5), "interpolated Paul" (1 Cor 14:34–35; 11:3–16), and "Paulinist" (1 Pet 3:1–7). For the sake of simplicity, however, I shall hereafter apply the label "Paulinist" to all except the authentically "Pauline" materials.

It is in the Paulinist, not the Pauline, passages that all of the material under consideration in this paper is to be found. Lest the significance of this fact be overlooked, it should be emphasized that, outside these Paulinist passages, there is not a single statement in the entire New Testament that supports the principle of male dominance and female subordination. This, like the four points previously cited, lends clear support to the case for a common source or origin, or at least a common tradition, underlying all such passages. Although the ultimate source of these materials may well have been Hellenistic or Hellenistic Jewish,[24] they

---

whole but also suggested some plausible reasons for its interpolation into the original text of 1 Corinthians; see his "On Attitudes toward Women in Paul and Paulinist Literature." It is my conviction that the case against Pauline authorship of 1 Cor 11:3–16 has now been cogently made, and I fully expect that this view will gain increasing acceptance by scholars in the field of NT studies.

21. Kümmel, *Introduction to the New Testament,* 423. Cf., e.g., Fuller, *Critical Introduction to the New Testament,* 157: "It has been said that but for the name 'Peter' in the opening address, 1 Pet would have been regarded as a deutero-Pauline letter. In fact, it is much more Pauline than the Past" (i.e., Pastorals).

22. On the pseudonymous character of 1 Peter, see n. 3 above.

23. Cleary, "Women in the New Testament."

24. See, e.g., Balch, *Let Wives Be Submissive,* esp. 1–62.

apparently entered the Christian tradition for the first time, not in the apostolic period, as Selwyn and others have assumed, but rather in the post-apostolic period and, even then, only through the Paulinist wing of Christianity, which, I have suggested, created a specific literary form for the express purpose of "keeping women in their place."

The fact that it was precisely within Paulinist Christianity that it was believed necessary to formulate a "theology of woman's place"[25] and to create a literary form to express this theology implies rather clearly that it was also within Paulinist Christianity that women were claiming and perhaps exercising the type of equality with men that was viewed as a problem.[26] This, in turn, has some rather clear implications for understanding of the nature of Pauline Christianity. The reason for the women's claims, no doubt, was the radically egalitarian teaching and practice of Paul himself, which apparently came to be viewed as a problem in the post-apostolic period, as the church lost much of its earlier eschatological and charismatic enthusiasm and sought to create for itself a measure of structure, order, and stability in the face

---

25. Trompf, "On Attitudes toward Women in Paul and Paulinist Literature," 210.

26. Cf., however, Balch, *Let Wives Be Submissive*, esp. 81–116, who argues that the function of the *Haustafeln*, especially in 1 Peter, was essentially apologetic: "Persons in Roman society were alienated and threatened by some of their slaves and wives who had converted to the new, despised religion, so they were accusing converts of impiety, immorality, and insubordination. As a defense, the author of 1 Peter encouraged the slaves and wives to play the social roles which Aristotle had outlined; this, he hoped, would shame those who were reviling their good behavior (3:16; 2:12). The conduct of the slaves was not expected to convert masters. However, the author hoped that the wives would convert their husbands by laudable behavior" (109). This may well be correct, but there would hardly be any need to command that wives be submissive if they were already behaving in this manner. Thus, it is more likely that the intended function of the *Haustafeln* was to repress certain types of behavior among Christians—behavior stimulated by the teaching and practice of Paul but regarded as a problem in the later Paulinist churches. See Balch's critique of this latter position, pp. 106–7, and the bibliographical references there cited.

of an increasingly hostile environment and growing internal pluralism. That Paul's own teaching and practice were, in fact, radically egalitarian, particularly as regards the status and role of women, has been made increasingly clear by recent studies of Gal 3:27–28, which asserts the absolute equality of the sexes in Christ,[27] 1 Corinthians 7, which insists that the two sexes have precisely the same freedom and the same responsibility in the marriage relationship,[28] and the various New Testament references to women as Paul's honored and esteemed co-workers in the church.[29] The authentically Pauline materials are consistently and radically egalitarian in their outlook; the later Paulinist materials are equally consistently "patriarchal." Here, as apparently at other points, Paul's views and practices were no longer acceptable to the developing Hellenistic churches, and Paulinist teachers and writers found it necessary to "tame" or "domesticate" the now deceased Apostle.[30]

In conclusion, while I agree with Selwyn and others that the New Testament passages supporting the principle of male dominance and female subordination have a common source or origin, I do not agree that this origin was apostolic. Rather, the passages

---

27. See, e.g., Scroggs, "Paul and the Eschatological Woman," 291–93.

28. See, e.g., Scroggs, "Paul and the Eschatological Woman," 294–97.

29. See, e.g., Furnish, *Moral Teaching of Paul*, 102–10; and Thomas, "The Place of Women."

30. On the general tendency in the post-apostolic church toward such a "domesticizing" of Paul, see, e.g., Wiles, *Divine Apostle*, esp. the Epilogue. Elaine Hiesey Pagels, among others, argues cogently that there were two conflicting traditions of interpreting Paul in the late first and the second centuries, the one a "Gnostic" tradition and the other "anti-Gnostic." The Pastoral Letters, for example, represent the "anti-Gnostic" tradition. Pagels also suggests that, largely because of his popularity among Gnostic exegetes, "ecclesiastical Christians" tended to revere Paul as a great apostle and martyr but to remain virtually silent (possibly even ignorant) regarding his theology. See her *Gnostic Paul*, esp. 1–12, 157–66. Such uneasiness with Paul's theology may well also have extended to his *praxis*. Clearly, one way to deal with such uneasiness could have been to create a Paulinist literature expressing the views of the "ecclesiastical Christians" as opposed to those of the Gnostics and (at least in some cases) of Paul himself.

in question were introduced in the post-apostolic period, within one particular "wing" of the Christian tradition, the Paulinist wing, and are directly at variance with the clearly articulated views and practices of the Apostle Paul.[31] For a variety of reasons, however, Paul's own views came to be interpreted in the light of the later Paulinist tradition, and the result was that the authentically Pauline insight and practice were largely forgotten in the post-apostolic church.

---

31. Even to speak of the "Paulinist wing" of the early church is an oversimplification, Paulinist Christianity seems to have evolved in several somewhat different directions. Thus, the Pastoral Letters represent one line of development, and the attitude toward women therein reflected is similar to that also found in 1 Cor 14:34–35 and 1 Pet 3:1–7 (cf. also 1 Cor 11:4–7, 10, 13, 16). On the other hand, Colossians and Ephesians represent a different line of development, and the attitude toward women therein reflected is similar to that also found in 1 Cor 11:3–16 (esp. vv. 3, 8–9, 11–12). In both cases, however, the attitude is "patriarchal" and stems, I suggest, from a common origin, source, or line of tradition. Acts of the Apostles, by way of contrast, appears to be closer to Paul's own radically egalitarian views regarding women. For the argument that the Pastoral Letters and The Acts of Paul and Thecla represent two different Pauline (or rather, Paulinist) schools of thought regarding women, the former insisting upon patriarchal marriage and childbearing and the latter offering celibacy as an alternative, see Brooten, "Feminine Perspectives in New Testament Exegesis," 58–59.

Bibliography

Aland, Kurt, and Barbara Aland. *The Text of the New Testament: An Introduction to the Critical Editions and to the Theory and Practice of Modern Textual Criticism.* Trans. Erroll F. Rhodes. 2d ed. Grand Rapids: Wm. B. Eerdmans Publishing Co.; Leiden: E. J. Brill, 1989.

Allison, Dale C. "Peter and Cephas: One and the Same." *JBL* 111 (1992) 489–95.

Baarda, T. "Openbaring-Traditie en Didachè." Pp. 152–67 in *Zelfstandig geloven: Studies voor Jaap Firet.* Ed. F. H. Kuiper et al. Kampen: J. H. Kok Publishers, 1987.

_____. "Ti eti diōkomai in Gal. 5:11: Apodosis or Parenthesis." *NovT* 35 (1992) 250–56.

Balch, David L. *Let Wives Be Submissive: The Domestic Code in 1 Peter.* SBLMS 26; Chico: Scholars Press, 1981.

Barnett, Paul. *The Second Epistle to the Corinthians.* NICNT; Grand Rapids/ Cambridge: Wm. B. Eerdmans Publishing Co., 1997.

Barnikol, Ernst. *Der nichtpaulinische Ursprung des Parallelismus der Apostel Petrus und Paulus (Galater 2 7-8).* Forschungen zur Entstehung des Urchristentums, des Neuen Testaments und der Kirche 5; Kiel: W. G. Mühlau, 1931. (English translation cited below: Barnikol, "The Non-Pauline Origin.")

_____. "The Non-Pauline Origin of the Parallelism of the Apostles Peter and Paul. Galatians 2:7-8." Trans. Darrell J. Doughty with B. Keith Brewer. *The Journal of Higher Criticism* 5 (1998) 285–300. (German original cited above: Barnikol, *Der nichtpaulinische Ursprung.*)

Barrett, Charles Kingsley. "Acts and the Pauline Corpus." *ExpT* 88 (1976–77) 2–5.

_____. *A Commentary on the Second Epistle to the Corinthians.* HNTC; New York: Harper & Row, 1973.

_____. *A Critical and Exegetical Commentary on the Acts of the Apostles.* 2 vols. ICC; Edinburgh: T & T Clark, 1994, 1998.

_____. *New Testament Essays.* London: SPCK, 1972.

_____. "Titus." Pp. 1–14 in *Neotestamentica et Semitica: Studies in Honour of Matthew Black.* Ed. E. Earle Ellis and Max Wilcox. Edinburgh: T & T Clark, 1969. Reprinted as pp. 118–31 in his *New Testament Essays.* London: SPCK, 1972.

Bartchy, S. Scott. *Mallon chrēsai: First-Century Slavery and the Interpretation of 1 Corinthians 7:21.* SBLDS 11; Missoula: Society of Biblical Literature, 1973.

Bartlet, Vernon. "Titus the Friend of Luke, and Other Related Questions." *The Expositor* Series 8,13 (1917) 367–75.

Bauernfeind, Otto. *Kommentar und Studien zur Apostelgeschichte.* Ed. Volker Mitelmann; WUNT 22; Tübingen: J. C. B. Mohr/Siebeck, 1980.

Beasley-Murray, G. R. *Baptism in the New Testament.* Grand Rapids: Wm. B. Eerdmans Publishing Co., 1962.

Behm, Johannes. Review of Barnikol, *Der nichtpaulinische Ursprung des Parallelismus der Apostel Paulus und Petrus (Galater 2, 7-8).* TLZ 58 (1933) 27–29.

Betz, Hans Dieter. *2 Corinthians 8 and 9: A Commentary on Two Administrative Letters of the Apostle Paul.* Ed. George W. MacRae. Hermeneia; Philadelphia: Fortress Press, 1985.

_____. "Corinthians, Second Epistle to the." Pp. 1.1148–54 in *ABD*.

_____. *Galatians: A Commentary on Paul's Letter to the Churches in Galatia.* Hermeneia; Philadelphia: Fortress Press, 1979.
Blommerde, A. C. M. "Is there an Ellipsis between Galatians 2,3 and 2,4?" *Bib* 56 (1975) 100–102.
Boring, M. Eugene. *An Introduction to the New Testament: History, Literature, Theology.* Louisville: Westminster John Knox Press, 2012.
Boucher, Madeleine. "Some Unexplored Parallels to 1 Cor 11,11–12 and Gal 3,38: The NT on the Role of Women." *CBQ* 31 (1969) 50–58.
Bouttier, Michel. "Complexio Oppositorum: Sur Les Formules de I Cor 12:13; Gal 3:26–28; Col 3:10, 11." *NTS* 23 (1976) 1–11.
Bowen, C. R. "I Fought with Beasts at Ephesus." *JBL* 42 (1923) 59–68.
Boys-Smith, E. P. "Titus and Luke." *ExpT* 18 (1906–7) 380–81.
Bray, Gerald, ed. *1–2 Corinthians.* Ancient Christian Commentary on Scripture: NT 7; Downers Grove: InterVarsity Press, 1999.
Brooten, Bernadette. "Feminine Perspectives in New Testament Exegesis." Pp. 55–61 in *Conflicting Ways of Interpreting the Bible.* Ed. Hans Küng and Jürgen Moltmann. Eng. Trans. Ed. Marcus Lefébure. Concilium 138; Edinburgh: T & T Clark/New York: Seabury Press, 1980.
Brown, Scott G. *Mark's Other Gospel: Rethinking Morton Smith's Controversial Discovery.* Studies in Christianity and Judaism 15; Waterloo: Wilfred Laurier University Press, 2005.
Bruce, F. F. *The Epistle of Paul to the Galatians: A Commentary on the Greek Text.* NIGTC; Exeter: Paternoster Press, 1982.
_____. *Paul: Apostle of the Heart Set Free.* Grand Rapids: Wm B. Eerdmans Publishing Co.; Carlisle and Cumbria: Paternoster Press, 1977.
Bultmann, Rudolf. Review of Ernst Barnikol, *Der nichtpaulinische Ursprung . . . (Galater 2 7-8).* ZKG 51 Series 3:2 (1932) 555.
_____. *The Second Letter to the Corinthians.* Trans. Roy A. Harrisville. Minneapolis: Augsburg Press, 1985.
Burchard, C. *Der dreizehnte Zeuge. Traditions- und kompositions-geschichtliche Untersuchungen zu Lukas' Darstellung der Früzeit des Paulus.* FRLANT 103. Göttingen: Vandenhoeck & Ruprecht, 1970.
Burton, Ernest de Witt. *A Critical and Exegetical Commentary on the Epistle to the Galatians.* ICC; Edinburgh: T & T Clark, 1921.
_____. *Syntax of the Moods and Tenses in New Testament Greek.* 3d ed. Edinburgh: T & T Clark, 1898.
Byrne, Brendan. *Romans.* SP 6; Collegeville; Liturgical Press, 1996.
Cadbury, Henry J. *The Making of Luke-Acts.* New York: Macmillan and Co., 1927.
Carlson, Stephen. *The Gospel Hoax: Morton Smith's Invention of Secret Mark.* Waco, TX: Baylor University Press, 2005.
Carrington, Philip. *The Primitive Christian Catechism: A Study in the Epistles.* Cambridge: Cambridge University Press, 1940.
Clabeaux, John J. "Marcion." Pp. 4.514–16 in *ABD.*
Cleary, Francis X. "Women in the New Testament: St. Paul and the Early Pauline Churches." *BTB* 10/2 (1980) 78–82.
Collins, Raymond F. *First Corinthians.* SP 7; Collegeville: Liturgical Press, 1999.
Comfort, Philip W., and David P. Barrett, eds. *The Text of the Earliest New Testament Greek Manuscripts.* Wheaton, IL: Tyndale House, 2001.
Conzelmann, Hans. *1 Corinthians: A Commentary on the First Epistle to the Corinthians.* Hermeneia; Philadelphia: Fortress Press, 1975.
_____. *Acts of the Apostles: A Commentary on the Acts of the Apostles.* Hermeneia; Philadelphia: Fortress Press, 1987.

Cope, Lamar. "1 Cor 11:2–16: One Step Further." *JBL* 97 (1978) 435–36.
Couchoud, P.-L. "La première édition de Saint Paul." *RHR* 94 (1926) 242–63.
Cousar, Charles B. "Jerusalem, Council of." Pp. 3.766–68 in *ABD*.
Cranfield, C. E. B. *A Critical and Exegetical Commentary on the Epistle to the Romans.* 2 vols. ICC; Edinburgh: T & T Clark, 1975–79.
Crouch, James E. *The Origin and Intention of the Colossian Haustafel.* FRLANT 109; Göttingen: Vandenhoeck & Ruprecht, 1972.
Cullmann, Oscar. "Πέτρος, Κηφᾶς." Pp. 6.100–112 in *TDNT*.
_____. *Peter: Disciple · Apostle · Martyr: A Historical and Theological Study.* Trans. Floyd V. Filson. 2d ed. Philadelphia: Westminster Press, 1962
Dana, H. E. and Julius R. Mantey. *A Manual Grammar of the Greek New Testament.* New York: Macmillan and Co., 1949.
D'Angelo, Mary Rose. "Reconstructing 'Real' Women from Gospel Literature: The Case of Mary Magdalene." Pp. 105–28 in *Women & Christian Origins.* Ed. Ross Shepard Kramer and Mary Rose D'Angelo. New York/Oxford: Oxford University Press, 1999.
_____. "(Re)presentations of Women in the Gospels: John and Mark." Pp. 129–49 in *Women & Christian Origins.* Ed. Ross Shepard Kramer and Mary Rose D'Angelo. New York/Oxford: Oxford University Press, 1999.
_____. "'(Re)presentations of Women in the Gospels of Matthew and Luke-Acts." Pp. 171–95 in *Women & Christian Origins.* Ed. Ross Shepard Kramer and Mary Rose D'Angelo. New York/Oxford: Oxford University Press, 1999.
_____. "Women in Luke-Acts: A Redactional View." *JBL* 109 (1990) 441–61.
Das, A. Andrew. "Another Look at ἐὰν μή in Galatians 2:16." *JBL* 119 (2000) 529–39.
Dautsenberg, Gerhard. "Da Ist Nicht Männlich und Weiblich. Zur Interpretation von Gal 3,28." *Kairós* n.s. 24 (1982) 181–206.
De Boer, Martinus C. *Galatians: A Commentary.* NTL; Louisville: Westminster John Knox Press, 2011.
Delafosse, Henri a.k.a. Joseph Turmel. *Les écrits de Saint Paul: traduction nouvelle avec introduction et notes, 3: La seconde épître aux Corinthiens, les épîtres aux Galates, aux Colossiens, aux Éphésiens, à Philemon.* Paris: F. Rieder et cie, 1927.
Dewey Arthur J., Roy W. Hoover, Lane C. McGaughy, and Daryl D. Schmidt. *The Authentic Letters of Paul: A New Reading of Paul's Rhetoric and Meaning: The Scholars Version.* Salem: Polebridge Press, 2010.
Dibelius, Martin. *An die Kolosser, Epheser, und Philemon.* Tübingen: J. C. B. Mohr, 1913.
_____. "The Conversion of Cornelius." Pp. 140–50 in *The Book of Acts: Form, Style, und Theology.* Ed. K. C. Hanson. Minneapolis: Fortress Press, 2004.
Dinkler, Erich. "Der Brief an die Galater. Zum Kommentar von Heinrich Schlier." *VF* 1–3 (1953–55) 175–83. Reprinted with "Nachtrag" as pp. 270–82 in his *Signum Crucis. Aufsätze zum Neuen Testament und zur Christlichen Archäologie.* Tübingen: J. C. B. Mohr (Paul Siebeck), 1967.
_____. "Die Petrus-Rom-Frage. Ein Forschungsbericht." *TRu* n.s. 25 (1959) 189–208.
_____. Dinkler, Erich. "Nachtrag." Pp. 270–82 in *Signum Crucis. Aufsätze zum Neuen Testament und zur Christlichen Archäologie.* Tübingen: J. C. B. Mohr (Paul Siebeck), 1967.
Duff, Paul B. "Glory in the Ministry of Death: Gentile Condemnation and Letters of Recommendation in 2 Cor. 3:6–18." *NovT* 46 (2004) 313–37.
Dungan, David L. *The Sayings of Jesus in the Churches of Paul: The Use of the Synoptic Tradition in the Regulation of Early Church Life.* Philadelphia: Fortress Press, 1971.

Dunn, James D. G. *Baptism in the Holy Spirit*. London: SCM Press, 1970.
_____. *A Commentary on the Epistle to the Galatians*. BNTC 9; London: A. C. Black, 1993.
_____. "The New Perspective on Paul." *BJRL* 65 (1983) 95–122.
Edmundson, George. "The Enigma of Titus." *The Expositor* Series 8,11 (1916) 321–34.
Ehrman, Bart D. "Cephas and Peter." *JBL* 109 (1990) 463–74.
Ellingworth, Paul, and Howard Hatton. *A Translator's Handbook on Paul's First Letter to the Corinthians*. Helps for Translators; London/New York/Stuttgart: United Bible Societies, 1985.
Elliott, J. K. "Κηφᾶς: Σίμων Πέτρος: ὁ Πέτρος: An Examination of New Testament Usage." *NovT* 14 (1972) 241–56.
Ellis, E. Earle. "Paul and His Co-Workers." Pp. 3–22 in *Prophecy and Hermeneutic in Early Christianity: New Testament Essays*. Grand Rapids: Wm. B. Eerdmans Publishing Co., 1978.
_____. "The Silenced Wives of Corinth (I Cor. 14:34-5)." Pp. 213–20 in *New Testament Textual Criticism: Its Significance for Exegesis: Essays in Honour of Bruce M. Metzger*. Ed. Eldon Jay Epp and Gordon D. Fee. Oxford: Clarendon Press and New York: Oxford University Press, 1980.
_____. "Traditions in 1 Corinthians." *NTS* 32 (1986) 481–502.
Enslin, Morton Scott. "'Luke' and Paul." *JAOS* 58 (1938) 81–91.
_____. "Once Again, Luke and Paul." *ZNW* 61 (1970) 253–71.
_____. *Reapproaching Paul*. Philadelphia: Westminster Press, 1972.
Epp, Eldon Jay. *Junia: The First Woman Apostle*. Minneapolis: Fortress Press, 2005.
Farmer, William R. *The Synoptic Problem: A Critical Analysis*. New York: Macmillan and Co., and London: Collier-Macmillan, 1964.
Fee, Gordon D. *The First Epistle to the Corinthians*. NICNT; Grand Rapids: Wm. B. Eerdmans Publishing Co., 1987.
Fitzgerald, John T. "Philippians, Epistle to the." Pp. 5.318–26 in *ABD*.
Fitzmyer, Joseph A. *The Acts of the Apostles: A New Translation with Introduction and Commentary*. AB 31; New York: Doubleday and Company, 1998.
_____. "Aramaic *Kêphā'* and Peter's Name in the New Testament." Pp. 112–24 in *To Advance the Gospel: New Testament Studies*. New York: Crossroad Publishing Co., 1981.
_____. *First Corinthians: A New Translation with Introduction and Commentary*. The Anchor Yale Bible 32; New Haven and London: Yale University Press, 2008.
_____. "Glory Reflected on the Face of Christ (2 Cor 3:7–4:6) and a Palestinian Jewish Motif." *TS* 42 (1981) 630–44. Reprinted as pp. 64–79 in *According to Paul: Studies in the Theology of the Apostle*. New York: Paulist Press, 1993.
_____. *Romans: A New Translation with Introduction and Commentary*. AB 33; New York: Doubleday, 1993.
Foakes-Jackson, F. J. *The Acts of the Apostles*. MNTC; London: Hodder and Stoughton; New York: Harper and Brothers, 1931.
Foakes-Jackson, F. J., and Kirsopp Lake, eds. The Beginnings of Christianity, Part I: *The Acts of the Apostles*. 5 vols (vols. 4 and 5 ed. Kirsopp Lake and Henry J. Cadbury). London: Macmillan and Co., 1929–1933.
Friedrich, Gerhard. "εὐαγγελίζομαι, εὐαγγέλιον, προευαγγελίζομαι, εὐαγγελιστής." Pp. 2.707–37 in *TDNT*.
Frye, Roland Mushat. "The Synoptic Problem and Analogies in Other Literatures." Pp. 261–302 in *The Relationships among the Gospels: An Interdisciplinary Dialogue*. Ed. William O. Walker, Jr. Trinity University Monograph Series in Religion 5; San Antonio: Trinity University Press, 1978.

Fuller, Reginald H. *A Critical Introduction to the New Testament.* Studies in Theology 55; London: Gerald Duckworth & Co., 1966.

Furnish, Victor Paul. *II Corinthians: Translated with Introduction, Notes, and Commentary.* AB 32A; Garden City: Doubleday, 1984.

_____. *The Moral Teaching of Paul.* Nashville: Abingdon Press, 1979.

Gaechter, Paul. *Petrus und seine Zeit. Neutestamentliche Studien.* Innsbruck: Tyrolia, 1958.

Gamble, Harry Y. "The Redaction of the Pauline Letters and the Formation of the Pauline Corpus." *JBL* 94 (1975) 403–18.

Gaventa, Beverly Roberts. *From Darkness to Light: Aspects of Conversion in the New Testament.* Philadelphia: Fortress Press, 1986.

Geer Jr., Thomas C. "Galatians 2:16: Paul's Continuity with or Radical Break from Judaism?" Unpublished paper presented to Southwest Biblical Studies Seminar, 1993.

Georgi, Dieter. *The Opponents of Paul in Second Corinthians.* Philadelphia: Fortress Press, 1986.

_____. *Remembering the Poor: The History of Paul's Collection for Jerusalem.* Nashville: Abingdon Press, 1992.

Goguel, Maurice. *La foi à la résurrection de Jésus dans le Christianisme primitif: étude d'histoire et de psychologie religieuses.* Paris: E. Leroux, 1933.

Goodenough, Erwin R. "The Perspective of Acts." Pp. 51–59 in *Studies in Luke-Acts: Essays Presented in Honor of Paul Schubert.* Ed. Leander E. Keck and J. Louis Martyn. Nashville: Abingdon Press, 1966.

Goodwin, William Watson. *Greek Grammar.* Rev. Charles Burton Gulick. Boston: Ginn and Company, 1930.

Goulder, Michael. *St. Paul versus St. Peter: A Tale of Two Missions.* Louisville: Westminster John Knox Press, 1994.

Gregory, Andrew. *The Reception of Luke and Acts in the Period before Irenaeus: Looking for Luke in the Second Century.* WUNT 2/169; Tübingen: J. C. B. Mohr/Siebeck, 2003.

Haenchen, Ernst. *The Acts of the Apostles: A Commentary.* Trans. and ed. Bernard Noble et al. Trans. rev. and updated R. McL. Wilson. Philadelphia: Westminster Press, 1971.

_____. "The Book of Acts as Source Material for the History of Early Christianity." Pp. 258–78 in *Studies in Luke-Acts: Essays Presented in Honor of Paul Schubert.* Ed. Leander E. Keck and J. Louis Martyn. Nashville: Abingdon Press, 1966.

_____. "Petrus-Probleme." *NTS* 7 (1960–61) 187–97. Reprinted as pp. 55–67 in *Gott und Mensch. Gesammelte Aufsätze.* Tübingen: J. C. B. Mohr (Paul Siebeck), 1965.

Hafemann, Scott. *Paul, Moses, and the History of Israel: The Letter/Spirit Contrast and the Argument from Scripture in 2 Corinthians 3.* WUNT 81; Tübingen: J. C. B. Mohr (Paul Siebeck), 1996.

_____. "Paul's Use of the Old Testament in 2 Corinthians." *Int* 52 (1998) 246–57.

_____. *Suffering and Ministry in the Spirit: Paul's Defense of His Ministry in II Corinthians 2:14-3:3.* Grand Rapids: Wm. B. Eerdmans Publishing Co., 1990.

Hansen, Bruce. "'All of you are one': The Social Vision of Gal 3:28, 1 Cor 12:13, and Col 3:33." Ph.D. diss., University of St. Andrews, 2007.

Hanson, A. T. "The Midrash in 2 Corinthians 3: A Reconsideration." *JSNT* 9 (1980) 2–28.

Harnack, Adolf von. *Marcion. Das Evangelium vom Fremden Gott. Eine Monographie zur Geschichte der Groundlegung der katholischen Kirche.* 2d ed. TUGAL 45; Leipzig: J. C. Hinrichs, 1924. Repr., Darmstadt: Wissenschaftliche Buchgesellschaft, 1985.

_____. *Marcion: The Gospel of the Alien God*. Trans. John E. Steely and Lyle D. Bierma. Durham: Labyrinth Press, 1990.
Harrill, J. Albert. "The Dramatic Function of the Running Slave Rhoda (Acts 12.13–16): A Piece of Greco-Roman Comedy." *NTS* 46 (2000) 150–57.
Hawkins, Robert Martyr. *The Recovery of the Historical Paul*. Nashville: Vanderbilt University Press, 1943.
Hays, Richard B. *The Faith of Jesus Christ: An Investigation of the Narrative Substructure of Galatians 3:1–4:11*. SBLDS 56; Chico: Scholars Press, 1983.
_____. *First Corinthians*. IBC; Louisville: John Knox Press, 1997.
_____. "The Letter to the Galatians: Introduction, Commentary, and Reflections." *NIB* 11.181–348.
Heinrici, C. F. G. *Der erste Brief an die Korinther*. 8th ed. KEK 5; Göttingen: Vandenhoeck & Ruprecht, 1896.
_____. *Der zweite Brief an die Korinther; Mit ein Anhang: Zum Hellenismus des Paulus*. 8th ed. KEK 6. Abteilung; Göttingen: Vandenhoeck & Ruprecht, 1900.
Hengel, Martin. *Acts and the History of Earliest Christianity*. Trans. John Bowden. Philadelphia: Fortress Press, 1979.
Henze, Clemens M. "Cephas seu Kephas non est Simon Petrus!" *Divus Thomas* 61 (1958) 63–67.
Holl, Karl. *Gesammelte Aufsätze zur Kirchengeschichte*, 2: *Der Osten*. 3 vols. Vols. 2 and 3 ed. Hans Lietzmann. Tübingen: J. C. B. Mohr (Paul Siebeck), 1921–30.
Howard, George. *Paul: Crisis in Galatia*. 2d ed. SNTSMS 35; Cambridge: Cambridge University Press, 1990.
Hughes, Philip Edgcumbe. *Paul's Second Epistle to the Corinthians: The English Text with Introduction, Exposition and Notes*. NICNT; Grand Rapids: Wm. B. Eerdmans Publishing Co., 1962.
Jewett, Robert. *Romans: A Commentary*. Ed. Eldon Jay Epp. Hermeneia; Minneapolis: Fortress Press, 2007.
Keck, Leander E., and J. Louis Martyn, eds. *Studies in Luke-Acts: Essays Presented in Honor of Paul Schubert*. Nashville: Abingdon Press, 1966.
Kilpatrick, G. D. "Apollos—Apelles." *JBL* 89 (1970) 77.
Klein, Günter. "Galater 2,6–9 und die Geschichte der Jerusalemer Urgemeinde." *ZTK* 57 (1960) 275–95. Reprinted with "Nachtrag" as pp. 99–128 in *Rekonstruktion und Interpretation. Gesammelte Aufsätze zum Neuen Testament*. Munich: Chr. Kaiser Verlag, 1969.
_____. "Nachtrag" to "Galater 2,6–9 und die Geschichte der Jerusalemer Urgemeinde." Pp. 118–28 in *Rekonstruktion und Interpretation. Gesammelte Aufsätze zum Neuen Testament*. Munich: Chr. Kaiser Verlag, 1969.
_____. *Die zwölf Apostel. Ursprung und Gehalt einer Idee* (FRLANT 59; Göttingen: Vandenhoeck & Ruprecht, 1961)
Knox, John. "Acts and the Pauline Letter Corpus." Pp. 279–87 in *Studies in Luke-Acts: Essays Presented in Honor of Paul Schubert*. Ed. Leander E. Keck and J. Louis Martyr. Nashville: Abingdon Press, 1966.
_____. *Chapters in a Life of Paul*. Rev. ed. Ed. D. R. A. Hare. Macon: Mercer University Press, 1987.
_____. "Galatians, Letter to the." Pp. 2.338–43 in *IDB*.
_____. *Marcion and the New Testament: An Essay in the Early History of the Canon*. Chicago: University of Chicago Press, 1942.
Kock, Theodor, ed. *Comicorum Atticorum Fragmenta*. 3 vols. Leipzig: B. G. Teubner, 1880–88.

Kramer, Ross Shepard and Mary Rose D'Angelo, eds. *Women and Christian Origins*. New York/Oxford: Oxford University Press, 1999.
Kümmel, Werner Georg. *Introduction to the New Testament*. Rev. ed. Trans. Howard Clark Kee. Nashville: Abingdon Press, 1975.
Lake, Kirsopp. *The Earlier Epistles of St. Paul: Their Motive and Origin*. 2d ed. London: Rivington's, 1914.
_____. "Note XVI. The Apostolic Council of Jerusalem." Pp. 191–212 in The Beginnings of Christianity, Part I: *The Acts of the Apostles*, Vol. 5: *Additional Notes to the Commentary*. Ed. Kirsopp Lake and Henry J. Cadbury. London: Macmillan and Co., 1933.
_____. "Simon, Cephas, Peter." *HTR* 14 (1921) 95–97.
Lake, Kirsopp, and Henry J. Cadbury. The Beginnings of Christianity, Part I: The *Acts of the Apostles*, Vol. 4: *English Translation and Commentary*. London: Macmillan and Co., 1933.
Lake, Kirsopp, and Henry J. Cadbury, eds. The Beginnings of Christianity, Part I: *The Acts of the Apostles*, Vol. 5: *Additional Notes to the Commentary*. London: Macmillan and Co., 1933.
Lambrecht, Jan. "Is Gal 5:11b a Parenthesis? A Response to T. Baarda." *NovT* 38 (1996) 237–41.
_____. *Second Corinthians*. Collegeville: Glazier and Liturgical Press, 1999.
Leppä, Outi. *The Making of Colossians: A Study on the Formation and Purpose of a Deutero-Pauline Letter*. Publications of the Finnish Exegetical Society 86; Helsinki: Finnish Exegetical Society; Göttingen: Vandenhoeck & Ruprecht, 2003.
Levine, Amy-Jill, with Marianne Blickenstaff, eds. *A Feminist Companion to the Acts of the Apostles*. Cleveland: Pilgrim Press, 2004.
Lietzmann, Hans. *An die Galater*. HNT 10; 3d ed. Tübingen: J. C. B. Mohr (Paul Siebeck), 1932.
_____. *An die Korinther II*. Ed. Werner G. Kümmel. 5th ed. HNT 9; Tübingen: J. C. B. Mohr (Paul Siebeck), 1969.
_____. "Notizen." *ZNW* 33 (1934) 93–96.
Lightfoot, Joseph Barber. *Biblical Essays*. London and New York: Macmillan and Co., 1893.
Lohse, Eduard. *Colossians and Philemon: A Commentary on the Epistles to the Colossians and to Philemon*. Trans. William R. Poehlmann and Robert J. Karris. Ed. Helmut Koester. Hermeneia. Philadelphia: Fortress Press, 1971.
_____. "Paränese und Kerygma im 1. Petrusbrief." *ZNW* 45 (1954) 68–89.
Longenecker, Richard N. *Galatians*. Word Biblical Commentary 42; Dallas: Word Books, 1990.
Lovering Jr., Eugene Harrison. "The Collection, Redaction, and Early Circulation of the Corpus Paulinum." Ph.D. diss., Southern Methodist University, 1988.
Lüdemann, Gerd. *Paul, Apostle to the Gentiles: Studies in Chronology*. Trans. F. Stanley Jones. Philadelphia: Fortress Press, 1984.
_____. with Tom Hall. *The Acts of the Apostles: What Really Happened in the Earliest Days of the Church*. Amherst: Prometheus Press, 2005.
MacDonald, Dennis R. "A Conjectural Emendation of 1 Cor 15:31-32: Or the Case of the Misplaced Lion Fight." *HTR* 73 (1980) 265–76.
_____. *There Is No Male and Female: The Fate of a Dominical Saying in Paul and Gnosticism*. Harvard Dissertations in Religion. Philadelphia: Fortress Press, 1987.

MacDonald, Margaret Y. "Reading Real Women through the Undisputed Letters of Paul." Pp. 199–220 in *Women & Christian Origins*. Ed. Ross Shepard Kramer and Mary Rose D'Angelo. New York/Oxford: Oxford University Press, 1999.

Malherbe, Abraham J. "The Beasts at Ephesus." *JBL* 87 (1968) 71–80.

Manson, T. W. *Studies in the Gospels and Epistles*. Ed. Matthew Black; Manchester: Manchester University Press, 1962.

Martin, Ralph P. *2 Corinthians*. Word Biblical Commentary 40; Waco, TX: Word Books, 1986.

Martin, Troy W. "The Covenant of Circumcision (Gen 17:9-14) and the Situational Antitheses in Gal 3:28." *JBL* 122 (2003) 111–25.

Martyn, J. Louis. *Galatians: A New Translation with Introduction and Commentary*. AB 33A; New York: Doubleday, 1997.

Matera, Frank J. *Galatians*. SP 9; Glazier: Collegeville; Liturgical Press, 1992.

McLean, Bradley H. "Galatians 2.7–9 and the Recognition of Paul's Apostolic Status at the Jerusalem Conference: A Critique of G. Luedemann's Solution." *NTS* 37 (1991) 67–76.

Meeks, Wayne A. "The Image of the Androgyne: Some Uses of a Symbol in Earliest Christianity." *HR* 13 (1974) 165–208.

Meier, John P. "On the Veiling of Hermeneutics (1 Cor 11:2–16)." *CBQ* 40 (1978) 212–16.

Merx, Adalbert. *Die vier kanonischen Evangelien nach ihrem ältesten bekannten Texte. Übersetzung und erläuterung der syrischen im Sinaikloster gefundenen Palimpsesthandschrift*. 2.1: *Das Evangelium des Matthäus*. Berlin: Georg Reimer, 1902.

Metzger, Bruce M. *The Text of the New Testament: Its Transmission, Corruption, and Restoration*. 3d ed. New York/Oxford: Oxford University Press, 1992.

———. *A Textual Commentary on the Greek New Testament*. 2d ed. Stuttgart: Deutsche Bibelgesellschaft/United Bible Societies, 1994.

Milinovich, Timothy. *Beyond What Is Written: The Performative Structure of 1 Corinthians*. Eugene: Pickwick Publications, 2013.

Miller, Donald G. *Live As Free Men: A Study Guide on Galatians*. Board of Christian Education, The United Presbyterian Church U.S.A., 1964.

Mitton, C. Leslie. *The Epistle to the Ephesians: Its Authorship, Origin and Purpose*. Oxford: Clarendon Press, 1951.

———. *The Formation of the Pauline Corpus of Letters*. London: Epworth Press, 1955.

Moffatt, James. *An Introduction to the Literature of the New Testament*. International Theological Library. 3d ed. Edinburgh: T & T Clark, 1918.

Moo, Douglas. "Romans, Letter to the." Pp. 4.841–52 in *NIDB*.

Moule, C. F. D. *The Birth of the New Testament*. 3d ed. San Francisco: Harper & Row, 1981.

———. "The Problem of the Pastoral Epistles: A Reappraisal." *BJRL* 47 (1964–65) 430–52.

———. *Worship in the New Testament*. Richmond, VA: John Knox Press, 1961.

Mount, Christopher. "1 Corinthians 11:3–16: Spirit Possession and Authority in a Non-Pauline Interpolation." *JBL* 124 (2005) 313–40.

Munck, Johannes. *Paul and the Salvation of Mankind*. Richmond, VA: John Knox Press, 1959.

Munro, Winsome. "Authority and Subjection in Early Christian Paideia." Ph.D. diss., Teachers College, Columbia University, 1974.

———. *Authority in Paul and Peter: The Identification of a Pastoral Stratum in the Pauline Corpus and 1 Peter*. SNTSMS 45; Cambridge: Cambridge University Press, l983.

_____. "Patriarchy and Charismatic Community in 'Paul.'" Pp. 141–59 in *Women and Religion: Papers of the Working Group on Women and Religion 1972–73*. Rev. ed. Ed. Judith Plaskow and Joan Arnold Romero. Missoula: American Academy of Religion/Scholars Press, 1974.

_____. "Post-Pauline Material in 1 Cor 10, 11, and 14 with Confirmation from 2 Cor 6:14–7:1." Unpublished paper, 1977.

_____. "Two Strata in 1 Cor 10 and 11." Unpublished paper presented at the annual Society of Biblical Literature meeting, Atlanta, Georgia, 1971.

_____. "Women, Text, and Canon: The Strange Case of 1 Corinthians 14:33–35." *BTB* 18 (1988) 26–31.

Murphy-O'Connor, Jerome. "Interpolations in 1 Corinthians." *CBQ* 48 (1986) 81–94.

_____. "The Non-Pauline Character of 1 Corinthians 11:2–16?" *JBL* 95 (1976) 615–21.

_____. *Paul the Letter-Writer: His World, His Options, His Skills*. Collegeville: Liturgical Press, 1995.

_____. "Prisca and Aquila." *BRev* 8 (1992) 40–51, 62.

_____. "Relating 2 Corinthians 6.14–7.1 to Its Context." *NTS* 33 (1987) 272–75.

_____. "Sex and Logic in 1 Corinthians 11:2–16." *CBQ* 42 (1980) 482–500.

Mussner, Franz. *Der Galaterbrief. Auslegung*. HTKNT 9; Freiburg: Herder & Herder, 1974.

Myers Jr., Charles D. "Romans, Epistle to the." Pp. 5.816–30 in *ABD*.

Nanos, Mark D. *The Irony of Galatians: Paul's Letter in First-Century Context*. Minneapolis: Fortress Press, 2002.

Nguyen, vanThanh. *Peter and Cornelius: A Story of Conversion and Mission*. American Society of Missiology Monograph Series 15; Eugene: Pickwick Publications, 2012.

Nguyen, V. Henry T. "The Identification of Paul's Spectacle of Death Metaphor in 1 Corinthians 4.9" *NTS* 53 (2007) 489–501.

Nickle, Keith F. *The Collection: A Study in Paul's Strategy*. SBT 48; London: SCM Press, 1966.

Oakley, E. H. "Contributions and Comments: Titus and the Acts." *ExpT* 22 (1910–11) 564.

Ogg, George. *The Chronology of the Life of Paul*. London: Epworth Press, 1968.

Ollrog, Wolf-Henning. *Paul und Seiner Mitarbeiter. Untersuchungen zu Theorie und Praxis der paulinischen Mission*. WMANT 50; Neukirchen-Vluyn: Neukirchener Verlag, 1979.

O'Neill, J. C. *Paul's Letter to the Romans*. Harmondsworth: Penguin Books, 1975.

_____. *The Recovery of Paul's Letter to the Galatians*. London: SPCK, 1972.

Orchard, J. Bernard. "Ellipsis and Parenthesis in Ga 2:1–10 and 2 Th 2:1-12." Pp. 249–58 in *Paul de Tarse: Apôtre de notre temps*. Ed. L. de Lorenzi. Rome: Abbaye de S. Paul h.l.m., 1979.

_____. "The Ellipsis between Galatians 2,3 and 2,4." *Bib* 54 (1973) 469–81.

_____. "A New Solution of the Galatians Problem." *BJRL* 28 (1944) 154–74.

_____. "A Note on the Meaning of Galatians ii.3–5." *JTS* 43 (1942) 173–77.

_____. "Once Again the Ellipsis between Gal. 2,3 and 2,4." *Bib* 57 (1976) 254–55.

Orr, William F., and James Arthur Walther. *I Corinthians: A New Translation: Introduction with a Study of the Life of Paul, Notes, and Commentary*. AB 32; Garden City: Doubleday, 1976.

Osborne, R. E. "Paul and the Wild Beasts." *JBL* 85 (1966) 225–30.

Osiek, Carolyn. *Galatians*. New Testament Message 12. Wilmington: Michael Glazier Books, 1980.

Pagels, Elaine. *The Gnostic Paul: Gnostic Exegesis of the Pauline Letters.* Philadelphia: Fortress Press, 1975.
Payne, Philip B. *Man and Woman, One in Christ: An Exegetical and Theological Study of Paul's Letters.* Grand Rapids: Zondervan, 2009.
Pervo, Richard I. *Acts: A Commentary.* Ed. Harold W. Attridge. Hermeneia; Minneapolis: Fortress Press, 2009.
_____. *Dating Acts: Between the Evangelists and the Apologists.* Santa Rosa: Polebridge Press, 2006.
_____. *Profit with Delight: The Literary Genre of the Acts of the Apostles.* Philadelphia: Fortress Press, 1987.
_____. "Social and Religious Aspects of the Western Text." Pp. 229–41 in *The Living Text: Essays in Honor of Ernest W. Saunders.* Ed. Dennis E. Groh and Robert Jewett; Lanham: University Press of America, 1985.
Plummer, Alfred. *A Critical and Exegetical Commentary on the Second Epistle of St. Paul to the Corinthians.* ICC; Edinburgh: T & T Clark, 1915.
Quinn, Jerome D. "The Last Volume of Luke: The Relation of Luke-Acts to the Pastoral Epistles." Pp. 62–75 in *Perspectives on Luke-Acts.* Ed. Charles H. Talbert. Danville, KY: Association of Baptist Professors of Religion; Edinburgh: T & T Clark, 1978.
_____. "Timothy and Titus, Epistles to." Pp. 6.560–71 in *ABD.*
Räisänen, Heikki. "Galatians 2.16 and Paul's Break with Judaism." *NTS* 31 (1985) 543–53.
Ramsay, William M. *A Historical Commentary on St. Paul's Epistle to the Galatians.* New York: G. P. Putnam's Sons, 1900.
_____. *Luke the Physician and Other Studies in the History of Religion.* New York: Hodder and Stoughton, 1908.
_____. *St. Paul the Traveller and the Roman Citizen.* 2d ed. London: Hodder and Stoughton; New York: G. P. Putnam's Sons, 1896.
Reimer, Ivoni Richter. *Women in the Acts of the Apostles: A Feminist Liberation Perspective.* Trans. Linda M. Maloney. Minneapolis: Fortress Press, 1995.
Riddle, Donald W. "The Cephas-Peter Problem, and a Possible Solution." *JBL* 59 (1940) 169–80.
Ropes, James Hardy. The Beginnings of Christianity, Part I: *The Acts of the Apostles,* Vol. 3: *The Text of Acts.* Ed. F. J. Foakes Jackson and Kirsopp Lake. London: Macmillan and Co., 1926.
Sabatier, Auguste. "L'auteur du livre des Actes des Apôtres a-t-il connu et utilizé dans son récit les Epîtres de saint Paul?" *Bibliothèque de l'École des Hautes Études. Sciences religieuses* 1 (1889) 205–29.
Sampley, J. Paul. "The First Letter to the Corinthians: Introduction, Commentary, and Reflections." P. 10.771–1003 in *NIB.*
Sanday, William, and Arthur C. Headlam. *A Critical and Exegetical Commentary on the Epistle to the Romans.* 5th ed. ICC; Edinburgh: T & T Clark, 1902.
Sandmel, Samuel. *Anti-Semitism in the New Testament?* Philadelphia: Fortress Press, 1978.
Schenke, Hans-Martin. "Das Weiterwirken des Paulus und die Pflege seines Erbes durch die Paulus-Schule." *NTS* 21 (1975) 505–18.
Schenke, Hans-Martin, and Karl Fischer. *Einleitung in die Schriften des Neuen Testaments, 1: Die Briefe des Paulus und Schriften des Paulismus.* Berlin: Evangelische Verlagsanstalt, 1978.
Schlier, Heinrich. *Der Brief an die Galater. Übersetzt und erklärt.* 12th ed. KEK 7; Göttingen: Vandenhoeck & Ruprecht, 1962.

_____. *Der Brief an die Galater. Übersetzt und erklärt.* 13th ed. KEK 7. Göttingen: Vandenhoeck & Ruprecht, 1965.

_____. *Der Brief an die Galater. Übersetzt und erklärt.* 14th ed. KEK 7: Göttingen: Vandenhoeck & Ruprecht, 1971.

Schmidt, Carl, and Wilhelm Schubart. *Acta Pauli nach dem Papyrus der Hamburger Staats- und Universitäts-Bibliothek.* Glückstadt/Hamburg: J. J. Augustin, 1936.

Schneemelcher, Wilhelm, ed. *New Testament Apocrypha*, 2: *Writings Relating to the Apostles, Apocalypses and Related Subjects.* Eng. trans. ed. R. McL. Wilson. Rev. ed. Louisville: Westminster John Knox Press, 1991.

Schnelle, Udo. *Apostle Paul: His Life and Theology.* Trans. M. Eugene Boring. Grand Rapids: Baker Academic Press, 2003.

Schrage, Wolfgang. *Der erste Brief an die Korinther.* 4 vols. EKKNT 7; Neukirchen-Vluyn: Neukirchener Verlag, 1991–2000.

Schroeder, David. "Die Haustafeln des Neuen Testaments. Ihre Herkunft und ihr theologischer Sinn." Ph.D. diss., Universität Hamburg, 1959.

Schulz, Siegfried. "Die Decke des Moses. Untersuchungen zu einer vorpaulinischen Überlieferung in II Cor 3.7–18." *ZNW* 49 (1958) 1–30.

Schulze-Kadelbach, Gerhard. "Die Stellung des Petrus in der Urchristenheit." *TLZ* 81 (1956) 1–12.

Schüssler Fiorenza, Elisabeth. *In Memory of Her: A Feminist Theological Reconstruction of Christian Origins.* New York: Crossroad Publishing Co., 1983.

_____. "The Study of Women in Early Christianity: Some Methodological Considerations." Pp. 30–58 in *Critical History and Biblical Faith: New Testament Perspectives.* Ed. Thomas J. Ryan. The Annual Publication of the College Theology Society; Villanova: The College Theology Society/Horizons, 1979.

Schwyzer, Eduard. *Griechische Grammatik. Auf der Grundlage von Karl Brugmanns Griechischer Grammatik.* 4 vols. Handbuch der Altertumswissenschaft; Munich: C. H. Beck, 1934–71.

Scroggs, Robin. "Paul and the Eschatological Woman." *JAAR* 40 (1972) 283–303.

Seeberg, Alfred. *Die beiden Wege und das Aposteldekret.* Leipzig: A. Deichert, 1906.

_____. *Die Didache des Judentums und der Urchristenheit.* Leipzig: A. Deichert, 1908.

_____. *Das Evangelium Christi.* Leipzig: A. Deichert, 1905.

_____. *Das Katechismus der Urchristenheit.* Leipzig: A. Deichert, 1903.

Seim, Turid Karlsen. *The Double Message: Patterns of Gender in Luke-Acts.* Edinburgh: T & T Clark, 1994.

Selwyn, Edward Gordon. *The First Epistle of St. Peter: The Greek Text with Introduction, Notes, and Essays.* 2d ed. London: Macmillan & Co./New York: St. Martin's Press, 1947.

Sieffert, Friedrich. *Der Brief an die Galater.* 9th ed. MeyerK; Göttingen: Vandenhoeck & Ruprecht, 1899.

Silva, Moisés. "Old Testament in Paul." Pp. 630–42 in *Dictionary of Paul and His Letters.* Ed. Gerald F. Hawthorne and Ralph P. Martin; Downers Grove/Leicester: InterVarsity Press, 1993.

Smyth, Herbert Weir. *Greek Grammar.* Rev. Gordon M. Messing. Cambridge: Harvard University Press, 1956.

Souter, Alexander. "The Relationship between Titus and Luke." *ExpT* 18 (1906–07) 335–36.

_____. "A Suggested Relationship between Titus and Luke." *ExpT* 18 (1906–7) 285.

Spencer, F. Scott. "Women of 'the Cloth' in Acts: Sewing the Word." Pp. 134–54 in *A Feminist Companion to the Acts of the Apostles.* Ed. Amy-Jill Levine with Marianne Blickenstaff. Cleveland: Pilgrim Press, 2004.

Stendahl, Krister. *The Bible and the Role of Women: A Case Study in Hermeneutics.* FBBS 15; Philadelphia: Fortress Press, 1966.

Strecker, Georg. "Das Evangelium Jesu Christi." Pp. 503–48 in *Jesus Christus in Historie und Theologie. Neutestamentliche Festschrift für Hans Conzelmann zum 60. Geburtstag.* Ed. Georg Strecker. Tübingen: J. C. B. Mohr (Paul Siebeck), 1975.

_____. *History of New Testament Literature.* Trans. Calvin Katter. Harrisburg: Trinity Press International, 1997.

Strobel, A. "Schreiben des Lukas? Zum sprachlichen Problem der Pastoralbriefe." *NTS* 15 (1968–69) 191–210.

Stuhlmacher, Peter. *Das Paulinische Evangelium, 1: Vorgeschichte.* FRLANT 95; Göttingen: Vandenhoeck & Ruprecht, 1968.

Swanson, Donald C. "Diminutives in the Greek New Testament." *JBL* 77 (1958) 134–51.

Szesnat, H. "What Did the σκηνοποιός Paul Produce?" *Neot* 27 (1993) 391–402.

Talbert, Charles H. *Luke and the Gnostics: An Examination of the Lucan Purpose.* Nashville: Abingdon Press, 1966.

Thiselton, Anthony C. *The First Epistle to the Corinthians: A Commentary on the Greek Text.* NIGTC; Grand Rapids and Cambridge: Wm. B. Eerdmans Publishing Co.; Carlisle: Paternoster Press, 2000.

_____. "Realized Eschatology at Corinth." *NTS* 24 (1978) 510–26.

Thomas, W. Derek. "The Place of Women in the Church at Philippi." *ExpT* 83 (1971–72) 117–20.

Thrall, Margaret E. "The Problem of II Cor. VI.14-VII.1 in Some Recent Discussion." *NTS* 24 (1977) 132–48.

Townsend, John T. "The Date of Luke-Acts." Pp. 47–62 in *Luke-Acts: New Perspectives from the Society of Biblical Literature.* Ed. Charles H. Talbert; New York: Crossroad Publishing Co., 1984.

Trebilco, Paul R. "Asia." Pp. 291–362 in *The Book of Acts in Its First Century Setting, 2: The Book of Acts in Its Graeco-Roman Setting.* Ed. David W. J. Gill and Conrad Gempf. Grand Rapids: Wm. B. Eerdmans Publishing Co.; Carlisle: Paternoster Press, 1994.

_____. *The Early Christians in Ephesus from Paul to Ignatius.* WUNT 166: Tübingen: J. C. B. Mohr/Siebeck, 2004.

Trobisch, David. *The First Edition of the New Testament.* New York: Oxford University Press, 2000.

_____. *Paul's Letter Collection: Tracing the Origins.* Minneapolis: Fortress Press, 1994.

Trompf, G. W. "On Attitudes toward Women in Paul and Paulinist Literature: 1 Corinthians 11:3–16 and Its Context." *CBQ* 42 (1980) 196–215.

Turmel, Joseph. *See* Henri Delafosse.

Tyson, Joseph B. "Literary Criticism and the Gospels: The Seminar." Pp. 323–41 in *The Relationships among the Gospels: An Interdisciplinary Dialogue.* Ed. William O. Walker, Jr. Trinity University Monograph Series in Religion 5. San Antonio: Trinity University Press, 1978.

_____. *Marcion and Luke-Acts: A Defining Struggle.* Columbia: University of South Carolina Press, 2006.

Van Manen, W. C. "Marcions Brief van Paulus aan de Galatiërs." *ThT* 21 (1887) 382–404, 450–533.

Vielhauer, Philipp. *Geschichte der urchristlichen Literatur. Einleitung in das Neue Testament, die Apokryphen und die Apostolischen Väter.* Berlin, New York: Walter de Gruyter, 1975.

_____. "On the 'Paulinism' of Acts." Pp. 33–50 in *Studies in Luke-Acts: Essays Presented in Honor of Paul Schubert*. Ed. Leander E. Keck and J. Louis Martyn. Nashville: Abingdon Press, 1966.

Von Weizsäcker, Karl H. *The Apostolic Age of the Christian Church*. 2 vols. Trans. James Millar. New York: G. P. Putnam's Sons, 1894–95.

Walasky, P. W. *"And So We Came to Rome": The Political Perspectives of St. Luke*. SNTSMS 49; Cambridge: Cambridge University Press, 1983.

Walker Jr., William O. "1 Corinthians 11:2-16 and Paul's Views regarding Women." *JBL* 94 (1975) 94–110.

_____. "1 Corinthians 15:29–34 as a Non-Pauline Interpolation." *CBQ* 69 (2007) 84–103.

_____. "2 Cor 6.14–7.1 and the Chiastic Structure of 6.11–13; 7.2–3." *NTS* 48 (2002) 142–44.

_____. "Acts and the Pauline Corpus Reconsidered." *JSNT* 24 (1985) 3–23. Reprinted as pp. 55–74 in *The Pauline Writings: A Sheffield Reader*. Eds. Stanley E. Porter and Craig A. Evans. The Biblical Seminar 34; Sheffield: Sheffield Academic Press, 1995.

_____. "Acts and the Pauline Corpus Revisited: Peter's Speech at the Jerusalem Conference." Pp. 77–86 in *Literary Studies in Luke-Acts: Essays in Honor of Joseph B. Tyson*. Ed. Richard P. Thompson and Thomas E. Phillips; Macon: Mercer University Press, 1998.

_____. "Apollos and Timothy as the Unnamed 'Brothers' in 2 Corinthians 8:18–24." *CBQ* 73 (2011) 318–38.

_____. "Does the 'We' in Gal 2.15–17 include Paul's Opponents." *NTS* 49 (2003) 560–65.

_____. "Galatians 2:7b–8 as a Non-Pauline Interpolation." *CBQ* 65 (2003) 568–87.

_____. "Galatians 2:8 and the Question of Paul's Apostleship." *JBL* 123 (2004) 323–27.

_____. *Interpolations in the Pauline Letters*. JSNTSup 213; London/New York: Sheffield Academic Press, 2001.

_____. "The 'Paulinization' of Peter in the Book of Acts." *The Fourth R* 22,3 (May/June 2009) 9–12, 14.

_____. "Paul on the Status and Role of Women: The Apostle as Radical Egalitarian." *The Fourth R* 25,2 (Mar/Apr 2012) 5–9, 22.

_____. "The Portrayal of Aquila and Priscilla in Acts: The Question of Sources." *NTS* 54 (2008) 479–95.

_____. "Romans 8:29-30 as a Non-Pauline Interpolation." *JSPL* 2 (2012) 27–40.

_____. "Second Corinthians 3:7-18 as a Non-Pauline Interpolation." *JSPL* 3 (2013) 67–89.

_____. "The 'Theology of Woman's Place' and the 'Paulinist' Tradition." *Trinity University Studies in Religion* 11 (1982) 131–52. Reprinted in *Semeia* 28 (1983) 101–12.

_____. "The Timothy-Titus Problem Reconsidered." *ExpT* 92 (1981) 231–35.

_____. "Translation and Interpretation of Ἐὰν Μή." *JBL* 116 (1997) 515–20.

_____. "The Vocabulary of 1 Corinthians 11.3-16: Pauline or Non-Pauline?" *JSNT*, 35 (1989) 75–88.

_____. "Why Paul Went to Jerusalem: The Interpretation of Galatians 2:1-5." *CBQ* 54 (1992) 503–10.

Webb, William J. *Returning Home: New Covenant and Second Exodus as the Context for 2 Corinthians 6.14–7.1*. JSNTSup 85; Sheffield: Sheffield Academic Press, 1993.

Weidinger, Karl. *Die Haustafeln. Ein Stück urchristlicher Paränese*. UNT 14; Leipzig: J. C. Hinrichs, 1928.

Wendland, Heinz-Dietrich. "Zur sozialethischen Bedeutung der neutestamentlichen Haustafeln." Pp. 34–46 in *Die Liebhaftigkeit des Wortes. Festgabe für Adolf Köberle*. Ed. O. Michel and U. Mann. Hamburg: Furche, 1958.

Werner, David. "Galatians ii.3–8: As an Interpolation." *ExpT* 62 (1950-51) 380.

Wilckens, Ulrich. "Der Ursprung der Überlieferung der Erscheinungen des Auferstandenen. Zur traditionsgeschichtlichen Analyse von 1 Kor 15, 1–11." Pp. 56–95 in *Dogma und Denkstrukturen, Edmund Schlink in Verehrung und Dankbarkeit zum sechzigsten Geburtstag* (dargebracht). Ed. Wilfried Joest and Wolfhart Pannenberg. Göttingen: Vandenhoeck & Ruprecht, 1963.

Wiles, Maurice F. *The Divine Apostle: The Interpretation of St. Paul's Epistles in the Early Church*. Cambridge: Cambridge University Press, 1967.

Wilson, Stephen G. *Luke and the Pastoral Epistles*. London: SPCK, 1979.

Windisch, Hans. *Der zweite Korintherbrief*. 9th ed. KEK 6; Göttingen: Vandenhoeck & Ruprecht, 1924.

Wisse, Frederik W. "Textual Limits to Redactional Theory in the Pauline Corpus." Pp. 167–78 in *Gospel Origins and Christian Beginnings: In Honor of James M. Robinson*. Ed. James E. Goehring et al. Forum Fascicles 1; Sonoma: Polebridge Press, 1990.

Witherington III, Ben. "The Anti-Feminist Tendencies of the 'Western' Text in Acts." *JBL* 103 (1984) 82–84.

_____. *Grace in Galatia: A Commentary on St. Paul's Letter to the Galatians*. Grand Rapids: Wm. B. Eerdmans Publishing Co, 1998.

Wolter, Michael. "Apollos und die ephesinischen Johannesjünger (Acts 18:24–19:7)." *ZNW* 78 (1987) 49–73.

Wright, N. T. *The Resurrection of the Son of God*, vol. 3: *Christian Origins and the Question of God*. Minneapolis: Fortress Press, 2003.

Yamauchi, Edwin M. "Hellenism." Pp. 383–88 in *DPL*.

Zahn, Theodor. *Der Brief des Paulus an die Galater*. Kommentar zum Neuen Testament 9; 3d ed. Leipzig: A. Deichert, 1922.

_____. *Introduction to the New Testament*. Trans. John Moore Trout et al. Edinburgh: T & T Clark, 1909.

Index of Modern Authors

Aland, Barbara, 44n28, 301
Aland, Kurt, 44n28, 301
Allison, Dale C., 252n8, 301
Baarda, T., 17, 17nn18–19, 301, 307
Balch, David L., 288n2, 297n24, 298n26, 301
Barnett, Paul, 129n21, 155, 155n18, 156n23, 301
Barnikol, Ernst, 35, 35n16, 40n15, 41–43, 41n19, 42n21, 43nn24–25, 45, 45n31, 46n37, 50–51, 50n51, 51n55, 52n56, 53–56, 54n67, 54nn69–70, 55n72, 56n75, 58, 61–62, 61nn90–91, 61nn93–95, 301–302
Barrett, Charles Kingsley, 154n16, 203, 203n2, 206, 206nn13–14, 208, 208n17, 214–17, 214n5, 214n10, 216n14, 216n17, 219–21, 220nn28–29, 231, 254n15, 267nn10–12, 271n30, 283n83, 301
Barrett, David P., 271n30, 302
Bartchy, S. Scott, 67n4, 301
Bartlet, Vernon, 204n7, 301
Bauernfeind, Otto, 250n4, 301
Beasley-Murray, G. R., 66n3, 301
Behm, Johannes, 42, 42n21, 61n94, 301
Betz, Hans Dieter, 4–5, 4n5, 21n1, 22n4, 29n1, 31n7, 38n5, 40, 40n13, 42n22, 52n56, 56n76, 57n79, 59, 59n86, 65n1, 67–69, 68nn7–8, 69n10, 69n13, 70, 70n14, 71–72, 74, 74n20, 87, 126n12, 152, 152nn14–6, 155–59, 155n19, 156n22, 158n28, 158nn30–31, 159nn32–33, 169n59, 175, 175n68, 301
Blickenstaff, Marianne, 279n67, 307, 311
Blommerde, A. C. M., 4n6, 302
Boring, M. Eugene, 68n9, 302, 311
Boucher, Madeleine, 291n10, 302
Bouttier, Michel, 65n1, 302
Bowen, C. R., 111n75, 302
Boys-Smith, E. P., 204n6, 302
Bray, Gerald, 107n64, 302

Brooten, Bernadette, 300n31, 302
Brown, Scott G., 285n91, 302
Bruce, F. F., 4n6, 5, 5n7, 7n13, 15, 15n9, 24n14, 38n5, 41n17, 42n22, 48n47, 66n3, 69n12, 207, 207n15, 238n6, 302
Bultmann, Rudolf, 61, 61n95, 93n7, 302
Burchard, C., 217n20,
Burton, Ernest de Witt, 3n3, 4n3, 5n8, 10, 10n22, 14–15, 15n8, 18n26, 19, 19nn26–27, 20n30, 29, 29n4, 32, 32nn8–10, 34n12, 52n60, 57n80, 59n86, 62n98, 302
Byrne, Brendan, 188n21, 188n23, 302

Cadbury, Henry J., 203, 203n1, 207n16, 260n29, 302, 304, 307
Carlson, Stephen, 285n91, 302
Carrington, Philip, 288n1, 302
Clabeaux, John J., 282n79, 302
Cleary, Francis X., 297, 297n23, 302
Collins, Raymond F., 67n5, 84n51, 95, 95n1, 97, 97nn9–10, 99, 99n16, 302
Comfort, Philip W., 271n30, 302
Conzelmann, Hans J., 95–96, 95n1, 96n6, 99n17, 103n48, 107n64, 109, 109nn69–70, 115n90, 237n3, 242n24, 302, 312
Cope, Lamar, 80n32, 296n20, 303
Couchoud, P.-L., 41–42, 41n19, 303
Cousar, Charles B., 237n3, 303
Cranfield, C. E. B., 188n21, 188n24, 303
Crouch, James E., 288n2, 303
Cullmann, Oscar, 38, 38n2, 48n46, 303

Dana, H. E., 19n27, 303
D'Angelo, Mary Rose, 78–79, 79nn26–27, 280n67, 303, 307–8
Das, A. Andrew, 22n6, 303
Dautsenberg, Gerhard, 65n1, 303
De Boer, Martinus C., 65n1, 303
Delafosse, Henri (a.k.a. Joseph Turmel), 41–42, 41n19, 303, 312
Dewey Arthur J., 80n32, 303

315

Dibelius, Martin, 249, 249n3, 250n4, 288n2, 303
Dinkler, Erich, 34n14, 38–40, 38n3, 38n7, 39n8, 40n12, 40n14, 42, 42n21, 48n49, 52n56, 59n87, 60, 60n89, 303
Duff, Paul B., 123–26, 123nn1–2, 124n2, 124nn6–8, 127nn13–14, 131, 303
Dungan, David L., 230n53, 303
Dunn, James D. G., 14–15, 14n5, 15nn11–12, 19, 34nn14–15, 42n23, 66n3, 304

Edmundson, George, 204n9, 304
Ehrman, Bart D., 252n8, 304
Ellingworth, Paul, 96, 96n6, 104, 104n54, 304
Elliott, J. K., 46n37, 48, 48n48, 304
Ellis, E. Earle, 44n28, 118n95, 154n14, 157n27, 301, 304
Enslin, Morton Scott, 8n14, 205, 205nn11–12, 214, 214n5, 214n7, 214n9, 215–22, 215n12, 216n14, 216n16, 218nn23–25, 222nn34–35, 223nn35–36, 225–27, 225nn39–40, 229–33, 229n50, 230n51, 304
Epp, Eldon Jay, 82n45, 164n43, 304, 306

Farmer, William R., 226n44, 304
Fee, Gordon D., 43n27, 80n32, 96, 96nn3–4, 96n7, 102n45, 103, 103nn48–49, 105, 105n56, 107, 107nn62–63, 107n65, 111, 111n77, 114, 114n88, 116, 116n93, 174, 175n67, 304
Fischer, Karl, 41n20, 310
Fitzgerald, John T., 193n35, 304
Fitzmyer, Joseph A., 43n27, 67n5, 83, 83n46, 129n22, 188n21, 251n8, 254n15, 266n8, 304
Foakes-Jackson, F. J., 234n57, 235n58, 239n12, 243, 243n32, 304
Friedrich, Gerhard. 155, 155n17, 304
Frye, Roland Mushat, 226n44, 304
Fuller, Reginald H., 297n21, 305
Furnish, Victor Paul, 91n2, 127–28, 127n15, 128n18, 129n19, 130nn27–30, 146n71, 147n74, 152, 152n4, 152nn7–9, 154, 154nn15–16, 159, 159n32, 176n69, 299n29, 305

Gaechter, Paul, 49n50, 305
Gamble, Harry Y., 44n28, 305
Gaventa, Beverly Roberts, 249n3, 305
Geer Jr., Thomas C., 13–14, 13nn3–4, 14n5, 305
Georgi, Dieter, 38n6, 124n6, 305
Goguel, Maurice, 48n46, 305
Goodwin, William Watson, 18n24, 305
Goulder, Michael, 55, 55n73, 305
Gregory, Andrew, 267n13, 305

Haenchen, Ernst, 7n14, 8, 8n18, 41n16, 214n3, 224n38, 234n57, 235n58, 237n3, 239n13, 246, 246n40, 254n15, 305
Hafemann, Scott, 124n8, 125n8, 135n41, 305
Hall, Tom, 267n10–12, 307
Hansen, Bruce, 65n2, 66n3, 305
Hanson, A. T., 129n21, 305
Hanson, K. C., 303
Harnack, Adolf von, 107n64, 121, 121nn103–4, 305–6
Harrill, J. Albert, 280n69, 306
Hatton, Howard, 96, 96n6, 104, 104n54, 304
Hawkins, Robert Martyr, 80n32, 99, 99n18, 183n8, 306
Hays, Richard B., 30, 30n6, 39–40, 39n9, 41n16, 84n51, 242n26, 306
Headlam, Arthur C., 188n25, 310
Heinrici, C. F. G., 109, 109n70, 152n8, 153n12, 306
Hengel, Martin, 7n14, 306
Henze, Clemens M., 48n46, 306
Holl, Karl, 48, 48n49, 306
Hoover, Roy W., 303
Howard, George, 242n26, 306
Hughes, Philip Edgcumbe, 152n8, 176n69, 306

Jewett, Robert, 183n8, 194n40, 198n54, 271n29, 306, 310

Keck, Leander E., 305–6, 313
Kilpatrick, G. D., 281n78, 306
Klein, Günter, 34n14, 38n4, 40, 40n14, 42, 42n21, 52n56, 217n20, 306
Knox, John, 8, 8n16, 13, 13n2, 58n83, 205, 205n10, 205n12, 214–19, 214n6, 214nn8–9, 216nn15–16, 219n26, 221–22, 222n32, 223n35, 225–27, 225nn41–43, 228n47, 229, 229n49, 231, 282, 282n79, 306
Kock, Theodor, 100n24, 306
Kramer, Ross Shepard, 303, 307–8
Kümmel, Werner Georg, 213, 213n1, 266n9, 288n3, 297n21, 307

Lake, Kirsopp, 8, 8n17, 47–48, 47n45, 48nn46–47, 203, 203n1, 207n16, 224n38, 234n57, 235n58, 304, 307, 310
Lambrecht, Jan, 17, 17n19, 17n23, 18n26, 123n2, 307
Leppä, Outi, 101n31, 307
Levine, Amy-Jill, 279n67, 307, 311
Lietzmann, Hans, 42n21, 61–62, 61n94, 62n96, 124n4, 306–7
Lightfoot, Joseph Barber, 204, 204n5, 307
Lohse, Eduard, 65n1, 288nn1–3, 307
Longenecker, Richard N., 21n1, 307
Lovering Jr., Eugene Harrison, 272n32, 307
Lüdemann, Gerd, 34n14, 38n6, 51n55, 52n62, 267, 267nn10–12, 307

MacDonald, Dennis R., 83n47, 103, 103n51, 105n57, 108, 108n66, 111, 111n76, 112, 112n78, 112n80, 113nn83–84, 307
MacDonald, Margaret Y., 79, 80n30, 308
Malherbe, Abraham J., 110–11, 110nn72–73, 111n75, 114–15, 115nn89–90, 308
Manson, T. W., 208–9, 209n19, 308
Mantey, Julius R., 19n27, 303
Martin, Ralph P., 129n23, 308, 311
Martin, Troy W., 65n1, 308
Martyn, J. Louis, 21–22, 21nn1–2, 22nn5–6, 27n21, 42n23, 65n1, 66n3, 69n12, 305–6, 308, 313
Matera, Frank J., 22n4, 30, 30n5, 42n23, 57n81, 244n34, 308
McLean, Bradley H., 29n3, 308
McGaughy, Lane C., 303
Meeks, Wayne A., 77n22, 308
Meier, John P., 296n20, 308
Merx, Adalbert, 48, 48n49, 308
Metzger, Bruce M., 77n23, 251n5, 266nn5–6, 270n21, 279n66, 304, 308
Milinovich, Timothy, 80n32, 308
Miller, Donald G., 13, 13n1, 308
Mitton, C. Leslie, 213n1, 231n54, 308
Moffatt, James, 62, 62nn97–98, 308
Moo, Douglas, 84n49, 308
Moule, C. F. D., 66n3, 129n23, 231n54, 308
Mount, Christopher, 80n32, 118, 119n96, 308
Munck, Johannes, 38n6, 238n8, 308
Munro, Winsome, 80n32, 120, 120n102, 289n6, 296n20, 308–9
Murphy-O'Connor, Jerome, 43n27, 92n4, 270, 270n22, 272, 272n33, 279, 279n65, 292n13, 296n20, 309
Mussner, Franz, 29n3, 309
Myers Jr., Charles D., 84n49, 188n25, 309

Nanos, Mark D., 23n12, 25–26, 25nn17–18, 26n19, 309
Nguyen, vanThanh, 249n3, 309
Nguyen, V. Henry T., 277n60, 309
Nickle, Keith F., 156n23, 309

Oakley, E. H., 204n8, 309
Ogg, George, 238n6, 309
Ollrog, Wolf-Henning, 154n14, 309
O'Neill, J. C., 3n3, 41n20, 181–84, 181nn2–3, 182nn4–7, 183n9, 183n11, 184n12, 184n14, 192n33, 197n47, 309
Orchard, J. Bernard, 4–5, 4n6, 208–9, 209n19, 309
Orr, William F., 100n20, 296n20, 309
Osborne, R. E., 110n73, 309
Osiek, Carolyn, 13, 13n3, 309

Pagels, Elaine, 299n30, 310
Payne, Philip B., 80n32, 310
Pervo, Richard I., 79n28, 162n39, 251n5, 252, 252n9, 257nn22–24, 258n25, 260, 260n28, 267n13, 268n14, 279n66, 280n69, 310
Plummer, Alfred, 156n22, 310

Quinn, Jerome D., 231n54, 286n92, 310

Räisänen, Heikki, 14–15, 14n5, 15n10, 310
Ramsay, William M., 3n1, 10n23, 203–4, 203n4, 204n6, 310
Reimer, Ivoni Richter, 280n67, 310
Riddle, Donald W., 48n46, 310
Ropes, James Hardy, 279n66, 310

Sabatier, Auguste, 214n5, 310
Sampley, J. Paul, 108, 108n66, 310
Sanday, William, 188n25, 310
Sandmel, Samuel, 211n21, 310
Schenke, Hans-Martin, 41n20, 310
Schlier, Heinrich, 29n3, 34n14, 38n4, 42, 42n21, 48n49, 61n94, 65n1, 310
Schmidt, Carl, 311
Schmidt, Daryl D., 303
Schnelle, Udo, 68n9, 311
Schrage, Wolfgang, 65n1, 311
Schroeder, David, 288n2, 311
Schubart, Wilhelm, 311
Schulz, Siegfried, 123n2, 124n5, 311
Schulze–Kadelbach, Gerhard, 48n49, 311
Schüssler Fiorenza, Elisabeth, 78n25, 296n20, 311
Schwyzer, Eduard, 29n3, 311
Scroggs, Robin, 66n3, 299nn27–28, 311
Seeberg, Alfred, 288n2, 311
Seim, Turid Karlsen, 280n67, 311
Selwyn, Edward Gordon, 287–88, 288n1, 290n8, 298–99, 311
Sieffert, Friedrich, 5n8, 311
Silva, Moisés, 114n86, 311
Smyth, Herbert Weir, 18n24, 19nn27–28, 279n64, 311
Souter, Alexander, 204n6, 204n8, 311

Spencer, F. Scott, 278n62, 280, 280n73, 311
Stendahl, Krister, 69n12, 73, 73nn17–18, 312
Strecker, Georg, 43n27, 44, 44n29, 312
Strobel, A., 231n54, 312
Stuhlmacher, Peter, 49, 49n50, 312
Swanson, Donald C., 279n64, 312
Szesnat, H., 277nn56–57, 312

Talbert, Charles H., 218n25, 310, 312
Thiselton, Anthony C., 81n35, 97n8, 104, 104n52, 109n68, 296n20, 312
Thomas, W. Derek, 299n29, 312
Thrall, Margaret E., 92n4, 312
Townsend, John T., 267n13, 312
Trebilco, Paul R., 112n79, 254n15, 312
Trobisch, David, 272, 272nn32–33, 312
Trompf, G. W., 80n32, 292n13, 293n14, 296n20, 298n25, 312
Turmel, Joseph (a.k.a. Henri Delafosse), 303, 312
Tyson, Joseph B., 58n83, 79n29, 226n44, 261n31, 267n13, 282–83, 282n79, 283n86, 312–13

Van Manen, W. C., 41–42, 41n19, 312
Vielhauer, Philipp, 214n3, 220, 220n29, 243n33, 312–13
Von Weizsäcker, Karl H., 228n48, 242n27, 313

Walasky, P. W., 260n30, 313
Walker Jr., William O., 17n21, 35n17, 43 nn.26–27, 44n30, 80n32, 81n33, 102n44, 119nn97–101, 126nn10–11, 150n77, 162n38, 183n10, 187n18, 192n31, 193n36, 227n45, 237nn1–2, 238n4, 238n10, 247n42, 248n44, 252n8, 255n16, 261n32, 261n34, 262n35, 289nn4–5, 292n11, 296n20, 304, 312–13
Walther, James Arthur, 100n20, 296n20, 309
Webb, William J., 91n2, 92nn3–4, 313
Weidinger, Karl, 288n2, 313
Wendland, Heinz-Dietrich, 288n2, 314

Werner, David, 41–42, 41n19, 314
Wilckens, Ulrich, 50, 51n52, 52, 52n62, 314
Wiles, Maurice F., 299n30, 314
Wilson, R. McL., 305, 311,
Wilson, Stephen G., 231n54, 314
Windisch, Hans, 123n2, 124n3, 127, 127n14, 129, 129nn20–22, 159n33, 176n69, 314
Wisse, Frederik W., 44n28, 118n95, 314
Witherington III, Ben, 21n1, 279n66, 314

Wolter, Michael, 166n49, 275n50, 276n52, 283n83, 314
Wright,nT., 96n5, 99–100, 100n19, 100n21, 314

Yamauchi, Edwin M., 115, 115n91, 314

Zahn, Theodor, 48n47, 213n3, 214n5, 314

About the Author

William O. Walker, Jr. (Ph.D., Duke University) is Jennie Farris Railey King Professor Emeritus of Religion at Trinity University in San Antonio, Texas. He has served as author, co-author, editor, associate editor, or assistant editor of a number of books, including *Interpolations in the Pauline Letters* (2001) and *The HarperCollins Bible Dictionary* (1996). He has also published more than sixty articles on New Testament topics. He is a member of *Studiorum Novi Testamenti Societas*, the Society of Biblical Literature, the Catholic Biblical Association of America, and is a Fellow of Westar Institute.